GEOS

the pearson custom library for geography & geology

Pearson Learning Solutions

New York   Boston   San Francisco
London   Toronto   Sydney   Tokyo   Singapore   Madrid
Mexico City   Munich   Paris   Cape Town   Hong Kong   Montreal

Senior Vice President, Editorial and Marketing: Patrick F. Boles
Executive Marketing Manager: Nathan L. Wilbur
Senior Acquisition Editor: Debbie Coniglio
Operations Manager: Eric M. Kenney
Development Editor: Christina Martin
Editorial Assistant: Jeanne Martin
Production Manager: Jennifer Berry
Art Director: Renée Sartell
Cover Designer: Kristen Kiley

Cover Art: Courtesy of Photoubrary.com, Robert Harding World Imagery, Getty Images/Photodisc.

This special edition published in cooperation with Pearson Learning Solutions.

Printed in the United States of America.
V092
Please visit our web site at *www.pearsoncustom.com/custom-library/geos.*

Attention bookstores: For permission to return any unsold stock, contact us at *pe-uscustomreturns@pearson.com.*

Pearson Learning Solutions, 501 Boylston Street, Suite 900, Boston, MA 02116
A Pearson Education Company
www.pearsoned.com

ISBN 10: 1-256-02444-9
ISBN 13: 978-1-256-02444-6

Contents

Observing and Measuring Earth Materials and Processes

CONTRIBUTING AUTHORS

Cynthia Fisher • *West Chester University of Pennsylvania*
C. Gil Wiswall • *West Chester University of Pennsylvania*

OBJECTIVES AND ACTIVITIES

A. Know how to make a scale model of Earth, calculate its fractional scale, and use it to understand the relative proportions of Earth's physical spheres.

ACTIVITY 1: Basketball Model of Earth's Spheres

B. Understand some basic principles and tools of direct and remote observation that are used by geoscientists and apply them to identify Earth materials, observe and describe processes of change, make a prediction, and describe a plan of field geology and lab work that you could use to test your prediction.

ACTIVITY 2: Remote Sensing of Earth and Exploring for Copper

C. Measure or calculate length, area, volume, mass, and density of Earth materials using basic scientific equipment and techniques.

ACTIVITY 3: Measuring Earth Materials and Relationships

D. Develop and test physical and quantitative models of isostasy based on floating wood blocks and icebergs. Then apply your quantitative model and your measurements of basalt and granite density to calculate the isostasy of average blocks of oceanic and continental crust.

ACTIVITY 4: Density, Gravity, and Isostasy

E. Analyze Earth's global topography in relation to your work and a hypsographic curve, and infer how Earth's global topography may be related to isostasy.

ACTIVITY 5: Isostasy and Earth's Global Topography

STUDENT MATERIALS

Pencil, eraser, calculator, metric ruler. **The following materials will be provided for you during the laboratory:** drafting compass, small (10 mL) graduated cylinder, large (500 mL) graduated cylinder, pieces of basalt and granite that will fit into the large graduated cylinder, small lump of modeling clay (marble size), water, wood block (about 8 cm × 10 cm × 4 cm), small bucket to float wood block, gram balance, and wash bottle or dropper (optional).

INTRODUCTION

Exploring and interacting with the natural world leads one to fundamental questions about the natural world and how it operates. **Science** is a way of answering these questions by *gathering information* (based on investigations and careful observations), *engaging in discourse* (verbal or written exchange, organization, and evaluation of information and ideas), *running tests* to verify or falsify tentative ideas, and *communicating inferences* (conclusions justified with information and an explanation of one's evaluation and interpretation of that information). **Geology** is the branch of science that deals with Earth: its rocky body, 4.55 billion-year-long history, and environmental changes that affect humans. Its name comes from two Greek words, *geo* = Earth and *logos* = discourse. So geologists are also Earth scientists or geoscientists.

Geologists use their senses and tools (microscopes, rock hammers, rulers, etc.) to make direct observations of Earth materials and processes of change. They also use computer-based technologies to make exact, automated, and even remote observations. These collective observations serve as a growing body of *data* (information, evidence) that enables geologists to characterize and classify Earth materials, identify relationships of cause (process) and effect (product), design models (physical, conceptual, mathematical, graphical, or artistic representations of something to test or demonstrate how it works), and publish inferences about Earth and how it operates. Geologists also apply their information and inferences to locate and manage resources, identify and mitigate hazards, predict change, and help communities plan for the future.

PART A: OBSERVING EARTH MATERIALS AND PROCESSES OF CHANGE THROUGH TIME

As you complete exercises in this laboratory manual, think of yourself as a geologist. Conduct tests and make careful observations. Record your observations carefully so that you have a body of information (data, evidence) to justify your ideas (hypotheses, inferences). The quality of your ideas depends on your logic (method of thinking) and the information that you use to justify them. Your ideas may change as you make new observations, locate new information, or apply a different method of thinking. Your instructor will not accept simple yes or no answers to questions. S/he will expect your answers to be complete inferences justified with information and an explanation of your logic. Show your work whenever you use mathematics to solve a problem so your method of thinking is obvious.

When making direct observations, you should observe and record **qualitative information,** by *describing* how things look, feel, smell, sound, taste, or behave. You should also collect and record **quantitative information,** by *measuring* materials, energy levels, and processes of change in time and space. This will require you to understand and use some scales and tools of measurement that professional geologists use in their work. You will also be expected to infer and quantify relationships by comparing one set of measurements to another.

Scales of Earth Observation

The most widely known geologic feature in the United States is undoubtedly the Grand Canyon (Figure 1). This canyon cuts a mile deep, through

FIGURE 1 Photograph of a portion of the Grand Canyon, Arizona. Rocks exposed at the base of the canyon are more than a billion years old, yet some layers of sand along the Colorado River that runs through the canyon may have formed just seconds ago. (Photo by Allen Johnson)

millions of rock layers that are like pages of an immense stone book of geologic history called the **geologic record.** These stone pages vary in thickness from millimeters to meters. Each page has distinguishing features—some as tiny as microscopic fossils or grains of sand and some as large as fossil trees, dinosaur skeletons, or ancient stream channels. Each successive stone page, from the bottom (oldest page) to the top (youngest page) of the canyon, is but one of millions of recorded events and times in Earth's long geologic history.

Geologists study all of Earth's materials, from the spatial scale of atoms (atomic scale) to the scale of our entire planet (global scale). At each spatial scale of observation, they identify materials and characterize relationships. Each scale is also related to the others. You should familiarize yourself with these **spatial scales of observation** as they are summarized in Figure 2.

Geologists also think about **temporal scales of observation.** As geologic detectives, they analyze the stone pages of the geologic record for evidence of events and relationships. As geologic historians, they group the events and relationships into paragraphs, chapters, sections, and parts of geologic history that occurred over epochs, periods, eras, and eons of time. The index to this text of geologic history is called the **geologic time scale** (Figure 3). Notice that the geologic time scale is a chart showing named intervals of the geologic record (rock units), the sequence in which they formed (oldest at the bottom), and their ages in millions of years. The eonothems, erathems, systems, and series of rock are the physical record of what happened during eons, eras, periods, and epochs of time. The intervals have been named and dated on the basis of more than a century of cooperative work among scientists of different nations, races, religions, genders, classes, and ethnic groups from throughout the world. What all of these scientists have had in common is the ability to do science and an intense desire to decipher Earth's long and complex history based on evidence contained in the stone pages that record geologic history.

Processes and Cycles of Change

Earth is characterized by energy flow and processes of change at every spatial and temporal scale of observation. Earth's surface is energized by geothermal energy (from inside the planet) and solar energy (from outside the planet). The energy flows from *sources* to *sinks* (materials that store or convert energy) and drives processes of change like the examples in Figure 4. Most of these processes involve organic (biological; parts of living or once living organisms) and inorganic (non-biological)

SPATIAL SCALES OF OBSERVATION USED BY GEOLOGISTS

Scale of observation	Used to study things like...	Measured in...
Global	Entire planet and its interactive "spheres"	Thousands of kilometers (km) or miles (mi)
Regional	Portions of oceans, continents, countries, provinces, states, islands	Kilometers (km), miles (mi)
Local (outcrop or field site)	Specific locations that can be "pin-pointed" on a map	Meters (m), feet (ft)
Hand sample (field/lab. sample)	Sample of a mineral, a rock, air, water, or an organism that can be held in your hand	Centimeters (cm), millimeters (mm), inches (in.) 0 1 cm 0 10 mm
Microscopic	Features of a hand sample that can only be seen with a hand lens (magnifier) or microscope	Fractions of millimeters (mm), micrometers (μm)
Atomic (or molecular)	Arrangements of the atoms or molecules in a substance	Nanometers (nm), angstroms (Å)

Macroscopic: visible with the naked eye (spanning the Global through Hand sample rows)

FIGURE 2 Spatial scales of observation used by geologists in their work.

materials in solid, liquid, and gaseous states, or *phases* (Figure 5). Note that many of the processes have opposites depending on the flow of energy to or from a material: melting and freezing, evaporation

THE GEOLOGIC TIME SCALE

A chart showing the sequence, names, and ages of Earth's rock layers (oldest at the bottom)

Eon of time Eonothem of rock	Era of time Erathem of rock	Period of time System of rock**	Epoch of time Series of rock	Millions of years ago (Ma)	Some notable fossils in named rock layers
Phanerozoic	Cenozoic: (new life) Age of Mammals	Quaternary (Q)	Holocene	.0117	First *Homo* fossils, 70–100% extant mollusks+
			Pleistocene	2.6	
		Tertiary — Neogene (N)	Pliocene	5.3	First humans (Hominidae), 15–70% extant mollusks+
			Miocene	23	
		Tertiary — Paleogene (PG)	Oligocene	34	More mammals than reptiles, <15% extant mollusks+
			Eocene	56	
			Paleocene	65	
	Mesozoic: (middle life) Age of Reptiles	Cretaceous (K)		145	Last dinosaur fossils: including *Tyrannosaurus rex*
		Jurassic (J)		200	First bird fossil: *Archaeopteryx*
		Triassic (Ŧ)		251	First dinosaur, mammal, turtle, and crocodile fossils
	Paleozoic: (old life) Age of Trilobites	Permian (P)		299	Last (youngest) trilobite fossils
		Carboniferous (C)* — Pennsylvanian (℗)		318	First reptile fossils
		Carboniferous (C)* — Mississippian (M)		359	First fossil conifer trees
		Devonian (D)		416	First amphibian, insect, tree, and shark fossils
		Silurian (S)		444	First true land plant fossils
		Ordovician (O)		488	First fossils of coral and fish
		Cambrian (Є)		542	First trilobite fossils First abundant visible fossils
Proterozoic	Precambrian: An informal name for all of this time and rock.			2500	Oldest fossils: mostly microscopic life, visible fossils rare
Archean				3850	
Hadean		Acasta Gneiss, northwestern Canada		4030	
		Nuvvuagittuq greenstone belt, Quebec, Canada		4280	
		Zircon mineral crystals in the Jack Hills Metaconglomerate, Western Australia		4400	
	Oldest meteorites			4550	

*European name
**Symbols in parentheses are abbreviations commonly used to designate the age of rock units on geologic maps.
+Extant mollusks are mollusks (clams, snails, squid, etc.) found as fossils and still living today.

FIGURE 3 The geologic time scale. Absolute ages of Phanerozoic boundaries on this chart are used courtesy of the International Commission on Stratigraphy (ICS, 2010) of the International Union of Geological Sciences (**http://www.iugs.org/**). Get the latest International Stratigraphic Chart and ICS publications and information from the IUGS Subcommission for Stratigraphic Information website (**https://engineering.purdue.edu/Stratigraphy/**).

COMMON PROCESSES OF CHANGE

Process	Kind of Change	Example
Melting	Solid phase changes to liquid phase.	Water ice turns to water.
Freezing	Liquid phase changes to solid phase.	Water turns to water ice.
Evaporation	Liquid phase changes to gas (vapor) phase.	Water turns to water vapor or steam (hot water vapor).
Condensation	Gas (vapor) phase changes to liquid phase.	Water vapor turns to water droplets.
Sublimation	Solid phase changes directly to a gas (vapor) phase.	Dry ice (carbon dioxide ice) turns to carbon dioxide gas.
Deposition	The laying down of solid material as when a gas phase changes into a solid phase or solid particles settle out of a fluid.	Frost is the deposition of ice (solid phase) from water vapor (gas). There is deposition of sand and gravel on beaches.
Dissolution	A substance becomes evenly dispersed into a liquid (or gas). The dispersed substance is called a solute, and the liquid (or gas) that causes the dissolution is called a solvent.	Table salt (solute) dissolves in water (solvent).
Vaporization	Solid or liquid changes into a gas (vapor), due to evaporation or sublimation.	Water turns to water vapor or water ice turns directly to water vapor.
Reaction	Any change that results in formation of a new chemical substance (by combining two or more different substances).	Sulfur dioxide (gas) combines with water vapor in the atmosphere to form sulfuric acid, one of the acids in rain.
Decomposition	An irreversible reaction. The different elements in a chemical compound are irreversibly split apart from one another to form new compounds.	Feldspar mineral crystals decompose to clay minerals and metal oxides (rust).
Dissociation	A reversible reaction in which some of the elements in a chemical compound are temporarily split up. They can combine again under the right conditions to form back into the starting compound.	The mineral gypsum dissociates into water and calcium sulfate, which can recombine to form gypsum again.
Chemical precipitation	A solid that forms when a liquid solution evaporates or reacts with another substance.	Salt forms as ocean water evaporates. Table salt forms when hydrochloric acid and sodium hydroxide solutions are mixed.
Photosynthesis	Sugar (glucose) and oxygen are produced from the reaction of carbon dioxide and water in the presence of sunlight (solar energy).	Plants produce glucose sugar and oxygen.
Respiration	Sugar (glucose) and oxygen undergo combustion (burning) without flames and change to carbon dioxide, water, and heat energy.	Plants and animals obtain their energy from respiration.
Transpiration	Water vapor is produced by the biological processes of animals and plants (respiration, photosynthesis).	Plants release water vapor to the atmosphere through their pores.
Evolution	Change in a specific direction (gradually or in stages).	Biological evolution, change in the shape of Earth's landforms through time.
Crystallization	Atoms, ions, or molecules arrange themselves into a regular repeating 3-dimensional pattern. The formation of a crystal.	Water vapor freezes into snowflakes. Liquid magma cools into a solid mass of crystals.
Weathering	Materials are fragmented, worn, or chemically decomposed.	Rocks break apart, get worn into pebbles or sand, dissolve, rust, or decompose to mud.
Transportation	Materials are pushed, bounced, or carried by water, wind, ice, or organisms.	Sand and soil are blown away. Streams push, bounce, and carry materials downstream.
Convection	Current motion (and heat transfer) within a body of material (gas, liquid, or soft solid). As part of the material is heated and rises, a cooler part of the material descends to replace it and form a cycle of convection (convection cell).	Warm air in the atmosphere rises and cooler air descends to replaces it; water boiling in a pot.

FIGURE 4 Some common processes of change on Earth.

and condensation, sublimation and deposition, dissolution and chemical precipitation, photosynthesis (food energy storage) and respiration (food energy release or "burning" without flames). And while some chemical reactions are irreversible, most are reversible (as in the process of dissociation). Thus, opposing processes of change cause chemical materials to be endlessly cycled and recycled between two or more

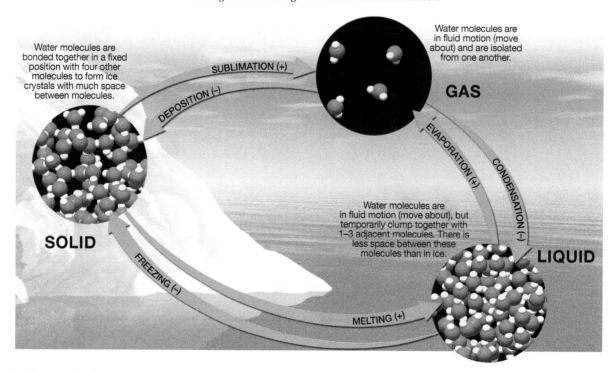

FIGURE 5 Ternary diagram showing the three states (*phases*) of water, plus six common processes that change states of matter by heating (+) and cooling (−). Note the distribution and packing of atoms and molecules in fluid (liquid and gas) versus solid states.

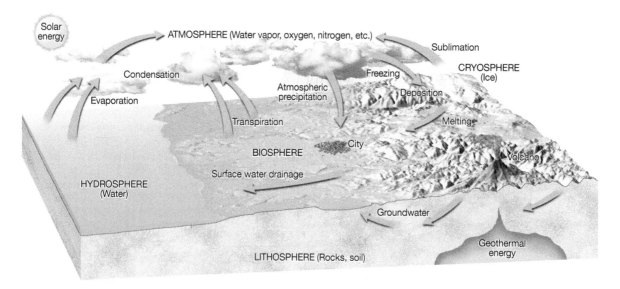

FIGURE 6 The hydrologic cycle (water cycle). Note the relationship of processes of change in the states of water (evaporation, condensation, etc.) to Earth's spheres (geosphere, cryosphere, hydrosphere, atmosphere, biosphere). Also note that the hydrologic cycle is driven (forced to operate) by energy from the Sun (solar energy), energy from Earth's interior (volcanoes and geothermal energy), and gravity.

phases. One of these cycles is the *hydrologic cycle,* or "water cycle" (Figure 6).

The hydrologic cycle involves several processes and changes in relation to all three phases of water and all of Earth's spheres (global subsystems). It is one of the most important cycles that geologists routinely consider in their work. The hydrologic cycle is generally thought to operate like this: water (hydrosphere) evaporating from Earth's surface produces water vapor (atmospheric gas). The water vapor eventually condenses in the atmosphere to form aerosol water droplets (clouds). The droplets combine to form raindrops or snowflakes (atmospheric precipitation). Snowflakes can accumulate to form ice (cryosphere) that sublimates back into the atmosphere or melts back into water. Both rainwater and meltwater soak into the ground (to form groundwater), evaporate back into the atmosphere, drain back into the ocean, or are consumed by plants and animals (which release the water back to the atmosphere via the process of transpiration).

In addition to water that is moving about the Earth system, there is also water that is stored and not circulating at any given time. For example, a very small portion of Earth's water (about 2% of the water volume in oceans) is currently stored in snow and glacial ice at the poles and on high mountaintops. Additional water (perhaps as much as 80% of the water now in oceans) is also stored in "hydrous" (water-bearing) minerals inside Earth. When glaciers melt, or rocks melt, the water can return to active circulation.

The endless exchange of energy and recycling of water undoubtedly has occurred since the first water bodies formed on Earth billions of years ago. Your next drink may include water molecules that once were part of a hydrous (water-bearing) mineral inside Earth or that once were consumed by a thirsty dinosaur!

Relating Scales of Understanding

The hydrologic cycle is a reminder that each thing on Earth is somehow related to everything else in space, time, or process. Geologists seek to understand these complex relationships relative to human lifetimes and the geologic time scale. For you to think like a geologist, you must consider many materials and processes over a broad range of temporal and spatial scales of observation. Some of these scales of observation may be unfamiliar to you, so you will need to convert unfamiliar sizes and rates to familiar ones. For example, a rate of "1000 meters per million years" is much easier to conceptualize if it is converted to "1 millimeter per year." You can also make scale models of things that are too large or small to visualize. A scale model is a physical representation of something that is actually much larger or smaller and has the same proportions as the actual object. For example, a toy car is a small model of an actual car. The scale of the model is the ratio by which the actual object was enlarged or reduced to make the scale model. If a toy car is 20 centimeters long and the actual car was 800 centimeters long, then the ratio scale of model to actual car is 20:800, which reduces to 1:40. The model has a fractional scale of 1/40, meaning that the actual car is 40 times (40×) larger than the model.

ACTIVITY 1

Basketball Model of Earth's Spheres

At the global scale of observation, geologists conceptualize Earth as a dynamic planetary system composed of interacting *spheres* (subsystems) of living and nonliving materials. The *geosphere* is Earth's rocky body, which has an average radius of 6371 km (kilometers, or thousands of meters). The geosphere is divided on the basis of chemical composition into the inner core, outer core, mantle, and crust. The inner core has a radius of 1196 km and is composed mostly of iron (Fe) in a solid state. The outer core is 2250 km thick and is composed mostly of iron (Fe) and nickel (Ni) in a liquid state. The mantle is 2900 km thick and is composed mostly of oxygen (O), silicon (Si), magnesium (Mg), and iron (Fe) in a solid state. The crust has an average thickness of about 25 km and is composed mostly of oxygen (O), silicon (Si), aluminum (Al), and iron (Fe) in a solid state. The *hydrosphere* is all of the liquid water on Earth's surface and in the ground (groundwater). Most of the hydrosphere is salt water in the world ocean, which has an average depth (thickness) of 3.7 km. The *cryosphere* is the snow and ice that forms from freezing parts of the hydrosphere or atmosphere. (Because ice is a mineral, the cryosphere can also be thought of as part of the lithosphere.) Most of it exists in the polar ice sheets (continental glaciers), permafrost (permanently frozen moisture in the ground), and sea ice (ice on the oceans). The *atmosphere* is the gaseous envelope that surrounds Earth. It consists of about 78% nitrogen (Ni), 21% oxygen (O), 0.9% argon (Ar), and trace amounts of other gases like carbon dioxide, water vapor, and methane. About 80% of these gases (including nearly all of the water vapor) occur in the lowest layer of the atmosphere (troposphere), which has an average thickness of about 16 km (10 miles). From there, the atmosphere thins and eventually ends (no air) at about 1000 km above sea level. The *biosphere* is the living part of Earth, the part that is organic and self-replicating. It includes all of the plants and animals, so you are a member of the biosphere.

Tear out the worksheet for Activity 1, and construct a scale model of Earth in which the geosphere is the same size as a basketball. The basketball image is the actual size of a men's basketball, which has a diameter of 238 mm (a radius of 119 mm). Draw and label the spheres as carefully and as exactly as you can so that you can understand their relative proportions.

PART B: DIRECT AND REMOTE INVESTIGATION OF GEOLOGY

The most reliable information about Earth is obtained by direct observation, investigation, and measurement in the field (out of doors, in natural context) and laboratory. Most geologists study *outcrops*—field sites where rocks *crop out* (stick out of the ground). The outcrops are made of rocks, and rocks are made of minerals.

Samples obtained "in the field" (from outcrops at field sites) are often removed to the laboratory for further analysis using basic science. Careful observation (use of your senses, tactile abilities, and tools to gather information) and critical thought lead to questions and hypotheses (tentative ideas to test). Investigations are then designed and carried out to test the hypotheses and gather data (information, evidence). Results of the investigations are analyzed to answer questions and justify logical conclusions.

Refer to the example of field and laboratory analysis in Figure 7. Observation 1 (in the field) reveals that Earth's rocky geosphere crops out at the surface of the land. Observation 2 reveals that outcrops are made of rocks. Observation 3 reveals that rocks are made of mineral crystals such as the mineral *chalcopyrite*. This line of reasoning leads to the next **logical question:** *What is chalcopyrite composed of?* Let us consider the two most logical possibilities, or **working hypotheses** (tentative ideas to investigate, test). It is always best to have more than one working hypothesis.

1. Chalcopyrite may be a pure substance, or chemical element. What investigating and gathering of evidence could we do to reasonably determine if this is true or false?

2. Chalcopyrite may be a *compound* composed of two or more elements. What investigating and gathering of evidence could we do to reasonably determine if this is true or false? If true, then how could we find out what elements make up chalcopyrite?

Let us conduct two **investigations** (activities planned and conducted to test hypotheses, gather and record data, make measurements, or control and explore variables). In Investigation 1, the chalcopyrite is ground to a powder and heated. This investigation reveals the presence of sulfur and at least one other substance. The remaining substance is attracted to a magnet, so it may be iron, or a compound containing iron. When the powder is leached (dissolved in acidic water) and subjected to electrolysis (Investigation 2), copper separates from the powder. The remaining powder is attracted to a magnet, indicating the presence of iron. **Analysis of the results** of these two investigations leads us to the **logical conclusion** that Hypothesis 2 was correct (chalcopyrite is a compound). The results are also evidence that chalcopyrite is composed of three different elements: sulfur (S), iron (Fe), and copper (Cu). Chemists call chalcopyrite, copper-iron sulfide ($CuFeS_2$). Because chalcopyrite contains a significant proportion of copper, it is also a *copper ore* (natural material from which copper can be extracted at a reasonable profit).

This same laboratory procedure is applied on a massive scale at copper mines. Because most copper-bearing rock contains only a few percent of chalcopyrite or another copper-bearing mineral, the rock is mined, crushed, and powdered. It is then mixed with water, detergents, and air bubbles that float the chalcopyrite grains to the surface of the water. When these grains are removed, they are smelted (roasted) to separate the copper from the other parts of the chalcopyrite and melted rock (that cool to form *slag*). The remaining copper powder is then leached in sulfuric acid and subjected to electrolysis, whereupon the copper is deposited as a mass of pure copper on the positive electrode (cathode).

Satellite Remote Sensing of Geology

There are times when geologists cannot make direct observations of Earth and must rely on a technology to acquire and record information remotely (from a distance, without direct contact). This is called *remote sensing*. One of the most common kinds of remote sensing used by geologists is satellite remote sensing. Some satellites, such as the space shuttle and International Space Station, are manned by astronauts who take photographs of Earth using cameras. However, most satellite remote sensing is done by scanners mounted on unmanned environmental satellites. These satellites scan Earth to obtain a digital data set, and the data are sent to ground stations that convert it into visual satellite images of Earth. Instruments aboard the satellites scan information from not only the visible part of the electromagnetic spectrum, but also parts of the spectrum that are not visible to humans (e.g., infrared).

The electromagnetic (EM) spectrum of radiation (Figure 8) is a spectrum of electric and magnetic waves that travel at the speed of light (300,000,000 meters/second, or 3×10^8 m/s). The spectrum is subdivided into **bands**—parts of the EM spectrum that are defined and named according to their wavelength (distance between two adjacent wave crests or troughs). Waves in the gamma ray and X-ray bands have the shortest wavelengths, which are measured in billionths of a meter (called nanometers, nm). Waves in the ultraviolet, visible, and infrared bands have wavelengths measured in millionths of a meter (called micrometers, μm). The long waves of the microwave and broadcast radio bands are measured in meters (m) and kilometers (km).

Earth materials may *emit* (send out) EM waves in the thermal (heat) infrared band (3–15 μm). Earth materials also *reflect* EM waves (like a mirror), *absorb* EM waves and convert them to another wavelength or form of energy (like sunlight converted to heat), or *transmit* EM waves (allow them to pass through, like a glass window). Many Earth materials can be identified from

Example of Geologic Field and Laboratory Investigation

OBSERVATION 1:
Earth's geosphere crops out in surface exposures called *outcrops*.

OBSERVATION 2:
Outcrops are composed of *rocks*.

OBSERVATION 3:
Rocks are composed of *mineral crystals*. Chalcopyrite is a kind of mineral crystal found in some rocks.

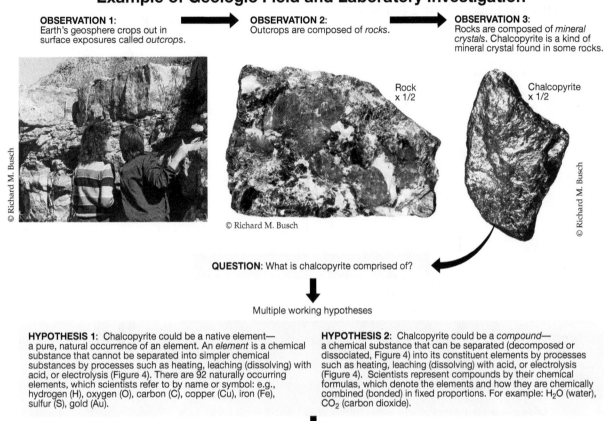

Rock x 1/2

© Richard M. Busch

Chalcopyrite x 1/2

© Richard M. Busch

© Richard M. Busch

QUESTION: What is chalcopyrite comprised of?

Multiple working hypotheses

HYPOTHESIS 1: Chalcopyrite could be a native element— a pure, natural occurrence of an element. An *element* is a chemical substance that cannot be separated into simpler chemical substances by processes such as heating, leaching (dissolving) with acid, or electrolysis (Figure 4). There are 92 naturally occurring elements, which scientists refer to by name or symbol: e.g., hydrogen (H), oxygen (O), carbon (C), copper (Cu), iron (Fe), sulfur (S), gold (Au).

HYPOTHESIS 2: Chalcopyrite could be a *compound*— a chemical substance that can be separated (decomposed or dissociated, Figure 4) into its constituent elements by processes such as heating, leaching (dissolving) with acid, or electrolysis (Figure 4). Scientists represent compounds by their chemical formulas, which denote the elements and how they are chemically combined (bonded) in fixed proportions. For example: H_2O (water), CO_2 (carbon dioxide).

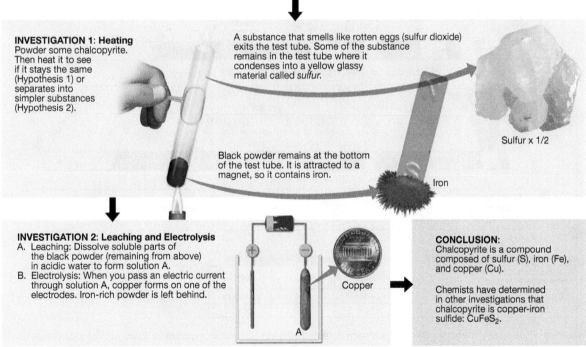

INVESTIGATION 1: Heating
Powder some chalcopyrite. Then heat it to see if it stays the same (Hypothesis 1) or separates into simpler substances (Hypothesis 2).

A substance that smells like rotten eggs (sulfur dioxide) exits the test tube. Some of the substance remains in the test tube where it condenses into a yellow glassy material called *sulfur*.

Sulfur x 1/2

Black powder remains at the bottom of the test tube. It is attracted to a magnet, so it contains iron.

Iron

INVESTIGATION 2: Leaching and Electrolysis
A. Leaching: Dissolve soluble parts of the black powder (remaining from above) in acidic water to form solution A.
B. Electrolysis: When you pass an electric current through solution A, copper forms on one of the electrodes. Iron-rich powder is left behind.

Copper

A

CONCLUSION:
Chalcopyrite is a compound composed of sulfur (S), iron (Fe), and copper (Cu).

Chemists have determined in other investigations that chalcopyrite is copper-iron sulfide: $CuFeS_2$.

FIGURE 7 Example of geologic field and laboratory investigation.

Bands of Electromagnetic (EM) Radiation Used to Image Earth's Surface

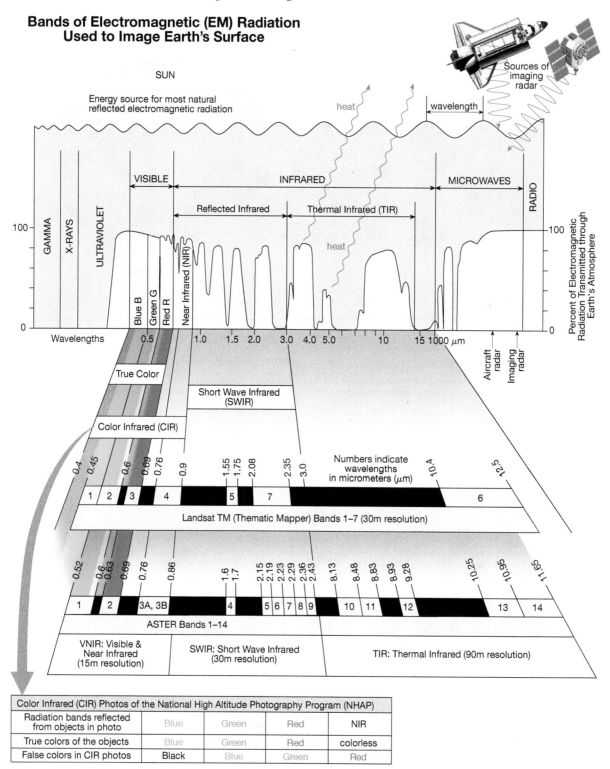

FIGURE 8 Bands of electromagnetic (EM) radiation detected with the human eye (true color), NHAP color-infrared film, and the Landsat TM and ASTER instruments on environmental satellites. Refer to text for discussion.

space by their characteristic wavelengths and intensities of emitted and reflected EM radiation. However, Earth's atmosphere is very effective at absorbing (not transmitting) EM radiation in the gamma ray, X-ray, most of the ultraviolet, and some parts of the infrared wavelengths. These absorbed bands cannot be used in satellite remote sensing. (Note how this is shown graphically at the top of Figure 8, which shows the percentage of EM radiation transmitted through Earth's atmosphere.) Therefore, satellite remote sensing is based on the use of EM radiation that is transmitted through Earth's atmosphere and provides the most useful information to identify and characterize Earth materials.

The most intense EM radiation that reaches Earth's surface is short wavelengths of EM radiation from our Sun. This includes some ultraviolet bands ($0.3-0.4\,\mu m$), all of the visible bands ($0.4-0.7\,\mu m$), and the reflected infrared bands [both NIR—near infrared ($0.7-0.9\,\mu m$) and SWIR—short wave infrared ($0.9-3.0\,\mu m$)]. The most intense solar radiation is the green visible band. Some solar EM radiation is absorbed by Earth materials or transmitted through them. What is not absorbed or transmitted is reflected back into space, where it is detected by satellite instruments that are remotely sensing the reflected bands of EM radiation. This is done during the day, when the reflections occur.

Some solar radiation is absorbed by Earth materials, converted to heat, and then emitted from those materials as long wavelengths of invisible, thermal (heat) infrared radiation (TIR radiation, $3-30\,\mu m$). Earth materials warmed in other ways (e.g., fire, body heat produced by respiration, volcanic heat from Earth's interior) also emit thermal (heat) infrared radiation (TIR). It is normally detected and measured by satellite instruments operating at night, when there is no sunlight to heat up surfaces. This allows geologists to see objects that emit heat on their own, even when they are not absorbing solar radiation and converting it to heat.

Microwaves ($0.1-30$ cm) are also invisible to humans. However, they are used in imaging radar instruments that measure the distance between a satellite (or aircraft) and points on Earth. Imaging radar is used to make images with a three-dimensional perspective.

True color photographs and satellite images (Figure 9) show objects in the colors that they appear to the human eye (visible spectrum of red, orange, yellow, green, blue, indigo, violet). Instruments aboard satellites also detect EM radiation in the bands that humans cannot see. Because they are invisible, they have no true color. These invisible bands must be given a **false color** in satellite images (Figure 10).

All instruments that measure spatial or temporal information have a **resolution**—ability to resolve and measure detail. The smaller the increments of measurement or imaging, the greater the resolution. Therefore, one way to tell the resolution of a photograph or image is to determine the smallest object that it reveals. Image resolution also depends on the resolution of the digital scanning instrument that collected the data for the image.

Scanners on environmental satellites are digital scanners that subdivide the field of view into rows of square picture elements, or *pixels*. The pixels are assembled row-by-row via computer to produce an image. All of the light (EM radiation) entering the scanner for the area represented by a single pixel is averaged into a single reading for that pixel. Therefore, satellite images are not exact copies of what was in the satellite's field of view. They are a grid of information averaged into pixels at some resolution. The easiest way to express the resolution of a satellite image is to determine the surface area that one of its pixels represents. If each pixel in an image represents a 100 m by 100 m square of land, then the satellite image is said to have a resolution of 100 m. At this resolution, each pixel is bigger than a house, so homes would not be visible in the image.

MODIS satellite images have a resolution of 250 m (bands 1–2, Figure 9A), 500 m (bands 3–7), and 1000 m (bands 8–36). This makes them useful for viewing large features of Earth at a regional scale of observation. MODIS instruments scan the entire Earth every 1–2 days.

Landsat TM instruments collect digital data at a resolution of 30 m from seven different bands. Bands 1, 2, and 3 are blue, green, and red bands useful for true color images. Band 4 is near infrared (NIR), useful for detecting vegetation that reflects NIR. Bands 5, 6, and 7 are thermal infrared (TIR) bands that can be used to measure and produce false color images of the temperature of water, clouds, volcanoes, or other objects of the landscape.

The ASTER instrument scans 14 bands of electromagnetic radiation at three different resolutions (Figure 8). Bands 1, 2, and 3 are visible (green, red) and NIR bands, collectively called VNIR, obtained at a resolution of 15 m. Bands 4–9 are short wave infrared (SWIR) obtained at a resolution of 30 m. Bands 10–14 are TIR obtained at a resolution of 90 m.

Satellite remote sensing is a tool used by geologists to help them view regions that are not accessible to them, connect sample and outcrop data to regional and global perspectives, or survey regions to devise a strategy for field work. Inferences made from satellite images must be ground truthed as much as possible with field geology and laboratory work. The more they are ground truthed, the more reliable they are as tools for understanding Earth.

ACTIVITY 2

Remote Sensing of Earth and Exploring for Copper

Refer to the images in Figures 9 and 10 to observe and describe processes of change, make a prediction, and describe a plan of field geology and lab work that you could use to test your prediction.

Mt. Etna, Sicily: Europe's largest and most active volcano, shown in true color

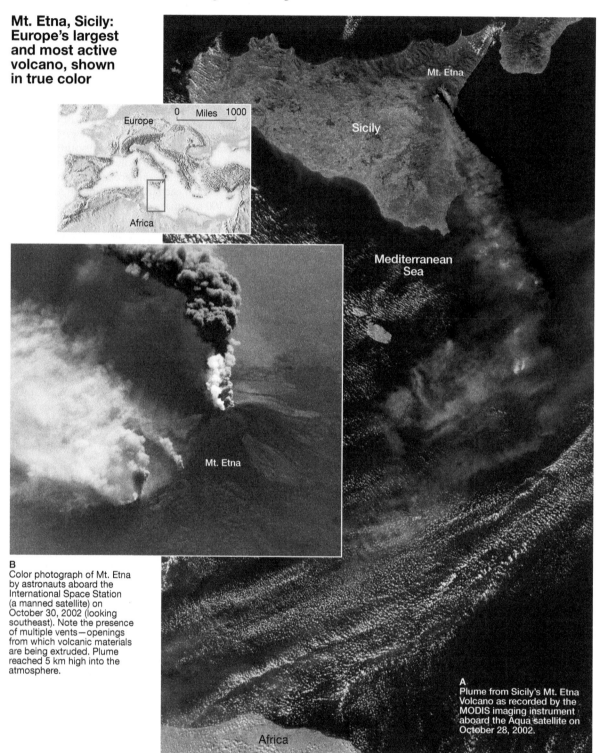

B
Color photograph of Mt. Etna by astronauts aboard the International Space Station (a manned satellite) on October 30, 2002 (looking southeast). Note the presence of multiple vents—openings from which volcanic materials are being extruded. Plume reached 5 km high into the atmosphere.

A
Plume from Sicily's Mt. Etna Volcano as recorded by the MODIS imaging instrument aboard the Aqua satellite on October 28, 2002.

FIGURE 9 True color pictures of Mt. Etna, on the island of Sicily, in the Mediterranean Sea. **A.** View on October 28, 2002, by the MODIS instrument on the Aqua satellite (Courtesy of Jacques Descloitres, MODIS Rapid Response Team, NASA GSFC). **B.** View on October 30, 2002, photographed by astronauts aboard the International Space Station. (Image ISS05-E-19024: Courtesy of Earth Science & Image Analysis Laboratory, NASA Johnson Space Center)

ASTER Bands 1, 2, 3 in Blue, Green, Red

ASTER Bands 4, 6, 8 (SWIR)
in Red, Green, Blue

**ASTER Satellite Images:
Escondida Open Pit Copper Mines, Chile**

0 _____ 10 km

0 _____ 10 mi

FIGURE 10 Escondida open pit copper mining region, northern Chile, as imaged by ASTER. Refer to Figure 8 to review what kind of EM radiation is detected by each of the ASTER bands. (Images courtesy of NASA/GSFC/METI/ERSDAC/JAROS, and U.S./Japan ASTER Science Team: **asterweb.jpl.nasa.gov**; photograph courtesy of Rio Tinto: **www.riotinto.com**)

PART C: MEASURING EARTH MATERIALS AND RELATIONSHIPS

Every material has a *mass* that can be weighed and a *volume* of space that it occupies. An object's mass can be measured by determining its weight under the pull of Earth's gravity (using a balance). An object's volume can be calculated by determining the multiple of its linear dimensions (measured using a ruler) or directly measured by determining the volume of water that it displaces (using a graduated cylinder). In this laboratory, you will use metric balances, rulers, and graduated cylinders to analyze and evaluate the dimensions and density of Earth materials. Refer to page viii at the front of this manual for illustrations of this basic laboratory equipment.

Metric System of Measurement

People in different parts of the world have historically used different systems of measurement. For example, people in the United States have historically used the English system of measurement based on units such as inches, feet, miles, pounds, gallons, and degrees Fahrenheit. However, for more than a century, most nations of the world have used the metric system of measurement based on units such as meters, liters, and degrees Celsius. In 1975, the U.S. Congress recognized the value of a global system of measurement and adopted the metric system as the official measurement system of the United States. This conversion is not yet complete, so Americans currently use both English and metric systems of measurement. In this laboratory we will only use the metric system.

Each kind of metric unit can be divided or multiplied by 10 and its powers to form the smaller or larger units of the metric system. Therefore, the metric system is also known as a base-10 or decimal system. The International System of Units (SI) is the modern version of metric system symbols, numbers, base-10 numerals, powers of ten, and prefixes.

Linear Measurements and Conversions

You must be able to use a metric ruler to make exact measurements of **length** (how long something is). This is called *linear measurement*. Most rulers in the United States are graduated in English units of length (inches) on one side and metric units of length (centimeters) on the other. For example, notice that one side of the ruler in Figure 11A is graduated in numbered inches, and each inch is subdivided into eighths and sixteenths. The other side of the ruler is graduated in numbered centimeters (hundredths of a meter), and each centimeter is subdivided into ten millimeters. The ruler provided for you in GeoTools Sheets 1 and 2 are graduated in exactly the same way.

Review the examples of linear metric measurement in Figure 11A to be sure that you understand how to make *exact* metric measurements. Note that the length of an object may not coincide with a specific centimeter or millimeter mark on the ruler, so you may have to estimate the fraction of a unit as exactly as you can. The length of the red rectangle in Figure 11A is between graduation marks for 106 and 107 millimeters (mm), so the most exact measurement of this length is 106.5 mm. Also, be sure that you measure lengths starting from the zero point on the ruler and *not from the end of the ruler*.

There will be times when you will need to convert a measurement from one unit of measure to another. This can be done with the aid of the mathematical conversions chart on page xi at the front of the manual. For example, you convert millimeters (mm) to meters (m) by multiplying the measurement in mm by 0.001 m/mm. Thus,

$$\frac{106.5 \text{ mm}}{1} \times \frac{0.001 \text{ m}}{1 \text{ mm}} = 0.1065 \text{ m}$$

so 106.5 millimeters is the same as 0.1065 meters.

Area and Volume

An **area** is a two-dimensional space, such as the surface of a table. The long dimension is the *length*, and the short dimension is the *width*. If the area is square or rectangular, then the size of the area is the product of its length multiplied times its width. For example, the blue rectangular area in Figure 11A is 7.3 cm long and 3.8 cm wide. So the size of the area is 7.3 cm $\times$ 3.8 cm, which equals 27.7 cm^2. This is called 27.7 square centimeters. Using this same method, the yellow front of the box in Figure 11B has an area of 9.0 cm $\times$ 4.0 cm, which equals 36.0 cm^2. The green side of this same box has an area of 4.0 cm $\times$ 4.0 cm, which equals 16.0 cm^2.

Three-dimensional objects are said to occupy a **volume** of space. Box shaped objects have *linear volume* because they take up three linear dimensions of space: their length (longest dimension), width (or depth), and height (or thickness). So, the volume of a box shaped object is the product of its length, width, and height. For example, the box in Figure 11B has a length of 9.0 cm, a width of 4.0 cm, and a height of 4.0 cm. Its volume is 9.0 cm $\times$ 4.0 cm $\times$ 4.0 cm, which equals 144 cm^3. This is called 144 cubic centimeters.

Most natural materials such as rocks do not have linear dimensions, so their volumes cannot be calculated from linear measurements. However, the volumes of these odd-shaped materials can be determined by measuring the volume of water they displace. This is often done in the laboratory with a *graduated cylinder* (Figure 11C), an instrument used to measure volumes of fluid (fluid volume). Most graduated cylinders are graduated in metric units called milliliters (mL), which are thousandths of a liter. *You should also note that 1 mL of fluid volume is exactly the same as 1 cm^3 of linear volume.*

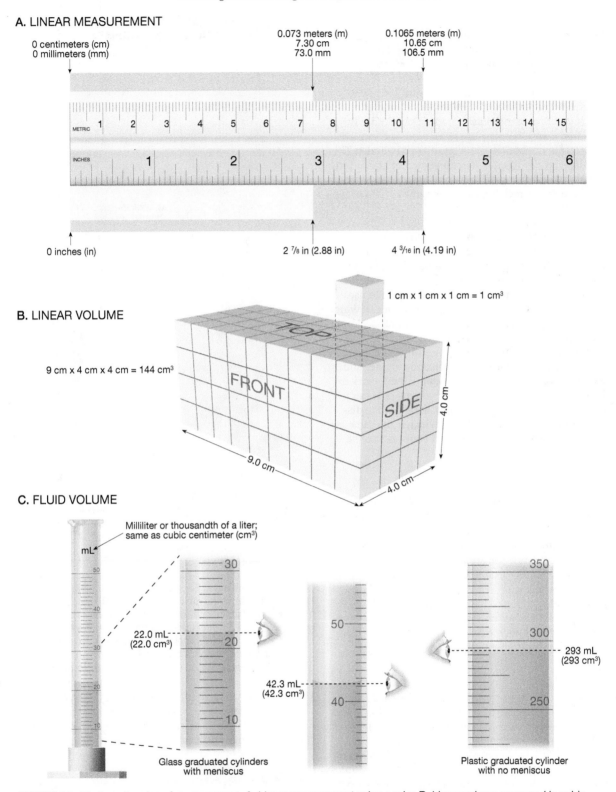

FIGURE 11 Tools and scales of measurement. **A.** Linear measurement using a ruler. **B.** Linear volume measured in cubic centimeters. **C.** Fluid volume measured with graduated cylinder (at base of meniscus). A milliliter (mL) is the same as a cubic centimeter (cm^3). Some manufacturers use the abbreviation ml (instead of mL) on their graduated cylinders and beakers.

When you pour water into a graduated cylinder, the surface of the liquid is usually a curved *meniscus*, and the volume is read at the bottom of the curve (Figure 11C: middle and left-hand examples). In some plastic graduated cylinders, however, there is no meniscus. The water level is flat (Figure 11C: right-hand example).

If you drop a rock into a graduated cylinder full of water, then it takes up space previously occupied by water at the bottom of the graduated cylinder. This displaced water has nowhere to go except higher into the graduated cylinder. Therefore, the volume of an object such as a rock is exactly the same as the volume of fluid (water) that it displaces.

The water displacement procedure for determining the volume of an object is illustrated in Figure 12. First place water in the bottom of a graduated cylinder. Choose a graduated cylinder into which the rock will fit easily, and add enough water to be able to totally immerse the rock. It is also helpful to use a dropper or wash bottle and bring the volume of water (before adding the rock) up to an exact graduation mark (5.0 mL mark in Figure 12A). Record this starting volume of water. Then carefully slide the rock sample down into the same graduated cylinder and record this ending level of the water (7.8 mL mark in Figure 12B). Subtract the starting volume of water from the ending volume of water, to obtain the displaced volume of water (2.8 mL, which is the same as 2.8 cm^3). This volume of displaced water is also the volume of the rock sample.

Mass

Earth materials do not just take up space (volume). They also have a mass of atoms that can be weighed. You will use a gram balance to measure the **mass** of materials (by determining their weight under the pull of Earth's gravity). The gram (g) is the basic unit of mass in the metric system, but instruments used to measure grams vary from triple-beam balances to spring scales to digital balances. Consult with your laboratory instructor or other students to be sure that you understand how to read the gram balance provided in your laboratory.

Density

Every material has a *mass* that can be weighed and a *volume* of space that it occupies. However, the relationship between a material's mass and volume tends to vary from one kind of material to another. For example, a bucket of rocks has much greater mass than an equal-sized bucket of air. Therefore, a useful way to describe an object is to determine its mass per unit of volume, called **density**. *Per* refers to division, as in miles *per* hour (distance divided by time). So, density is the measure of an object's mass divided by its volume (density = mass ÷ volume). Scientists and mathematicians use the Greek character rho (ρ) to

VOLUME DETERMINATION BY WATER DISPLACEMENT

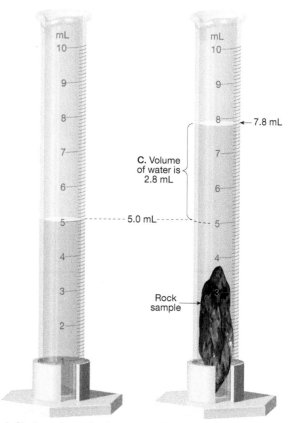

A. Starting volume of water   B. Ending volume of water

FIGURE 12   Procedure for determining volume of a rock sample by water displacement. **A.** Place water in the bottom of a graduated cylinder. Choose a graduated cylinder into which the rock will fit easily and add enough water to be able to totally immerse the rock. It is also helpful to use a dropper or wash bottle and bring the volume of water (before adding the rock) up to an exact graduation mark like the 5.0 mL mark. Record this starting volume of water. **B.** Carefully slide the rock sample down into the same graduated cylinder and record this ending level of the water (7.8 mL mark). Subtract the starting volume of water from the ending volume of water to obtain the displaced volume of water (2.8 mL, which is the same as 2.8 cm^3). This volume of displaced water is also the volume of the rock sample.

represent density. Also, the gram (g) is the basic metric unit of mass, and the cubic centimeter (cm^3) is the basic unit of metric volume. So, density (ρ) is usually expressed in grams per cubic centimeter (g/cm^3).

ACTIVITY 3

Measuring Earth Materials and Relationships

Tear out the activity sheet and complete it as indicated on the sheet.

PART D: DENSITY, GRAVITY, AND ISOSTASY

Scientists have wondered for centuries about how the distribution of Earth materials is related to their density and gravity. For example, Greek scientist and mathematician, Archimedes, experimented with floating objects around 225 B.C. When he placed a block of wood in a bucket of water, he noticed that the block floated and the water level rose (Figure 13A). When he pushed down on the wood block, the water level rose even more. When he removed his fingers from the wood block, the water pushed it back up to its original level of floating. Archimedes eventually

A. FLOATING WOOD BLOCK

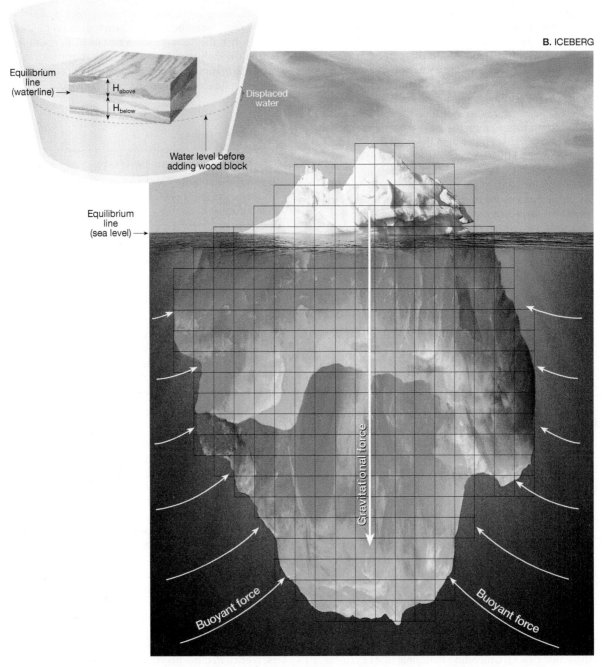

FIGURE 13 Isostasy relationships **A.** of a floating wood block and **B.** an iceberg. Refer to text for discussion. (Iceberg image © Ralph A. Clavenger/CORBIS. All rights reserved.)

17

realized that every floating object is pulled down (toward Earth's center) by gravity, so the object displaces fluid and causes the fluid level to rise. However, Archimedes also realized that every floating object is also pushed upward by a buoyant force that is equal to the weight of the displaced fluid. This is now called Archimedes' Principle.

Buoyant force (buoyancy) is caused as gravity pulls on the mass of a fluid, causing it to exert a *fluid pressure* on submerged objects that increases steadily with increasing depth in the fluid. The deeper (greater amount of) a fluid, the more it weighs, so deep water exerts greater fluid pressure than shallow water. Therefore, the lowest surfaces of a submerged object are squeezed more (by the fluid pressure) than the upper surfaces. This creates the wedge of buoyant force that pushes the object upward and opposes the downward pull of gravity (white arrows in Figure 13B). An object will sink if it is heavier than the fluid it displaces (is denser than the fluid it displaces). An object will rise if it is lighter than the fluid it displaces (is less dense than the fluid it displaces). But a floating object is balanced between sinking and rising. The object sinks until it displaces a volume of fluid that has the same mass as the entire floating object. When the object achieves a motionless floating condition, it is balanced between the downward pull of gravity and the upward push of the buoyant force.

Isostasy

In the 1880s, geologists began to realize the abundant evidence that levels of shoreline along lakes and oceans had changed often throughout geologic time in all parts of the world. Geologists like Edward Suess hypothesized that changes in sea level can occur if *the volume of ocean water changes* in response to climate. Global atmospheric warming leads to sea level rise caused by melting of glaciers (cryosphere), and global atmospheric cooling leads to a drop in sea level as more of Earth's hydrosphere gets stored in thicker glaciers. However, an American geologist named Clarence Dutton suggested that shorelines can also change *if the level of the land changes* (and the volume of water remains the same).

Dutton reasoned that if blocks of Earth's crust are supported by fluid materials beneath them, then they must float according to Archimedes' Principle (like wood blocks, icebergs, and boats floating in water). Therefore, he proposed that Earth's crust consists of buoyant blocks of rock that float in gravitational balance on top of the mantle. He called this floating condition **isostasy** (Greek for "equal standing"). Loading a crustal block (by adding lava flows, sediments, glaciers, water, etc.) will decrease its buoyancy, and the block will sink (like pushing down on a floating wood block). Unloading materials from a crustal block will increase its buoyancy, and the block will rise. Therefore, you can also think of isostasy as the

equilibrium (balancing) condition between any floating object (such as the iceberg in Figure 13) and the more dense fluid in which it is floating (such as the water in Figure 13). Gravity pulls the iceberg down toward Earth's center (this is called *gravitational force*), so the submerged root of the iceberg displaces water. At the same time, gravity also tries to pull the displaced water back into its original place (now occupied by the iceberg's root). This creates fluid pressure that increases with depth along the iceberg's root, so the iceberg is squeezed and wedged (pushed) upward. This squeezing and upward-pushing force is called *buoyant force*. **Isostatic equilibrium** (balanced floating) occurs when the buoyant force equals (is in equilibrium with) the gravitational force that opposes it. An **equilibrium line** (like the waterline on a boat) separates the iceberg's submerged root from its exposed top.

ACTIVITY 4

Density, Gravity, and Isostasy

Tear out the activity sheet and complete it as indicated on the sheet using materials provided in laboratory.

PART E: ISOSTASY AND EARTH'S GLOBAL TOPOGRAPHY

Clarence Dutton applied his isostasy hypothesis in 1889 to explain how the shorelines of lakes or oceans could be elevated by vertical motions of Earth's crust. At that time, little was known about Earth's mantle or the topography of the seafloor. Modern data show that Dutton's isostasy hypothesis has broader application for understanding global topography.

Global Topography

Radar and laser imaging technologies carried aboard satellites now measure Earth's topography very exactly, and the data can be used to form very precise relief images of the height of landforms and depths of ocean basins. For example, satellite data were used to construct the image in Figure 14A of Earth with ocean water removed. The seafloor is shaded blue and includes features such as shallow continental shelves, submarine mountains (mid-ocean ridges), deep abyssal plains, and even deeper trenches. Land areas (continents) are shaded green (lowlands) and brown (mountains).

The histogram (bar diagram) of Earth's topography in Figure 14B shows the percentage of Earth's surface for each depth or height class (bar) in kilometers. Notice that the histogram is bimodal (shows two levels of elevation that are most common on Earth). One of the elevation modes occurs above sea level

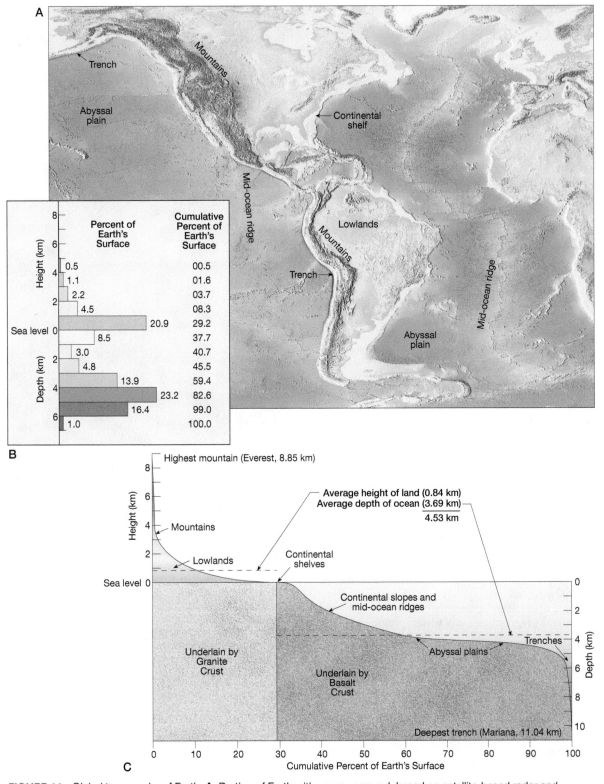

FIGURE 14 Global topography of Earth. **A.** Portion of Earth with ocean removed, based on satellite-based radar and laser technologies. **B.** Histogram of global topography. **C.** Hypsographic curve of Earth's global topography. (Refer to text for discussion.)

and corresponds to the continents. The other elevation mode occurs below sea level and corresponds to the ocean floor.

Figure 14C is called a *hypsographic curve* and shows the cumulative percentage of Earth's spherical surface that occurs at specific elevations or depths in relation to sea level. This curve is not the profile of a continent, because it represents Earth's entire spherical surface. Notice that the cumulative percentage of land is only 29.2% of Earth's surface, and most of the land is lowlands. The remaining 70.8 cumulative percent of Earth's surface is covered by ocean, and most of the seafloor is more than 3 km deep.

Global Isostasy

The average elevation of the continents is about 0.84 km above sea level (+0.84 km), but the average elevation of the ocean basins is 3.87 km below sea level (−3.87 km). Therefore, the difference between the average continental and ocean basin elevations is 4.71 km! If the continents did not sit so much higher than the floor of the ocean basins, then Earth would have no dry land and there would be no humans. What could account for this elevation difference? One clue may be the difference between crustal granite and basalt in relation to mantle peridotite.

Granite (light-colored, coarse-grained igneous rock) and basalt (dark-colored, fine-grained igneous rock) make up nearly all of Earth's crust (Figure 15). *Basaltic rocks* form the crust of the oceans, beneath a thin veneer of sediment. *Granitic rocks* form the crust of the continents, usually beneath a thin veneer of sediment and other rock types. Therefore, you can think of the continents (green and brown) in Figure 14A as granitic islands surrounded by a low sea of basaltic ocean crust (blue). All of these rocky bodies rest on mantle rock called *peridotite* (Figure 15B). Could differences among the three rock types making up Earth's outer edge explain Earth's bimodal global topography? Let's investigate. You will need a 500 mL or 1000 mL graduated cylinder, small samples (about 30–50 g) of basalt and granite that fit into the graduated cylinder, a gram balance, and water (provided in lab.).

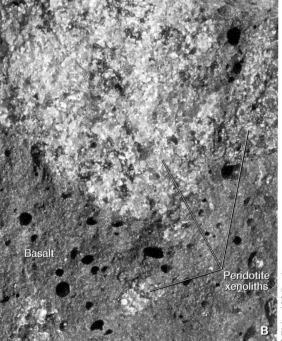

FIGURE 15 The most abundant rocks of Earth's crust and mantle. **A. Granite** is a light-colored igneous rock that forms the crust of continents, beneath layers of sedimentary and metamorphic rocks like those shown in Figure 1.
B. Basalt is an igneous rock that forms the crust of all oceans, beneath layers of sand and mud. The upper mantle consists of **peridotite** rock like these *xenoliths*—pieces of rock carried to Earth's surface by magma in a volcanic eruption. The magma cooled to form a body of basalt with the xenoliths (and gas bubbles) trapped inside.

ACTIVITY 5

Isostasy and Earth's Global Topography

Tear out the activity sheet and complete it as indicated on the sheet using materials provided in laboratory.

ACTIVITY 1 Basketball Model of Earth's Spheres

Name: _____   Course/Section: _____

Materials: Calculator, drafting compass, ruler, pencil, blue pencil or pen.

A. Geoscientists conceptualize Earth as a dynamic system of interacting material spheres (subsystems). The rocky body of Earth (geosphere) has an average radius of 6371 km and consists of four main compositional layers: inner core, outer core, mantle, and crust. These are overlain by the hydrosphere and atmosphere. If Earth's geosphere had the radius of a men's basketball (119 mm), then how thick would each sphere be? Fill in the chart below, then draw (with a ruler and drafting compass) and label each sphere on the pie-shaped slice of this basketball. Label each sphere. For example, the inner core has already been done.

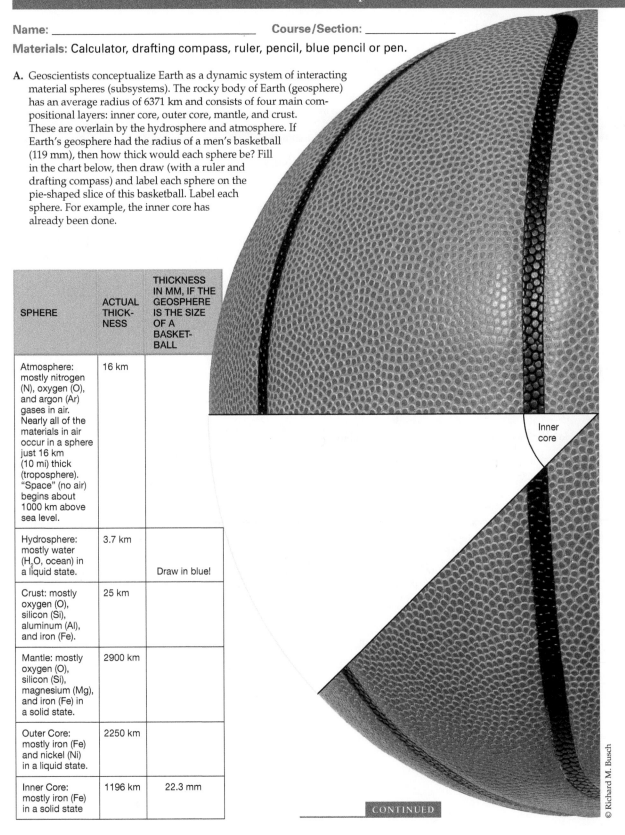

SPHERE	ACTUAL THICK-NESS	THICKNESS IN MM, IF THE GEOSPHERE IS THE SIZE OF A BASKET-BALL
Atmosphere: mostly nitrogen (N), oxygen (O), and argon (Ar) gases in air. Nearly all of the materials in air occur in a sphere just 16 km (10 mi) thick (troposphere). "Space" (no air) begins about 1000 km above sea level.	16 km	
Hydrosphere: mostly water (H$_2$O, ocean) in a liquid state.	3.7 km	Draw in blue!
Crust: mostly oxygen (O), silicon (Si), aluminum (Al), and iron (Fe).	25 km	
Mantle: mostly oxygen (O), silicon (Si), magnesium (Mg), and iron (Fe) in a solid state.	2900 km	
Outer Core: mostly iron (Fe) and nickel (Ni) in a liquid state.	2250 km	
Inner Core: mostly iron (Fe) in a solid state	1196 km	22.3 mm

Inner core

CONTINUED

© Richard M. Busch

B. Recall that Earth's actual average radius is 6371 km (6,371,000 meters) and that the radius of the basketball is only 119 mm (0.119 meters). Calculate the fractional scale (show your work) and ratio scale of the basketball model shown earlier in the chapter.

Fractional scale: Ratio scale:

ACTIVITY 2   Remote Sensing of Earth and Exploring for Copper

Name: _____   Course/Section: _____

Materials: Ruler, pencil.

A. Analyze Figure 9, an astronaut's photograph and MODIS satellite image of the eruption of Sicily's Mt. Etna in the Mediterranean Sea in 2002.

    1. Volcanic "vents" are openings from which volcanic materials are extruded. Analyze Figure 9B (October 30, 2002 eruption of Mt. Etna). What two kinds of materials do you think are being extruded from Mt. Etna's vents and how can you recognize them?

    2. What distance has the brown extruded material traveled so far, and where do you predict it will land?

    3. How did this eruption affect the atmosphere and hydrosphere?

B. Analyze Figure 10, true and false colored ASTER images of Chile's Escondida Mine and vicinity. This is primarily a copper mine, but it also produces some silver and gold. The copper ore is mined from large open pits. Notice how these pits appear in the images.

    1. Imagine that you have been hired by Escondida Mine to find the best location for a new pit. Which location, A, B, or C, is probably the best site for a new pit? How can you tell?

    2. What plan of scientific investigation would you carry out to see if the location you chose above is actually a good source for more copper ore?

ACTIVITY 3 Measuring Earth Materials and Relationships

Name: _____   Course/Section: _____

Materials: Calculator, pencil. Other materials provided in lab.

A. Make the following unit conversions.

    1. 10 miles = _____ kilometers

    2. 1 foot = _____ meters

    3. 16 kilometers = _____ m

    4. 25 meters = _____ cm

    5. 25.4 mL = _____ cm^3

    6. 1.3 liters = _____ cm^3

B. Using a ruler, draw a line segment that has a length of exactly 1 cm (1 centimeter). A line occupies only one dimension of space, so a line that is 1 cm long is 1 cm^1.

C. Using a ruler, draw a square area that has a length of exactly 1 cm and a width of exactly 1 cm. An area occupies two dimensions of space, so a square that is 1 cm long and 1 cm wide is 1 cm^2 of area (1 cm $\times$ 1 cm = 1 cm^2).

D. Using a ruler, draw a cube that has a length of 1 cm, width of 1 cm, and height of 1 cm. This cube made of centimeters occupies three dimensions of space, so it is 1 cm^3 (1 cubic centimeter) of volume.

E. Explain how you could use a small graduated cylinder and a gram balance to determine the density of water (ρ_{water}) in g/cm^3. Then use your procedures to calculate the density of water as exactly as you can. Show your data and calculations.

F. Obtain a small lump of clay (grease-based modeling clay) and determine its density (ρ_{clay}) in g/cm^3. There is more than one way to do this, so develop and apply a procedure that makes the most sense to you. Explain the procedure that you use, show your data, and show your calculations.

CONTINUED

G. Reconsider your answers to items E and F and the fact that modeling clay sinks in water.

    1. Why does modeling clay sink in water?

    2. What could you do to a lump of modeling clay to get it to float in water? Try your hypothesis and experiment until you get the clay to float.

    3. When you got the clay to float, why did it float?

H. Compared to your answer in item E, what is the density of Earth's atmosphere ($\rho_{atmosphere}$), and lithosphere ($\rho_{lithosphere}$)?

    1. $(\rho_{atmosphere}) = $ ——————— g/cm^3 **2.** $(\rho_{lithosphere}) = $ ——————— g/cm^3

I. How is the distribution of Earth's spheres related to their relative densities?

ACTIVITY 4 Density, Gravity, and Isostasy

Name: _____   Course/Section: _____

Materials: Calculator, pencil. Other materials provided in lab.

A. Obtain one of the wood blocks provided at your table. Determine the density of the wood block (ρ_{wood}) in g/cm³. Show your calculations.

B. Float the same wood block in a bowl of water (like Figure 13A) and mark the equilibrium line (waterline).

   1. Draw an exact sketch of the side view of the wood block and show the exact position of the waterline (equilibrium line). Label the total height of the wood block (H_{block}), the height of the wood block that is submerged below the waterline (H_{below}), and the height of the wood block that is exposed above the waterline (H_{above}).

   2. Measure and record H_{block} in cm: ———————— cm

   3. Measure and record H_{below} in cm: ———————— cm

   4. Measure and record H_{above} in cm: ———————— cm

C. Write an isostasy equation (mathematical model) that expresses how the density of the wood block (ρ_{wood}) compared to the density of the water (ρ_{water}) is related to the height of the wood block that floats *below* the equilibrium line (H_{below}). [*Hint:* Recall that the wood block achieves isostatic equilibrium (motionless balanced floating) when it displaces a volume of water that has the same mass as the entire wood block. For example, if the wood block is 80% as dense as the water, then only 80% of the wood block will be below the equilibrium line (waterline). Therefore, the portion of the wood block's height that is below the equilibrium line (H_{below}) is equal to the total height of the wood block (H_{block}) times the ratio of the density of the wood block (ρ_{wood}) to the density of water (ρ_{water}).]

D. Change your answer in Part C to an equation (mathematical model) that expresses how the density of the wood block (ρ_{wood}) compared to the density of the water (ρ_{water}) is related to the height of the wood block that floats *above* the equilibrium line (H_{above}).

CONTINUED

E. The density of water ice (in icebergs) is 0.917 g/cm³. The average density of (salty) ocean water is 1.025 g/cm³.

1. Use your isostasy equation for H_{below} (Part C) to calculate how much of an iceberg is exposed below sea level. Show your work.

2. Use your isostasy equation for H_{above} (Part D) to calculate how much of an iceberg is exposed above sea level. Show your work.

3. Notice the graph paper grid overlay on the picture of an iceberg in Figure 13B. Use this grid to determine and record the cross-sectional area of this iceberg that is below sea level and the cross-sectional area that is above sea level (by adding together all of the whole boxes and fractions of boxes that overlay the root of the iceberg or the exposed top of the iceberg). Use these data to calculate what proportion of the iceberg is below sea level (the equilibrium line) and what proportion is above sea level. How do your results compare to your calculations in Parts E1 and E2?

4. What will happen as the top of the iceberg melts?

5. Clarence Dutton proposed his isostasy hypothesis to explain how some ancient shorelines have been elevated to where they now occur on the slopes of adjacent mountains. Use *your* understanding of isostasy and icebergs to explain how this may happen.

ACTIVITY 5 Isostasy and Earth's Global Topography

Name: _____   Course/Section: _____

Materials: Calculator, pencil. Other materials provided in lab.

A. *As exactly as you can*, weigh (grams) and determine the volume (by water displacement, Figure 12) of a sample of basalt. Add your data to the basalt density chart below. Calculate the density of your sample of basalt to tenths of a g/cm³. Then determine the average density of basalt using all ten lines of sample data in the basalt density chart.

B. *As exactly as you can*, weigh (grams) and determine the volume (by water displacement, Figure 12) of a sample of granite. Add your data to the granite density chart below. Calculate the density of your sample of granite to tenths of a g/cm³. Then determine the average density of granite using all ten lines of sample data in the granite density chart.

A. BASALT DENSITY CHART

Basalt Sample Number	Sample Weight (g)	Sample Volume (cm³)	Sample Density (g/cm³)
1	40.5	13	3.1
2	29.5	10	3.0
3	46.6	15	3.0
4	31.5	10	3.2
5	37.6	12	3.1
6	34.3	11	3.1
7	78.3	25	3.1
8	28.2	9	3.1
9	55.6	18	3.1
10			

Average density of basalt = _____

B. GRANITE DENSITY CHART

Granite Sample Number	Sample Weight (g)	Sample Volume (cm³)	Sample Density (g/cm³)
1	32.1	12	2.7
2	27.8	10	2.8
3	27.6	10	2.8
4	31.1	11	2.8
5	58.6	20	2.9
6	62.1	22	2.8
7	28.8	10	2.9
8	82.8	30	2.8
9	52.2	20	2.6
10			

Average density of granite = _____

CONTINUED

C. Seismology (the study of Earth's structure and composition using earthquake waves), mantle xenoliths (Figure 15B), and laboratory experiments indicate that the upper mantle is peridotite rock. The peridotite has an average density of about 3.3 g/cm^3 and is capable of slow flow. Seismology also reveals the thicknesses of crust and mantle layers.

    1. Seismology indicates that the average thickness of basaltic ocean crust is about 5.0 km. Use the average density of basalt (Figure 15B) and your isostasy equation (Activity 4, item D) to calculate how high (in kilometers) basalt floats in the mantle. Show your work.

    2. Seismology indicates that the average thickness of granitic continental crust is about 30.0 kilometers. Use the average density of granite (Figure 15B) and your isostasy equation (Activity 4, item D) to calculate how high (in kilometers) granite floats in the mantle. Show your work.

    3. What is the difference (in km) between your answers in C1 and C2?

    4. How does this difference between C1 and C2 compare to the actual difference between the average height of continents and average depth of oceans on the hypsographic curve (Figure 14C)?

D. Reflect on all of your work in this laboratory. Explain why Earth has a bimodal global topography.

E. How is a mountain like the iceberg in Figure 13B?

F. Clarence Dutton was not the first person to develop the concept of a floating crust in equilibrium balance with the mantle, which he called *isostasy* in 1889. Two other people proposed floating crust (isostasy) hypotheses in 1855 (Figure 16). John Pratt (a British physicist and Archdeacon of Calcutta) studied the Himalaya Mountains and hypothesized that floating blocks of Earth's crust have different densities, but they all sink to the same *compensation level* within the mantle. The continental blocks are higher because they are less dense. George Airy (a British astronomer and mathematician) hypothesized that floating blocks of Earth's crust have the same density but different thicknesses. The continental blocks are higher because they are thicker. Do you think that one of these two hypotheses (Pratt vs. Airy) is correct, or would you propose a compromise between them? Explain.

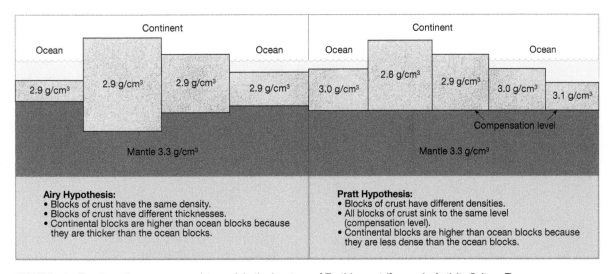

FIGURE 16 Two hypotheses proposed to explain the isostasy of Earth's crust (for use in Activity 5, item F).

Plate Tectonics and the Origin of Magma

CONTRIBUTING AUTHORS

Edward A. Hay • *De Anza College*
Cherukupalli E. Nehru • *Brooklyn College (CUNY)*
C. Gil Wiswall • *West Chester University of Pennsylvania*

OBJECTIVES AND ACTIVITIES

A. Infer whether expanding-Earth or shrinking-Earth hypotheses could explain plate tectonics and how mantle convection plays a role in causing plate tectonics.

ACTIVITY 1: Is Plate Tectonics Caused by a Change in Earth's Size?

ACTIVITY 2: Evaluate a Lava Lamp Model of Earth

B. Understand how plate boundaries are identified and be able to measure and calculate some plate tectonic processes.

ACTIVITY 3: Using Earthquakes to Identify Plate Boundaries

ACTIVITY 4: Analysis of Atlantic Seafloor Spreading

ACTIVITY 5: Plate Motions Along the San Andreas Fault

ACTIVITY 6: The Hawaiian Hot Spot and Pacific Plate Motion

ACTIVITY 7: Plate Tectonics of the Northwest United States

C. Use physical and graphical models of rock melting to infer how magma forms in relation to pressure, temperature, water, and plate tectonics.

ACTIVITY 8: The Origin of Magma

STUDENT MATERIALS

Pencil, eraser, ruler, calculator, and red and blue colored pencils. Hot plate, aluminum foil or two aluminum foil baking cups, sugar cubes (2), dropper with water, and permanent felt-tipped marker provided in lab.

INTRODUCTION

Ever since the first reasonably accurate world maps were constructed in the 1600s, people have proposed models to explain the origin of Earth's mountain belts, continents, ocean basins, rifts, and trenches. For example, some people proposed that surficial processes, like catastrophic global floods, had carved our ocean basins and deposited mountains of gravel. Others proposed that global relief was the result of what is now called **tectonism:** large-scale (regional, global) movements and deformation of Earth's crust. What kinds of tectonic movements occur on Earth, and what process(es) cause them?

German scientist, Alfred Wegener, noticed that the shapes of the continents matched up like pieces of a global jig-saw puzzle. In 1915, he hypothesized that all continents were once part of a single supercontinent, *Pangea*, parts of which drifted apart to form the smaller modern continents. However, most scientists were immediately skeptical of Wegener's **Continental Drift Hypothesis,** because he could not think of a natural process that could force the continents to drift apart. These "anti-drift" scientists viewed continents as stationary landforms that could rise and fall but not drift sideways.

The anti-drift scientists argued that it was impossible for continents to drift or plow through solid oceanic rocks. They also reasoned that Earth was cooling from an older semi-molten state, so it must be shrinking. Their **Shrinking Earth Hypothesis** suggested that the continents were moving together, rather than drifting apart. As Earth's crust shrank into less space, flat rock layers in ocean basins would have been squeezed and folded between the continents (as observed in the Alps).

Two other German scientists, Bernard Lindemann (in 1927) and Otto Hilgenberg (in 1933), independently evaluated the Continental Drift and Shrinking Earth Hypotheses. Both men agreed with Wegener's notion that the continents seemed to fit together like a jig-saw puzzle, but they also felt that the ocean basins were best explained by a new **Expanding Earth Hypothesis** (that they developed and published separately). According to this hypothesis, Earth was once much smaller (about 60% of its modern size) and covered entirely by granitic crust. As Earth expanded, the granitic crust split apart into the shapes of the modern continents and basaltic ocean crust was exposed between them (and covered by ocean).

During the 1960s more data emerged in favor of the Continental Drift Hypothesis. For example, geologists found that it was not only the shapes (outlines) of the continents that matched up like pieces of a Pangea jig-saw puzzle. Similar bodies of rock and the patterns they make at Earth's surface also matched up like a picture on the puzzle pieces. Abundant studies also revealed that ocean basins were generally younger than the continents. An American geologist, Harry Hess, even developed a **Seafloor-Spreading Hypothesis** to explain this. According to Hess' hypothesis, seafloor crust is created along mid-ocean ridges above regions of up-welling magma from Earth's mantle. As old seafloor crust moves from the elevated mid-ocean ridges to the trenches, new magma rises and fills fractures along the mid-ocean ridge. This creates new crust while old crust at the trenches begins descending back into the mantle.

Harry Hess' hypothesis was supported by studies showing that although Earth's rocky body (geosphere) has distinct compositional layers (inner core, outer core, mantle, crust), it can also be divided into layers that have distinct physical behaviors. Two of these physical layers are the lithosphere and asthenosphere (Figure 1). The **lithosphere** (Greek *lithos* = rock) is a physical layer of rock that is composed of Earth's brittle crust and brittle uppermost mantle, called *lithospheric mantle*. It normally has a thickness of 70–150 km but has an average thickness of about 100 km. The lithosphere rests on the **asthenosphere** (Greek *asthenēs* = weak), a physical layer of the mantle about 100–250 km thick that has plastic (ductile) behavior. It tends to flow rather than fracture. Tectonic plates are plates of lithosphere that rest and move upon the weak asthenosphere. Zones of abundant earthquake and volcanic activity are also concentrated along the unstable boundaries (plate boundaries) between rigid stable plates/sheets of lithosphere (lithospheric plates). Thus, by the end of the 1960s a new hypothesis of global tectonics had emerged called the

Plate Tectonics Hypothesis. It is now the prevailing model of Earth's global tectonism.

According to the developing Plate Tectonics Model, the continents are parts of rigid lithospheric plates that move about relative to one another. Plates form and spread apart along **divergent boundaries** such as mid-ocean ridges (Figure 1), where magma rises up between plates that are spreading apart. The magma cools to form new rock on the edges of both plates. Plates are destroyed along **convergent boundaries,** where the edge of one plate may *subduct* (descend beneath the edge of another plate) back into the mantle (Figure 1) or both plates may crumple and merge to form a mountain belt. Plates slide past one another along **transform fault boundaries,** where plates are neither formed nor destroyed (Figure 1).

Most evidence for plate tectonics has come from the detailed observations, maps, and measurements made by field geologists studying Earth's surface directly. However, some of the best modern evidence of lithospheric plate motions is now obtained remotely with satellites orbiting thousands of kilometers above Earth's surface. Several different kinds of satellite technologies and measurement techniques are used, but the most common is the Global Positioning System (GPS).

The Global Positioning System (GPS) is a constellation of 24 satellites in orbit above Earth. These satellites transmit their own radio signals that can be detected by a fixed or hand-held GPS receiver. Most hand-held GPS receivers, including the ones used in many cell phones, are exact to meters or tens-of-meters of accuracy. The most expensive GPS receivers are much more exact. They are used to measure plate motions (movement of specific points over years) within fractions of a millimeter of accuracy.

PART A: WHAT COULD CAUSE PLATE TECTONICS?

Recall that geoscientists have historically tried to understand the cause of Earth's oceans, mountains, and global tectonics by questioning if Earth could be shrinking, expanding, or staying the same in size. This question can be evaluated by studying Earth's natural forces and faults in relation to those that you might predict to occur if the size of Earth were changing. By comparing your predictions to observations of the kinds of strains and faults actually observed, it is possible to determine if Earth's size is changing and infer whether a change in Earth's size could cause plate tectonics.

Earth Forces and the Faults They Produce

Three kinds of directed force (stress) can be applied to a solid mass of rock and cause it to deform (strain) by bending or even faulting (Figure 2). **Compression** compacts a block of rock and squeezes it into less

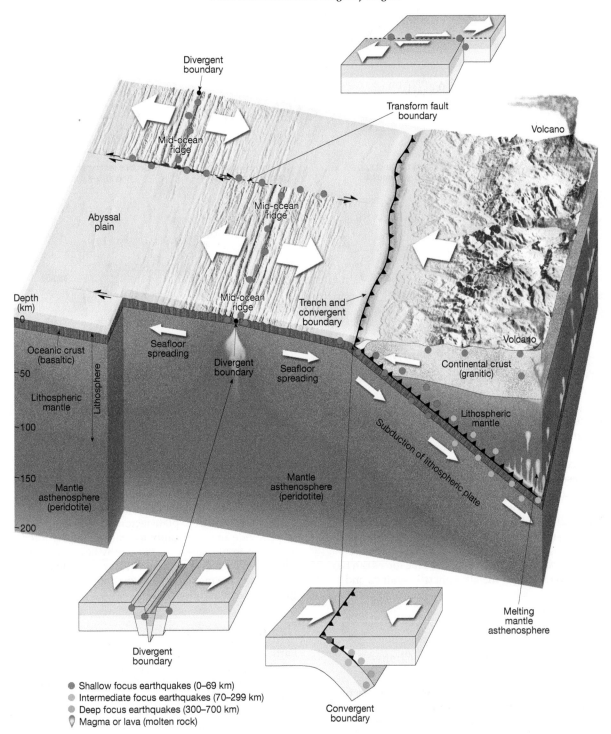

Shallow focus earthquakes (0–69 km)
Intermediate focus earthquakes (70–299 km)
Deep focus earthquakes (300–700 km)
Magma or lava (molten rock)

FIGURE 1 Three kinds of plate boundaries: divergent, convergent, and transform fault boundaries. White arrows indicate motions of the lithospheric plates. Half arrows on the transform fault boundary indicate relative motion of the two blocks on either side of the fault. The focus of an earthquake is the exact location where an earthquake occurred. Shallow focus earthquakes (0–69 km deep) are common along all three kinds of plate boundaries, but intermediate focus earthquakes (70–299 km deep) and deep focus earthquakes (300–700 km deep) occur only in subduction zones (where lithospheric plates return to the mantle). Water from the subducted plate can lower the melting point of rock just above it at intermediate depths and lead to formation of volcanoes.

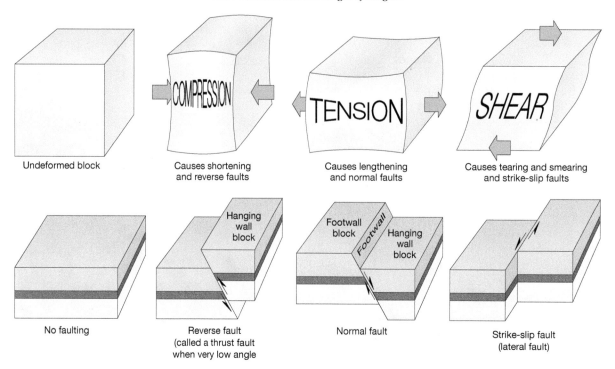

FIGURE 2 Three kinds of stress (applied force, as indicated by arrows) and the kinds of strain (deformation) and faulting that they cause.

space. This can cause *reverse faulting,* in which the hanging wall block is forced up the footwall block in opposition to the pull of gravity (Figure 2). **Tension** (also called *dilation*) pulls a block of rock apart and increases its length. This can cause *normal faulting*, in which gravity pulls the hanging wall block down and forces it to slide down off of the footwall block (see Figure 2). **Shear** smears a block of rock from side to side and may eventually tear it apart into two blocks of rock that slide past each other along a lateral or *strike-slip fault* (Figure 2). Plate tectonic forces can be understood by how the lithosphere is strained and faulted.

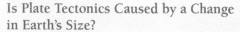

Is Plate Tectonics Caused by a Change in Earth's Size?

Conduct this activity to determine if Earth may be expanding or shrinking in size, and if changing Earth's size could be causing plate tectonics.

Mantle Convection as a Cause of Plate Tectonics

While much is known about plate tectonics, and the plates have been identified and named (Figure 3), there has been uncertainty about how mantle rocks beneath the asthenosphere may influence this

process. In the 1930s, an English geologist named Arthur Holmes speculated that the mantle may experience circular (convection cell) flow like a boiling pot of soup. He proposed that such flow could carry continents about the Earth like a giant conveyor belt. This idea was also adapted in the 1960s by Harry Hess, who hypothesized that mantle flow is the driving mechanism of plate tectonics. New technologies provide an opportunity to evaluate this hypothesis. For example, seismic tomography now provides sound evidence that processes at least 660 kilometers deep inside the mantle may have dramatic effects on plate tectonics at the surface.

Seismic Tomography

Earth's mantle is nearly 3000 km thick and occurs between the crust and the molten outer core. Although mantle rocks behave like a brittle solid on short timescales associated with earthquakes, they seem to flow like a very thick (viscous) fluid on longer timescales of days to years. Geologists use a technique called *seismic tomography* to detect this mantle flow.

The word *tomography* (Greek: *tomos* = slice, *graphe* = drawing) refers to the process of making drawings of slices through an object or person. Geologists use seismic tomography to view slices of Earth's interior similar to the way that medical technologists view slices of the human body. The human body slices are known as CAT (computer axial tomography) scans and are constructed using X-rays to penetrate and image the human body. The tomography scans of Earth's interior are constructed using seismic waves to penetrate and image the body of Earth.

In seismic tomography, geologists collect data on the velocity (rate and direction) of many thousands of seismic waves as they pass through Earth. The waves travel fastest through rocks that are the most dense and presumed to be coolest. The waves travel slower through rocks that are less dense and presumed to be warmer. When a computer is used to analyze all of the data, from all directions, it is possible to generate seismic tomography images of Earth. These images can be viewed individually or combined to form three-dimensional perspectives. The computer can also assist in false coloring seismic tomography images to show bodies of mantle rock that are significantly warmer (red) and cooler (blue) than the rest of the mantle (Figure 4).

ACTIVITY 2
Evaluate a Lava Lamp Model of Earth
Conduct this activity to evaluate if mantle convection could be a cause of plate tectonics.

PART B: EVALUATING PLATE TECTONICS AND HOT SPOTS

The Plate Tectonics Model is widely applied by geoscientists to help explain many regional and global features of the geosphere. Another regional feature of Earth is hot spots, centers of volcanic activity that persist in a stationary location for tens-of-millions of years. Geologists think they are either: a) the result of long-lived narrow *plumes* of hot rock rising rapidly from Earth's mantle (like a stream of heated lava rising in a lava lamp), or b) the slow melting of a large mass of hot mantle rock in the upper mantle that persists for a long interval of geologic time.

The following activities are designed for you to evaluate plate tectonic and hot spot processes:

ACTIVITY 3
Using Earthquakes to Identify Plate Boundaries
Earthquakes occur at depths of 0–700 km inside Earth. Most occur along the mobile boundaries of plates (interplate earthquakes). Only a few occur within the rigid plates themselves (intraplate earthquakes). In this activity, you are expected to use earthquake data from South America to define plate boundaries, identify plates, construct a cross section of a subduction zone, and determine how volcanoes can be related to plate subduction.

ACTIVITY 4
Analysis of Atlantic Seafloor Spreading
Observe how fracture zones and shapes of coastlines provide clues about how North America and Africa were once part of the same continent, and determine rates of seafloor spreading between North America and Africa.

ACTIVITY 5
Plate Motions Along the San Andreas Fault
Use aerial photographs and GPS data to understand absolute and relative plate motions along the San Andreas Fault.

ACTIVITY 6
The Hawaiian Hot Spot and Pacific Plate Motion
As a lithospheric plate migrates across a stationary hot spot, a volcano develops directly above the hot spot. When the plate slides on, the volcano that was over the hot spot becomes dormant, and over time, it migrates many kilometers from the hot spot. Meanwhile, a new volcano arises as new lithosphere passes over the hot spot. The result is a string of volcanoes, with one end of the line located over the hot spot and quite active, and the other end distant and inactive. In between is a succession of volcanoes that are progressively older with distance from the hot spot. The Hawaiian Islands and Emperor Seamount chain (Figure 5) are thought to represent such a line of volcanoes that formed over the Hawaiian hot spot. You are expected to determine rates and directions that the Pacific Plate moved over the hot spot through time.

ACTIVITY 7
Plate Tectonics of the Northwest United States
The northwestern region of the United States is characterized by another hot spot, located beneath Yellowstone National Park, and a volcanic arc (Cascade Range) associated with modern subduction of the Juan de Fuca Plate (Figure 6). You are expected to analyze and evaluate the interaction of these processes.

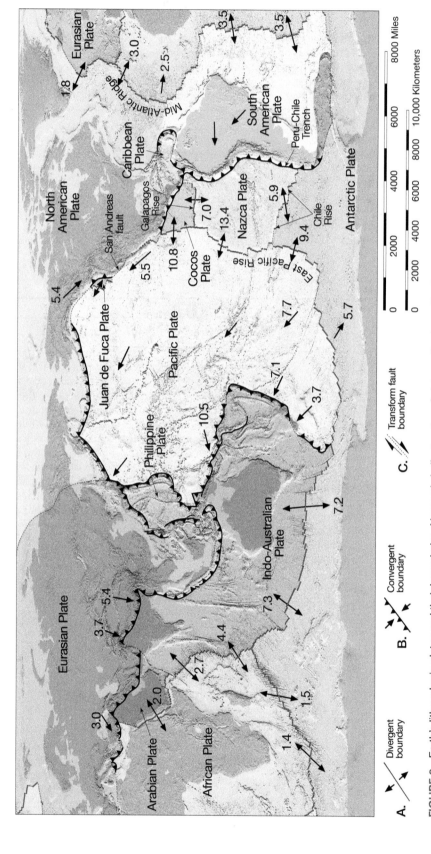

FIGURE 3 Earth's lithospheric plates and their boundaries. Numerals indicate rates of plate motion in centimeters per year (cm/yr) based on satellite measurements (Courtesy of NASA). Divergent boundaries (red) occur where two adjacent plates form and move apart (diverge) from each other. Convergent boundaries (hachured with triangular "teeth") occur where two adjacent plates move together. Transform fault boundaries (dashed) occur along faults where two adjacent plates slide past each other. Refer back to Figure 1 for another perspective of the three kinds of plate boundaries.

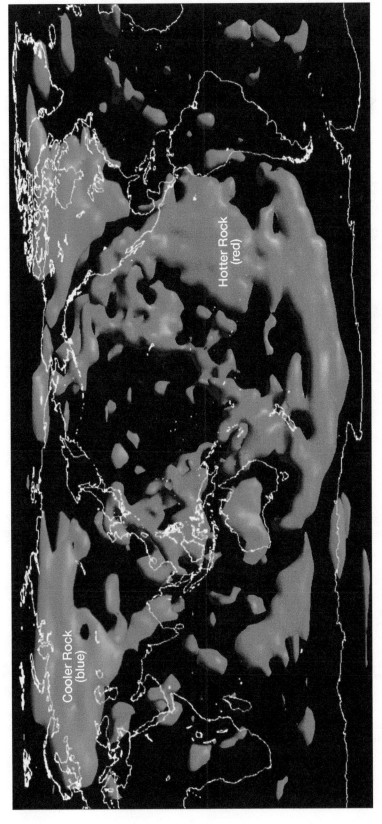

FIGURE 4 Seismic tomography image (horizontal slice) of Earth's mantle at a depth of 350 km. Red false coloring indicates hot rock that is less dense and ascending. Blue false coloring indicates cooler rock that is static or descending. See text for discussion. (Courtesy of Paul J. Morin, University of Minnesota)

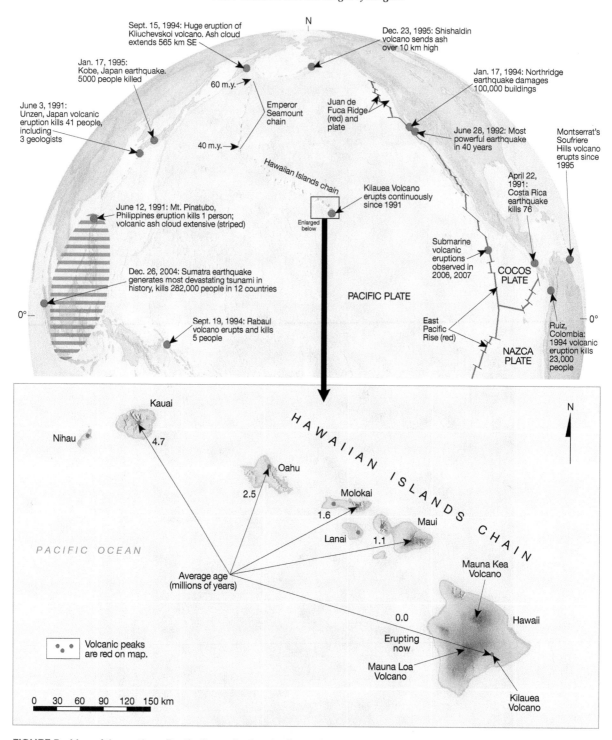

FIGURE 5 Map of the northern Pacific Ocean (top) and adjacent landmasses showing some notable geologic hazards (natural disasters) from the 1990s, the Hawaiian Islands chain, and the Emperor Seamount chain. Lower map shows details of the Hawaiian Islands chain, including locations of volcanic peaks.

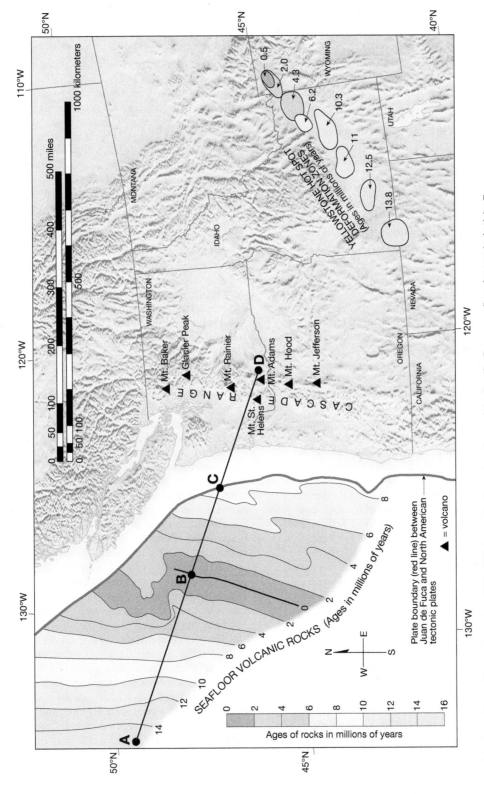

FIGURE 6 Map of the northwestern United States and adjacent portions of the Pacific Ocean seafloor for use in Activity 7.

PART C: THE ORIGIN OF MAGMA

Seismic studies indicate that Earth's outer core contains a substantial proportion of melted rock called *magma*. However, this magma is so deep inside Earth that it cannot erupt to the surface. Seismic studies also indicate that nearly all of Earth's mantle and crust are solid rock—not magma. Therefore, except for some specific locations where active volcanoes occur, there is no reservoir or layer of magma beneath Earth's surface just waiting to erupt. On a global scale, the volume of magma that feeds active volcanoes is actually very small. What, then, are the special conditions that cause these rare bodies of upper mantle and lower crust magma to form?

Magma generally forms in three plate tectonic settings (divergent plate boundaries, convergent plate boundaries, and hot spots). Its origin (rock melting) is also influenced by underground temperature, underground pressure (lithostatic pressure), and the kind of minerals that comprise underground rocks.

Temperature (T)

Rocks are mostly masses of solid mineral crystals. Therefore, some or all of the mineral crystals must melt to form magma. According to the Kinetic Theory, a solid mineral crystal will melt if its kinetic energy (motion of its atoms and molecules) exceeds the attractive forces that hold together its orderly crystalline structure. Heating a crystal is the most obvious way to melt it. If enough heat energy is applied to the crystal, then its kinetic energy level may rise enough to cause melting. The specific temperature at which crystals of a given mineral begin to melt is the mineral's **melting point.**

All minerals have different melting points. So when heating a rock comprised of several different kinds of mineral crystals, one part of the rock (one kind of mineral crystal) will melt before another part (another kind of mineral crystal). Geologists call this **partial melting** of rock. But where would the heat come from to begin melting rocks below the ground?

Unless you live near a volcano or hot spring, you probably are not aware of Earth's body heat. But South African gold miners know all about it. The deeper they mine, the hotter it gets. In the deepest mine, 3.8 kilometers below ground, temperatures reach 60 °C (140 °F) and the mines must be air conditioned. This gradient of increasing temperature with depth is called the **geothermal gradient.** This gradient also varies between ocean crust and continental crust, but the global average for all of Earth's crust is about 25 °C (77 °F) per kilometer. In other words, rocks located 1 kilometer below your house are about 25 °C warmer than the foundation of your house. If the geothermal gradient continued at this rate through the mantle, then the mantle would eventually melt at depths of 100–150 kilometers. Seismology shows that this

does not occur, so temperature is not the only factor that determines whether a rock melts or remains solid. Pressure is also a factor.

Pressure (P)

When you press your hand against something like a bookshelf, you can apply all of your body *weight* against the surface *area* under your hand. Therefore, **pressure** is expressed as amount of weight applied per unit of area. For example, imagine that you weigh 100 pounds and that your hand is 5 inches long and 4 inches wide. If you exert all of your weight against a wall by leaning against the wall with one hand, then you are exerting 100 pounds of weight over an area of 20 square inches (5 inches $\times$ 4 inches = 20 square inches). This means that you are exerting 5 pounds of pressure per square inch of your hand.

Atoms and molecules of air (atmosphere) are masses of matter that are pulled by gravity toward the center of Earth. But they cannot reach Earth's center because water, rocks, and your body are in their path. As a result, the weight of the air presses against surfaces of water, rocks, and your body. If you stand at sea level, then your body is confined by 14.7 pounds of weight pressing on every square inch of your body (14 lbs./inch^2). This is called atmospheric **confining pressure.** Scientists also refer to this as one *atmosphere* (1 atm) of pressure.

You do not normally feel one atmosphere of confining pressure, because your body exerts the same pressure to keep you in equilibrium (balance) with your surroundings. But if you ever dove into the deep end of a swimming pool, then you experienced the confining pressure exerted by the water plus the confining pressure of the atmosphere. The deeper you dove, the more pressure you felt. It takes 10 m (33.9 ft) of water to exert another 1 atm of confining pressure on your body.

Rocks are about three times denser than water, so it takes only about 3.3 m of rock to exert a force equal to that of 10 m of water or the entire thickness of the atmosphere! 100 m of rock exert a confining pressure of about 30 atm, and 1 km (1000 m) of rock exerts a confining pressure of about 300 atm. At 300 atm/km, a rock buried 5 km underground is confined by 1500 atm of pressure!

The confining pressure under kilometers of rock is so great that a mineral crystal cannot melt at its "normal" melting point observed on Earth's surface. The pressure confines the atoms and molecules and prevents them from flowing apart. More heat is required to raise the kinetic energy level of atoms and molecules in the crystal enough to melt the crystal. Consequently, an increase in confining pressure causes an increase in the melting point of a mineral. Reducing confining pressure lowers the melting point of a mineral. This means that if a mineral is already near its melting point, and its confining pressure decreases enough, then it will melt. This is called **decompression melting.**

Pressure-Temperature (P-T) Diagrams

Geologists understand that rock melting (the origin of magma) is related to both temperature and pressure. Therefore, they heat and pressurize rock samples under controlled conditions in geochemical laboratories to determine how rock melting is influenced by specific combinations of both pressure and temperature. Samples are pressurized and heated to specific P-T points to determine if they remain solid, undergo partial melting, or melt completely. The data are then plotted as specific points on a **pressure-temperature (P-T) diagram** such as the one in Figure 7 for mantle peridotite. Mantle peridotite is made of olivine, pyroxene, amphibole, and garnet mineral crystals. Therefore, this diagram also shows the combined effects of pressure and temperature on a rock made of several different minerals. At P-T points below (to the left of) the *solidus*, all mineral crystals in the rock remain solid. At P-T points above (to the right of) the *liquidus,* all mineral crystals in the rock melt to liquid. At

P-T points between the solidus and liquidus, the rock undergoes partial melting—one kind of mineral at a time. Therefore, a P-T diagram also reveals stability fields for states (phases) of matter. In this case (see Figure 7), there are stability fields for solid, solid + liquid, and liquid.

Notice that lines for the continental and oceanic geothermal gradients are also plotted on Figure 7. They show how temperature normally varies according to depth below the continents and ocean basins. Temperatures along both of these geothermal gradients are not great enough to begin melting peridotite. Both gradients occur along temperatures below (to the left of) the peridotite solidus.

ACTIVITY 8

The Origin of Magma

Explore ways that magma forms in relation to plate tectonics. (Figure 8)

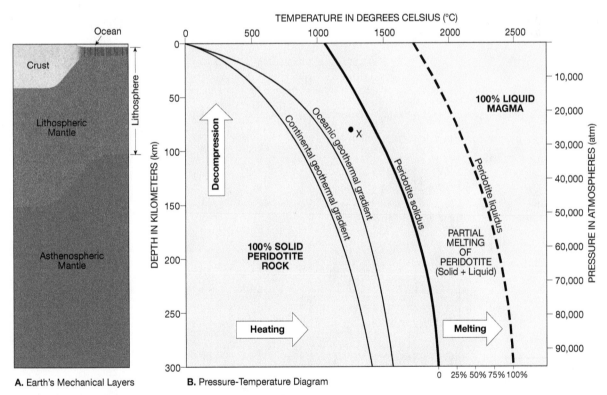

FIGURE 7 **A.** Mechanical layers at the edge of Earth's rocky body, **B.** Pressure-temperature (P-T) diagram of environmental conditions that exist across the mechanical layers shown in A. The diagram shows how P-T conditions affect peridotite rock (made of olivine, pyroxene, amphibole, and garnet mineral crystals). At P-T points below (to the left of) the *peridotite solidus,* all mineral crystals in the rock remain solid. At P-T points above (to the right of) the *peridotite liquidus,* all mineral crystals in the rock melt to liquid. At P-T points between the solidus and liquidus, the rock undergoes partial melting—one kind of mineral at a time, so solid and liquid are present. Continental and oceanic geothermal gradients are curves showing how temperature normally varies according to depth below the continents and ocean basins. Temperatures along both of these geothermal gradients are too cool to begin partial melting of peridotite. Both gradients occur below (to the left of) the peridotite solidus. (1 atm = about 1 bar)

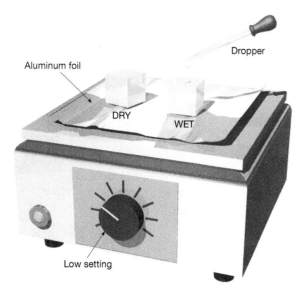

FIGURE 8 Procedures for melting experiment in Activity 8. Turn the hot plate on a low setting (about 2 or 3 on most commercial hot plates) and allow it to heat up in a safe location (be careful not to touch hot surfaces directly). Next, place two sugar cubes on a flat piece of aluminum foil or in aluminum foil baking cups. Label (on the foil) one sugar cube "dry." Moisten the second sugar cube with about 4 or 5 drops of water and label it "wet." Carefully place the aluminum foil with the labeled sugar cubes onto the hot plate and observe what happens. When one of the sugar cubes begins to melt, use crucible tongs and/or hot pads to remove the foil and sugar cubes from the hot plate and avoid burning the sugar. Turn off and un-plug the hot plate while being careful not to touch the hot surface!

ACTIVITY 1 Is Plate Tectonics Caused by a Change in Earth's Size?

Name: _____   Course/Section: _____

Materials: Pencil.

A. Analyze Figure 2 to see how three kinds of faults are caused by three kinds of stress (applied force). Now recall that geoscientists have historically tried to understand the cause of oceans, mountains, and global tectonics by questioning if Earth could be shrinking, expanding, or staying the same in size. This question can be evaluated by studying Earth's natural forces and faults in relation to those that you might predict to occur if the size of Earth were changing. To the right of this diagram, predict what kind of faulting you would expect to find in Earth's lithosphere if Earth were expanding, contracting (shrinking), or staying the same in size.

What kind of faulting would you expect to find in the lithosphere if:

1. Earth is expanding?

2. Earth is contracting?

3. Earth's lithosphere fractures but there is no expansion or contraction in size?

Original size of Earth

B. Refer to Figures 1 and Fill in the table below to indicate what kind of stress and faulting characterizes each kind of plate boundary.

Plate Boundary Type	Main Stress (applied force)	Main Fault Type
Divergent		
Convergent		
Transform		

C. Refer to Figure 3, a map showing the distribution of kind of Earth's lithospheric plates and plate boundaries. Study this figure to determine the location, distribution, and length of Earth's three kinds of plate boundaries: divergent (red), convergent (hachured), and transform (dashed). Then visually estimate the following data.

1. What percentage (based on length) of Earth's plate boundaries are transform fault boundaries?

2. What percentage (based on length) of Earth's plate boundaries are divergent boundaries?

3. What percentage (based on length) of Earth's plate boundaries are convergent boundaries?

CONTINUED

D. Do you think Earth's size is increasing (expanding), decreasing (shrinking), or staying about the same? Justify your answer by citing evidence from your work above.

E. Do you think that plate tectonics is being caused by a change in Earth's size? Why?

ACTIVITY 2 Evaluate a Lava Lamp Model of Earth

Name: _____   Course/Section: _____

Materials: Pencil, red and blue colored pencils, lava lamp (provided in laboratory).

A. A "lava lamp" is inactive when the light is off, but a lighted lava lamp is dynamic and ever changing. Observe the rising and sinking motion of the lava-like wax in a lighted lava lamp.

   1. Describe the motions of the "lava" that occur over one full minute of time, starting with lava at the bottom of the lamp and its path through the lamp.

   2. What causes the "lava" to move from the base of the lamp to the top of the lamp? (Be as specific and complete as you can.)

   3. What causes the "lava" to move from the top of the lamp to the base of the lamp? (Be as specific and complete as you can.)

   4. What is the name applied to this kind of cycle of change?

B. Observe the seismic tomography image in Figure 4: a slice through Earth's mantle at a depth of 350 kilometers. Unlike the lava lamp that you viewed in a vertical profile from the side of the lamp, this image is a horizontal slice of Earth's mantle viewed from above. This image is also false colored to show where rocks are significantly warmer and less dense (colored red) versus cooler and more dense (colored blue).

   1. How is Earth's mantle like a lava lamp?

   2. How is Earth's mantle different from a lava lamp?

C. Compare the tectonic plates and plate boundaries in Figure 3 to the red and blue regions of the seismic tomography image in Figure 4.

   1. Under what kind of plate tectonic feature do the warm, less dense rocks (red) occur most often?

   2. Under what kind of plate tectonic feature do the cool, more dense rocks (blue) occur most often?

CONTINUED

D. Based on your work in **A–C**, draw a vertical cross section (vertical slice) of Earth that shows how mantle convection may be related to plate tectonics. Include and label the following features in your drawing: lithospheric plates, a mid-ocean ridge (divergent plate boundary), a subduction zone (convergent plate boundary), continental crust, ocean crust, and locations of slab pull. Use colored pencils to show where the mantle rocks in your vertical cross section would be red and blue like the false colored mantle rocks in Figure 4.

ACTIVITY 3 Using Earthquakes to Identify Plate Boundaries

Name: _____   **Course/Section:** _____

Materials: Pencil, red pencil or pen, ruler.

A. Refer to Figure 1 for background on how the depth of earthquake foci is related to plate tectonics. On the map below, use a red colored pencil or pen to draw lines (as exactly as you can) that indicate where plate boundaries occur at Earth's surface. Then label the East Pacific Rise, Galapagos Rise, Chile Rise, and all of the plates (Refer to Figure 3).

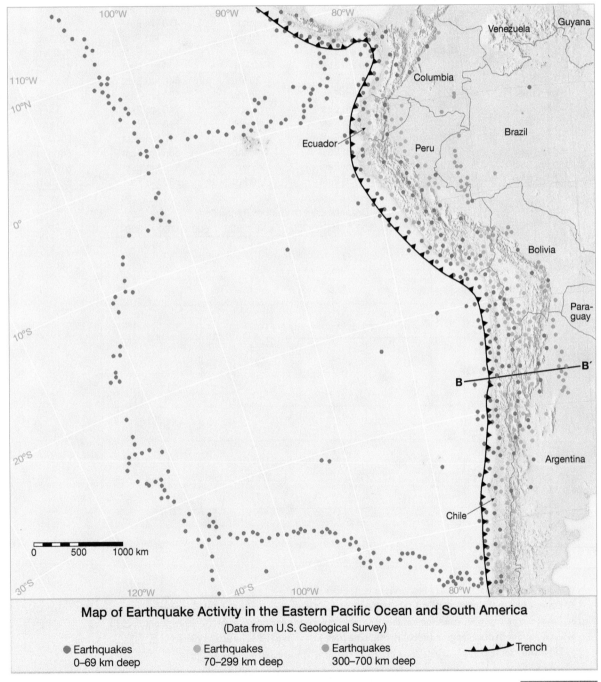

Map of Earthquake Activity in the Eastern Pacific Ocean and South America
(Data from U.S. Geological Survey)

- Earthquakes 0–69 km deep
- Earthquakes 70–299 km deep
- Earthquakes 300–700 km deep
- ▲▲▲ Trench

CONTINUED

Plate Tectonics and the Origin of Magma

B. Notice line B–B' on the map in Part **A** and the fact that shallow, intermediate, and deep earthquakes occur along it. Volcanoes also occur at Earth's surface along this line. Plot the locations of earthquake foci (depth of earthquake vs. its location east or west of the trench) on the cross section below using data in the accompanying table (provided by the U.S. Geological Survey). For volcanoes, draw a small triangle on the surface (depth of zero).

Location East or West of Trench	Depth of Earthquake (or volcano location)	Location East or West of Trench	Depth of Earthquake (or volcano location)	Location East or West of Trench	Depth of Earthquake (or volcano location)
200 km West	20 km	220 km East	30 km	410 km East	150 km
160 km West	25 km	250 km East	volcano	450 km East	50 km
60 km West	10 km	260 km East	120 km	450 km East	150 km
30 km West	25 km	300 km East	volcano	470 km East	180 km
0 (trench)	20 km	300 km East	110 km	500 km East	30 km
10 km East	40 km	330 km East	volcano	500 km East	160 km
20 km East	30 km	330 km East	40 km	500 km East	180 km
50 km East	60 km	330 km East	120 km	540 km East	30 km
51 km East	10 km	350 km East	volcano	590 km East	20 km
55 km East	30 km	390 km East	volcano	640 km East	10 km
60 km East	20 km	390 km East	40 km	710 km East	30 km
80 km East	70 km	390 km East	140 km	780 km East	530 km
100 km East	10 km	410 km East	volcano	800 km East	560 km
120 km East	80 km	410 km East	25 km	820 km East	610 km
200 km East	110 km	410 km East	110 km	880 km East	620 km

1. What kind of plate boundary is shown in your cross section?_____
2. Draw a line in the cross section to show the probable top surface of the subducting plate.
3. Label the part of your cross section that probably represents earthquakes in the lithosphere.
4. At what depth does magma probably originate here just above the subducting plate: _____ km How can you tell?

ACTIVITY 4 Analysis of Atlantic Seafloor Spreading

Name: _____   Course/Section: _____

Materials: Pencil, ruler, calculator, red pencil or pen, blue pencil or pen.

A. The map below shows the ages of seafloor basalt (the actual floor of the ocean, beneath the modern mud and sand) between North America and Africa.

    1. Draw a red line on the map to show the exact location of the divergent plate boundary between the North American Plate and the African and Eurasian Plates. Refer to Figures 1 and 3 for assistance as needed.

    2. Draw two blue lines on the map to show the exact position of two different transform fault plate boundaries. Refer to Figure 1 for assistance as needed.

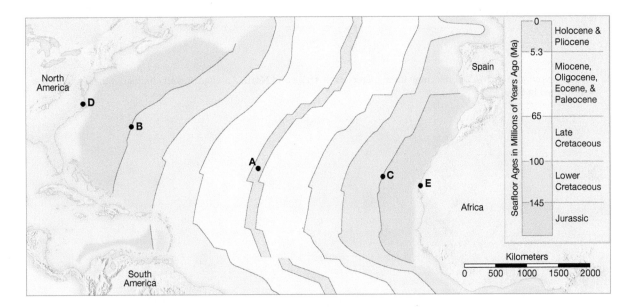

B. Notice that points B and C were together 145 million years ago, but did the sea floor spread apart at exactly the same rate on both sides of the mid-ocean ridge? How can you tell?

C. How far apart are points B and C today, in kilometers? _____ km

    1. Calculate the average rate, in km per million years, that points B and C have moved apart over the past 145 million years. Show your work.

    2. Convert your answer above from km per million years to mm per year.

CONTINUED

D. Based on your answer in **C1** above, how many millions of years ago and in what geologic period of time were Africa and North America part of the same continent? Show your work.

E. Based on your answer in **C2** above, how far in meters have Africa and North America moved apart since the United States was formed in 1776?

ACTIVITY 5 Plate Motions Along the San Andreas Fault

51

Name: _____   Course/Section: _____

Materials: Pencil, ruler, calculator. Other materials provided in lab.

Study the geologic map of southern California below, showing the position of the famous San Andreas Fault, a transform plate boundary between the North American Plate (east side) and the Pacific Plate (west side). It is well known to all who live in southern California that plate motions along the fault cause frequent earthquakes, which place at risk humans and their properties.

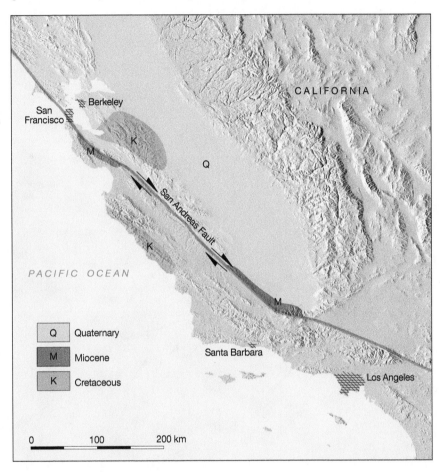

A. The two bodies of Late Miocene rocks (about 25 million years old) located along either side of the San Andreas Fault (map above) were one body of rock that has been separated by motions along the fault. Note that arrows have been placed along the sides of the fault to show the relative sense of movement.

    1. You can estimate the average annual rate of movement along the San Andreas Fault by measuring how much the Late Miocene rocks have been offset by the fault and by assuming that these rocks began separating soon after they formed. What is the average rate of fault movement in centimeters per year (cm/yr)? Show your work.

CONTINUED

2. An average movement of about 5 m (16 ft) along the San Andreas Fault was associated with the devastating 1906 San Francisco earthquake that killed people and destroyed properties. Assuming that all displacement along the fault was produced by Earth motions of this magnitude, how often must such earthquakes have occurred in order to account for the total displacement? Show your work.

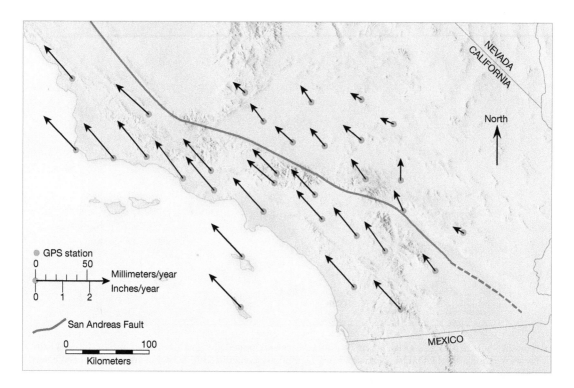

B. The above map shows some Global Positioning System (GPS) reference stations and observations of the former Southern California Integrated GPS Network (SCIGN), now operated by the U.S. Geological Survey, NASA Jet Propulsion Laboratory, and the UNAVCO Plate Boundary Observatory. Length of the arrows indicates the actual direction and rate that bedrock beneath the reference point is moving in mm/yr.

1. Notice that both plates are moving northwest here. Estimate in mm/year how much faster the Pacific Plate is moving than the North American Plate. _____ mm/yr

2. Add half arrows to the San Andreas Fault to show the relative motion of the fault.

ACTIVITY 6 The Hawaiian Hot Spot and Pacific Plate Motion

Name: _____   Course/Section: _____

Materials: Pencil, ruler, calculator. Other materials provided in lab.

As a lithospheric plate migrates across a stationary hot spot, a volcano develops directly above the hot spot. When the plate slides on, the volcano that was over the hot spot becomes dormant, and over time, it migrates many kilometers from the hot spot. Meanwhile, a new volcano arises as new lithosphere passes over the hot spot. The result is a string of volcanoes, with one end of the line located over the hot spot and quite active, and the other end distant and inactive. In between is a succession of volcanoes that are progressively older with distance from the hot spot. The Hawaiian Islands and Emperor Seamount chains are thought to represent such a line of volcanoes that formed over the Hawaiian hot spot (Figure 5). You are expected to determine rates and directions that the Pacific Plate moved over the hot spot through time.

A. Figure 5 shows the distribution of the Hawaiian Islands chain and Emperor Seamount chain. The numbers indicate the age of each island in millions of years (m.y.), obtained from the basaltic igneous rock of which each island is composed.

    1. What was the rate in centimeters per year (cm/yr) and direction of plate motion in the Hawaiian region from 4.7 to 1.6 million years (m.y.) ago?

    2. What was the rate in centimeters per year (cm/yr) and direction of plate motion from 1.6 million years ago to the present time?

    3. How does the rate and direction of Pacific Plate movement during the past 1.6 million years differ from the older rate and direction (4.7–1.6 m.y.) of plate motion?

    4. Locate the Hawaiian Island chain and the Emperor Seamount chain (submerged volcanic islands) in the top part of Figure 5. How are the two island chains related?

    5. Based on the distribution of the Hawaiian Islands and Emperor Seamount chains, suggest how the direction of Pacific Plate movement has generally changed over the past 60 million years.

ACTIVITY 7 Plate Tectonics of the Northwest United States

Name: _____   Course/Section: _____

Materials: Pencil, ruler, calculator. Other materials provided in lab.

Refer to Figure 6. A hot spot is located beneath Yellowstone National Park in the United States. There are no erupting volcanoes on the Yellowstone hot spot today, but there are hot springs and geysers. The high heat flow also causes buckling and faulting of Earth's crust. Geologist Mark Anders has observed that as the North American Plate slides over this hot spot, it causes development of a U-shaped set of faults (with the closed end of the U pointing northeast). Also, as layers of volcanic ash and lava flows accumulate on deforming crust, they tilt. By dating the layers of tilted rocks, and mapping the U-shaped fault systems that moved beneath them, Anders has been able to compose a map of circular regions that were once centered over the hot spot at specific times. Figure 6 also shows the ages of seafloor rocks in the adjacent Pacific Ocean.

A. Examine the part of Figure 6 showing the distribution of circular areas that were centers of crustal faulting and buckling when they were located over the Yellowstone hot spot. The numbers indicate the ages of deformation, as determined by Mark Anders.

　　1. What direction is the North American Plate moving, according to Anders' data?

　　2. What was the average rate in centimeters per year (cm/yr) that the North American Plate has moved over the past 11 million years?

B. Notice the ages of seafloor volcanic rocks in Figure 6. The modern seafloor rocks of this region (located at 0 million years old) are forming along a divergent plate boundary called the Juan de Fuca Ridge. The farther one moves away from the plate boundary (B in Figure 6), the older are the seafloor rocks.

　　1. What has been the average rate and direction of seafloor spreading in centimeters per year (cm/yr) east of the Juan de Fuca Ridge (along line B–D) over the past 8 million years?

　　2. Notice that seafloor rocks older than 8 million years are present west of the Juan de Fuca Ridge but not east of the ridge. What could be happening to the seafloor rocks along line C–D that would explain their absence from the map?

　　3. Based on your reasoning above, what kind of plate boundary is represented by the red line running through location C on Figure 6?

　　4. Notice the line of volcanoes in the Cascade Range located at the center of the map. How could magma form beneath these volcanoes? (Be as specific as you can.)

ACTIVITY 8 The Origin of Magma

Name: _____   Course/Section: _____

Materials: Pencil, ruler. Other materials provided in lab.

A. Examine the pressure-temperature (P-T) diagram for mantle peridotite in Figure 7, and locate point **X**. This point represents a mass of peridotite buried 80 km underground.

    1. According to the continental geothermal gradient, rocks buried 80 km beneath a continent would normally be heated to what temperature? _____

    2. According to the oceanic geothermal gradient, rocks buried 80 km beneath an ocean basin would normally be heated to what temperature? _____

    3. Is the peridotite at point **X** a mass of solid, a mixture of solid and liquid, or a mass of liquid? How do you know?

    4. What would happen to the mass of peridotite at point **X** if it were heated to 1750 °C? How do you know?

    5. What would happen to the mass of peridotite at point **X** if it were heated to 2250 °C? How do you know?

B. At its current depth, the peridotite at point **X** in Figure 7 is under about 25,000 atm of pressure.

    1. At what depth and pressure will this peridotite begin to melt if it is uplifted closer to Earth's surface and its temperature remains the same?
    Depth: _____   Pressure: _____

    2. What is the name applied to this kind of melting?

    3. Name and describe a process that could uplift mantle peridotite to start it melting in this way, and name a specific plate tectonic setting where this may be happening now. (*Hint:* Study Figures 1, 3, and 4.)

C. Based on your answers above, what are two environmental changes that can cause the peridotite at point **X** (see Figure 7) to begin partial melting?

CONTINUED

D. Obtain the materials shown in Figure 8. Turn the hot plate on a low setting (about 3 on most commercial hot plates) and allow it to heat up in a safe location. Next place two sugar cubes on a flat piece of aluminum foil. Label (on the foil) one sugar cube "dry." Moisten the second sugar cube with a few drops of water, and label it "wet." Carefully place the aluminum foil (with the sugar cubes) onto the hot plate and observe what happens. (*Note:* Turn off the hot plate when one cube begins to melt.)

1. Which sugar cube melted first?

2. The rapid melting that you observed in 12a is called "**flux melting**," because flux is something that speeds up a process. What was the flux?

3. How would the P-T diagram in Figure 7 change if all of the peridotite in the diagram was "wet" peridotite?

4. In what specific kind of plate tectonic setting could water enter Earth's mantle and cause flux melting of mantle peridotite? (*Hint:* Figure 1)

E. Examine this cross section of a plate boundary.

1. What kind of plate boundary is this?

2. Name the specific process that led to the formation of magma in this cross section.

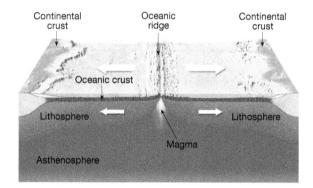

3. Describe the sequence of plate tectonic and magma generating processes that led to formation of the volcanoes (oceanic ridge) in this cross section.

F. Examine this cross section of a plate boundary.

1. What kind of plate boundary is this?

2. Name the specific process that led to the formation of magma in this cross section.

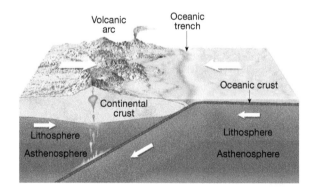

3. Describe the sequence of plate tectonic and magma generating processes that led to formation of the volcanoes (oceanic ridge) in this cross section.

Mineral Properties, Uses, and Identification

CONTRIBUTING AUTHORS

Jane L. Boger • *SUNY, College at Geneseo*

Philip D. Boger • *SUNY, College at Geneseo*

Roseann J. Carlson • *Tidewater Community College*

Charles I. Frye • *Northwest Missouri State University*

Michael F. Hochella, Jr. • *Virginia Polytechnic Institute*

OBJECTIVES AND ACTIVITIES

A. Understand how to analyze samples of minerals for seven common properties (color, crystal habit and form, luster, streak, hardness, cleavage, fracture) and six other properties (tenacity, reaction with acid, magnetism, striations, exsolution lamellae, specific gravity).

ACTIVITY 1: Mineral Properties

ACTIVITY 2: Analysis and Classification of Crystal Forms

ACTIVITY 3: Determining Specific Gravity (SG)

B. Be able to identify common minerals (in hand samples) on the basis of their properties and infer how they are (or could be) used by people.

ACTIVITY 4: Mineral Analysis, Identification, and Uses

STUDENT MATERIALS

Pencil, eraser, laboratory notebook, calculator, cleavage goniometer (cut from GeoTools Sheet 1), and mineral and rock samples (purchased or provided by your instructor and marked with an identifying number or letter). Obtain mineral analysis tools as directed by your instructor: steel masonry nail, common wire nail, glass plate, streak plate, copper penny, small magnet, dilute (1–3%) hydrochloric acid (HCl)

in a dropper bottle, 500 mL graduated cylinder, gram balance, wash or dropper bottle, water.

INTRODUCTION

You may know minerals as the beautiful gemstones in jewelry or natural crystals displayed in museums. However, most **rocks** are aggregates of one or more kinds of minerals (Figure 1). Minerals are also the natural materials from which every inorganic item in our industrialized society has been manufactured. Therefore, minerals are the physical foundation of both our planet and our human societies.

All **minerals** are inorganic, naturally occurring substances that have a characteristic chemical composition, distinctive physical properties, and crystalline structure. *Crystalline structure* is an orderly three-dimensional arrangement of atoms or molecules (Figure 2), and materials with crystalline structure form *crystals*. A few "minerals," such as limonite (rust) and opal (Figure 3), do not have crystalline structure and never form crystals, so they are not true minerals. They are sometimes called *mineraloids*.

More than 4000 different kinds of minerals have been identified and named based on their characteristic chemical composition and physical properties. Some are best known as *rock-forming minerals*,

From Laboratory 3 of *Laboratory Manual in Physical Geology*, Ninth Edition, American Geological Institute, National Association of Geoscience Teachers, Richard M. Busch, Dennis Tasa. Copyright © 2011 by Pearson Education, Inc. Published by Pearson Prentice Hall. All rights reserved.

FIGURE 1 Most rocks are made of mineral crystals, as in these four examples. **A.** Rock made of numerous mineral crystals of amethyst, a purple variety of quartz. Two crystals have been outlined to emphasize their *crystal form* (geometric shape), and dots show the boundaries between their *crystal faces* (the flat surfaces on the outside of a crystal). **B.** Rock (called marble) made of intergrown calcite mineral crystals. The calcite crystals are so tightly intergrown that their crystal form is not visible. **C.** Rock made of red-brown potassium-feldspar ("K-spar") crystals, white plagioclase feldspar crystals, gray quartz crystals, and black biotite crystals. Like rock B, the crystals grew together so closely that their crystal form is obscured. **D.** A variety of quartz called agate. It is made of variously colored quartz crystals that are *cryptocrystalline* (so tiny that they are not visible in hand sample) in most of the bands of the agate.

meaning that they are the main minerals observed in rocks. Others are best known as *industrial minerals,* meaning that they are the main minerals used to manufacture physical materials of industrialized societies.

Although all minerals are inorganic, *biochemical minerals* can be manufactured by organisms. A good example is the mineral aragonite, which clams and other mollusks use to construct their shells.

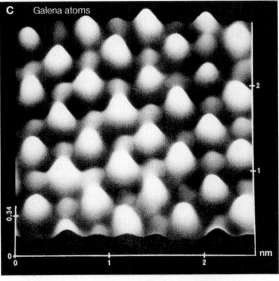

Blue = S (sulfur) atoms, Orange = Pb (lead) atoms
nm = nanometer = 1 millionth of a millimeter

FIGURE 2   Galena is lead sulfide—PbS, an ore of lead **A.** This mineral forms cubic (cube-shaped) crystals that are the color of dull tarnished lead metal. **B.** Galena crystals are brittle. When struck with a hammer, they shatter into silvery gray fragments with cubic shapes. **C.** The orderly arrangement of lead and sulfur atoms in galena can be seen in this atomic-resolution image of galena taken with a scanning tunneling microscope (STM) by C. M. Eggleston, University of Wyoming. Each *sulfur* atom is bonded to four lead atoms in the image, plus another lead atom beneath it. Similarly, each *lead* atom is bonded to four sulfur atoms in the image, plus a sulfur atom beneath it.

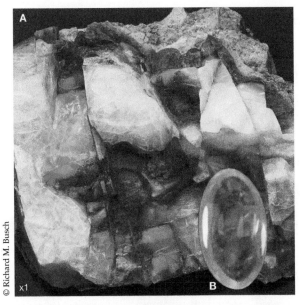

FIGURE 3   Opal is hydrated silicon dioxide—$SiO_2 \cdot nH_2O$. Opal is not a true mineral because it is an *amorphous* (without crystalline structure) solid. It is sometimes referred to as a mineraloid (mineral-like) material. **A.** This sample of Australian opal formed on brown rock and ranges from colorless to translucent white and blue. **B.** This *precious opal* from Mexico has "fire" (internal flashes of color) and has been artificially shaped into a cabochon (oval shape with a rounded top and flat back) to be set in jewelry.

PART A: MINERAL PROPERTIES AND USES

Seven properties are commonly used to identify minerals and determine how they may be used. You should be able to analyze minerals for all of these common properties (color, crystal habit and form, luster, streak, hardness, cleavage, fracture). It will also be useful for you to be familiar with ways to analyze minerals for six other properties that may be used to distinguish specific minerals or specific groups of minerals (tenacity, reaction with acid, magnetism, striations, exsolution lamellae, specific gravity).

Color and Clarity

Color of a mineral is usually its most noticeable property and may be a clue to its identity. A rock made up of one color of mineral crystals is usually made up of one kind of mineral (Figure 1A, 1B), and a rock made of more than one color of mineral crystals is usually made up of more than one kind of mineral (Figure 1C). However, there are exceptions. The rock in Figure 1D has many colors, but they are simply *varieties* (var.)—different forms or colors—of the mineral quartz. This means that a mineral cannot be identified solely on the basis of its color. The mineral's other properties must also be observed, recorded, and used collectively to identify it. Most minerals also tend to exhibit one color on freshly broken surfaces and a different color on tarnished or weathered surfaces. Be sure to note this difference, if present, to aid your identification.

Mineral crystals may vary in their **clarity** (also called diaphaneity), clearness, or ability to transmit light. They may be *transparent* (clear and see-through, like window glass), *translucent* (foggy, like looking through a steamed-up shower door), or *opaque* (impervious to light, like concrete and metals). It is good practice to record not only a mineral's color, but also its clarity. For example, the crystals in Figure 1A are purple in color and have transparent to translucent clarity. Galena mineral crystals (Figure 2) are opaque.

Crystal Habits and Forms

Crystal form is the geometric shape of a crystal. The flat outer surfaces of the crystal forms are called *crystal faces*. They are the outward reflection of the way that atoms or groups of atoms bonded together in a dimensional pattern as the crystal grew under specific environmental conditions. Under different environmental conditions, the mineral may have developed a different crystal form. **Crystal habit** refers to the general crystal form(s) and combinations in which a mineral habitually forms. A mineral's crystal habit is a clue that can be used to identify the mineral

and the environmental conditions under which its crystals grew.

These common crystal habits are illustrated in Figure 4.

- Acicular—long narrow crystals, like needles
- Bladed—crystals shaped like a sword or knife blade
- Botryoidal—smooth bubble-like shapes
- Cubic—crystals shaped like cubes (6 faces)
- Dendritic—a pattern of crystal growth that resembles the branches of a tree
- Dipyramidal—crystal shapes made of two pyramids connected by their bases
- Dipyramid prismatic—crystal shape made of a prism with pyramid shapes at both ends
- Equant—said of crystals that have all of their symmetrical faces spaced apart equally (includes many forms such as dodecahedrons, pyritohedrons, and some tetrahedrons)
- Fibrous—masses of long flexible crystals that resemble clumps of thread or cloth
- Prismatic—crystal forms dominated by three, four, six, eight, or twelve long, parallel faces

Crystal Habits (General Forms and Combinations)

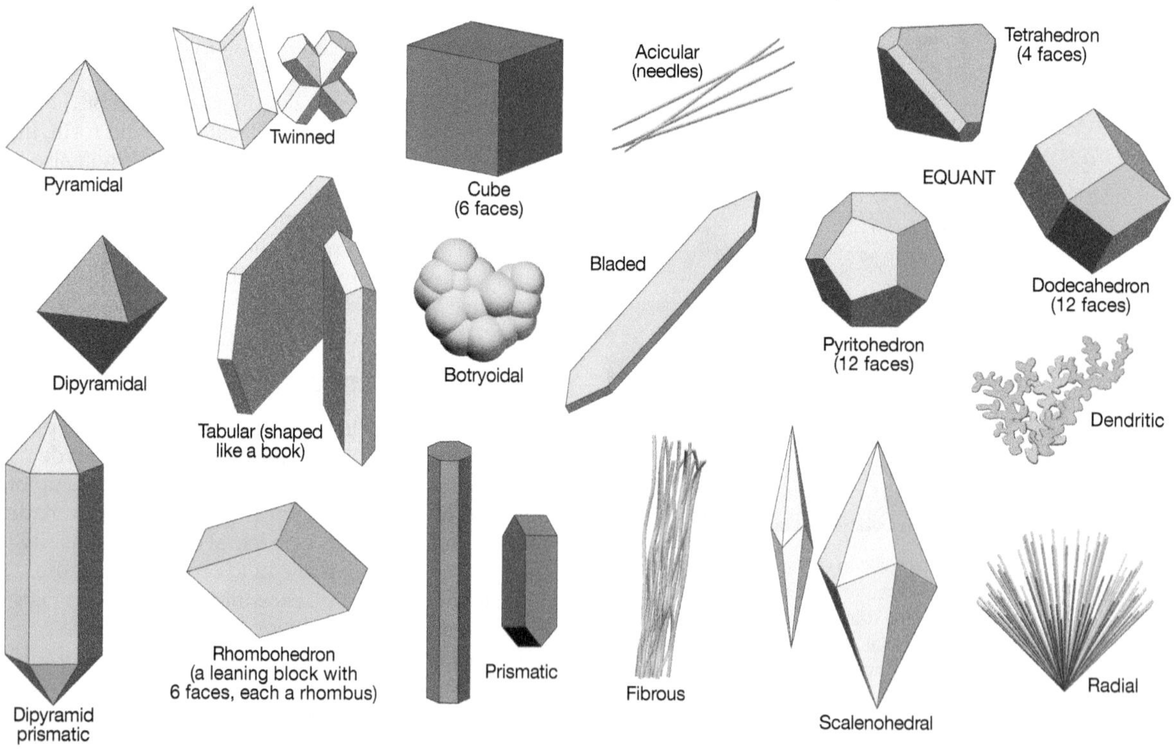

FIGURE 4   Common crystal **habits,** general geometric forms and combinations of crystals. See text (above and on next page) for a description of each habit.

60

- Pyramidal—crystals having three, four, six, eight, or twelve faces that intersect in a point

- Radial—said of masses of crystals that grew outward from a central point

- Rhombohedral—crystal forms that resemble leaning blocks and have six faces

- Scalenohedral—crystals with faces that are long scalene (no sides of equal length) triangles

- Tabular—crystals forms dominated by two very large parallel faces, like a book or tablet

- Twinned—two crystals of identical shape that have grown together

Crystal habit refers to general forms and combinations of crystals. Each specific crystal form can be classified into one of six **crystal systems** (Figure 5) according to the number, lengths, and angular relationships of imaginary geometric axes along which its crystal faces grew. The crystal systems comprise 32 classes of crystal forms, but only the common crystal forms are illustrated in Figure 5.

Note that crystal form is an external feature of mineral crystals. Perfect crystal forms can only develop if a mineral crystal is unrestricted as it grows. This is rare. It is more common for mineral crystals to crowd together as they grow, resulting in a *massive* network of intergrown crystals that do not exhibit their crystal form. For example, calcite normally forms 12-sided scalenohedrons (Figures 4, 5). But the calcite crystals in Figure 1B crowded together so much as they grew that none of them exhibits its crystal form. Most crystalline rocks form in this way. Even if crystal forms develop, the crystals may be *cryptocrystalline*—too small to see with the naked eye (Figure 1D). Most of the laboratory samples of minerals that you will analyze do not exhibit their crystal forms either, because they are small broken pieces of larger crystals. However, whenever the habit, form, or system of crystals in a mineral sample can be detected, then it should be noted and used as evidence for mineral identification.

Luster

Luster is a description of how light reflects from the surface of an object, such as a mineral. Luster is of two main types—metallic and nonmetallic—that vary in intensity from bright (very reflective, shiny, polished) to dull (not very reflective, not very shiny, not polished). For example, if you make a list of objects in your home that are made of unpainted metal that has not tarnished (e.g., new coins, knives, keys, jewelry, aluminum foil), then you are already familiar with metallic luster. Yet the metallic objects can vary from bright (very reflective—like polished jewelry, the polished side of aluminum foil, or new coins) to dull (non-reflective—like unpolished jewelry or the unpolished side of aluminum foil).

Minerals with a **metallic luster (M)** reflect light just like the metal objects in your home—they have opaque, reflective surfaces with a silvery, gold, brassy, or coppery sheen (Figures 2B, 6C, 7). All other minerals have a **nonmetallic luster (NM)**—a luster unlike that of the metal objects in your home (Figures 1, 2A, 3). The luster of nonmetallic minerals can also be described with the more specific terms below:

- Vitreous—resembling the luster of freshly broken glass or a glossy photograph

- Waxy—resembling the luster of a candle

- Pearly—resembling the luster of a pearl

- Satiny—resembling the luster of satin or silk cloth

- Earthy—lacking reflection, completely dull, like dry soil

- Greasy—resembling the luster of grease, oily

- Porcelaneous—resembling the luster of porcelain (translucent white ceramic ware)

Exposed surfaces of most minerals, especially metallic minerals, will normally tarnish or weather to a more dull or earthy nonmetallic luster. Notice how the exposed metallic copper crystals in Figure 6A, 6B, and the galena crystals in Figure 2A, have tarnished to a nonmetallic luster. Always observe freshly broken surfaces of a mineral (e.g., Figure 2B) to determine whether it has a metallic or nonmetallic luster. It is also useful to note a mineral's luster on fresh versus tarnished surfaces when possible. If you think that a mineral's luster is *submetallic*, between metallic and nonmetallic, then it should be treated as metallic for identification purposes.

Streak

Streak is the color of a substance after it has been ground to a fine powder (so fine that you cannot see the grains of powder). The easiest way to do this is simply by scratching the mineral back and forth across a hard surface such as concrete, or a square of unglazed porcelain (called a *streak plate*). The color of the mineral's fine powder is its streak. Note that the brassy mineral in Figure 7 has a dark gray streak, but the reddish silver mineral has a red-brown streak. A mineral's streak is usually similar even among all of that mineral's varieties.

If you encounter a mineral that is harder than the streak plate, it will scratch the streak plate and make a white streak of powder from the streak plate. The streak of such hard minerals can be determined by crushing a tiny piece of them with a hammer (if available). Otherwise, record the streak as unknown.

Crystal Forms (Specific Geometric Shapes) and Classification into Six Systems

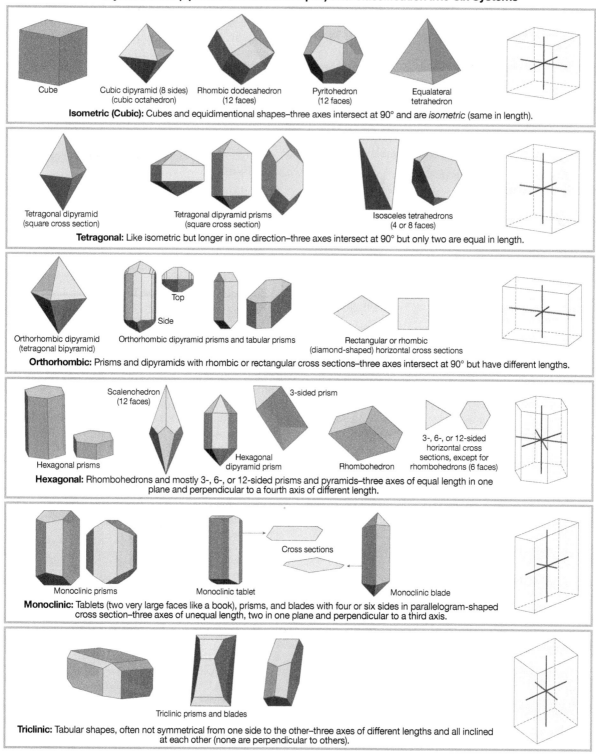

Cube   Cubic dipyramid (8 sides) (cubic octahedron)   Rhombic dodecahedron (12 faces)   Pyritohedron (12 faces)   Equalateral tetrahedron

Isometric (Cubic): Cubes and equidimentional shapes–three axes intersect at 90° and are *isometric* (same in length).

Tetragonal dipyramid (square cross section)   Tetragonal dipyramid prisms (square cross section)   Isosceles tetrahedrons (4 or 8 faces)

Tetragonal: Like isometric but longer in one direction–three axes intersect at 90° but only two are equal in length.

Orthorhombic dipyramid (tetragonal bipyramid)   Top   Side   Orthorhombic dipyramid prisms and tabular prisms   Rectangular or rhombic (diamond-shaped) horizontal cross sections

Orthorhombic: Prisms and dipyramids with rhombic or rectangular cross sections–three axes intersect at 90° but have different lengths.

Hexagonal prisms   Scalenohedron (12 faces)   Hexagonal dipyramid prism   3-sided prism   Rhombohedron   3-, 6-, or 12-sided horizontal cross sections, except for rhombohedrons (6 faces)

Hexagonal: Rhombohedrons and mostly 3-, 6-, or 12-sided prisms and pyramids–three axes of equal length in one plane and perpendicular to a fourth axis of different length.

Monoclinic prisms   Monoclinic tablet   Cross sections   Monoclinic blade

Monoclinic: Tablets (two very large faces like a book), prisms, and blades with four or six sides in parallelogram-shaped cross section–three axes of unequal length, two in one plane and perpendicular to a third axis.

Triclinic prisms and blades

Triclinic: Tabular shapes, often not symmetrical from one side to the other–three axes of different lengths and all inclined at each other (none are perpendicular to others).

FIGURE 5 Each specific crystal form can be classified into one of six **crystal systems** (major groups) according to the number, lengths, and angular relationships of imaginary geometric axes along which its crystal faces grew (red lines in the right-hand models of each system above). Only the common crystal forms are illustrated and named above.

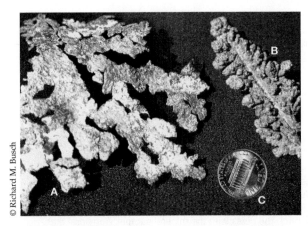

FIGURE 6 Native copper—Cu (naturally occurring pure copper) has a metallic luster until it tarnishes. **A.** Copper crystals tarnished brown and nonmetallic. **B.** Tarnished copper crystals with a thin coating of green malachite (copper carbonate) also have a nonmetallic luster. **C.** A freshly minted copper coin has a bright metallic luster (until it tarnishes).

Hardness (H)

Hardness is a measure of resistance to scratching. A harder substance will scratch a softer one (Figure 8). German mineralogist Friedrich Mohs (1773–1839) developed a quantitative scale of relative mineral hardness on which the softest mineral (talc) has an arbitrary hardness of 1 and the hardest mineral (diamond) has an arbitrary hardness of 10. Higher-numbered minerals will scratch lower-numbered minerals (e.g., diamond will scratch talc, but talc cannot scratch diamond).

Mohs Scale of Hardness (Figure 9) is now widely used by geologists and engineers. When identifying a mineral, you should mainly be able to distinguish minerals that are relatively hard (6.0 or higher on Mohs Scale) from minerals that are relatively soft (less than or equal to 5.5 on Mohs Scale). You can use common objects such as a glass plate (Figure 8), pocketknife or steel masonry nail to make this distinction as follows.

- **Hard minerals:** Will scratch glass. Cannot be scratched with a knife blade or masonry nail (or glass).
- **Soft minerals:** Will not scratch glass. Can be scratched with a knife blade or masonry nail (or glass).

You can determine a mineral's hardness number on Mohs Scale by comparing the mineral to common objects shown in Figure 9 or pieces of the minerals in Mohs Scale. Commercial *hardness kits* contain a set of all of the minerals in Figure 9 or a set of metal scribes of known hardnesses. When using such kits to make hardness comparisons, remember that the harder mineral/object is the one that scratches and the softer mineral/object is the one that is scratched.

Cleavage and Fractures

Cleavage is the tendency of some minerals to break (*cleave*) along flat, parallel surfaces (**cleavage planes**) like the flat surfaces on broken pieces of galena (Figure 2B). The cleavage can be described as excellent,

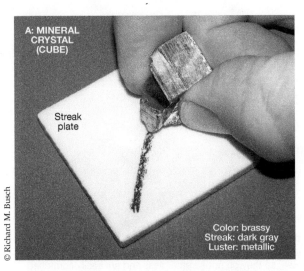

FIGURE 7 Streak tests. **A.** This mineral has a brassy color and metallic *luster* (surface reflection), but its *streak* (color in powdered form) is dark gray. **B.** This mineral has a reddish silver color and silvery or steel-gray metallic luster, but its streak is red-brown. If you do not have a streak plate, then determine the streak color by crushing or scratching part of the sample to see the color of its powdered form.

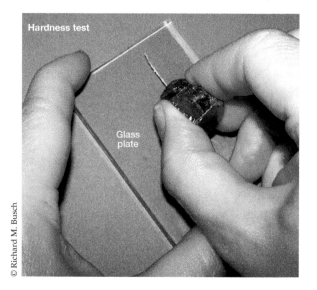

Hardness test

Glass plate

© Richard M. Busch

FIGURE 8 *Hardness* (resistance to scratching) test using a glass plate, which has a hardness of 5.5 on Mohs Scale of Hardness (Figure 9). Be sure the edges of the glass have been dulled. If not, then wrap the edges in masking tape or duct tape. Hold the glass plate firmly against a flat tabletop (do NOT hold it in the palm of your hand), then try to scratch the glass with the mineral sample. A mineral that scratches the glass (this image) is a *hard* mineral (i.e., harder than 5.5 on Mohs Scale of Hardness). A mineral that does not scratch the glass is a *soft* mineral (i.e., less than or equal to 5.5 on Mohs Scale of Hardness).

Mohs Scale of Hardness*	Hardness of Some Common Objects (Harder objects scratch softer objects)
HARD 10 Diamond	
9 Corundum	
8 Topaz	
7 Quartz	
6 Orthoclase Feldspar	6.5 Streak plate
	5.5 Glass, Masonry nail, Knife blade
SOFT 5 Apatite	4.5 Wire (iron) nail
4 Fluorite	
3 Calcite	3.5 Brass (wood screw, washer)
	2.9 Copper coin (penny)
	2.5 Fingernail
2 Gypsum	
1 Talc	

* A scale for measuring relative mineral hardness (resistance to scratching).

FIGURE 9 Mohs Scale of Hardness (resistance to scratching) and the hardness of some common objects. *Hard minerals* have a Mohs hardness number greater than 5.5, so they scratch glass and cannot be scratched with a knife blade or masonry (steel) nail. *Soft minerals* have a Mohs hardness number of 5.5 or less, so they do not scratch glass and are easily scratched by a knife blade or masonry (steel) nail. Mohs hardness numbers can be determined for hard or soft minerals by comparing them to the hardness of other common objects or minerals of Mohs Scale of Hardness.

Light rays

A. Cleavage excellent or perfect (large, parallel, flat surfaces)

Light rays

B. Cleavage good or imperfect (small, parallel, flat, stair-like surfaces)

Light rays

C. Cleavage poor (a few small, flat surfaces difficult to detect)

Light rays

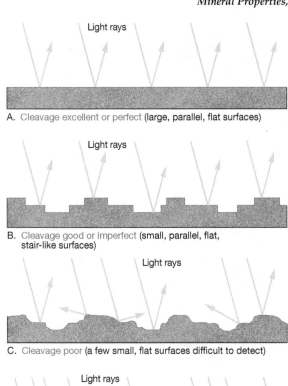

| conchoidal | uneven | hackly | splintery | fibrous |

D. Fractures (broken surfaces lacking cleavage planes)

FIGURE 10 Cross sections of mineral samples to illustrate degrees of development of cleavage—the tendency for a mineral to break along one or more sets of parallel planar surfaces called *cleavage planes*. The cleavage planes are surfaces of weak chemical bonding (attraction) between repeating, parallel layers of atoms in a crystal. Each different set of parallel cleavage planes is referred to as a *cleavage direction*. **A.** An *excellent cleavage* direction reflects light in one direction from a set of large, obvious, flat, parallel surfaces. **B.** A *good cleavage* direction reflects light in one direction from a set of small, flat, parallel, stair-like surfaces. A good example is galena (Figure 2). **C.** A *poor cleavage* direction reflects only a small amount of light from a set of very small, flat, parallel, surfaces that are not obvious. Remaining rays of light are reflected in all directions from fracture surfaces. **D.** *Fracture* refers to any break in a mineral that does not occur along a cleavage plane. Therefore, fracture surfaces are normally not flat and they never occur in parallel sets. Fracture can be characterized as conchoidal, uneven, hackly, splintery, or fibrous.

good, or poor (Figure 10). An *excellent cleavage* direction reflects light in one direction from a set of obvious, large, flat, parallel surfaces. A *good cleavage* direction reflects light in one direction from a set of many small, obvious, flat, parallel surfaces. A *poor cleavage* direction reflects light from a set of small, flat, parallel surfaces that are difficult to detect. Some

A: Milky quartz (x1)

B: Pure quartz (x1)

FIGURE 11 Quartz (silicon dioxide). These two samples are broken pieces of quartz mineral crystals that do not exhibit any crystal form. **A.** Milky quartz forms when the quartz has microscopic fluid inclusions, usually water. Note the nonmetallic (vitreous) luster and uneven fracture. **B.** Pure quartz (var. rock crystal) is colorless, transparent, nonmetallic, and exhibits excellent conchoidal fracture.

of the light is reflected in one direction from the small cleavage surfaces, but most of the light is scattered randomly by fracture surfaces separating the cleavage surfaces. **Fracture** refers to any break in a mineral that does not occur along a cleavage plane. Therefore, fracture surfaces are normally not flat and they never occur in parallel sets. Fracture can be described as *uneven* (rough, like the milky quartz in Figure 11A), *splintery* (like splintered wood), or *hackly* (having jagged edges). Opal (Figure 3A) and pure quartz (Figure 11B) both tend to fracture like glass—along ribbed, smoothly curved surfaces called *conchoidal fractures*.

The cleavage planes are parallel surfaces of weak chemical bonding (attraction) between repeating, parallel layers of atoms in a crystal, and more than one set of cleavage planes can be present in a crystal. Each different set has an orientation relative to the crystalline structure and is referred to as a **cleavage direction** (Figure 12). For example, muscovite

Number of Cleavages and Their Directions	Name and Description of How the Mineral Breaks	Shape of Broken Pieces (cleavage directions are numbered)	Illustration of Cleavage Directions
No cleavage (fractures only)	No parallel broken surfaces; may have conchoidal fracture (like glass)	 Quartz	None (no cleavage)
1 cleavage	**Basal (book) cleavage** "Books" that split apart along flat sheets	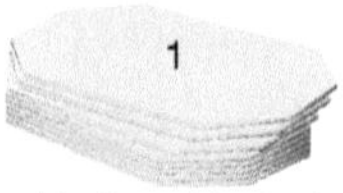 Muscovite, biotite, chlorite (micas)	
2 cleavages intersect at or near 90°	**Prismatic cleavage** Elongated forms that fracture along short *rectangular* cross sections	Orthoclase 90° (K-spar) 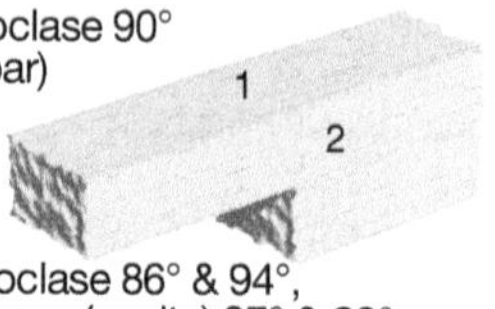 Plagioclase 86° & 94°, pyroxene (augite) 87° & 93°	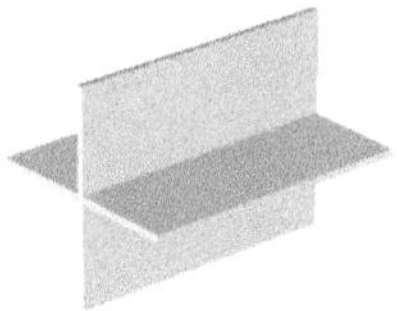
2 cleavages do not intersect at 90°	**Prismatic cleavage** Elongated forms that fracture along short *parallelogram* cross sections	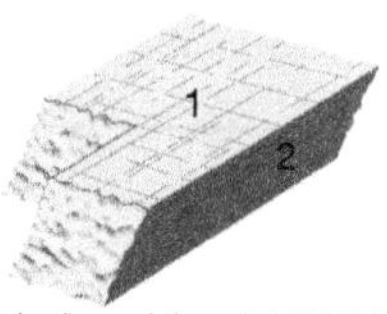 Amphibole (hornblende) 56° & 124°	
3 cleavages intersect at 90°	**Cubic cleavage** Shapes made of cubes and parts of cubes	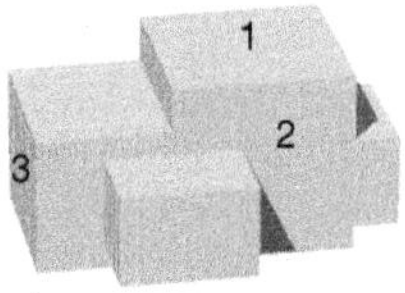 Halite, galena	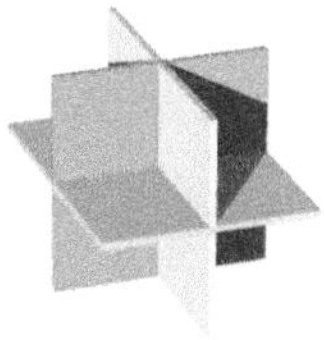
3 cleavages do not intersect at 90°	**Rhombohedral cleavage** Shapes made of rhombohedrons and parts of rhombohedrons	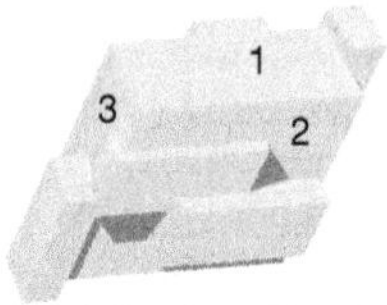 Calcite and dolomite 75° & 105°	
4 main cleavages intersect at 71° and 109° to form octahedrons, which split along hexagon-shaped surfaces; may have secondary cleavages at 60° and 120°	**Octahedral cleavage** Shapes made of octahedrons and parts of octahedrons	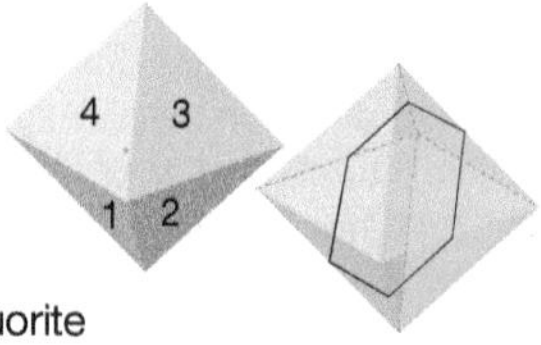 Fluorite	
6 cleavages intersect at 60° and 120°	**Dodecahedral cleavage** Shapes made of dodecahedrons and parts of dodecahedrons	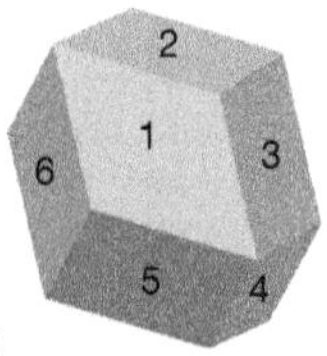 Sphalerite	

FIGURE 12 Cleavage in minerals.

© Richard M. Busch

x0.5

FIGURE 13 Muscovite (white mica). Micas are aluminum silicate minerals that form stout crystals with *book* (basal) cleavage, because they split easily into paper-thin, transparent, flexible sheets, along planes of one excellent cleavage direction. Muscovite is a light-colored, colorless to brown (as in this photograph) mica, in contrast to black biotite mica.

(Figure 13) has one excellent cleavage direction and splits apart like pages of a book (book cleavage). Galena (Figure 2) breaks into small cubes and shapes made of cubes, so it has three cleavage directions developed at right angles to one another. This is called cubic cleavage (Figure 12).

Minerals of the pyroxene (e.g., augite) and amphibole (e.g., hornblende) groups generally are both dark-colored (dark green to black), opaque, nonmetallic minerals that have two good cleavage directions. The two groups of minerals are sometimes difficult to distinguish, so some people identify them collectively as *pyriboles*. However, pyroxenes can be distinguished from amphiboles on the basis of their cleavage. The two cleavages of pyroxenes intersect at 87° and 93°, or nearly right angles (Figure 14A). The two cleavages of amphiboles intersect at angles of 56° and 124° (Figure 14B). These angles can be measured in hand samples using the cleavage goniometer from GeoTools Sheet 1. Notice how a green cleavage goniometer was used to measure angles between cleavage directions in Figures 14 and 15.

Garnet (Figure 16) has no cleavage, but it fractures along very low angle, slightly curved *parting surfaces* that resemble cleavage. Parting surfaces develop along planes of chemical change or imperfection, so they are not developed in all samples of garnet. Parting surfaces do not occur in flat parallel sets the way cleavage planes do. They are generally subparallel and discontinuous.

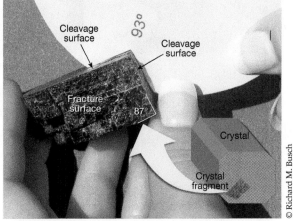

© Richard M. Busch

A. Cleavage in Pyroxenes (e.g., Augite)

© Richard M. Busch

B. Cleavage in Amphiboles (e.g., Hornblende)

FIGURE 14 Pyroxenes and amphiboles are two groups of minerals with many similar properties. Minerals in both groups have similar hardness (5.5–6.0), color (usually green to black), luster (vitreous nonmetallic), and streak (white to pale gray). Minerals in both groups are also complex silicates containing some proportion of iron (Fe) and magnesium (Mg), so they are dark-colored *ferromagnesian silicates*. The main feature that distinguishes the two groups is their cleavage. Augite and other pyroxenes have two prominent cleavage directions that intersect at 87° and 93° (nearly right angles). Hornblende and other amphiboles have two prominent cleavage directions that intersect at 56° and 124°. These cleavage differences are the main way to distinguish pyroxenes (e.g., augite) from amphiboles (e.g., hornblende) in hand samples.

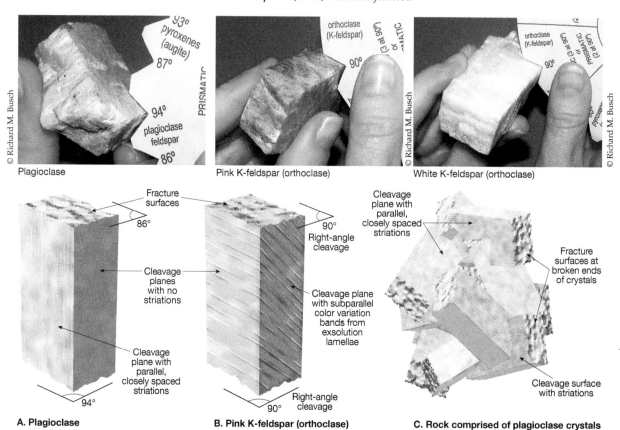

A. Plagioclase

B. Pink K-feldspar (orthoclase)

C. Rock comprised of plagioclase crystals

FIGURE 15 Common feldspars and rock. Note how the cleavage goniometer can be used to distinguish potassium feldspar (K-feldspar, orthoclase) from plagioclase. The K-feldspar or orthoclase (Greek, *ortho* = right angle and *clase* = break) has perfect right-angle cleavage. Plagioclase (Greek, *plagio* = oblique angle and *clase* = break) does not. **A.** Illustration of a fragment of a plagioclase feldspar crystal showing two excellent cleavage directions, fractured ends, angles between cleavage directions, and *hairline striations* on a cleavage surface. The striations are caused by *twinning*: microscopic intergrowths between symmetrically paired microcrystalline portions of the larger crystal. The striations occur only along one of the cleavage directions. They are not present in all samples of plagioclase. **B.** Broken piece of a K-feldspar (orthoclase) crystal showing two excellent cleavage directions, fractured ends, angles between cleavage directions, and intergrowths of thin, discontinuous, subparallel lamellae of plagioclase, called *exsolution lamellae*. The lamellae are actually microscopic layers of plagioclase that form as the mineral cools, like fat separates from soup when it is refrigerated. **C.** Hand sample of a rock that is an aggregate of intergrown plagioclase mineral crystals. Individual mineral crystals are discernible within the rock, particularly the cleavage surfaces that have characteristic hairline striations.

FIGURE 16 Garnet, a hard (H = 7), complex silicate mineral used for sandpaper and as a gemstone. Garnet is brittle and has no cleavage. Some samples, such as this one, break along subparallel *parting* surfaces developed along planes of chemical change or imperfection. Parting does not occur along parallel even surfaces the way cleavage does.

Other Properties

Tenacity is the manner in which a substance resists breakage. Terms used to describe mineral tenacity include *brittle* (shatters like glass), *malleable* (like modeling clay or gold; can be hammered or bent permanently into new shapes), *elastic* or *flexible* (like a plastic comb; bends but returns to its original shape), and *sectile* (can be carved with a knife).

Reaction to acid differs among minerals. Cool, dilute (1–3%) hydrochloric acid (HCl) applied from a dropper bottle is a common "acid test." All of the so-called *carbonate minerals* (minerals whose chemical composition includes carbonate, CO_3) will effervesce ("fizz") when a drop of dilute HCl is applied to one of their freshly exposed surfaces (Figure 17). Calcite $CaCO_3$ is the most commonly encountered carbonate mineral and effervesces in the acid test. Dolomite $[Ca, Mg(CO_3)_2]$ is another carbonate mineral that resembles calcite, but it will effervesce in dilute HCl only if the mineral is first powdered. (It can be powdered for this test by simply scratching the mineral's surface with the tip of a rock pick, pocketknife, or nail.) If HCl is not available, then undiluted vinegar can be used for the acid test.

x1

FIGURE 17 Acid test (placing a drop of weak hydrochloric acid on the sample) was positive for this mineral (i.e., caused the mineral to effervesce), so this is a carbonate (CO_3-containing) mineral. Also note that the mineral occurs in several different colors and can be scratched by a wire (iron) nail. The yellow sample is a crystal of this mineral, but the other samples are fragments that reveal the mineral's characteristic cleavage angles.

© Richard M. Busch

It contains acetic acid (but the effervescence will be much less violent).

Striations are straight "hairline" grooves on the cleavage surfaces of some minerals. This can be helpful in mineral identification. For example, you can use the striations of plagioclase feldspar (Figure 15A) to distinguish it from potassium feldspar (K-feldspar, Figure 15B). *Plagioclase feldspars* have striations on surfaces of one of their two cleavage directions. *K-feldspars* may have lines that resemble striations at a glance. However, they are thin, discontinuous, subparallel exsolution lamellae (thin, discontinuous layers) of plagioclase within the K-feldspar.

Magnetism influences some minerals, such as magnetite. The test is simple: magnetite is attracted to a magnet. Lodestone is a variety of magnetite that is itself a natural magnet. It will attract steel paperclips. Some other minerals (e.g., hematite, bornite) may be weakly attracted to a magnet after they are heated.

Density is a measure of an object's mass (weighed in grams, g) divided by its volume (in cubic centimeters, cm^3). **Specific gravity (SG)** is the ratio of the density of a substance divided by the density of water. Because water has a density of $1 g/cm^3$ and the units cancel out, specific gravity is the same number as density but without any units. For example, the mineral quartz has a density of $2.65 g/cm^3$ so its specific gravity is 2.65 (i.e., SG = 2.65). *Hefting* is an easy way to judge the specific gravity of one mineral relative to another. This is done by holding a piece of the first mineral in one hand and holding an equal-sized piece of the second mineral in your other hand. Feel the difference in weight between the two samples (i.e., heft the samples). The sample that feels heavier has a higher specific gravity than the other. Most metallic minerals have higher specific gravities than non-metallic minerals.

ACTIVITY 1

Mineral Properties

Complete this activity to review mineral properties and develop some familiarity with the mineral identification tables (Figures 18–20) and Mineral Database (Figure 21) before you proceed to Part B of this laboratory.

METALLIC AND SUBMETALLIC (M) MINERALS

Step 1: What is the mineral's hardness?	Step 2: What is the mineral's streak?	Step 3: Compare the mineral's physical properties to other characteristic properties below.	Step 4: Find mineral name(s) and check the mineral database for additional properties (Figure 21).
HARD (H > 5.5) Scratches glass Not scratched by masonry nail or knife blade	Dark gray	Color silvery gold; tarnishes brown; H 6–6.5; Cleavage absent to poor; Brittle; Crystals: cubes (often striated) or pyritohedrons	Pyrite
		Silvery dark gray to black; Tarnishes gray or rusty yellow-brown; Strongly attracted to a magnet and may be magnetized; H 6–6.5; No cleavage; Crystals: octahedrons	Magnetite
HARD **or** **SOFT**	Yellow-brown	Color silvery brown to dark brown; Tarnishes dull yellow-brown to brown; Amorphous; H 1–5.5; More common in softer (H 1–5) nonmetallic yellow-brown forms	Limonite
	Brown	Color silvery black to black; Tarnishes gray to black; H 5.5–6; No cleavage; May be weakly attracted to a magnet; Crystals: octahedrons	Chromite
	Red to red-brown	Color steel gray to glittery silver (var. specular); Tarnishes gray to dull red; May be attracted to a magnet; H 5–6.0; Also occurs in soft (H 1–5) nonmetallic earthy red forms	Hematite
SOFT (H ≤ 5.5) Does not scratch glass Scratched by masonry nail or knife blade	Dark gray	Color bright silvery gold; Tarnishes bronze brown brassy gold, or iridescent blue-green and red; H 3.5–4.0; Brittle; No cleavage; Crystals: tetrahedrons	Chalcopyrite
		Color brownish bronze; Tarnishes bright purple, blue, and/or red; May be weakly attracted to a magnet; H 3; Cleavage absent or poor; Rarely forms crystals	Bornite
		Color bright silvery gray; Tarnishes dull gray; Cleavage good to excellent; H 2.5; Crystals: cubes or octahedrons	Galena
		Color dark silvery gray to black; Can be scratched with your fingernail; Easily rubs off on your fingers and clothes, making them gray; H 1–2	Graphite
	Yellow-brown	Color dark brown to black; Forms layers of radiating microscopic crystals; H 5–5.5	Goethite
	White to pale yellow-brown	Color silvery yellow-brown, silvery red, or black; Tarnishes brown or black; H 3.5–4.0; Cleavage excellent to good; Smells like rotten eggs when scratched/powdered	Sphalerite
	Copper	Color copper; Tarnishes dark brown or green; Malleable; No cleavage; H 2.5–3.0; Forms odd-shaped masses, nuggets, or dendritic forms	Copper (Native Copper)
	Gold	Color yellow gold; Does not tarnish; Malleable; No cleavage; H 2.5–3.0; Forms odd-shaped masses, nuggets, or dendritic forms	Gold (Native Gold)

FIGURE 18 Flowchart for identification of opaque minerals having a metallic or submetallic luster (M).

LIGHT-COLORED NONMETALLIC (NM) MINERALS

Step 1: What is the mineral's hardness?	Step 2: What is the mineral's cleavage?	Step 3: Compare the mineral's physical properties to other distinctive properties below.	Step 4: Find mineral name(s) and check the mineral database for additional properties (Figure 21).
HARD (H > 5.5) Scratches glass Not scratched by masonry nail or knife blade	Cleavage excellent or good	White or gray; 2 cleavages at nearly right angles and with striations; H 6	Plagioclase feldspar
		Orange, brown, white, gray, green, or pink; H 6; 2 cleavages at nearly right angles; Exsolution lamellae	Potassium feldspar
		Pale brown, white, or gray; Long slender prisms; 1 excellent cleavage plus fracture surfaces; H 6–7	Sillimanite
		Blue, very pale green, white, or gray; Crystals are blades; H 4–7	Kyanite
	Cleavage poor or absent	Gray, white, or colored (dark red, blue, brown) hexagonal prisms with flat striated ends; H 9	Corundum Ruby (red var.), Sapphire (blue var.)
		Colorless, white, gray, or other colors; Greasy luster; Massive or hexagonal prisms and pyramids; Transparent or translucent; H 7	Quartz Milky quartz (white var.), Citrine quartz (yellow var.), Rose quartz (pink var.)
		Opaque gray or white; Luster waxy; H 7	Chert (variety of quartz)
		Colorless, white, yellow, light brown, or pastel colors; Translucent or opaque; Laminated or massive; Cryptocrystalline; Luster waxy; H 7	Chalcedony (variety of quartz)
		Pale olive green to yellow; Conchoidal fracture; Transparent or translucent; Forms short stout prisms; H 7	Olivine
SOFT (H ≤ 5.5) Does not scratch glass Scratched by masonry nail or knife blade	Cleavage excellent or good	Colorless, white, yellow, green, pink, or brown; 3 excellent cleavages; Breaks into rhombohedrons; Effervesces in dilute HCl; H 3	Calcite
		Colorless, white, gray, creme, or pink; 3 excellent cleavages; Breaks into rhombohedrons; Effervesces in dilute HCl only if powdered; H 3.5–4	Dolomite
		Colorless or white with tints of brown, yellow, blue, black; Short tabular crystals and roses; Very heavy; H 3–3.5	Barite
		Colorless, white, or pastel colors; Massive or tabular crystals, blades, or needles; Transparent to opaque; Can be scratched with your fingernail; H 2	Gypsum Selenite (colorless transparent var.) Alabaster (opaque white or pastel var.) Satin spar (fibrous silky translucent var.)
		Colorless, white, gray, or pale green, yellow, or red; Spheres of radiating needles; Luster silky; H 5–5.5	Natrolite
		Colorless, white, yellow, blue, brown, or red; Cubic crystals; Breaks into cubes; Salty taste; H 2.5	Halite
		Colorless, purple, blue, gray, green, yellow; Cubes with octahedral cleavage; H 4	Fluorite
		Colorless, yellow, brown, or red-brown; Short opaque prisms; Splits along 1 excellent cleavage into thin flexible transparent sheets; H 2–2.5	Muscovite (white mica)
	Cleavage poor or absent	Yellow crystals or earthy masses; Luster greasy; H 1.5–2.5; Smells like rotten eggs when powdered	Sulfur (Native sulfur)
		Opaque pale blue to blue-green; Amorphous crusts or massive; Very light blue streak; H 2–4	Chrysocolla
		Opaque green, yellow, or gray; Dull or silky masses or asbestos; White streak; H 2–5	Serpentine
		Opaque white, gray, green, or brown; Can be scratched with fingernail; Greasy or soapy feel; H 1	Talc
		Opaque earthy white to very light brown; Powdery, greasy feel; H 1–2	Kaolinite
		Colorless to white, orange, yellow, brown, blue, gray, green, or red; May have play of colors; Conchoidal fracture; H 5–5.5	Opal
		Colorless or pale green, brown, blue, white, or purple; Brittle hexagonal prisms; Conchoidal fracture; H 5	Apatite

FIGURE 19 Flowchart for identification of light-colored minerals with nonmetallic (NM) luster.

DARK-COLORED NONMETALLIC (NM) MINERALS

Step 1: What is the mineral's hardness?	Step 2: What is the mineral's cleavage?	Step 3: Compare the mineral's physical properties to other distinctive properties below.	Step 4: Find mineral name(s) and check the mineral database for additional properties (Figure 21).
HARD (H > 5.5) Scratches glass Not scratched by masonry nail or knife blade	Cleavage excellent or good	Translucent dark gray, blue-gray, or black; May have silvery iridescence; 2 cleavages at nearly 90° and with striations; H 6	Plagioclase feldspar
		Translucent brown, gray, green, or red; 2 cleavages at nearly right angles; Exsolution lamellae; H 6	Potassium feldspar (K-spar)
		Dark green to black; 2 cleavages at about 56° and 124°; H 5.5–6	Actinolite (Amphibole)
		Dark gray to black; 2 cleavages at about 56° and 124°; H 5.5–6	Hornblende (Amphibole)
		Dark green to black; 2 cleavages at nearly right angles (93° and 87°); H 5.5–6	Augite (Pyroxene)
	Cleavage poor or absent	Transparent or translucent gray, brown, or purple; Greasy luster; Massive or hexagonal prisms and pyramids; H 7	Quartz Smoky quartz (black/brown var.), Amethyst (purple var.)
		Gray, black, or colored (dark red, blue, brown) hexagonal prisms with flat striated ends; H 9	Corundum Emery (black impure var.) Ruby (red var.), Sapphire (blue var.)
		Opaque red-brown or brown; Luster waxy; Cryptocrystalline; H 7	Jasper (variety of quartz)
		Transparent to translucent dark red to black; Equant (dodecahedron) crystal form or massive; H 7	Garnet
		Opaque gray; Luster waxy; Cryptocrystalline; H 7	Chert (gray variety of quartz)
		Opaque black; Luster waxy; Cryptocrystalline; H 7	Flint (black variety of quartz)
		Black or dark green; Long striated prisms; H 7–7.5	Tourmaline
		Transparent or translucent olive green; Conchoidal fracture; Transparent or translucent; H 7	Olivine
		Opaque dark gray to black; Tarnishes gray to rusty yellow-brown; Cleavage absent; Strongly attracted to a magnet; May be magnetized; H 6–6.5	Magnetite
		Opaque green; Poor cleavage; H 6–7	Epidote
		Opaque brown prisms and cross-shaped twins; H 7	Staurolite
SOFT (H ≤ 5.5) Does not scratch glass Scratched by masonry nail or knife blade	Cleavage excellent or good	Translucent to opaque yellow-brown to brown; May appear submetallic; Dodecahedral cleavage; H 3.5–4	Sphalerite
		Purple cubes or octahedrons; Octahedral cleavage; H 4	Fluorite
		Black short opaque prisms; Splits easily along 1 excellent cleavage into thin sheets; H 2.5–3	Biotite (black mica)
		Green short opaque prisms; Splits easily along 1 excellent cleavage into thin sheets; H 2–3	Chlorite
	Cleavage poor or absent	Opaque rusty brown or yellow-brown; Massive and amorphous; Yellow-brown streak; H 1–5.5	Limonite
		Opaque rusty brown to brown-gray rock with shades of gray, yellow, and white; Contains pea-sized spheres that are laminated internally; Pale brown streak; H 1–3	Bauxite
		Deep blue; Crusts, small crystals, or massive; Light blue streak; H 3.5–4	Azurite
		Opaque green or gray-green; Dull or silky masses or asbestos; White streak; H 2–5	Serpentine
		Opaque green in laminated crusts or massive; Streak pale green; Effervesces in dilute HCl; H 3.5–4	Malachite
		Translucent or opaque dark green; Can be scratched with your fingernail; Feels greasy or soapy; H 1	Talc
		Transparent or translucent green, brown, blue, or purple; Brittle hexagonal prisms; Conchoidal fracture; H 5	Apatite
		Opaque red or red-gray; H 1.5–5	Hematite

FIGURE 20 Flowchart for identification of dark- and medium-colored minerals with nonmetallic (NM) luster.

MINERAL DATABASE (Alphabetical Listing)

Mineral	Luster and Crystal System	Hardness	Streak	Distinctive Properties	Some Uses
ACTINOLITE (amphibole)	Nonmetallic (NM) Monoclinic	5.5–6	White	Color dark green or pale green; Forms needles, prisms, and asbestose fibers; Good cleavage at 56° and 124°; SG = 3.1	Gemstone (Nephrite), Asbestos products
AMPHIBOLE: See HORNEBLENDE and ACTINOLITE					
APATITE $Ca_5F(PO_4)_3$ calcium fluorophosphate	Nonmetallic (NM) Hexagonal	5	White	Color pale or dark green, brown, blue, white, or purple; Sometimes colorless; Transparent or opaque; Brittle; Conchoidal fracture; Forms hexagonal prisms; SG = 3.1–3.4	Used for pesticides and fertilizers
ASBESTOS: fibrous varieties of AMPHIBOLE and SERPENTINE					
AUGITE (pyroxene) calcium ferromagnesian silicate	Nonmetallic (NM) Monoclinic	5.5–6	White to pale gray	Color dark green to gray; Forms short, 8-sided prisms; Two good cleavages that intersect at 87° and 93° (nearly right angles); SG = 3.2–3.5	Some pyroxene mined as an ore of lithium, for making steel
AZURITE $Cu_3(CO_3)_2(OH)_2$ hydrous copper carbonate	Nonmetallic (NM) Monoclinic	3.5–4	Light blue	Color a distinctive deep blue; Forms crusts of small crystals, opaque earthy masses, or short and long prisms; Brittle; Effervesces in dilute HCl; SG = 3.7–3.8	Ore of copper for pipes, electrical circuits, coins, ammunition, gemstone
BARITE $BaSO_4$ barium sulfate	Nonmetallic (NM) Orthorhombic	3–3.5	White	Colorless to white, with tints of brown, yellow, blue, or red; Forms short tabular crystals and rose-shaped masses (Barite roses); Brittle; Cleavage good to excellent; Very heavy, SG = 4.3–4.6	Used in rubber, paint, glass, oil-well drilling fluids
BAUXITE Mixture of aluminum hydroxides	Nonmetallic (NM) No visible crystals	1–3	White	Brown earthy rock with shades of gray, white, and yellow; Amorphous; Often contains rounded pea-sized structures with laminations; SG = 2.0–3.0	Ore of aluminum
BIOTITE MICA ferromagnesian potassium, hydrous aluminum silicate $K(Mg,Fe)_3 (Al,Si_3O_{10})(OH,F)_2$	Nonmetallic (NM) Monoclinic	2.5–3	Gray-brown	Color black, green-black, or brown-black; Cleavage excellent; Forms very short prisms that split easily into very thin, flexible sheets; SG = 2.7–3.1	Used for fire-resistant tiles, rubber, paint
BORNITE Cu_5FeS_4 copper-iron sulfide	Metallic (M) Isometric	3	Dark gray to black	Color brownish bronze; Tarnishes bright purple, blue, and/or red; May be weakly attracted to a magnet; H 3; Cleavage absent or poor; Forms dense brittle masses; Rarely forms crystals	Ore of copper for pipes, electrical circuits, coins, ammunition, brass, bronze
CALCITE $CaCO_3$ calcium carbonate	Nonmetallic (NM) Hexagonal	3	White	Usually colorless, white, or yellow, but may be green, brown, or pink; Opaque or transparent; Excellent cleavage in 3 directions not at 90°; Forms prisms, rhombohedrons, or scalenohedrons that break into rhombohedrons; Effervesces in dilute HCl; SG = 2.7	Used to make antacid tablets, fertilizer, cement; Ore of calcium
CHALCEDONY SiO_2 cryptocrystalline quartz	Nonmetallic (NM) No visible crystals	7	White*	Colorless, white, yellow, light brown, or other pastel colors in laminations; Often translucent; Conchoidal fracture; Luster waxy; Cryptocrystalline; SG = 2.5–2.8	Used as an abrasive; Used to make glass, gemstones (agate, chrysoprase)

*Streak cannot be determined with a streak plate for minerals harder than 6.5. They scratch the streak plate.

FIGURE 21 Mineral Database—alphabetical list of minerals and their properties and uses.

MINERAL DATABASE (Alphabetical Listing)

Mineral	Luster and Crystal System	Hardness	Streak	Distinctive Properties	Some Uses
CHALCOPYRITE $CuFeS_2$ copper-iron sulfide	Metallic (M) Tetragonal	3.5–4	Dark gray	Color bright silvery gold; Tarnishes bronze brown, brassy gold, or iridescent blue-green and red; Brittle; No cleavage; Forms dense masses or elongate tetrahedrons; SG = 4.1–4.3	Ore of copper for pipes, electrical circuits, coins, ammunition, brass, bronze
CHERT SiO_2 cryptocrystalline quartz	Nonmetallic (NM) No visible crystals	7	White*	Opaque gray or white; Luster waxy; Conchoidal fracture; SG = 2.5–2.8	Used as an abrasive; Used to make glass, gemstones
CHLORITE ferromagnesian aluminum silicate $(Mg,Fe,Al)_6(Si,Al)_4O_{10}(OH)_8$	Nonmetallic (NM) Monoclinic	2–2.5	White	Color dark green; Cleavage excellent; Forms short prisms that split easily into thin flexible sheets; Luster bright or dull; SG = 2–3	Used for fire-resistant tiles, rubber, paint, art sculpture medium
CHROMITE $FeCr_2O_4$ iron-chromium oxide	Metallic (M) Isometric	5.5–6	Dark brown	Color silvery black to black; Tarnishes gray to black; No cleavage; May be weakly attracted to a magnet; Forms dense masses or granular masses of small crystals (octahedrons)	Ore of chromium for making chrome, stainless steel, mirrors, paint and used in leather tanning
CHRYSOCOLLA $CuSiO_3 \cdot 2H_2O$ hydrated copper silicate	Nonmetallic (NM) Orthorhombic	2–4	Very light blue	Color pale blue to blue-green; Opaque; Forms cryptocrystalline crusts or may be massive; Conchoidal fracture; Luster shiny or earthy; SG = 2.0–4.0	Ore of copper for pipes, electrical circuits, coins, ammunition; gemstone
COPPER (NATIVE COPPER) Cu copper	Metallic (M) Isometric	2.5–3	Copper	Color copper; Tarnishes brown or green; Malleable; No cleavage; Forms odd-shaped masses, nuggets, or dendritic forms; SG = 8.8–9.0	Ore of copper for pipes, electrical circuits, coins, ammunition, brass, bronze
CORUNDUM Al_2O_3 aluminum oxide	Nonmetallic (NM) Hexagonal	9	White*	Gray, white, black, or colored (red, blue, brown, yellow) hexagonal prisms with flat striated ends; Opaque to transparent; Cleavage absent; SG = 3.9–4.1 H 9	Used for abrasive powders to polish lenses; gemstones (red ruby, blue sapphire); emery cloth
DOLOMITE $CaMg(CO_3)_2$ magnesian calcium carbonate	Nonmetallic (NM) Hexagonal	3.5–4	White	Color white, gray, creme, or pink; Usually opaque; Cleavage excellent in 3 directions; Breaks into rhombohedrons; Resembles calcite, but will effervesce in dilute HCl only if powdered; SG = 2.8–2.9	Ore of magnesium metal; soft abrasive; used to make paper
EPIDOTE complex silicate	Nonmetallic (NM) Monoclinic	6–7	White*	Color pale or dark green to yellow-green; Massive or forms striated prisms; Cleavage poor; SG = 3.3–3.5	Gemstone

FELDSPAR: See PLAGIOCLASE (Na-Ca Feldspars) and POTASSIUM FELDSPAR (K-Spar)

Mineral	Luster and Crystal System	Hardness	Streak	Distinctive Properties	Some Uses
FLINT SiO_2 cryptocrystalline quartz	Nonmetallic (NM) No visible crystals	7	White*	Color black to very dark gray; Opaque to translucent; Conchoidal fracture; Crypto-crystalline; SG = 2.5–2.8	Used as an abrasive; Used to make glass, gemstones
FLUORITE CaF_2 calcium fluoride	Nonmetallic (NM) Isometric	4	White	Colorless, purple, blue, gray, green, or yellow; Cleavage excellent; Crystals usually cubes; Transparent or opaque; Brittle; SG = 3.0–3.3	Source of fluorine for processing aluminum; flux in steel making

*Streak cannot be determined with a streak plate for minerals harder than 6.5. They scratch the streak plate.

FIGURE 21 (continued)

MINERAL DATABASE (Alphabetical Listing)

Mineral	Luster and Crystal System	Hardness	Streak	Distinctive Properties	Some Uses
GALENA PbS lead sulfide	Metallic (M) Isometric	2.5	Gray to dark gray	Color bright silvery gray; Tarnishes dull gray; Forms cubes and octahedrons; Brittle; Cleavage good in three directions, so breaks into cubes; SG = 7.4–7.6	Ore of lead for TV glass, auto batteries, solder, ammunition, paint
GARNET complex silicate	Nonmetallic (NM) Isometric	7	White*	Color usually red, black, or brown, sometimes yellow, green, pink; Forms dodecahedrons; Cleavage absent but may have parting; Brittle; Translucent to opaque; SG = 3.5–4.3	Used as an abrasive; gemstone
GOETHITE FeO(OH) iron oxide hydroxide	Metallic (M) Orthorhombic	5–5.5	Yellow-brown	Color dark brown to black; Tarnishes yellow-brown; Forms layers of radiating microscopic crystals; SG = 3.3–4.3	Ore of iron for steel, brass, bronze, tools, vehicles, nails and bolts, bridges, etc.
GRAPHITE C carbon	Metallic (M) Hexagonal	1	Dark gray	Color dark silvery gray to black; Forms flakes, short hexagonal prisms, and earthy masses; Greasy feel; Very soft; Cleavage excellent in 1 direction; SG = 2.0–2.3	Used as a lubricant (as in graphite oil), pencil leads, fishing rods
GYPSUM $CaSO_4 \cdot 2H_2O$ hydrated calcium sulfate	Nonmetallic (NM) Monoclinic	2	White	Colorless, white, or gray; Forms tabular crystals, prisms, blades, or needles (satin spar variety); Transparent to translucent; Very soft; Cleavage good; SG = 2.3	Plaster-of-paris, wallboard, drywall, art sculpture medium (alabaster)
HALITE NaCl sodium chloride	Nonmetallic (NM) Isometric	2.5	White	Colorless, white, yellow, blue, brown, or red; Transparent to translucent; Brittle; Forms cubes; Cleavage excellent in 3 directions, so breaks into cubes; Salty taste; SG = 2.1–2.6	Table salt, road salt; Used in water softeners and as a preservative; Sodium ore
HEMATITE Fe_2O_3 iron oxide	Metallic (M) or Nonmetallic (NM) Hexagonal	1–6	Red to red-brown	Color silvery gray, reddish silver, black, or brick red; Tarnishes red; Opaque; Soft (earthy) and hard (metallic) varieties have same streak; Forms thin tabular crystals or massive; May be attracted to a magnet; SG = 4.9–5.3	Rouge makeup and polish: red pigment in paints, ore of iron for steel tools, vehicles, nails and bolts, bridges, etc.
HORNBLENDE (amphibole) calcium ferromagnesian aluminum silicate	Nonmetallic (NM) Monoclinic	5.5	White to pale gray	Color dark gray to black; Forms prisms with good cleavage at 56° and 124°; Brittle; Splintery or asbestos forms; SG = 3.0–3.3	Fibrous varieties used for fire-resistant clothing, tiles, brake linings
JASPER SiO_2 cryptocrystalline quartz	Nonmetallic (NM) No visible crystals	7	White*	Color red-brown, or yellow; Opaque; Waxy luster; Conchoidal fracture; Cryptocrystalline; SG = 2.5–2.8	Used as an abrasive; Used to make glass, gemstones
KAOLINITE $Al_4(Si_4O_{10})(OH)_8$ hydrous aluminum silicate	Nonmetallic (NM) Triclinic	1–2	White	Color white to very light brown; Commonly forms earthy, microcrystalline masses; Cleavage excellent but absent in hand samples; SG = 2.6	Used for pottery, clays, polishing compounds, pencil leads, paper
K-SPAR: See POTASSIUM FELSDPAR					
KYANITE $Al_2(SiO_4)O$ aluminum silicate	Nonmetallic (NM) Triclinic	4–7	White*	Color blue, pale green, white, or gray; Translucent to transparent; Forms blades; SG = 3.6–3.7	High temperature ceramics, spark plugs

*Streak cannot be determined with a streak plate for minerals harder than 6.5. They scratch the streak plate.

FIGURE 21 (continued)

MINERAL DATABASE (Alphabetical Listing)

Mineral	Luster and Crystal System	Hardness	Streak	Distinctive Properties	Some Uses
LIMONITE $Fe_2O_3 \cdot nH_2O$ hydrated iron oxide and/or $FeO(OH) \cdot nH_2O$ hydrated iron oxide hydroxide	Metallic (M) or Nonmetallic (NM) Amorphous	1–5.5	Yellow-brown	Color yellow-brown to dark brown; Tarnishes yellow to brown; Amorphous masses; Luster dull or earthy; Hard or soft; SG = 3.3–4.3	Yellow pigment; Ore of iron for steel tools, vehicles, nails and bolts, bridges, etc.
MAGNETITE Fe_3O_4 iron oxide	Metallic (M) Isometric	6–6.5	Dark gray	Color silvery gray to black; Opaque; Forms octahedrons; Tarnishes gray; No cleavage; Attracted to a magnet and can be magnetized; SG = 5.0–5.2	Ore of iron for steel, brass, bronze, tools, vehicles, nails and bolts, bridges, etc.
MALACHITE $Cu_2CO_3(OH)_2$ hydrous copper carbonate	Nonmetallic (NM) Monoclinic	3.5–4	Green	Color green, pale green, or gray-green; Usually in crusts, laminated masses, or microcrystals; Effervesces in dilute HCl; SG = 3.6–4.0	Ore of copper for pipes, electrical circuits, coins, ammunition; Gemstone

MICA: See BIOTITE and MUSCOVITE

NATIVE COPPER: See COPPER

NATIVE SULFUR: See SULFUR

Mineral	Luster and Crystal System	Hardness	Streak	Distinctive Properties	Some Uses
NATROLITE (ZEOLITE) $Na_2(Al_2Si_3O_{10}) \cdot 2H_2O$ hydrous sodium aluminum silicate	Nonmetallic (NM) Orthorhombic	5–5.5	White	Colorless, white, gray, or pale green, yellow, or red; Forms masses of radiating needles; Silky luster; SG = 2.2–2.4	Water softeners
MUSCOVITE MICA potassium hydrous aluminum silicate $KAl_2(Al,Si_3O_{10})(OH,F)_2$	Nonmetallic (NM) Monoclinic	2–2.5	White	Colorless, yellow, brown, or red-brown; Forms short opaque prisms; Cleavage excellent in 1 direction, can be split into thin flexible transparent sheets; SG = 2.7–3.0	Computer chip substrates, electrical insulation, roof shingles, facial makeup
OLIVINE $(Fe,Mg)_2SiO_4$ ferromagnesian silicate	Nonmetallic (NM) Orthorhombic	7	White*	Color pale or dark olive-green to yellow, or brown; Forms short crystals that may resemble sand grains; Conchoidal fracture; Cleavage absent; Brittle; SG = 3.3–3.4	Gemstone (peridot); Ore of magnesium metal
OPAL $SiO_2 \cdot nH_2O$ hydrated silicon dioxide	Nonmetallic (NM) Amorphous	5–5.5	White	Colorless to white, orange, yellow, brown, blue, gray, green, or red; may have play of colors (opalescence); Amorphous; Cleavage absent; Conchoidal fracture; SG = 1.9–2.3	Gemstone
PLAGIOCLASE FELDSPAR $NaAlSi_3O_8$ to $CaAl_2Si_2O_8$ calcium-sodium aluminum silicate	Nonmetallic (NM) Triclinic	6	White	Colorless, white, gray, or black; May have iridescent play of color from within; Translucent; Forms striated tabular crystals or blades; Cleavage good in two directions at nearly 90°; SG = 2.6–2.8	Used to make ceramics, glass, enamel, soap, false teeth, scouring powders
POTASSIUM FELDSPAR $KAlSi_3O_8$ potassium aluminum silicate	Nonmetallic (NM) Monoclinic	6	White	Color orange, brown, white, green, or pink; Forms translucent prisms with subparallel exsolution lamellae; Cleavage excellent in two directions at nearly 90°; SG = 2.5–2.6	Used to make ceramics, glass, enamel, soap, false teeth, scouring powders
PYRITE ("fool's gold") FeS_2 iron sulfide	Metallic (M) Isometric	6–6.5	Dark gray	Color silvery gold; Tarnishes brown; H 6–6.5; Cleavage absent to poor; Brittle; Forms opaque masses, cubes (often striated), or pyritohedrons; SG = 4.9–5.2	Ore of sulfur, for sulfuric acid, explosives, fertilizers, pulp processing, insecticides

*Streak cannot be determined with a streak plate for minerals harder than 6.5. They scratch the streak plate.

FIGURE 21   (continued)

MINERAL DATABASE (Alphabetical Listing)

Mineral	Luster and Crystal System	Hardness	Streak	Distinctive Properties	Some Uses
PYROXENE: See AUGITE					
QUARTZ SiO_2 silicon dioxide	Nonmetallic (NM) Hexagonal	7	White*	Usually colorless, white, or gray but uncommon varieties occur in all colors; Transparent to translucent; Luster greasy; No cleavage; Forms hexagonal prism and pyramids; SG = 2.6–2.7 Some quartz varieties are: • var. flint (opaque black or dark gray) • var. smoky (transparent gray) • var. citrine (transparent yellow-brown) • var. amethyst (purple) • var. chert (opaque gray) • var. milky (white) • var. jasper (opaque red or yellow) • var. rock crystal (colorless) • var. rose (pink) • var. chalcedony (translucent, waxy luster)	Used as an abrasive; Used to make glass, gemstones
SERPENTINE $Mg_6Si_4O_{10}(OH)_8$ hydrous magnesian silicate group	Nonmetallic (NM) Monoclinic	2–5	White	Color pale or dark green, yellow, gray; Forms dull or silky masses and asbestos forms; No cleavage; SG = 2.2–2.6	Fibrous varieties used for fire-resistant clothing, tiles, brake linings
SILLIMANITE $Al_2(SiO_4)O$ aluminum silicate	Nonmetallic (NM) Orthorhombic	6–7	White	Color pale brown, white, or gray; One good cleavage plus fracture surfaces; Forms slender prisms; SG = 3.2	High-temperature ceramics
SPHALERITE ZnS zinc sulfide	Metallic (M) or Nonmetallic (NM) Isometric	3.5–4	White to pale yellow-brown	Color silvery yellow-brown, dark red, or black; Tarnishes brown or black; Dodecahedral cleavage excellent to good; Smells like rotten eggs when scratched/powdered; Forms misshapen tetrahedrons or dodecahedrons; SG = 3.9–4.1	Ore of zinc for die-cast automobile parts, brass, galvanizing, batteries
STAUROLITE iron magnesium zinc aluminum silicate	Nonmetallic (NM) Monoclinic	7	White to gray*	Color brown to gray-brown; Tarnishes dull brown; Forms prisms that interpenetrate to form natural crosses; Cleavage poor; SG = 3.7–3.8	Gemstone crosses called "fairy crosses"
SULFUR (NATIVE SULFUR) S sulfur	Nonmetallic (NM) Orthorhombic	1.5–2.5	Pale yellow	Color bright yellow; Forms transparent to translucent crystals or earthy masses; Cleavage poor; Luster greasy to earthy; Brittle; SG = 2.1	Used for drugs, sulfuric acid, explosives, fertilizers, pulp processing, insecticides
TALC $Mg_3Si_4O_{10}(OH)_2$ hydrous magnesian silicate	Nonmetallic (NM) Monoclinic	1	White	Color white, gray, pale green, or brown; Forms cryptocrystalline masses that show no cleavage; Luster silky to greasy; Feels greasy or soapy (talcum powder); Very soft; SG = 2.7–2.8	Used for talcum powder, facial makeup, ceramics, paint, sculptures
TOURMALINE complex silicate	Nonmetallic (NM) Hexagonal	7–7.5	White*	Color usually opaque black or green, but may be transparent or translucent green, red, yellow, pink or blue; Forms long striated prisms with triangular cross sections; Cleavage absent; SG = 3.0–3.2	Crystals used in radio transmitters; gemstone
ZEOLITE: A group of calcium or sodium hydrous aluminum silicates. See NATROLITE.					

*Streak cannot be determined with a streak plate for minerals harder than 6.5. They scratch the streak plate.

FIGURE 21   (continued)

ACTIVITY 2

Analysis and Classification of Crystal Forms

Analyze and classify crystals of some common minerals.

ACTIVITY 3

Determining Specific Gravity (SG)

Conduct this activity to practice your hefting skills and be sure that you understand how to determine the specific gravity of mineral samples.

PART B: MINERAL IDENTIFICATION AND APPRECIATION

The ability to identify minerals is one of the most fundamental skills of an Earth scientist. It also is fundamental to identifying rocks, for you must first identify the minerals comprising them. Only after minerals and rocks have been identified can their origin, classification, and alteration be adequately understood. Mineral identification is based on your ability to describe mineral properties, using identification charts (Figures 18–20) and the Mineral Database (Figure 21), as you did in Part A.

ACTIVITY 4

Mineral Analysis, Identification, and Uses

Obtain a set of mineral samples according to your instructor's instructions. For each sample, fill in the Mineral Data Chart using the mineral identification procedures provided below.

Mineral Identification Procedures

To identify a mineral and its uses, use this step-by-step procedure:

A. Determine which minerals are metallic or sub-metallic (M) and which ones are nonmetallic (NM). Remember that metallic minerals are opaque (and resemble metal), so all transparent and translucent samples are nonmetallic. If you

are uncertain about a mineral's luster, then it is probably nonmetallic. If you are looking at a rock, then consider each mineral separately.

B. For the *metallic* minerals (Figure 18):
   1. Determine the mineral's hardness and record it in your Mineral Data Chart.
   2. Determine the mineral's streak and record it in your Mineral Data Chart.
   3. Determine and record other properties, such as color on fresh and tarnished surfaces, presence or absence of cleavage (and type of cleavage, if present), presence or absence of magnetism, tenacity, specific gravity, and crystal habit, form, and system (if visible).
   4. Use the mineral properties to determine the probable name of the mineral in Figure 18. Check the Mineral Database (Figure 21) for that mineral name and compare its other properties against the properties you have recorded. If your mineral has different properties than those listed in the database, then repeat your analysis to determine a more reasonable identification. Also note mineral uses.
   5. Record the name, chemical formula, and uses of the mineral in your Mineral Data Chart.

C. For the *nonmetallic* minerals (Figures 19 and 20):
   1. Determine the mineral's hardness and record it in your Mineral Data Chart.
   2. Determine the mineral's cleavage and record it (or the lack of it) in your Mineral Data Chart.
   3. Determine and record the mineral's additional properties, such as color, tenacity, result of acid test, crystal form/habit/system (if visible), presence of striations or exsolution lamellae (if any), specific gravity, and specific kinds of nonmetallic luster.
   4. Use the mineral properties to determine the probable name of the mineral in Figure 19 (light-colored nonmetallic minerals) or 20 (dark-colored nonmetallic minerals). Check the Mineral Database (Figure 21) entry for that mineral name and compare its other properties against those you have recorded. If your mineral has different properties, then repeat your analysis to determine a more reasonable identification. Also note mineral uses.
   5. Record the name, chemical formula, and uses of the mineral in your Mineral Data Chart.

ACTIVITY 1 Mineral Properties

Name: _____   Course/Section: _____

Materials: Pencil.

A. Indicate whether the luster of each of the following materials is metallic (M) or nonmetallic (NM):

1. a brick: _____

2. butter or margarine: _____

3. ice: _____

4. sharpened pencil lead: _____

5. a seashell: _____

6. a mirror: _____

B. What is the streak color of each of the following substances?

1. salt: _____

2. wheat: _____

3. pencil lead: _____

4. charcoal: _____

C. What is the crystal habit (Figure 4) of the:

1. quartz in Figure 1A? _____

2. native copper in Figure 6? _____

D. Analyze the agate in Figure 1D, a massive form of quartz that is multicolored and banded. Also look up quartz in the Mineral Database (Figure 21) to find a list of some common varieties (var.) of quartz. Make a list of the names and descriptions of all of the varieties of quartz that are present in the agate in Figure 1D.

E. A mineral can be scratched by a masonry nail or knife blade but not by a wire (iron) nail (Figure 9).

1. Is this mineral hard or soft? _____

2. What is the hardness number of this mineral on Mohs Scale? _____

3. What mineral on Mohs Scale has this hardness? _____

F. A mineral can scratch calcite, and it can be scratched by a wire (iron) nail.

1. What is the hardness number of this mineral on Mohs Scale? _____

2. What mineral on Mohs Scale has this hardness? _____

G. The brassy, opaque, metallic mineral in Figure 7A is the same as the mineral in Figure 8.

1. What is this mineral's hardness, and how can you tell?

2. What is the crystal form (habit) of this mineral? _____

3. Based on the mineral identification tables, what is the name of this mineral? _____

4. Based on the Mineral Database, what is the chemical name and formula for this mineral?

5. Based on the Mineral Database, how is this mineral used by society?

CONTINUED

H. Analyze the mineral and figure caption in Figure 17.

    1. What is this mineral's hardness and how can you tell?

    2. Very carefully cut out the cleavage goniometer from GeoTools Sheet 1. Be sure to cut the angles as exactly as possible. Use the cleavage goniometer to measure the angles between the flat cleavage surfaces of this mineral. What is the name of this kind of cleavage? (**Keep your cleavage goniometer for Part B of this laboratory.**)

    3. Based on the mineral identification tables, what is the name of this mineral? ———————————

    4. Based on the Mineral Database, what is the chemical name and formula for this mineral?

    5. Based on the Mineral Database, how is this mineral used by society?

I. A mineral sample weighs 27 grams and takes up 10.4 cubic centimeters of space. The SG (specific gravity) of this mineral is (show your work):

J. What products in your house or dormitory might be made from each of the minerals listed below? (Examine laboratory samples of them, if available. Also refer to the Mineral Database in Figure 21 as needed.)

    1. muscovite

    2. halite

    3. hematite

    4. feldspar

    5. galena

ACTIVITY 2 Analysis and Classification of Crystal Forms

Name: _____   Course/Section: _____

Materials: Pencil, colored pencils. Other materials provided in lab.

A. Analyze these photomicrographs of ice crystals (snowflakes) provided by the Electron and Confocal Microscopy Laboratory. Agricultural Research Service, U. S. Department of Agriculture.

  1. Based on Figure 4, what is the habit of the top crystal?

  2. Notice that the top crystal is symmetrical, but not exactly. Using two colors of colored pencils color two parts of the crystal that are symmetrical mirror images of one another yet not exactly the same.

  3. Imperfections are common in crystals, but their underlying crystal form can still be detected. To what crystal system in Figure 5 do ice crystals belong? How can you tell?

  4. Ice crystals have many different habits. Why are they not all the same?

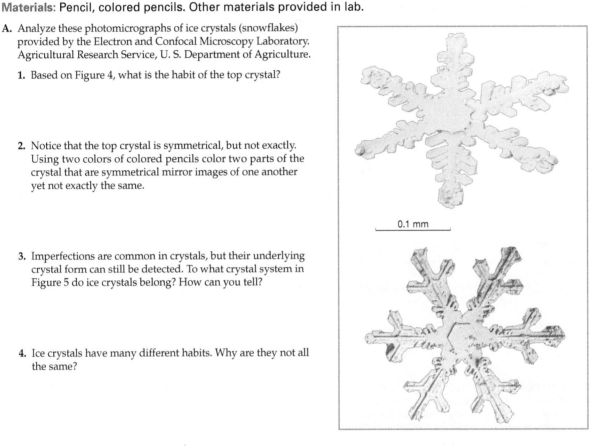

0.1 mm

B. Analyze samples of these crystalline household materials with a hand lens or microscope and identify what crystal system each one belongs to. (If samples are not available, then use the images below.)

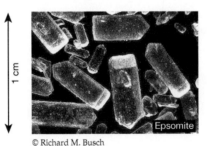

© Richard M. Busch

  1. Sucrose (table sugar) belongs to the _____ crystal system. How can you tell?

  2. Epsomite (Epsom salt) belongs to the _____ crystal system. How can you tell?

  3. Halite (table salt) belongs to the _____ crystal system. How can you tell?

ACTIVITY 3 Determining Specific Gravity (SG)

Name: _____   Course/Section: _____

Materials: Pencil. Provided in lab: 500 mL graduated cylinder, three mineral samples that will easily fit into the graduated cylinder, water, gram balance, calculator, optional wash bottle or dropper bottle.

A. Imagine that you want to buy a box of breakfast cereal and get the most cereal for your money. You have narrowed your search to two brands of cereal that are sold in boxes of the exact same size and price. The boxes are made of opaque cardboard that is sealed tight. Without opening the boxes, how can you tell which box has the most cereal inside?

B. Like the cereal boxes above, equal-sized samples of different minerals often have different weights. If you hold a mineral sample in one hand and an equal-sized sample of a different mineral in the other hand, then it is possible to act like a human balance and detect that one may be heavier than the other. This is called **hefting**, and it is used to estimate the relative densities of two objects. Heft the three mineral samples provided to you, then write sample numbers/letters on the lines below to indicate the sample densities from least dense to most dense.

   (Least dense) ————————————   ————————————   ———————————— (Most dense)

C. In more exact terms, **density** is a measure of an object's mass (weighed in grams, g) divided by its volume (how much space it takes up in cubic centimeters, cm³). Scientists use the Greek character rho (ρ) to represent density, which is always expressed in g/cm³. What is the density of a box of cereal that is 20 cm by 25 cm by 5 cm and weighs 0.453 kg? Show your work.

D. Mineralogists compare the relative densities of minerals according to their **specific gravity (SG)**: the ratio of the density of a mineral divided by the density of water. Because water has a density of 1 g/cm³, and the units cancel out, specific gravity is the same number as density but without any units. For example, the density of quartz is 2.6 g/cm³, so the specific gravity of quartz is 2.6. Return to the three mineral samples that you hefted above, and do the following:

1. First (while they are still dry), determine and record the mass (weight) of each sample in grams.

2. Use the water displacement method to measure and record the volume of each sample (Figure 15). Recall that one fluid milliliter (mL or ml on the graduated cylinder) equals one cubic centimeter.

3. Calculate the specific gravity of each sample.

4. Identify each sample based on the list of specific gravities of some common minerals.

Sample	Mass in Grams (g)	Volume in Cubic cm (cm³)	Specific Gravity (SG)	Mineral Name

SG OF SOME MINERALS	
2.1	Sulfur
2.6–2.7	Quartz
3.0–3.3	Fluorite
3.5–4.3	Garnet
4.4–4.6	Barite
4.9–5.2	Pyrite
7.4–7.6	Galena
8.8–9.0	Native copper
10.5	Native silver
19.3	Native gold

Name: _____   Course/Section: _____

ACTIVITY 4 Mineral Analysis, Identification, and Uses

MINERAL DATA CHART

Sample Letter or Number	Luster*	Hardness	Cleavage	Color / Streak	Other Properties	Name (Fig. 18, 19, or 20)	Some Uses (Fig. 21)

CONTINUED

*M = metallic or submetallic, NM = nonmetallic

ACTIVITY 4 Mineral Analysis, Identification, and Uses (continued)

MINERAL DATA CHART

Sample Letter or Number	Luster*	Hardness	Cleavage	Color / Streak	Other Properties	Name (Fig. 18, 19, or 20)	Some Uses (Fig. 21)

*M = metallic or submetallic, NM = nonmetallic

Name: _____   Course/Section: _____

ACTIVITY 4 Mineral Analysis, Identification, and Uses

MINERAL DATA CHART

Sample Letter or Number	Luster*	Hardness	Cleavage	Color / Streak	Other Properties	Name (Fig. 18, 19, or 20)	Some Uses (Fig. 21)

*M = metallic or submetallic, NM = nonmetallic

CONTINUED

ACTIVITY 4 Mineral Analysis, Identification, and Uses (continued)

MINERAL DATA CHART

Sample Letter or Number	Luster*	Hardness	Cleavage	Color / Streak	Other Properties	Name (Fig. 18, 19, or 20)	Some Uses (Fig. 21)

*M = metallic or submetallic, NM = nonmetallic

Name: _____   Course/Section: _____

ACTIVITY 4 Mineral Analysis, Identification, and Uses

MINERAL DATA CHART

Sample Letter or Number	Luster*	Hardness	Cleavage	Color	Streak	Other Properties	Name (Fig. 18, 19, or 20)	Some Uses (Fig. 21)

*M = metallic or submetallic, NM = nonmetallic

CONTINUED

ACTIVITY 4 Mineral Analysis, Identification, and Uses (continued)

MINERAL DATA CHART

Sample Letter or Number	Luster*	Hardness	Cleavage	Color	Streak	Other Properties	Name (Fig. 18, 19, or 20)	Some Uses (Fig. 21)

*M = metallic or submetallic, NM = nonmetallic

Igneous Rocks and Volcanic Hazards

CONTRIBUTING AUTHORS

Harold E. Andrews • *Wellesley College*

James R. Besancon • *Wellesley College*

Claude E. Bolze • *Tulsa Community College*

Margaret D. Thompson • *Wellesley College*

OBJECTIVES AND ACTIVITIES

A. Be able to identify and interpret the origin of igneous rock textures and classify igneous rocks on the basis of their mineralogical composition and texture.

ACTIVITY 1: Glassy and Vesicular Textures of Igneous Rocks

ACTIVITY 2: Crystalline Textures of Igneous Rocks

ACTIVITY 3: Rock Analysis, Classification, and Textural Interpretation

B. Apply your knowledge of igneous rock textures, minerals, mafic color index (MCI), Bowen's Reaction Series, and the origin of magma to classify and infer the origin of igneous rock samples.

ACTIVITY 4: Thin Section Analysis and Bowen's Reaction Series

ACTIVITY 5: Igneous Rocks Worksheet (for hand sample analysis)

C. Infer how lava viscosity affects the eruptions and shapes of volcanoes, and infer the origin of igneous rock bodies observed on aerial photographs and geologic maps.

ACTIVITY 6: Modeling Lava Behavior and Volcanic Landforms

ACTIVITY 7: Infer the Geologic History of Shiprock, New Mexico (aerial photographs)

ACTIVITY 8: Infer the Geologic History of Southeastern Pennsylvania (geologic map)

STUDENT MATERIALS

Pencil, eraser, metric ruler and a chart for visual estimation of percent (cut from GeoTools Sheets 1 and 2), and a hand magnifying lens (optional). A collection of numbered igneous rock samples, mineral-identification tools (hardness kit, streak plate, etc.), and other materials should be obtained as directed by your instructor.

INTRODUCTION

Igneous rocks form when molten rock (rock liquefied by intense heat and pressure) cools to a solid state. When the molten rock cools, it always forms a mass of inter-grown crystals and/or glass. Therefore, all igneous rocks and fragments of igneous rocks have crystalline or glassy textures. Even volcanic ash is microscopic fragments of igneous rock (mostly volcanic glass pulverized by an explosive volcanic eruption).

From Laboratory 5 of *Laboratory Manual in Physical Geology*, Ninth Edition, American Geological Institute, National Association of Geoscience Teachers, Richard M. Busch, Dennis Tasa. Copyright © 2011 by Pearson Education, Inc. Published by Pearson Prentice Hall. All rights reserved.

PART A: IGNEOUS ROCK TEXTURES, MINERALOGICAL COMPOSITION, AND CLASSIFICATION

A body of mostly molten (heated until liquefied) rock below Earth's surface is called **magma**. In addition to its liquid molten rock portion, or **melt**, magma contains dissolved gases (e.g., water, carbon dioxide, sulfur dioxide) and solid particles. The solid particles may be pieces of rock that have not yet melted and/or mineral crystals that may grow in size or abundance as the magma cools. **Texture** of an igneous rock is a description of its constituent parts and their sizes, shapes, and arrangement.

ACTIVITY 1

Glassy and Vesicular Textures of Igneous Rocks

Sugar is not a mineral (because it is an organic material), but when melted it behaves much like magma/lava containing abundant silica (SiO_2). Molten (heated until it melts) sugar and silica both form long chains of molecules as they cool. This impedes their flow as they cool to a solid state. In this activity, you will experiment with molten sugar to model the behavior of silica-rich magma/lava and form a solid material with glassy and vesicular textures.

ACTIVITY 2

Crystalline Textures of Igneous Rocks

Conduct this activity to understand how aphanitic, phaneritic, pegmatitic, and porphyritic crystalline textures form and be able recognize them in hand samples of igneous rocks.

Textures of Igneous Rocks

You must be able to identify the common textures of igneous rocks (highlighted in bold text below) and understand how they form (Figures 1 and 2). This will help you to classify *and* infer the origin of igneous rocks.

The size of mineral crystals in an igneous rock generally indicates the rate at which the lava or magma cooled to form a rock and the availability of the chemicals required to form the crystals. Large crystals require a long time to grow, so their presence generally means that a body of molten rock cooled slowly and contained ample atoms of the chemicals

required to form the crystals. Tiny crystals generally indicate that the magma cooled more rapidly (there was not enough time for large crystals to form). Volcanic glass (no crystals) can indicate that a magma was quenched (cooled immediately), but most volcanic glass is the result of poor nucleation as described below.

The crystallization process depends on the ability of atoms in lava or magma to *nucleate*. *Nucleation* is the initial formation of a microscopic crystal, to which other atoms progressively bond. This is how a crystal grows. Atoms are mobile in a fluid magma, so they are free to nucleate. If such a fluid magma cools slowly, then crystals have time to grow—sometimes to many centimeters in length. However, if a magma is very viscous (thick and resistant to flow), then atoms cannot easily move to nucleation sites. Crystals may not form even by slow cooling. Rapid cooling of very viscous magma (with poor nucleation) can produce igneous rocks with a **glassy texture** (see Figure 1).

Several common terms are used to describe igneous rock texture on the basis of crystal size (Figure 1). Igneous rocks made of crystals that are too small to identify with the naked eye or a hand lens (generally <1 mm) have a very fine-grained **aphanitic texture** (from the Greek word for invisible). Those made of visible crystals that can be identified are said to have a **phaneritic texture** (coarse-grained; crystals 1–10 mm) or **pegmatitic texture** (very coarse-grained; >1 cm).

Some igneous rocks have two distinct sizes of crystals. This is called **porphyritic texture** (see Figure 1). The large crystals are called *phenocrysts*, and the smaller, more numerous crystals form the *groundmass*, or *matrix*. Porphyritic textures may generally indicate that a body of magma cooled slowly at first (to form the large crystals) and more rapidly later (to form the small crystals). However, recall from above that crystal size can also be influenced by changes in magma composition or viscosity.

Combinations of igneous-rock textures also occur. For example, a *porphyritic-aphanitic* texture signifies that phenocrysts occur within an aphanitic matrix. A *porphyritic-phaneritic* texture signifies that phenocrysts occur within a phaneritic matrix.

When gas bubbles get trapped in cooling lava they are called *vesicles*, and the rock is said to have a **vesicular texture.** Scoria is a textural name for a rock having so many vesicles that it resembles a sponge. Pumice has a glassy texture and so many tiny vesicles (like frothy meringue on a pie) that it floats in water.

Pyroclasts (from Greek meaning "fire broken") are rocky materials that have been fragmented and/or ejected by explosive volcanic eruptions. They include *volcanic ash* fragments (pyroclasts < 2 mm), *lapilli* or *cinders* (pyroclasts 2–64 mm), and *volcanic bombs* or

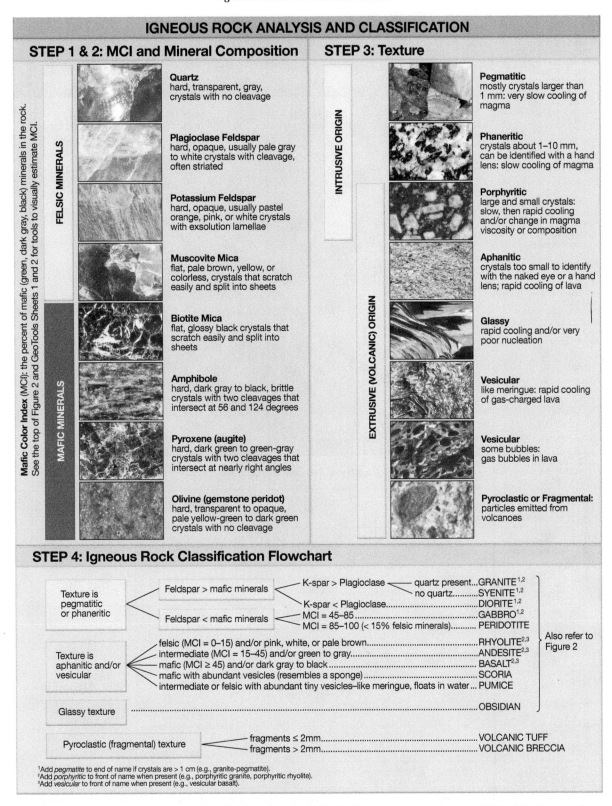

FIGURE 1 Igneous rock analysis and classification. **Step 1**—Estimate the rock's mafic color index (MCI). **Step 2**—Identify the main rock-forming minerals if the mineral crystals are large enough to do so, and estimate the relative abundance of each mineral (using a Visual Estimation of Percent chart from GeoTools Sheet 1 or 2). **Step 3**—Identify the texture(s) of the rock. **Step 4**—Use the Igneous Rock Classification Flowchart to name the rock. Start on the left side of the flowchart, and work toward the right side to the rock name.

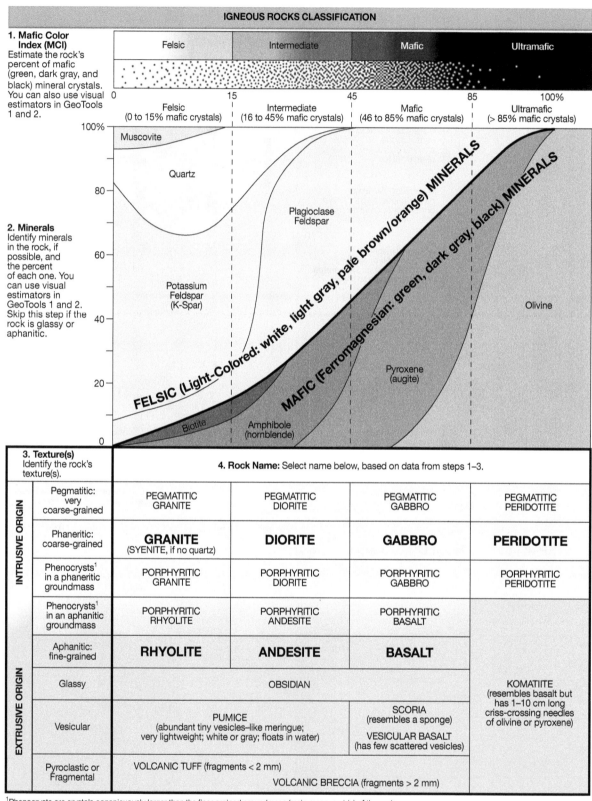

FIGURE 2 Igneous rock classification chart. Obtain data about the rock in Steps 1–3, then use that data to select the name of the rock (Step 4). Also refer to Figure 1 and the examples of classified igneous rocks in Figures 5–11.

blocks (pyroclasts > 64 mm). Igneous rocks composed of pyroclasts have a **pyroclastic texture** (see Figure 1). They include *tuff* (made of volcanic ash) and *volcanic breccia* (made chiefly of cinders and volcanic bombs).

Mineral Composition of Igneous Rocks

Mineral composition of an igneous rock is a description of the kinds of the mineral crystals that make up the rock and their abundance. You can estimate the abundance of any mineral in a rock using charts for visual estimation of percent provided at the back of the manual (GeoTools Sheets 1 and 2).

Eight rock-forming minerals make up most igneous rocks (Figures 1, 2). Gray *quartz*, light gray *plagioclase feldspar*, pale orange to pink *potassium feldspar*, and pale brown *muscovite* are light-colored **felsic minerals.** The name *felsic* refers to feldspars (*fel-*) and other silica-rich (*-sic*) minerals. Glossy black *biotite*, dark gray to black *amphibole*, dark green to green-gray *pyroxene*, and green *olivine* are **mafic minerals.** The name *mafic* refers to the magnesium (*ma-*) and iron (*-fic*) in their chemical formulas, so they are also called *ferromagnesian* minerals.

Notice at the top of Figure 2 that the mineralogy of an igneous rock can be approximated based on a mafic color index. A rock's **mafic color index (MCI)** is the percentage of its green, dark gray, and black mafic (ferromagnesian) mineral crystals.

The mafic color index of an igneous rock is only an approximation of the rock's mineral composition, because there are some exceptions to the generalization that "light-colored equals felsic" and "dark-colored equals mafic." For example, labradorite feldspar (felsic) can be dark gray to black. Luckily, it can be identified by its characteristic play of iridescent colors that flash on and off as the mineral is rotated and reflects light! Olivine (mafic) is sometimes a pale yellow-green color (instead of medium to dark green). Volcanic glass (obsidian) is also an exception to the mafic color index rules. Its dark color suggests that it is mafic when, in fact, most obsidian has a very high weight percentage of silica and less than 15% ferromagnesian constituents. (Ferromagnesian-rich obsidian does occur, but only rarely.)

Therefore mafic color index is a generalization often used to estimate the mineralogy of aphanitic (fine-grained) igneous rocks, which have crystals too small to identify with the naked eye or a hand lens. The larger mineral crystals in phaneritic and pegmatitic igneous rocks can be identified with the naked eye and a hand lens, so the relative percentage of specific minerals or groups of minerals (felsic vs. mafic) can be determined by "point counting." Point counting is counting the number of times that each kind of mineral crystal occurs in a specified area of the sample, then calculating the relative percentage of each mineral.

Classifying Igneous Rocks

The classification of an igneous rock is based on its texture and mineral composition (Figures 1, 2). Mineral composition can be estimated on the basis of the rock's mafic color index, but the identity and abundance of each kind of mineral should be determined whenever possible. Unfortunately, hand samples of aphanitic igneous rocks have mineral crystals that are too small to identify with a hand lens. Their classification can only be based on texture and MCI.

The composition of igneous rocks can be generally classified as felsic, intermediate, mafic, or ultramafic. **Felsic igneous rocks** have almost no mafic minerals, so they have a low MCI (0–15%). Quartz and/or feldspars are the most abundant mineral crystals in felsic rocks (Figure 2). **Intermediate igneous rocks** have more felsic minerals than mafic minerals (MCI of 16–45%). Plagioclase is the most abundant mineral, followed by amphibole (Figure 2). **Mafic igneous rocks** have more mafic minerals than felsic minerals (MCI of 45–85%) and are usually dark-colored (green-gray to very dark gray). Pyroxene is the most abundant mineral, followed by plagioclase (Figure 2). **Ultramafic igneous rocks** have a mafic color index of 85–100%, so they usually appear green to very dark gray or black. Olivine (yellow-green to dark green) and/or pyroxene (green-gray to dark gray) are the most abundant mineral crystals in ultramafic igneous rocks (Figure 2).

Follow these steps to classify an igneous rock:

Steps 1 and 2: Identify the rock's mafic color index (MCI). Then, if possible, identify the minerals that make up the rock and estimate the percentage of each.

- If the rock is very fine-grained (aphanitic or porphyritic-aphanitic), then you must estimate mineralogy based on the rock's mafic color index. *Felsic* fine-grained rocks tend to be pink, white, or pale gray/brown. *Intermediate* fine-grained rocks tend to be greenish gray to medium gray. *Mafic* and *ultramafic* fine-grained rocks tend to be green, dark gray, or black.

- If the rock is coarse-grained (phaneritic or pegmatitic), then estimate the mafic color index (MCI) and percentage abundance of each of the specific felsic and mafic minerals. With this information, you can also characterize the rock as felsic, intermediate, mafic, or ultramafic.

Step 3: Identify the rock's texture(s) using Figure 1.

Step 4: Determine the name of the rock using the flowchart in Figure 1 or the expanded classification chart in Figure 2.

- Use textural terms, such as porphyritic or vesicular, as adjectives. For example, you might identify a pink, aphanitic (fine-grained), igneous rock as a rhyolite. If it contains scattered phenocrysts, then you would call it a *porphyritic rhyolite*. Similarly, you should call a basalt with vesicles a *vesicular basalt*.

- The textural information can also be used to infer the origin of a rock. For example, vesicles (vesicular textures) imply that the rock formed by cooling of a gas-rich lava (vesicular and aphanitic). Pyroclastic texture implies violent volcanic eruption. Aphanitic texture implies more rapid cooling than phaneritic texture.

ACTIVITY 3

Rock Analysis, Classification, and Textural Interpretation

Practice analyzing, classifying, and using a rock's texture as evidence of its origin.

Bowen's Reaction Series as a Model for Interpreting Igneous Rocks

When magma intrudes Earth's crust, it cools into a mass of mineral crystals and/or glass. Yet when geologists observe and analyze the igneous rocks in a single dike, sill, or batholith, they often find that it contains more than just one kind of igneous rock. Apparently, more than one kind of igneous rock can form from a single homogeneous body of magma as it cools. American geologist, Norman L. Bowen made such observations in the early 1900s. He then devised and carried out laboratory experiments to study how magmas might evolve in ways that could explain the differentiation of multiple rock types from a single magma.

Other geologic investigations had already suggested that the top of Earth's mantle is made of peridotite. So Bowen placed pieces of peridotite into *bombs*, strong pressurized ovens used to melt the rocks at high temperatures (1200–1400° C). Once melted to form peridotite magma, he would allow the magma to cool to a given temperature and remain at that temperature for a while in hopes of having it begin to crystallize. The rock was then quickly removed from the bomb and quenched (cooled by dunking it in water) to make any remaining molten rock form glass. Bowen then identified the mineral crystals that had formed at each temperature. His experiments showed that as magma cools in an otherwise unchanging environment, two series of silicate minerals crystallize in a predictable order.

The left branch of **Bowen's Reaction Series** (Figure 3) shows the predictable series of mafic minerals that crystallize from a peridotite magma that is allowed to cool slowly. This series is discontinuous because one mafic mineral replaces another as the magma cools. For example, olivine is first to crystallize at very high temperature. But if the magma cools to about 1100° C, then the olivine starts to react with it and dissolve as pyroxene (next mineral in the series) starts to crystallize. More cooling of the magma causes pyroxene to react with the magma as amphibole (next mineral in the series) starts to crystallize, and so on. If the magma cools too quickly, then rock can form while one reaction is in progress and before any remaining reactions even have time to start.

The right branch of Bowen's Reaction Series (Figure 3) shows that plagioclase feldspar crystallizes continuously from high to low temperatures (~1100–800° C),

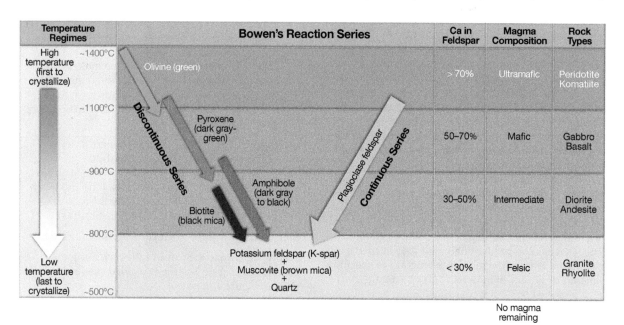

FIGURE 3 Bowen's Reaction Series—a laboratory-based conceptual model of one way that different kinds of igneous rocks can differentiate from a single, homogeneous body of magma as it cools. See text for discussion (above).

but this is accompanied by a series of continuous change in the composition of the plagioclase. The high temperature plagioclase is calcium rich and sodium poor, and the low temperature plagioclase is sodium rich and calcium poor. If the magma cools too quickly for the plagioclase to react with the magma, then a single plagioclase crystal can have a more calcium rich center and a more sodium rich rim.

Finally, notice what happens at the bottom of Bowen's Reaction Series (Figure 3). At the lowest temperatures, where the last crystallization of magma occurs, the remaining elements form abundant potassium feldspar (K-spar), muscovite, and quartz.

Bowen's laboratory investigations showed that if magma cools very slowly, and all other environmental and chemical factors remain the same, then an orderly series of different minerals will form and react. However, Bowen's work also showed how different kinds of igneous rocks can form from a single body of magma by simply removing (erupting and freezing) some of the magma at different temperatures along its path of cooling and reacting. For example, if part of a mafic magma is erupted to Earth's surface, then it freezes into a mafic rock (gabbro or basalt) before it can react. It is laboratory-based evidence that ultramafic igneous rocks (peridotite, komatiite) form at the highest temperatures, followed at lower temperatures by mafic rocks (gabbro, basalt), intermediate rocks (diorite, andesite), and felsic rocks (granite, rhyolite) (Figure 3).

Different kinds of igneous rocks can also form from a single body of magma by *fractional crystallization:* the process of physically separating early-formed mineral crystals from the magma in which they

formed. These crystals also take with them some of the chemicals that originally existed in the magma and leave the remaining body of cooling magma with a different combination of elements to form the next crystals. This is one way that intermediate and felsic magmas/rocks can differentiate from what started out as a mafic magma.

Bowen's Reaction Series is very generally reversed when rocks are heated. Earth materials react with their surroundings and melt at different temperatures as they are heated. An analogy is a plastic tray of ice cubes, heated in an oven. The ice cubes would melt long before the plastic tray would melt (i.e., the ice cubes melt at a much lower temperature). As rocks are heated, their different mineral crystals melt at different temperatures. Therefore, at a given temperature, it is possible to have rocks that are partly molten and partly solid. This phenomenon is known as *partial melting* and Bowen's Reaction Series can be used to predict the sequence of melting for mineral crystals in a rock that is undergoing heating. Mineral crystals formed at low temperatures will melt at low temperatures, and mineral crystals formed at high temperatures will melt at high temperatures. However, the minerals in a particular group, say felsic or intermediate, do not all melt at once. Each mineral in the group has its own unique melting point at specific pressures. Thus, partial melting of mantle peridotite beneath hot spots and mid-ocean ridges produces mafic magma rather than ultramafic magma. When the mafic magma erupts as mafic lava along the mid-ocean ridges and hot spots (e.g., Hawaiian Islands), it cools to form basalt (Figure 4). A contributing factor in melting is water, which can lower the melting point of

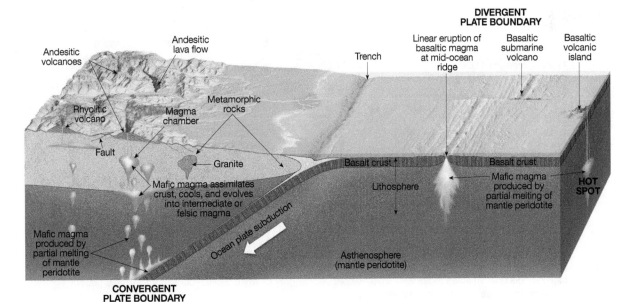

FIGURE 4 Formation of igneous rocks at a hot spot (such as the Hawaiian Islands), divergent plate boundary (mid-ocean ridge), and convergent plate boundary (subduction zone). See text for discussion.

rocks. This may be how mantle peridotite in the mantle wedge is partially melted above subducting plates at convergent plate boundaries to form mafic magma (Figure 4). Upon fractional crystallization and cooling along Bowen's Reaction Series, the mafic magma then follows Bowen's Reaction Series of crystallization and reaction to form intermediate or felsic magma that can erupt to form andesitic or rhyolitic volcanoes.

ACTIVITY 4

Thin Section Analysis and Bowen's Reaction Series

Analyze and interpret the origin of two thin sectioned rocks. Thin sections are rocks that have been sliced so thin as to allow light to pass through them. Geologists analyze and interpret the thin sections for information that cannot be seen in hand samples.

PART B: ANALYSIS AND INTERPRETATION OF IGNEOUS ROCK SAMPLES

Before you begin this activity, compare the named rock types in Figures 5–11 with the igneous rock classification charts in Figures 1 and 2. Also consider the origin of each rock type relative to Bowen's Reaction Series (Figure 3) and plate tectonic setting (Figure 4).

Hand sample
(actual size)

Photomicrograph (× 26.6)
Original sample width is 1.23 mm

Quartz crystals —

Mica crystals —

Feldspar crystals —

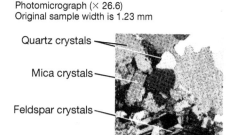

© Richard M. Busch

FIGURE 5 Granite—an intrusive, phaneritic igneous rock that has a low MCI (light color) and is made up chiefly of quartz and feldspar mineral crystals. Mafic (ferromagnesian) mineral crystals in granites generally include biotite and amphibole (hornblende). This sample contains pink potassium feldspar (K-spar), white plagioclase feldspar, gray quartz, and black biotite mica. Granites rich in pink potassium feldspar appear pink like this one, whereas those with white K-spar appear gray or white. Felsic rocks that resemble granite, but contain no quartz, are called *syenites*.

FIGURE 6 Rhyolite—a felsic, aphanitic igneous rock that is the extrusive equivalent of a granite. It is usually light gray or pink. Some rhyolites resemble andesite (see Figure 8), so their exact identification must be finalized where possible by microscopic examination to verify the abundance of quartz and feldspar mineral crystals.

Hand sample (actual size)

© Richard M. Busch

Quartz crystals

Feldspar crystals

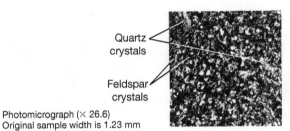

Photomicrograph (× 26.6)
Original sample width is 1.23 mm

FIGURE 7 Diorite—an intrusive, phaneritic igneous rock that has an intermediate MCI and is made up chiefly of plagioclase feldspar and ferromagnesian mineral crystals. The ferromagnesian mineral crystals are chiefly amphibole (hornblende). Quartz is only rarely present and only in small amounts (<5%).

Hand sample (actual size)

© Richard M. Busch

Feldspar crystals

Amphibole crystals

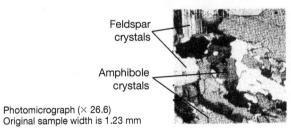

Photomicrograph (× 26.6)
Original sample width is 1.23 mm

97

FIGURE 8 Andesite—an intermediate, aphanitic igneous rock that is the extrusive equivalent of diorite. It is usually medium gray. Some andesites resemble rhyolite (Figure 6), so their identification must be finalized by microscopic examination to verify the abundance of plagioclase feldspar and ferromagnesian mineral crystals. This sample has a porphyritic-aphanitic texture, because it contains phenocrysts of black amphibole (hornblende) set in the aphanitic groundmass.

Hand sample (actual size)

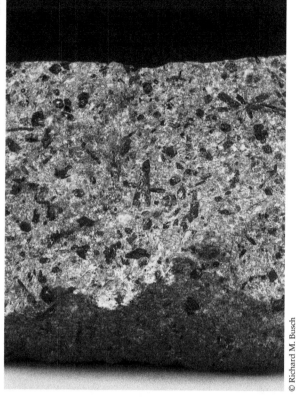

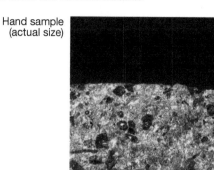

Amphibole phenocryst

Groundmass of feldspar and ferromagnesian mineral crystals

Feldspar phenocrysts

Photomicrograph (× 26.6)
Original sample width is 1.23 mm

FIGURE 9 Gabbro—a mafic, phaneritic igneous rock made up chiefly of ferromagnesian and plagioclase mineral crystals. The ferromagnesian mineral crystals usually are pyroxene (augite). Quartz is absent.

Hand sample (actual size)

Plagioclase feldspar crystals

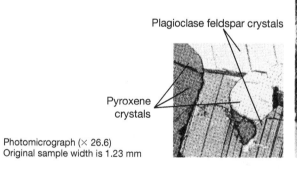

Pyroxene crystals

Photomicrograph (× 26.6)
Original sample width is 1.23 mm

FIGURE 10 Basalt—a mafic, aphanitic igneous rock that is the extrusive equivalent of gabbro, so it is dark gray to black. This sample has a vesicular (bubbly) texture. Microscopic examination of basalts reveals that they are made up chiefly of plagioclase and ferromagnesian mineral crystals. The ferromagnesian mineral crystals generally are pyroxene, but they also may include olivine or magnetite. Glass also may be visible between mineral crystals. Basalt forms the floors of all modern oceans (beneath the mud and sand) and is the most abundant aphanitic igneous rock on Earth.

Hand sample (actual size)

© Richard M. Busch

Photomicrograph (× 26.6)
Original sample width is 1.23 mm

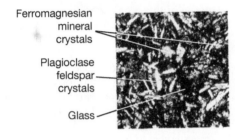

Ferromagnesian mineral crystals

Plagioclase feldspar crystals

Glass

© Richard M. Busch

10× close-up of peridotite

Hand sample (actual size)

FIGURE 11 Peridotite—an intrusive, phaneritic igneous rock having a very high MCI (>85%) and mostly made of ferromagnesian mineral crystals. This sample is a peridotite almost entirely made up of olivine mineral crystals; such a peridotite also is called *dunite*.

ACTIVITY 5

Igneous Rocks Worksheet (for hand sample analysis)

Obtain a set of numbered igneous rocks as directed by your instructor. Then fill in the information below on the Igneous Rocks Worksheet. For each rock in the set:

a. Record the rock's sample identification number.

b. Estimate the rock's mafic color index (MCI) using the visual estimation bars at the top of Figure 2 and/or the Visual Estimation of Percent cut-out in GeoTools Sheets 1 and 2.

c. For phaneritic and pegmatitic rocks, identify and list the minerals present (Figure 1, Step 2) and visually estimate the percent abundance of each one.

d. Describe the rock's texture(s). Refer to Figure 1, Step 3.

e. Determine the rock's name (Step 4 in Figures 1 or 2).

f. Describe how the rock may have formed (Figures 3, 4).

PART C: INTRUSION, ERUPTION, AND VOLCANIC LANDFORMS

Magma is under great pressure (like a bottled soft drink that has been shaken) and is less dense than the rocks that confine it. Like the blobs of heated "lava" in a lava lamp, the magma tends to rise and squeeze into Earth's cooler crust along any fractures or zones of weakness that it encounters. A body of magma that pushes its way through Earth's crust is called an **intrusion,** and it will eventually cool to form a body of igneous rock.

Intrusions have different sizes and shapes. *Batholiths* (Figure 12) are massive intrusions (often covering regions of 100 km² or more in map view) that have no visible bottom. They form when small bodies of lava amalgamate (mix together) into one large body. To observe one model of this amalgamation process, watch the blobs of "lava" in a lighted lava lamp as they rise and merge into one large body (batholith) at the top of the lamp.

Smaller intrusions (see Figure 12) include *sills* (sheet-like intrusions that force their way between layers of bedrock), *laccoliths* (blister-like sills), *pipes* (vertical tubes or pipe-like intrusions that feed volcanoes), and *dikes* (sheet-like intrusions that cut across layers of bedrock). The dikes can occur as

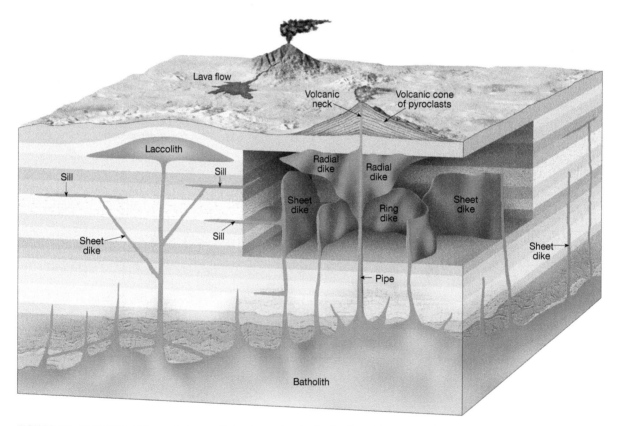

FIGURE 12 Illustration of the main types of intrusive and extrusive bodies of igneous rock.

FIGURE 13 Color-infrared stereogram of national high-altitude aerial photographs (NHAP) of Shiprock, New Mexico, 1991. Scale 1:58,000. To view in stereo: (a) note that the figure is two images, (b) hold figure at arm's length, (c) cross your eyes until the two images become four images, (d) slightly relax your eyes so the two center images merge in stereo. (Image Courtesy of U.S. Geological Survey)

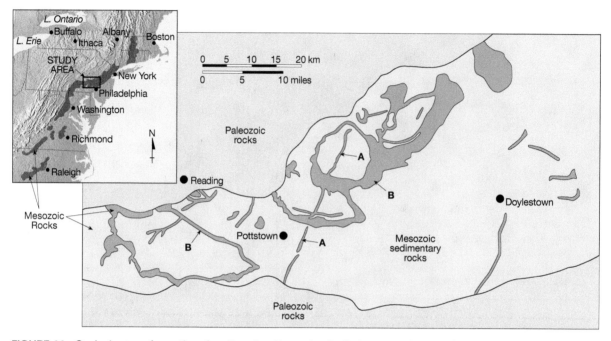

FIGURE 14 Geologic map of a portion of southeastern Pennsylvania. Red areas are bodies of Mesozoic igneous rock (basalt, Figure 10) about 190 million years old (Jurassic). Green areas are Mesozoic (Triassic) sands and muds (hardened into sandstones and mudstones) that are about 200–220 million years old. Older Paleozoic and Precambrian rocks are colored pale brown.

sheet dikes (nearly planar dikes that often occur in parallel pairs or groups), *ring dikes* (curved dikes that form circular patterns when viewed from above; they typically form under volcanoes), or *radial dikes* (dikes that develop from the pipe feeding a volcano; when viewed from above, they radiate away from the pipe).

When magma is extruded onto Earth's surface it is called **lava**. The lava may erupt gradually and cause a blister-like *lava dome* to form in the neck of a volcano or a *lava flow* to run from a volcano. The lava may also erupt explosively to form *pyroclastic deposits* (accumulations of rocky materials that have been fragmented and ejected by explosive volcanic eruptions). All of these extrusive (volcanic) igneous processes present geologic hazards that place humans at risk.

When you examine an unopened pressurized bottle of soft drink, no bubbles are present. But when you open the bottle (and hear a "swish" sound), you are releasing the pressure on the drink and allowing bubbles of carbon dioxide gas to escape from the liquid. Recall that magma behaves similarly. When its pressure is released near Earth's surface, it's dissolved gases expand and make bubbly lava that may erupt from a volcano. In fact, early stages of volcanic eruptions are eruptions of steam and other gases separated from magma just beneath Earth's surface. If the hot, bubbly lava cannot escape normally from the volcano, then the volcano may explode (like the top blowing off of a champagne bottle).

ACTIVITY 6

Modeling Lava Behavior and Volcanic Landforms

How a volcano erupts depends largely on factors that affect the viscosity of its lava. Recall from Activity 1 that increasing temperature tends to make magma/lava flow more easily (decrease viscosity) and cooling magma/lava makes it thicken (increase viscosity) and eventually stop flowing.

Also recall from Activity 1 that watery "sugar magma" was more fluid (had lower viscosity) than the sugar magma from which the water had boiled off. So *volatiles* (easily evaporated chemicals like water and carbon dioxide) tend to decrease lava viscosity. They break apart clumps of molecules like the silica (SiO_2) in magma/lava and the sugar in the watery sugar magma. Magmas that have high silica contents tend to be very viscous (resist flow) if volatiles are absent from them.

Geologists Don Baker, Claude Dalpé, and Glenn Poirer found that the viscosities of natural magma/lava are between that of smooth peanut butter and ketchup (*Journal of Geoscience Education*, v.52, no. 4, 2004). Smooth peanut butter has the viscosity of a typical rhyolitic lava. Ketchup has the viscosity of a typical basaltic lava.

In Activity 6, you can use this knowledge to experiment and infer why some lavas create explosive composite cones (stratovolcanoes), while others create broad shield volcanoes from layers of flowing lava.

ACTIVITY 7

Infer the Geologic History of Shiprock, New Mexico

Analyze aerial photographs of bodies of igneous rock and infer their origin.

ACTIVITY 8

Infer the Geologic History of Southeastern Pennsylvania

Analyze bodies of igneous rock in a geologic map and infer their origin.

ACTIVITY 1 Glassy and Vesicular Textures of Igneous Rocks

Name: _____   Course/Section: _____

Materials: Sugar (~50 ml, 1/8 cup), hot plate, small metal sauce pan with handle or 500 mL Pyrex™ beaker and tongs, water (~50ml), safety goggles, aluminum foil, collection of numbered igneous rock samples, hand lens.

Place equal parts of sugar (sucrose, $C_{12}H_{22}O_{11}$) and water in the pan/beaker and heat on medium high. Do not touch the hot plate, beaker/pan, or boiling sugar, because it is very hot! Notice that steam is given off after the sugar dissolves and the solution boils. After a few minutes there will be no more steam, and the remaining molten sugar will be have a very thick (viscous) consistency. At this point (before the sugar begins to burn), pour the thick molten sugar onto a piece of aluminum foil on a flat table. DO NOT TOUCH the molten sugar, but lift a corner of the foil to observe how it flows and behaves until it hardens (2–3 minutes).

A. Viscosity is a measure of how much a fluid resists flow. Water has low viscosity. Honey is more viscous than water. How did the viscosity of the sugar solution change as the water boiled off?

B. What happened to the viscosity of the molten sugar as it cooled on the aluminum foil?

C. When the molten sugar has cooled to a solid state, break it in half and observe its texture. Look about the room where you are now seated and name two objects that have this same texture.

D. Now observe the texture of the cooled solid mass of sugar with a hand lens. Notice that there are some tiny bubbles of gas within it. Geoscientists call these "vesicles," and rocks containing vesicles are said to have a "vesicular texture." What prevented the gas bubbles from escaping to the atmosphere?

E. When a sugar solution is permitted to slowly evaporate, sugar crystals form. The process of crystallization depends on the ability of atoms to move about in the solution and bond together in an orderly array. What two things may have prevented crystals from forming in the molten sugar as it cooled on the aluminum foil?

F. In your collection of numbered igneous rock samples, do any of the samples have the texture that you just observed in 5C? If yes, which one(s)?

G. In your collection of numbered igneous rock samples, do any of the samples have the texture that you just observed in 5D? If yes, which one(s)?

ACTIVITY 2 Crystalline Textures of Igneous Rocks

Name: _____   Course/Section: _____

John and Sarah are doing an experiment to find out if crystal size in igneous rocks can be related to the speed of cooling a magma/lava. They did not have equipment to melt rock, so they used thymol to model pieces of rock. Thymol melts easily at low temperature on a hot plate, and it cools and recrystallizes quickly. Thymol is a transparent, crystalline organic substance derived from the herb, thyme, and is used in antiseptics and disinfectants. It is not toxic, but does give off a very strong pungent odor that can irritate skin and eyes and cause headaches. Therefore, John and Sarah used a spoon to handle the thymol and did all of their work under a fume hood with supervision from their teacher. Sarah placed some thymol in a small Pyrex beaker and melted it completely under a fume hood to model the formation of magma. John poured one half of the molten thymol into a cold Petri dish and the other half into a hot Petri dish of the same size.

A. The results of John and Sarah's experiment are shown below. Notice that the images are enlarged. Beside each image below, measure and record the actual size range of the crystals (in mm) that formed.

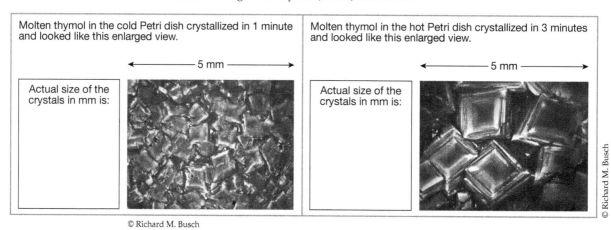

Molten thymol in the cold Petri dish crystallized in 1 minute and looked like this enlarged view.

◄——— 5 mm ———►

Actual size of the crystals in mm is:

Molten thymol in the hot Petri dish crystallized in 3 minutes and looked like this enlarged view.

◄——— 5 mm ———►

Actual size of the crystals in mm is:

© Richard M. Busch

© Richard M. Busch

B. Igneous rocks that are made of crystals too small to see with your naked eyes or hand lens are said to have an **aphanitic texture** (from the Greek word for invisible). Those made of visible crystals are said to have a **phaneritic texture** (crystals ~1–10 mm) or **pegmatitic texture** (crystals > 1 cm). Which of these three igneous rock textures probably represents the most rapid cooling of magma/lava?

C. This rock has a "**porphyritic texture,**" which means that it contains two sizes of crystals. The large white plagioclase crystals are called phenocrysts and sit in a green-gray "groundmass" of more abundant, smaller (aphanitic) crystals. Explain how this texture may have formed (more than one answer is possible).

×1

© Richard M. Busch

D. In your collection of numbered igneous rock samples, record the sample numbers with these textures:

Sample(s) with porphyritic texture:	Sample(s) with phaneritic texture:
Sample(s) with pegmatitic texture:	Sample(s) with aphanitic texture:

ACTIVITY 3 Rock Analysis, Classification, and Textural Interpretation

Name: _____   Course/Section: _____

A. Analyze and classify each igneous rock below, then infer the origin of each rock based on its texture. Refer to Figures 1 and 2 as needed. The rocks are shown ×1 (actual size).

© Richard M. Busch

Mafic color index (MCI, percentage of mafic mineral crystals):	Mafic color index (MCI, percentage of mafic mineral crystals):	Mafic color index (MCI, percentage of mafic mineral crystals):	Mafic color index (MCI, percentage of mafic mineral crystals):
Would you describe the rock as mafic, intermediate, or felsic?	Would you describe the rock as mafic, intermediate, or felsic?	Would you describe the rock as mafic, intermediate, or felsic?	Would you describe the rock as mafic, intermediate, or felsic?
Texture(s) present:	Texture(s) present:	Texture(s) present:	Name and percent abundance of mineral crystals:
			Texture present:
The name of this rock is:	The name of this rock is:	The name of this rock is:	The name of this rock is:
Based on its texture, how did this rock form?	Based on its texture, how did this rock form?	Based on its texture, how did this rock form?	Based on its texture, how did this rock form?

ACTIVITY 4 Thin Section Analysis and Bowen's Reaction Series

Name: _____   Course/Section: _____

A thin section of a rock can be made by grinding one side of it flat, gluing the flat side to a glass slide, and then grinding the rock so thin that light passes through it. The thin section is then viewed with a polarizing microscope. The view in plane polarized light is the same as looking at the thin section through a pair of sunglasses. If you place a second pair of sunglasses behind the thin section and hold it perpendicular to the first pair, then you are viewing the thin section through cross polarized light. These images of thin sections were made by geologist LeeAnn Srogi, West Chester University of Pennsylvania.

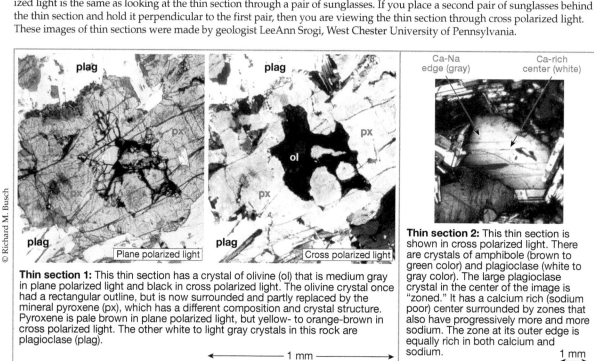

© Richard M. Busch

Thin section 1: This thin section has a crystal of olivine (ol) that is medium gray in plane polarized light and black in cross polarized light. The olivine crystal once had a rectangular outline, but is now surrounded and partly replaced by the mineral pyroxene (px), which has a different composition and crystal structure. Pyroxene is pale brown in plane polarized light, but yellow- to orange-brown in cross polarized light. The other white to light gray crystals in this rock are plagioclase (plag).

← 1 mm →

Thin section 2: This thin section is shown in cross polarized light. There are crystals of amphibole (brown to green color) and plagioclase (white to gray color). The large plagioclase crystal in the center of the image is "zoned." It has a calcium rich (sodium poor) center surrounded by zones that also have progressively more and more sodium. The zone at its outer edge is equally rich in both calcium and sodium.

1 mm
← →

A. Based on Bowen's Reaction Series (Figure 3), explain as exactly as you can what may have caused the relationship between olivine and pyroxene observed in thin section 1.

B. Based on Bowen's Reaction Series (Figure 3), explain as exactly as you can what may have caused the large plagioclase crystal in thin section 2 to be zoned as it is.

C. On the right-hand side of this Bowen's Reaction Series diagram, add brackets and labels to indicate the exact path of crystallization and reaction represented in thin section 1, and then 2. Refer to Figure 3 as needed.

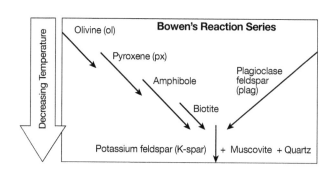

Name: _____   Course/Section: _____

ACTIVITY 5 Igneous Rocks Worksheet

IGNEOUS ROCKS WORKSHEET

Sample Number or Letter	Texture(s) Present (Figure 1)	Minerals Present and Their % Abundance (Figure 1)	Mafic Color Index (Figure 2)	Rock Name from Figure 1 or 2	How Did the Rock Form Relative to Bowen's Reaction Series (Figure 3) and Intrusive/Extrusive Processes?

Igneous Rocks and Volcanic Hazards

Name: _____   Course/Section: _____

IGNEOUS ROCKS WORKSHEET

Sample Number or Letter	Texture(s) Present (Figure 1)	Minerals Present and Their % Abundance (Figure 1)	Mafic Color Index (Figure 2)	Rock Name from Figure 1 or 2	How Did the Rock Form Relative to Bowen's Reaction Series (Figure 3) and Intrusive/Extrusive Processes?

ACTIVITY 6 Modeling Lava Behavior and Volcanic Landforms

Name: _____   Course/Section: _____

Materials: Heinz® ketchup, Kraft® smooth peanut butter, stiff paper plates (10-inch or larger), metric ruler, drinking straws, 50 ml beaker, small paper cups (2), paper bag.

Magmas/lavas are called mafic (basaltic), intermediate (andesitic), or felsic (granitic/rhyolitic), depending on their composition and temperature. Your challenge is to determine how their viscosity varies and infer how viscosity affects lava behavior and the development of volcanic landforms.

Composition	Temperature	Weight % Volatiles	Weight % Silica	Relative Viscosity (low vs. high)
Mafic (gabbroic/basaltic)	~900°–1100° C	1–2%	Low (≤ 50%)	
Intermediate (andesitic)	~800°–900° C	2–4%	50–65%	intermediate
Felsic (granitic/rhyolitic)	~less than 800° C	2–6%	High (≥ 65%)	

A. Geologists Don Baker, Claude Dalpé, and Glenn Poirer have already determined that Heinz® ketchup has the same viscosity as a typical basaltic (mafic) lava, and Skippy® smooth peanut butter has the viscosity of a typical rhyolitic (felsic) lava (*Journal of Geoscience Education*, v.52, no. 4, 2004). Place an equal amount of this ketchup and peanut butter in separate piles on one end of a paper plate. Tilt the plate at about 45 degrees and observe the viscosity (resistance to flow) of each material. Then write the word "low" or "high" in the right-hand column above to describe the relative viscosity of the two kinds of lava.

B. Carefully try to make a volcano from 50 ml of the ketchup (basaltic lava) on one plate. At the same time try to make a volcano from 5 tablespoons of peanut butter on another plate. Make a scale (actual size) drawing of the side view of each pile after it stops spreading out for 2 minutes.

C. Below is a profile of a shield volcano (Mauna Loa, Hawaii) and a composite cone (stratovolcano, Mt. Rainier, Washington). Based on your work, circle the one that likely formed from basaltic lava flows.

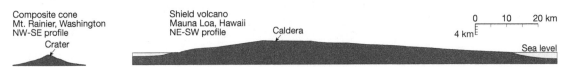

D. Fill one paper cup about 4 cm deep with ketchup and another paper cup about 4 cm deep with peanut butter. Use one of the straws to pipette about 3 cm of peanut butter from the cup of peanut butter. Now imagine that the straw is the neck of a volcano. Open a paper bag and try to shoot the peanut butter into the bag by blowing into the straw (volcanic neck). Repeat procedure using the ketchup. Based on your experimental models, explain why rhyolitic (felsic) and andesitic volcanoes tend to erupt explosively.

ACTIVITY 7 Infer the Geologic History of Shiprock, New Mexico

Name: _____   Course/Section: _____

Carefully study the various kinds of intrusive and extrusive igneous bodies in Figure 12 to understand their shapes and origins. Then analyze the stereogram (stereo pair of photographs) of Shiprock, New Mexico, in Figure 13. This "shiprock" feature is known to Navahos as *Tse Bi dahi*, or Rock with Wings. The light-colored portions of this stereogram are modern sand and gravel being transported by temporary streams after infrequent rains. The dark-colored features of this Rock (labeled A) with Wings (labeled B) are basalt about 27 million years old.

A. What kind of igneous body is labeled A?

B. What kind of igneous body is labeled B?

C. What was the main feature of the landscape that existed here about 27 million years ago (when these bodies of igneous rock were lava)?

ACTIVITY 8 Infer the Geologic History of Southeastern Pennsylvania

Name: _____   Course/Section: _____

Review Figure 12. Then study the portion of a geologic map of Pennsylvania (Figure 14). The green-colored areas are exposures of 200–220 million-year-old Mesozoic sand and mud that were deposited in lakes, streams, and fields of a long, narrow valley. The red-colored areas are bodies of basalt about 200 million years old.

A. Based on their geometries (as viewed from above, in map view), what kind of igneous bodies on the map are labeled A?

B. Based on their geometries (as viewed from above, in map view), what kind of igneous bodies on the map are labeled B (more than one answer is possible)?

C. If you could have seen the landscape that existed in this part of Pennsylvania about 200 million years ago (when the bodies of igneous rock were lava), then what else would you have seen on the landscape besides valleys, streams, lakes, and fields? Explain your reasoning.

Sedimentary Rocks, Processes, and Environments

CONTRIBUTING AUTHORS

Harold Andrews • *Wellesley College*

James R. Besancon • *Wellesley College*

Pamela J.W. Gore • *Dekalb College*

Margaret D. Thompson • *Wellesley College*

OBJECTIVES AND ACTIVITIES

A. Be able to describe, classify, and interpret textural and compositional features of detrital (siliciclastic), biochemical (bioclastic), and chemical sediment.

    ACTIVITY 1: Clastic and Detrital Sediment

    ACTIVITY 2: Biochemical Sediment and Rock

    ACTIVITY 3: Chemical Sediment and Rock

    ACTIVITY 4: Sediment Analysis, Classification, and Interpretation

B. Be able to describe textural and compositional features of sedimentary rocks, classify them by group (detrital, biochemical, or chemical) and specific name, and describe how they formed.

    ACTIVITY 5: Hand Sample Analysis and Interpretation (worksheet)

C. Apply the Principle of Uniformitarianism and knowledge of common sedimentary structures to interpret sedimentary rocks.

    ACTIVITY 6: Outcrop Analysis and Interpretation

    ACTIVITY 7: Using the Present to Imagine the Past—Dogs and Dinosaurs

    ACTIVITY 8: Using the Present to Imagine the Past—Cape Cod to Kansas

D. Infer Earth history by "reading" (interpreting) a sequence of strata, from bottom to top.

    ACTIVITY 9: "Reading" Earth History from a Sequence of Strata

STUDENT MATERIALS

Pencil, eraser, laboratory notebook, hand magnifying lens (optional), metric ruler and sediment grain-size scale (from GeoTools Sheets 1 or 2), and samples of sedimentary rocks (obtain as directed by your instructor). Additional materials and equipment will be provided in the laboratory room.

INTRODUCTION

Sediments are loose grains and chemical residues of Earth materials, including rock fragments, mineral grains, parts of plants or animals like seashells and twigs, and chemical residues like rust (hydrated iron oxide residue). Grains of sediment are affected by chemical and physical weathering processes until they are buried in a sedimentary deposit or else disintegrate to invisible atoms and molecules in aqueous (watery) solutions underground (groundwater) or on Earth's surface (lakes, streams, ocean).

    Chemical weathering is the decomposition or dissolution of Earth materials. For example, feldspars

From Laboratory 6 of *Laboratory Manual in Physical Geology*, Ninth Edition, American Geological Institute, National Association of Geoscience Teachers, Richard M. Busch, Dennis Tasa. Copyright © 2011 by Pearson Education, Inc. Published by Pearson Prentice Hall. All rights reserved.

like potassium feldspar ($KAlSi_3O_8$) decompose in acidic water to clay minerals [kaolinite: $Al_2Si_2O_5(OH)_4$] and an aqueous (water) solution of metal ions (K: potassium) and silica (hydrosilicic acid: H_4SiO_4). This is the main way that clay forms in soils of landscapes. Olivine [$(Fe,Mg)_2SiO_4$] decomposes to iron oxide residues and magnesium oxide residues. Halite (sodium chloride: $NaCl$) dissolves to form salt water (sodium chloride in aqueous solution). Chemical residues commonly coat the surfaces of visible grains of sediment and either discolor them or serve as a cement to "glue" them together and form sedimentary rock. When aqueous solutions full of dissolved chemicals evaporate, the chemicals combine to precipitate (form solids from the solution) mineral crystals and amorphous residues known as **chemical sediment.**

Physical (mechanical) weathering is the cracking, crushing, and wearing away (scratching, abrasion) of Earth materials. Cracking and crushing processes cause big rocks to be fragmented into *clasts* (broken pieces: from the Greek *klastós*, meaning broken in pieces) or **clastic sediment,** including *rock fragments* and *mineral grains* (whole crystals or fragments of crystals). The continental bedrock, rich in silicate minerals, is fragmented into *siliciclastic sediment* made of quartz grains, feldspar grains, and rock fragments. Plants and animals are fragmented into bioclastic **biochemical sediment** made of things like twigs, leaves, shells, and fragmented shells. Scratching and abrasion of grains and bedrock surfaces wears away sediment from the land and rounds sharp edges of individual grains. This is called **detrital sediment** (from the Latin *detritus*, participle of *detero*, meaning to weaken, wear away, rub off). Because detrital sediment is generally worn from the land (terrigenous), it is mostly siliciclastic grains and clay minerals.

Sedimentary rocks form when sediments are compressed, cemented, or otherwise hardened together (like mud hardened by the Sun forms *adobe*), or when masses of intergrown mineral crystals precipitate from aqueous solutions (like the rock salt that remains when ocean water is evaporated).

PART A: SEDIMENTARY PROCESSES AND ROCKS

Wherever sediments accumulate, or crystals precipitate from aqueous solutions, they form a deposit or *sedimentary unit.* Some sedimentary units are unconsolidated (unhardened), and some are consolidated (hardened) into sedimentary rock. Therefore, every sedimentary unit is made of sediment or sedimentary rock and can be described, identified, and interpreted on the basis of its texture (Figure 1) and composition (Figures 2, 3).

ACTIVITY 1

Clastic and Detrital Sediment

Make and analyze clastic and detrital sediment, then infer what clues you can use to tell detrital grains shaped in a glacial environment (ice) from detrital grains shaped in streams (water) or sand dunes (air).

ACTIVITY 2

Biochemical Sediment and Rock

Make some biochemical sediment and infer where and how biochemical sediments form.

ACTIVITY 3

Chemical Sediment and Rock

Do an experiment to understand the difference between two iron oxide minerals that commonly color and cement together sedimentary rocks.

Textures of Sediments and Sedimentary Rocks

Processes of weathering, transportation, precipitation, and *deposition* (settling to rest and forming a deposit) that contribute to the formation of a sediment or sedimentary rock also contribute to forming its texture. The **texture** of a sediment or sedimentary rock is a description of its constituent parts and their sizes, shapes, and arrangement (Figure 1).

Grain size (Figure 1) usually is expressed in *Wentworth classes*, named after C. K. Wentworth, an American geologist who devised the scale in 1922. Here are the Wentworth grain-size classes commonly used by geologists in describing sediments:

- **Gravel** includes grains larger than 2 mm in diameter (granules, pebbles, cobbles, and boulders).

- **Sand** includes grains from 1/16 mm to 2 mm in diameter (in decimal form, 0.0625 mm to 2.000 mm). This is the size range of grains in a sandbox. The grains are visible and feel very gritty when rubbed between your fingers.

- **Silt** includes grains from 1/256 mm to 1/16 mm in diameter (in decimal form, 0.0039 mm to 0.0625 mm). Grains of silt are usually too small to see, but you can still feel them as very tiny gritty grains when you rub them between your fingers or teeth.

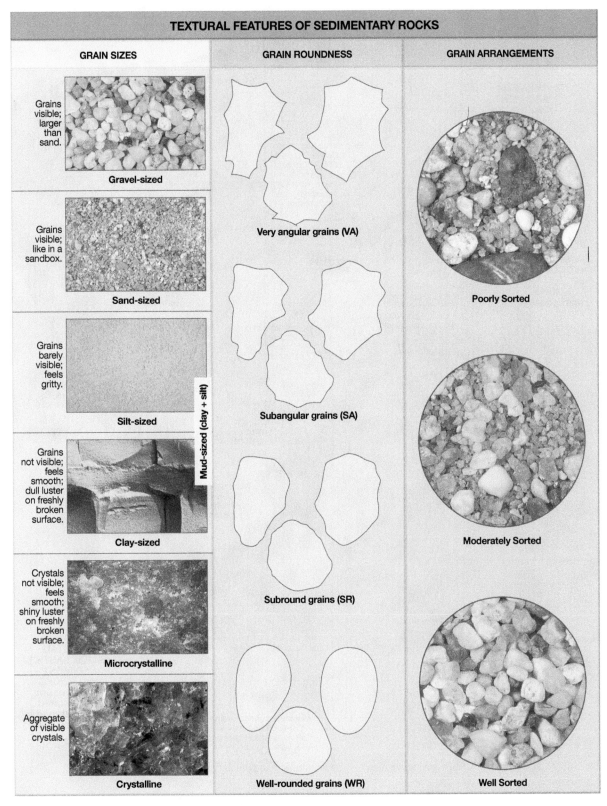

FIGURE 1   Textural features of sedimentary rocks. Scale for all images is ×1.

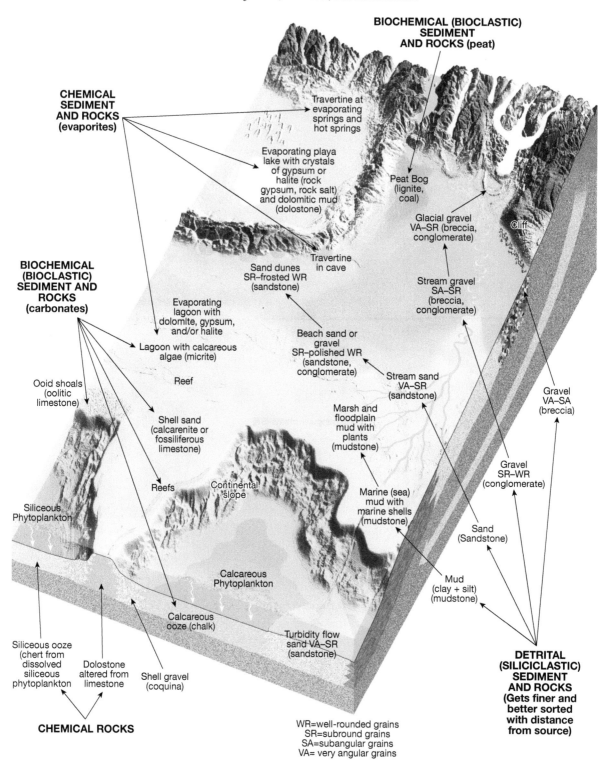

FIGURE 2 Some named modern environments where sediments and sedimentary rocks are forming.

SEDIMENTARY ROCK ANALYSIS AND CLASSIFICATION

STEP 1: Composition. What materials comprise most of the rock?	STEP 2: What are the rock's texture and other distinctive properties?			STEP 3: Name the rock based on your analysis in steps 1 and 2.		
Detrital (Siliciclastic) sediment grains: fragmented rocks and/or silicate mineral crystals — Rock fragments and/or quartz grains and/or feldspar grains and/or clay minerals (e.g., kaolinite). Detrital sediment is derived from the mechanical and chemical weathering of continental (land) rocks, which consist mostly of silicate minerals. Detrital sediment is also called terrigenous (land derived) sediment.	Mostly angular and/or subangular gravel (grains larger than 2 mm)			BRECCIA*		Detrital (Siliciclastic) sedimentary rocks / clastic rocks
	Mostly subround and/or well rounded gravel (grains larger than 2 mm)			CONGLOMERATE*		
	Mostly sand (1/16–2 mm grains). May contain fossils	Mostly quartz sand		QUARTZ SANDSTONE	SANDSTONE	
		Mostly feldspar sand		ARKOSE		
		Mostly rock fragment sand		LITHIC SANDSTONE		
		Sand is mixed with much mud		WACKE (GRAYWACKE)		
	No visible grains	Mud (< 1/16 mm)	Mostly silt. May contain fossils	Breaks into blocks or layers	SILTSTONE	MUDSTONE
			Mostly clay. May contain fossils	Fissile (splits easily into layers)	SHALE	
				Crumbles into blocks	CLAYSTONE	
Biochemical (Bioclastic) sediment grains: fragments/shells of organisms	Plant fragments and/or charcoal	Brown porous rock with visible plant fragments that are easily broken apart from one another		PEAT		Biochemical (Bioclastic) sedimentary rocks
		Dull, dark brown, brittle rock; fossil plant fragments may be visible		LIGNITE		
		Black, layered, brittle rock; may be sooty or bright		BITUMINOUS COAL		
	Shells and shell/coral fragments, and/or calcareous microfossils	Mostly gravel-sized shells and shell or coral fragments; (Figure 6)		COQUINA	LIMESTONE	carbonate/calcareous rocks
		Mostly sand-sized shell fragments; often contains a few larger whole fossil shells		CALCARENITE (FOSSILIFEROUS LIMESTONE)		
		Silty, earthy rock comprised of the microscopic shells of calcareous phytoplankton (microfossils); may contain a few visible fossils		CHALK		
	No visible grains	No visible grains in most of the rock. May break with conchoidal fracture. May contain a few visible fossils in the micrite		MICRITE		
Mineral crystals (inorganic) or chemical residues (e.g., rust) — rocks that effervesce in dilute HCl	Calcite crystals and/or calcite spheres and/or microcrystalline calcite/aragonite	Mostly spherical grains that resemble miniature pearls (< 2 mm), called ooliths or ooids		OOLITIC LIMESTONE	LIMESTONE	Chemical sedimentary rocks / evaporite rocks
		Masses of visible crystals and/or microcrystalline; may have cavities, pores, or color banding (Figure 8); usually light colored		TRAVERTINE		
	Microcrystalline dolomite	Effervesces in dilute HCl only if powdered. Usually light colored. (Commonly forms from alteration of limestone)		DOLOSTONE		
	Halite mineral crystals	Visible cubic crystals, translucent, salty taste (Figure 7)		ROCK SALT		
	Gypsum mineral crystals	Gray, white, or colorless. Visible crystals or microcrystalline. Can be scratched with your fingernail		ROCK GYPSUM		
	Iron-bearing minerals crystals or residues	Dark-colored, dense, amorphous masses (e.g. limonite), microcrystalline nodules or inter-layered with quartz or red chert (banded iron formation)		IRONSTONE		
	Microcrystalline varieties of quartz (flint, chalcedony, chert, jasper)	Microcrystalline, may break with a conchoidal fracture. Hard (scratches glass). Usually gray, brown, black, or mottled mixture of those colors. May contain fossils, as the silica in most chert is derived from dissolution of siliceous phytoplankton ooze (diatoms, radiolaria)		CHERT (a siliceous rock)		

*Modify name as quartz breccia/conglomerate, arkose breccia/conglomerate, lithic breccia/conglomerate, or wacke breccia/conglomerate as done for sandstones.

FIGURE 3 Sedimentary rock analysis and classification. See Part B (Activity 5) for steps to analyze and name a sedimentary rock.

- **Clay** includes grains less than 1/256 mm diameter (in decimal form, 0.0039 mm). Clay-sized grains are too small to see, and they feel smooth (like chalk dust) when rubbed between your fingers or teeth. Note that the word *clay* is used not only to denote a grain size, but also a clay mineral. However, clay mineral crystals are usually clay-sized.

Sedimentary rocks that form when crystals precipitate from aqueous solutions have a **crystalline texture** (clearly visible crystals; see Figure 1) or **microcrystalline texture** (crystals too small to identify; see Figure 1). As the crystals grow, they interfere with each other and form an intergrown and interlocking texture that also holds the rock together.

All sediment has a source (place of origin, provenance; Figure 2). Sediments deposited quickly at or near their source tend to lack abrasion. Sediments that have been moved about locally (as in waves on a beach) or transported away from their source are abraded (worn). **Roundness** is a description of the degree to which the sharp corners and points of a fragmented grain have been worn away and its profile has become round (Figure 1). A newly formed clast is *very angular*. As it is transported and worn it will become *subangular*, then *subround*, then *well rounded*. A freshly broken rock fragment, mineral grain, or seashell has sharp edges and is described as *angular*. The more rounded a grain becomes, the smaller it generally becomes. Gravel gets broken and abraded down into sand, sand gets broken and abraded into silt and clay-sized grains.

Different velocities of wind and water currents are capable of transporting and naturally separating different densities and sizes of sediments from one another. **Sorting** is a description of the degree to which one size class of sediment has been separated from the others (Figure 1). *Poorly sorted* sediments consist of a mixture of many different sizes of grains. *Well-sorted* sediments consist of grains that are of similar size and/or density.

Composition of Sediments and Sedimentary Rocks

The **composition** of a sediment or sedimentary rock is a description of the kinds and abundances of grains that compose it. Sediments and sedimentary rocks are classified as biochemical (bioclastic), chemical, or detrital (siliciclastic) based on their composition (Figure 3). **Biochemical** sediments and rocks consist of whole and **bioclastic** remains of organisms, such as shells and plant fragments. **Chemical** sediments and rocks consist of chemical residues and intergrown mineral crystals precipitated from aqueous solutions. The precipitated minerals commonly include gypsum, halite, hematite, limonite, calcite, dolomite, and chert (microcrystalline variety of quartz). **Detrital** sediments and rocks consist of **siliciclastic** and *detrital*

grains—worn rock fragments and mineral grains that were worn away from the landscape.

ACTIVITY 4

Sediment Analysis, Classification, and Interpretation

Analyze and interpret these sediment samples before proceeding on to rock analysis.

Formation of Sedimentary Rocks

Lithification is the hardening of sediment (masses of loose Earth materials such as pebbles, gravel, sand, silt, mud, shells, plant fragments, mineral crystals, and products of chemical decay) to produce rock. The lithification process usually occurs as layers of sediment are **compacted** (pressure-hardened, Figure 4) or **cemented** together (glued together by tiny crystals or chemical residues precipitated from fluids in the pores of sediment, Figures 5, 6). However, it is also possible to form a dense hard mass of intergrown crystals directly, as they precipitate from aqueous solutions (Figures 7 and 8).

A. Start with a handful of mud.

B. Compact the mud by squeezing it in your fist.

C. Release your grip to observe a piece of mudstone.

FIGURE 4 Compaction of a handful of mud to form a lump of mudstone. The more the mud is compacted, the harder it will become.

Quartz sand (sediment)

×2

CEMENTATION

SEDIMENTARY ROCK:

1. Sandstone with white calcite or quartz cement.

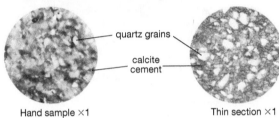

quartz grains

calcite cement

Hand sample ×1   Thin section ×1

2. Sandstone with reddish hematite cement.

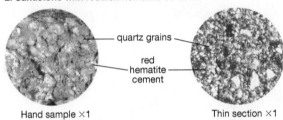

quartz grains

red hematite cement

Hand sample ×1   Thin section ×1

3. Sandstone with brown, black, or yellow limonite cement.

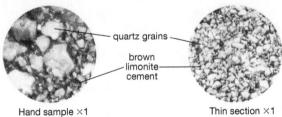

quartz grains

brown limonite cement

Hand sample ×1   Thin section ×1

FIGURE 5 Cementation of quartz sand to form sandstone.

×1

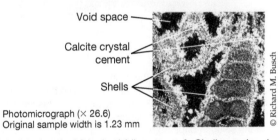

Void space

Calcite crystal cement

Shells

Photomicrograph (× 26.6)
Original sample width is 1.23 mm

FIGURE 6 Formation of the biochemical (bioclastic) limestone. **A.** Shell gravel and blades of the sea grass *Thalassia* have accumulated on a modern beach of Crane Key, Florida. Note pen (12 cm long) for scale. **B.** Sample of gravel like that shown in part A, but it is somewhat older and has been cemented together with calcite to form limestone. **C.** Photomicrograph of a thin section of the sample shown in B. Note that the rock is very porous and that it is cemented with films of microscopic calcite crystals that have essentially glued the shells together.

119

A. Rock salt (×1)

© Richard M. Busch

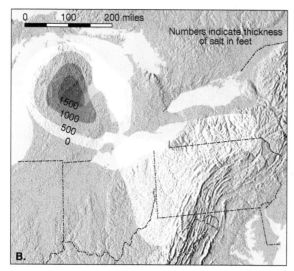

0   100   200 miles

Numbers indicate thickness
of salt in feet

1500
1000
500
0

B.

FIGURE 7 Rock salt, a chemical sedimentary rock with crystalline texture. **A.** Hand sample from salt mines deep below Lake Erie reveals that rock salt is an aggregate of intergrown halite mineral crystals. **B.** Map showing the thickness and distribution of rock salt deposits formed about 400 million years ago, when a portion of the ocean was trapped and evaporated in what is now the Great Lakes region, millions of years before any lakes existed.

FIGURE 8 Formation of the chemical sedimentary rock, travertine. **A.** Limestone bedrock is dissolved by acidic rain near the Earth's surface. **B.** The resulting aqueous solution of water, calcium ions, and bicarbonate ions seeps into caves. As the solution drips from the roof of a cave, it forms icicle-shaped stalactites. **C.** Broken end of a stalactite reveals that it is actually an aggregate of chemically precipitated calcite crystals. **D.** Thin section photomicrograph reveals that the concentric laminations of the stalactite are caused by variations in iron impurity and porosity of the calcite layers.

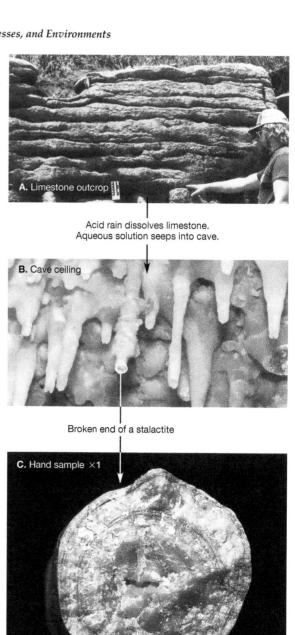

A. Limestone outcrop

Acid rain dissolves limestone.
Aqueous solution seeps into cave.

B. Cave ceiling

Broken end of a stalactite

C. Hand sample ×1

Photomicrograph of laminations

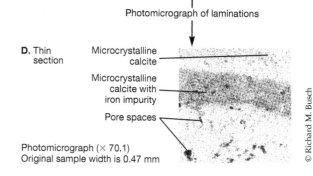

D. Thin
section

Microcrystalline
calcite

Microcrystalline
calcite with
iron impurity

Pore spaces

Photomicrograph (× 70.1)
Original sample width is 0.47 mm

© Richard M. Busch

Sand (a sediment) can be *compacted* until it is pressure-hardened into sandstone (a sedimentary rock). Alternatively, sandstone can form when sand grains are *cemented* together by chemical residues or the growth of interlocking microscopic crystals in pore spaces of the rock (void spaces among the grains). Rock salt and rock gypsum are examples of sedimentary rocks that form by the *precipitation* of aggregates of intergrown and interlocking crystals during the evaporation of salt water or brine.

Ocean water is the most common aqueous solution and variety of salt water on Earth. As it evaporates, a variety of minerals precipitate in a particular sequence. The first mineral to form in this sequence is aragonite (calcium carbonate). Gypsum forms when about 50–75% of the ocean water has evaporated, and halite (table salt) forms when 90% has evaporated. Ancient rock salt units buried under modern Lake Erie probably formed from evaporation of an ancient ocean. The salt units were then buried under superjacent layers of mud and sand, long before Lake Erie formed on top of them (see Figure 7).

Classifying Sedimentary Rocks

The main kinds of biochemical (bioclastic) sedimentary rocks are limestone, peat, lignite, and coal. Biochemical limestone is made of animal skeletons (usually seashells, coral, or microscopic shells), as in Figure 6. Differences in the density and size of the constituent grains of a biochemical (bioclastic) limestone can also be used to call it a **coquina, calcarenite (fossiliferous limestone), micrite,** or **chalk** (Figure 3). **Peat** is a very porous brown rock with visible plant fragments that can easily be pulled apart from the rock. **Lignite** is brown but more dense than peat. Its plant fragments cannot be pulled apart from the rock. **Bituminous coal** is a black rock made of sooty charcoal-like or else shiny brittle layers of carbon and plant fragments.

There are seven main kinds of chemical (inorganic) sedimentary rocks in the classification in Figure 3. **Chemical limestone** refers to any mass of crystalline limestone that has no color banding or visible internal structures. **Travertine** is a mass of intergrown calcite crystals that may have light and dark color banding, cavities, or pores (Figure 8C). **Oolitic limestone** is composed mostly of tiny spherical grains that resemble beads or miniature pearls and are made of concentric layers of microcrystalline aragonite or calcite. They form in intertidal zones of some marine regions (Figure 2) where the water is warm and detrital sediment is lacking. **Dolostone** (Figure 3) is an aggregate of dolomite mineral crystals that are usually microcrystalline. It forms in hypersaline lagoons and desert playa lakes (Figure 2). Because calcite and dolomite closely resemble one another, the best way to tell them apart is with the "acid test." Calcite will effervesce (fizz) in dilute HCl, but dolomite will effervesce *only* if it is powdered first. **Rock gypsum** is an aggregate of gypsum crystals, and **rock salt** is an aggregate of halite crystals (Figure 7). Two other chemical sedimentary rocks are **chert** (microcrystalline or even cryptocrystalline quartz) and **ironstone** (rock made mostly of hematite, limonite, or other iron-bearing minerals or chemical residues).

The main kinds of detrital (siliciclastic) sedimentary rocks are mudstone, sandstone, breccia, and conglomerate (Figure 3). It is very difficult to tell the percentage of clay or silt in a sedimentary rock with the naked eye, so sedimentary rocks made of clay and/or silt are commonly called **mudstone.** Mudstone that is *fissile* (splits apart easily into layers) can be called **shale.** Mudstone can also be called siltstone or claystone, depending upon whether silt or clay is the most abundant grain size. Any detrital rock composed mostly of sand-sized grains is simply called **sandstone** (Figures 3 and 5); although you can distinguish among *quartz sandstone* (made mostly of quartz grains), *arkose* (made mostly of feldspar grains), *lithic sandstone* (made mostly of rock fragments), or *wacke* (made of a mixture of sand-sized and mud-sized grains). **Breccia** and **conglomerate** are both made of gravel-sized grains and are often poorly sorted or moderately sorted. The grains in breccia are very angular and/or subangular, and the grains in conglomerate are subrounded and/or well rounded.

PART B: HAND SAMPLE ANALYSIS AND INTERPRETATION

The complete classification of a sedimentary rock requires knowledge of its composition, texture(s), and other distinctive properties that you learned in Part A. The same information used to name the rock can also be used to infer where and how it formed (Figure 2).

ACTIVITY 5

Hand Sample Analysis and Interpretation (worksheet)

Obtain a set of sedimentary rocks (as directed by your instructor) and analyze the rocks one at a time. For each sample, complete a row on the activity worksheets using the steps below. Refer to the example for sample X (Figure 9 and Activity 5 worksheet).

Follow these steps to classify a sedimentary rock using the Activity 5 worksheet:

Step 1: Determine and record the rock's general composition as *biochemical (bioclastic), chemical,* or *detrital (siliciclastic)* with reference to Figure 3, and record a description of the specific kinds and

Quartz grains (translucent gray)

© Richard M. Busch

K-feldspar grains (orange)

0   1   2   3 cm

FIGURE 9 Photograph of hand sample X (actual size). Refer to the first row of the Activity 5 worksheet to see the example of how this rock's composition, texture, and origin were described.

abundances of grains that make up the rock. Refer to the categories for composition in the left-hand column of Figure 3.

Step 2: Record a description of the rock's texture(s) with reference to Figure 1. Also record any other of the rock's distinctive properties as categorized in the center columns of Figure 3.

Step 3: Determine the name of the sedimentary rock by categorizing the rock from left to right across Figure 3. Use the compositional, textural, and special properties data from Steps 1 and 2 (left side of Figure 3) to deduce the rock name (right side of Figure 3).

Step 4: After you have named the rock, then you can use Figure 2 and information from Steps 1 and 2 to infer where and how the rock formed. See the example for sample X (Figure 9 and the Activity 5 worksheet).

PART C: SEDIMENTARY STRUCTURES AND ENVIRONMENTS

A variety of structures occur in sedimentary rocks (Figure 10). Some form by purely physical processes, and others form as a result of the activities of plants or animals. Therefore, the specific kinds of sedimentary structures can be used as indicators of environments where they normally form today.

Sedimentary Structures

One of the most obvious sedimentary structures is layering of sediments. Most layers of sediment, or **strata** (plural of *stratum*, a single layer), accumulate in nearly horizontal sheets. Strata less than 1 cm thick are called *laminations*; strata 1 cm or more thick are called *beds* (see Figure 10).

Surfaces between strata are called **bedding planes.** These represent surfaces of exposure that occurred between sedimentary depositional events. To illustrate, imagine a series of storms, each of which causes sediment to be deposited in puddles. Each storm is a sedimentary depositional event. Between storms, deposition stops, and the surface of the sediment in the puddles (bedding plane surface) becomes exposed to the sorting action of water in the puddles or to the processes of weathering as dry surfaces after the puddles evaporate.

Most strata are deposited in nearly horizontal sheets. However, some stratification is inclined and is referred to as **cross-stratification** or **cross-bedding** (see Figure 10). Sediment transported in a single direction by water or air currents commonly forms **current ripple marks** or sand dunes. Sediment transported by back-and-forth water motions or very gentle waves skimming the bottom of a lake or ocean commonly forms **oscillatory ripple marks** (Figure 10). Both types of ripple marks are internally cross-stratified, and the cross-strata are inclined in the direction of water/air flow. This information is useful for interpreting the kinds of environments in which the strata formed. For example, cross-strata inclined in just one general direction indicate flow of air or water in just one direction (downstream or downwind). If a sequence of cross-strata is inclined in opposite directions (**bimodal cross-bedding** in Figure 10), then the environment in which the sequence formed must have water/wind that changed direction back and forth. An example would be water currents associated with tides.

Individual strata also may be **graded** (Figure 10). Normally, graded beds are sorted from coarse at the bottom to fine at the top. This feature is caused when sediment-laden currents suddenly slow as they enter a standing body of water, or as current flow terminates abruptly.

Flutes (Figure 10) are scoop-shaped or V-shaped depressions scoured into a sediment surface by the erosional, winnowing action of currents. Sediment-filled flutes are called **flute casts.** Flutes and flute casts indicate current direction, because they flare out (widen) in the down-current direction.

Many sedimentary rocks also contain structures that formed shortly after deposition of the sediments that compose them. For example, **mudcracks** often form while moist deposits of mud dry and shrink, and **raindrop impressions** may form on terrestrial (land) surfaces (Figure 10). Animals make tracks, trails, and burrows (Figure 10) that can be preserved in sedimentary rocks. Such traces of former life are called **trace fossils.**

Sedimentary Environments

Sediments are deposited in many different environments. Some of these environments are illustrated in Figure 2. Each environment has characteristic sediments, sedimentary structures, and organisms that can become **fossils** (any evidence of prehistoric life). The information gained from grain characteristics, sedimentary structures, and fossils can be used to infer what ancient environments (**paleoenvironments**) were like in comparison to modern ones. The process of understanding where and how a body of sediment was deposited depends on the *Principle of Uniformitarianism*—the assumption that processes that shaped Earth and its environments in the past are the same as processes operating today. Often stated as, "the present is the key to the past," you can think of processes operating in modern ecosystems and then imagine how those same processes may have operated in past ecosystems with different organisms. You can also look at sediment, sedimentary structures, and fossils in a sedimentary rock and infer how it formed on the basis of where such sediment, sedimentary structures, and organisms are found together today.

ACTIVITY 6

Outcrop Analysis and Interpretation

Analyze and interpret an outcrop of sedimentary rock on the basis of its rock type and sedimentary structures.

ACTIVITY 7

Using the Present to Imagine the Past—Dogs and Dinosaurs

Analyze and interpret a Triassic rock compared to your knowledge of a modern environment where a dog lived.

ACTIVITY 8

Using the Present to Imagine the Past—Cape Cod to Kansas

Analyze and interpret a Pennsylvanian-age rock from Kansas compared to your knowledge of the modern seafloor near Cape Cod, Massachusetts. (Photograph from Cape Cod was provided by the U.S. Geological Survey, Open File Report OFR 00-427.)

PART D: INTERPRETATION OF A STRATIGRAPHIC SEQUENCE

As sediments accumulate, they cover up the sediments that were already deposited at an earlier (older) time. Environments also change through time, as layers of sediment accumulate. Therefore, at any particular location, bodies of sediment have accumulated in different times and environments. These bodies of sediment then changed into rock units, which have different textures, compositions, and sedimentary structures.

A succession of rock strata or units, one on top of the other, is called a *stratigraphic sequence*. If you interpret each rock unit of the stratigraphic sequence in order, from oldest (at the base) to youngest (at the top), then you will know what happened over a given portion of geologic history for the site where the stratigraphic sequence is located.

ACTIVITY 9

"Reading" Earth History from a Sequence of Strata

Analyze a stratigraphic sequence of Permian rocks (approximately 270 million years old) from northeast Kansas using pictures of hand samples and field descriptions of the rock units. The rock units are stacked one atop the other, from oldest at the bottom to youngest at the top. Your job is to "read" the units like pages of a stone book and interpret the changes that occurred here in Permian time. Use all of the information that is provided to fill in the paleoenvironment represented by each rock unit in the sequence. Then work from bottom to top, and shade in the narrow right-hand columns to indicate the "record of change." When you are done, you will see how environments changed in Kansas over about 400,000 years of the Permian Period.

SEDIMENTARY STRUCTURES

ILLUSTRATIONS	DESCRIPTIONS	ENVIRONMENTS

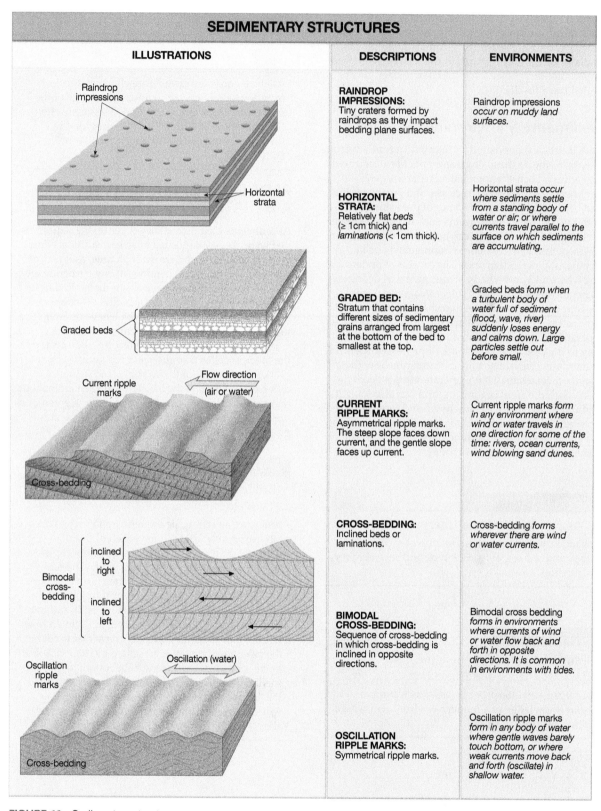

RAINDROP IMPRESSIONS:
Tiny craters formed by raindrops as they impact bedding plane surfaces.

Raindrop impressions *occur on muddy land surfaces.*

HORIZONTAL STRATA:
Relatively flat *beds* (≥ 1cm thick) and *laminations* (< 1cm thick).

Horizontal strata *occur where sediments settle from a standing body of water or air; or where currents travel parallel to the surface on which sediments are accumulating.*

GRADED BED:
Stratum that contains different sizes of sedimentary grains arranged from largest at the bottom of the bed to smallest at the top.

Graded beds *form when a turbulent body of water full of sediment (flood, wave, river) suddenly loses energy and calms down. Large particles settle out before small.*

CURRENT RIPPLE MARKS:
Asymmetrical ripple marks. The steep slope faces down current, and the gentle slope faces up current.

Current ripple marks *form in any environment where wind or water travels in one direction for some of the time: rivers, ocean currents, wind blowing sand dunes.*

CROSS-BEDDING:
Inclined beds or laminations.

Cross-bedding *forms wherever there are wind or water currents.*

BIMODAL CROSS-BEDDING:
Sequence of cross-bedding in which cross-bedding is inclined in opposite directions.

Bimodal cross bedding *forms in environments where currents of wind or water flow back and forth in opposite directions. It is common in environments with tides.*

OSCILLATION RIPPLE MARKS:
Symmetrical ripple marks.

Oscillation ripple marks *form in any body of water where gentle waves barely touch bottom, or where weak currents move back and forth (oscillate) in shallow water.*

FIGURE 10 Sedimentary structures.

SEDIMENTARY STRUCTURES

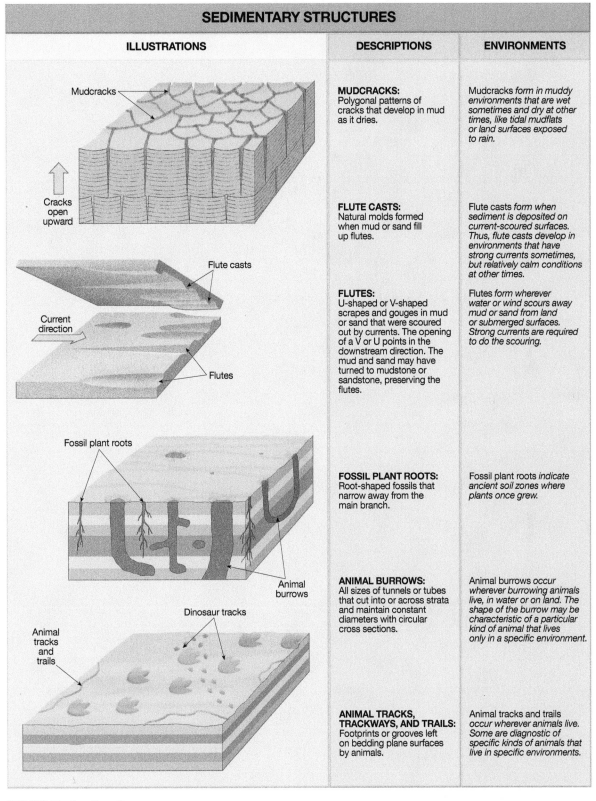

ILLUSTRATIONS	DESCRIPTIONS	ENVIRONMENTS
Mudcracks / Cracks open upward	**MUDCRACKS:** Polygonal patterns of cracks that develop in mud as it dries.	Mudcracks *form in muddy environments that are wet sometimes and dry at other times, like tidal mudflats or land surfaces exposed to rain.*
Flute casts / Current direction / Flutes	**FLUTE CASTS:** Natural molds formed when mud or sand fill up flutes.	Flute casts *form when sediment is deposited on current-scoured surfaces. Thus, flute casts develop in environments that have strong currents sometimes, but relatively calm conditions at other times.*
	FLUTES: U-shaped or V-shaped scrapes and gouges in mud or sand that were scoured out by currents. The opening of a V or U points in the downstream direction. The mud and sand may have turned to mudstone or sandstone, preserving the flutes.	Flutes *form wherever water or wind scours away mud or sand from land or submerged surfaces. Strong currents are required to do the scouring.*
Fossil plant roots / Animal burrows	**FOSSIL PLANT ROOTS:** Root-shaped fossils that narrow away from the main branch.	Fossil plant roots *indicate ancient soil zones where plants once grew.*
	ANIMAL BURROWS: All sizes of tunnels or tubes that cut into or across strata and maintain constant diameters with circular cross sections.	Animal burrows *occur wherever burrowing animals live, in water or on land. The shape of the burrow may be characteristic of a particular kind of animal that lives only in a specific environment.*
Dinosaur tracks / Animal tracks and trails	**ANIMAL TRACKS, TRACKWAYS, AND TRAILS:** Footprints or grooves left on bedding plane surfaces by animals.	Animal tracks and trails *occur wherever animals live. Some are diagnostic of specific kinds of animals that live in specific environments.*

FIGURE 10 (continued)

ACTIVITY 1 Clastic and Detrital Sediment

Name: _____   Course/Section: _____

Materials: Pencil; obtain a hand lens (or microscope), metric ruler and grain size scale (GeoTools 1, 2), a small piece of flat shale, medium quartz sandpaper, and two small pieces of granite or diorite as noted by your instructor.

A. Obtain two pieces of granite or diorite. Hold one in each hand and tap them together over a piece of paper. As you do this you should notice that you are breaking tiny sedimentary grains from the larger rock samples. These broken pieces of rocks and minerals are called **clasts** (from the Greek *klastós*, meaning "broken in pieces").

1. Using a hand lens or microscope, observe the tiny clasts that you just broke from the larger rock samples. Describe what minerals make up the clasts and whether or not the clasts are fragments of mineral crystals, rock fragments, or a mixture of both.

2. Geologists commonly refer to several different kinds of clastic sediment. Circle the one that you just made.
   - **pyroclastic sediment**—volcanic bombs and/or volcanic rocks fragmented by volcanic eruption
   - **bioclastic sediment**—broken pieces of shells, plants, and/or other parts of organisms
   - **siliciclastic sediment**—broken pieces of silicate mineral crystals and/or rocks containing them

3. **Roundness** is a measure of how much the profile of a grain of sediment resembles a circle. It is most often visually estimated using a chart like this one. Re-examine your clasts from Part A1 and sketch the outline of several of them. Compared to the chart, what is the roundness of the clasts that you sketched?

GRAIN ROUNDNESS — Very angular, Subangular, Subrounded, Well-rounded

4. Using a grain size scale (from GeoTools 1 or 2), circle the Wentworth size class(es) of the clastic sediment that you made above.

gravel	**sand**	**silt**	**clay**
(grains > 2 mm)	(grains 1/16 to 2 mm)	(grains too small to see but you can feel them)	(grains too small to see or feel; like chalk dust)

5. Obtain a piece of quartz sandpaper and lay it flat on the table. Find a sharp corner on one of the granite/diorite samples that you used above and sketch its outline in the "before abrasion" box below. Next, rub that corner against the quartz sandpaper for about 10 seconds. Sketch its profile in the "after abrasion" box. What did this abrasion process do to the sharp corner?

Before abrasion   After abrasion

CONTINUED

6. The sediment that you just made by wearing down the corner of a rock clast is called **detrital sediment** (from the Latin *detritus*, participle of *detero*, meaning "to weaken, wear away, rub off"). The term is also used to refer to all sediment that is terrigenous (from the land)—worn away or rubbed off of landscapes, including rock material that has been weakened and decomposed by chemical weathering (e.g., soil).

The Mississippi River carries detrital sediment that has been weathered from bedrock and worn away from the landscape of much of the United States. The river flows downhill under the influence of gravity and eventually flows into the Gulf of Mexico, where its load of detrital sediment temporarily accumulates at the mouth of the river on the edge of the Mississippi Delta. On this NASA satellite image of the Mississippi Delta, write a "D" to indicate where the main load of terrigenous detrital sediment is being deposited at the edge of the delta. How do you think the roundness of sediment in the river will change from a place upstream where it was broken from bedrock to the location where you placed your "D" on the image?

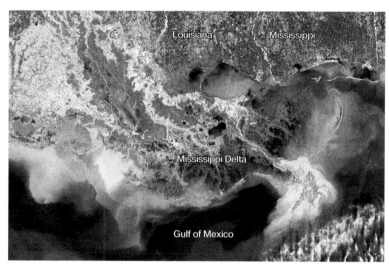

B. Sediment falls and slides (rockslides) downhill under the influence of gravity and is transported by flowing agents like water, wind, and ice (glaciers). As grains are transported, they scrape, chip, brake, and generally increase in roundness.

1. Glacial ice holds detrital grains of sediment in its firm grip while the weight of the glacier exerts tremendous downward force and gravity pulls the glacier downhill. You can model this process and see what it does to grains of sediment. Place a piece of sandpaper flat on the table. Next, firmly grip (like glacial ice) a piece of shale with a somewhat flat side pointing down. In one motion press the shale firmly against the sandpaper and push it forward one time. Then use a hand lens to observe the shale surface that you just scraped over the sandpaper. To the right of this paragraph, draw the pattern of scratches that you observe. What would happen to the shale surface if you kept grinding it straight ahead on a 10-meter-long strip of sandpaper?

2. Grains of sediment carried by water and wind move generally in one main direction but are free to quickly change direction and roll about so that all of their sides scrape and impact other grains often. Imagine that the piece of shale above has been dropped from a melting glacier and is being transported by a melt water stream. To model what might happen to the shale grain, place it onto the sandpaper, grip it lightly, and move it about against the sandpaper in multiple directions. Turn the shale to a different side and repeat. Now observe the newly scraped surfaces with a hand lens. To the right of this paragraph, draw the pattern of scratches that you observe.

3. Based on your work above, how could you tell a grain of sediment that was abraded and shaped in a glacial environment from one that was abraded and shaped while being transported by water or wind?

ACTIVITY 2 Biochemical Sediment and Rock

Name: _____   Course/Section: _____

Materials: (Provided in lab): dilute HCl (hydrochloric acid) in dropper bottle, seashells, charcoal briquette, coal, dolomite, hand lens, plastic sandwich bags, piece of chalk from a chalkboard.

A. Seashells are grains of sediment made by the biochemical processes of organisms, so they are grains of biochemical sediment. When you find a rock with a fossil seashell, then you have found evidence that the rock contains sediment deposited where the sea animal lived (i.e., in the ocean, in a marine environment). Some limestone is entirely made of the seashells or broken pieces of seashells. Obtain a seashell (e.g., hard clam shell) and draw it to the right of this paragraph. It may be easiest to trace it, then fill in the outline with details of what the shell looks like inside or out. Next, place the shell into a plastic sandwich bag and take the bag to the hammering station in your lab. Lightly tap the bag with the hammer to break up the shell into pieces. Return to your table and view the broken pieces of shell with a hand lens.

1. The shell fragments that you just made are called **clasts** (from the Greek *klastós*, meaning "broken in pieces"). Geologists commonly refer to several different kinds of clastic sediment. Circle the one that you just made.
   - **pyroclastic sediment**—volcanic bombs and/or volcanic rocks fragmented by volcanic eruption
   - **bioclastic sediment**—broken pieces of shells, plants, and/or other parts of organisms
   - **siliciclastic sediment**—broken pieces of silicate mineral crystals and/or rocks containing them

2. Compared to Figure 1, what is the roundness of your clasts? _____

3. What is the roundness of the clasts in this picture ($\times$ 1 scale)? _____
   Explain how and in what environment the shell clasts could have attained their roundness.

© Richard M. Busch

4. Some limestone is made of shells that are calcareous (calcite or aragonite), like visible seashells, but they are microscopic and cannot even be seen with a hand lens. Chalk is such a limestone. Some chalk used with modern blackboards is clay or plaster-of-Paris, rather than real chalk. Obtain a piece of chalk from your lab room or instructor. Explain how dilute HCl (hydrochloric acid) can be used to help you test your chalk and find out if it is real chalk or not. Then conduct your test and report the results of your test.

5. Based on Figure 2, how and where does chalk form?

CONTINUED

B. Place a charcoal briquette into a plastic sandwich bag and take it to the hammering station in your lab. Lightly hammer the bag enough to break apart the briquette. Return to your table with the bag of charcoal.

    1. View the broken pieces of charcoal with a hand lens. What do you see?

    2. Charcoal is made by allowing wood to smolder just enough that an impure mass of carbon remains. In the presence of oxygen, the charcoal briquette will naturally combine with oxygen to make carbon dioxide. Over a period of many years, it will all react with oxygen and chemically weather to carbon dioxide. When you burn charcoal in your grill, you are simply speeding up the process. However, if plant fragments are buried beneath layers of sediment that keep oxygen away from them, then they can slowly convert to a charcoal-like rock (peat, lignite, or coal) and remain so for millions of years. Obtain a piece of coal and compare it to your charcoal. How is it different? Why?

ACTIVITY 3 Chemical Sediment and Rock

Name: _____   Course/Section: _____

Materials (Provided in lab): limonite, hematite, Bunsen burner, Pyrex test tube with metal holder, mortar and pestle, safety glasses, fume hood or glass shield, square of aluminum foil about the size of your hand.

A. Bedrock can remain buried underground for millions to billions of years. However, when it is exposed to water and air at Earth's surface it weathers chemically and physically. For example, acidic water reacts with potassium and plagioclase feldspars to make clay minerals plus water containing dissolved silica (hydrosilicic acid) and metallic ions (K, Na, Ca). This is one of the main sources of clay found in soil and worn away into rivers and the ocean. The metals in many minerals oxidize (combine with oxygen) to form metal oxides like limonite ("rusty" iron) and hematite. Obtain and observe samples of both.

    1. What is the color and chemical formula for hematite?

sandstone ×1

© Richard M. Busch

    2. What is the color and chemical formula for limonite?

    3. As iron oxides form, they act like glue to cement together grains of sediment, like the "sandstone" above. Which iron oxide mineral has cemented together this sandstone?

    4. Powder some limonite in a mortar and pestle, and note its true streak color (yellow-brown). Put on safety goggles. In a fume hood or behind a glass shield, heat some of the powder in the Pyrex test tube over the Bunsen burner. Be sure to point the test tube at an angle, away from people. After about a minute of heating, pour the hot limonite powder onto the foil on the table. What happened to the limonite? Why?

    5. The rapid chemical change that you observed above can occur quickly only at temperatures like those above the Bunsen burner. However, some modern soils do contain hematite and appear red. How can that be?

ACTIVITY 4 Sediment Analysis, Classification, and Interpretation

Name: _____   Course/Section: _____

Materials: Pencil, ruler, Visual Estimation of Percent card (GeoTools 1, 2).

Sample A

0   5   10 cm

1. Grain size range in mm: _____
2. Percent of each Wentworth size class:

   clay _____   silt _____   sand _____   gravel _____
3. Grain sorting (circle):   Poor   Moderate   Well
4. Grain roundness (circle):   Angular   Subround   Well-rounded
5. Sediment composition (circle): Detrital   Biochemical   Chemical
                                  (Siliciclastic) (Bioclastic)
6. Describe how and in what environment (Figure 2) this sediment may have formed.

Sample B

0   2   4 cm

1. Grain size range in mm: _____
2. Percent of each Wentworth size class:

   clay _____   silt _____   sand _____   gravel _____
3. Grain sorting (circle):   Poor   Moderate   Well
4. Grain roundness (circle):   Angular   Subround   Well-rounded
5. Sediment composition (circle): Detrital   Biochemical   Chemical
                                  (Siliciclastic) (Bioclastic)
6. Describe how and in what environment (Figure 2) this sediment may have formed.

Sample C

0   1   2 mm

1. Grain size range in mm: _____
2. Percent of each Wentworth size class:

   clay _____   silt _____   sand _____   gravel _____
3. Grain sorting (circle):   Poor   Moderate   Well
4. Grain roundness (circle):   Angular   Subround   Well-rounded
5. Sediment composition (circle): Detrital   Biochemical   Chemical
                                  (Siliciclastic) (Bioclastic)
6. Describe how and in what environment (Figure 2) this sediment may have formed.

© Richard M. Busch

Sample D

0   1 mm

Ooids

© Richard M. Busch

1. Grain size range in mm: _____
2. Percent of each Wentworth size class:
   clay _____   silt _____   sand _____   gravel _____
3. Grain sorting (circle):   Poor   Moderate   Well
4. Grain roundness (circle):   Angular   Subround   Well-rounded
5. Sediment composition (circle):   Detrital   Biochemical   Chemical
                                    (Siliciclastic) (Bioclastic)
6. Describe how and in what environment (Figure 2) this sediment may have formed.

Sample E

0   10 mm

© Richard M. Busch

1. Grain size range in mm: _____
2. Percent of each Wentworth size class:
   clay _____   silt _____   sand _____   gravel _____
3. Grain sorting (circle):   Poor   Moderate   Well
4. Grain roundness (circle):   Angular   Subround   Well-rounded
5. Sediment composition (circle):   Detrital   Biochemical   Chemical
                                    (Siliciclastic) (Bioclastic)
6. Describe how and in what environment (Figure 2) this sediment may have formed.

Sample F

0   4   8 cm

© Richard M. Busch

1. Grain size range in mm: _____
2. Percent of each Wentworth size class:
   clay _____   silt _____   sand _____   gravel _____
3. Grain sorting (circle):   Poor   Moderate   Well
4. Grain roundness (circle):   Angular   Subround   Well-rounded
5. Sediment composition (circle):   Detrital   Biochemical   Chemical
                                    (Siliciclastic) (Bioclastic)
6. Describe how and in what environment (Figure 2) this sediment may have formed.

ACTIVITY 5 Hand Sample Analysis and Interpretation

Name: _____   **Course/Section:** _____

SEDIMENTARY ROCKS WORKSHEET

Sample Number or Letter	Composition (Figures 2 and 3)	Textural and Other Distinctive Properties (Figures 1 and 3)	Rock Name (Figure 3)	How Did the Rock Form? (See Figures 1, 4–8)
Fig. 9	Detrital (Siliciclastic): • Mostly orange feldspar grains (~85%) • Some quartz (~10%) • Green silty matrix (~5%)	• Mostly (~95%) angular to subangular gravel-sized grains • Poorly sorted (The gravel is mixed with some sand and green silt)	Breccia (Arkose breccia)	Preexisting rock (probably granite) was weathered. Grains were not rounded or sorted much, so they were not transported very far from their source. Grains were mixed with some green silt, deposited, and hardened (compaction?) into rock.

Sample Number or Letter	Composition (Figures 2 and 3)	Textural and Other Distinctive Properties (Figures 1 and 3)	Rock Name (Figure 3)	How Did the Rock Form? (See Figures 1, 4–8)

SEDIMENTARY ROCKS WORKSHEET

SEDIMENTARY ROCKS WORKSHEET

Sample Number or Letter	Composition (Figures 2 and 3)	Textural and Other Distinctive Properties (Figures 1 and 3)	Rock Name (Figure 3)	How Did the Rock Form? (See Figures 1, 4–8)

	Sample Number or Letter	Composition (Figures 2 and 3)	Textural and Other Distinctive Properties (Figures 1 and 3)	Rock Name (Figure 3)	How Did the Rock Form? (See Figures 1, 4–8)
SEDIMENTARY ROCKS WORKSHEET					

ACTIVITY 6 Outcrop Analysis and Interpretation

Name: _____   Course/Section: _____

A. The rock exposed in this Pennsylvania outcrop is calcarenite (fossiliferous limestone). The fossils in the rock are sand-sized fragments of seashells. The rock unit is named the Loyalhanna Member of the Mauch Chunk Formation. It is of Mississippian age (about 340 million years old).

© Richard M. Busch

1. Notice that the strata (sedimentary layers) are not horizontal. Draw arrows on the picture to show the direction(s) that the ocean water moved to deposit the two main parts (lower and upper) of the outcrop. Refer to Figure 10 as needed.

2. What is the name of this kind of stratification (Figure 10)? _____

3. Think about modern marine environments. What do you think caused the water to flow as you indicated in Part A1 to make this kind of stratification?

4. Today, this part of Pennsylvania is the Appalachian Mountains. Describe (as well as you can) what the environment was like here about 340 million years ago when these strata were deposited.

ACTIVITY 7 Using the Present to Imagine the Past—Dogs and Dinosaurs

Name: _____   Course/Section: _____

A. Analyze photographs A and B below.

A. **Modern dog tracks in mud with mudcracks on a tidal flat, St Catherines Island, Georgia (×1)**

B. **Triassic rock (about 215 m.y. old) from southeast Pennsylvania with the track of a three-toed *Coelophysis* dinosaur (×1)**

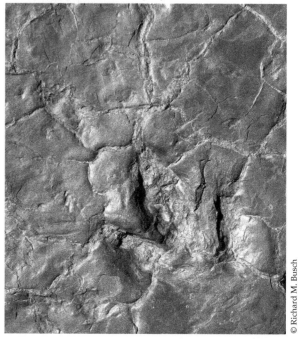

© Richard M. Busch

1. How are the modern environment (Photograph A) and Triassic rock (Photograph B) the same?

2. How are the modern environment (Photograph A) and Triassic rock (Photograph B) different?

3. Describe what the Pennsylvania ecosystem (environment + organisms) was like when *Coelophysis* walked there about 215 million years ago.

138

ACTIVITY 8 Using the Present to Imagine the Past—Cape Cod to Kansas

Name: _____   Course/Section: _____

A. Analyze photographs A and B below of a Kansas rock and the modern-day seafloor near Cape Cod.

A. Pennsylvanian-age rock from Kansas (290 m.y. old)

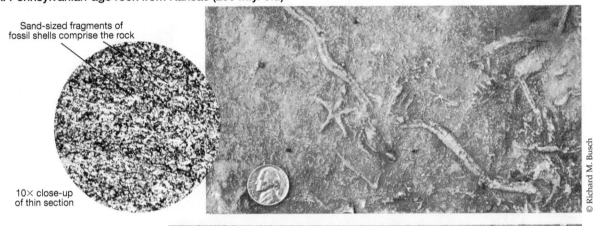

Sand-sized fragments of fossil shells comprise the rock

10× close-up of thin section

© Richard M. Busch

B. Modern sea-floor environment, 40 m (130 ft) deep, near Massachusetts (10 miles north of Cape Cod). Detrital (siliciclastic) sediment:
- 1% gravel
- 90% sand
- 9% mud

0   10 cm

© Richard M. Busch

1. How are the modern environment (Photograph B) and Kansas rock (Photograph A) the same?

2. How are the modern environment (Photograph B) and Kansas rock (Photograph A) different?

3. Today, this part of Kansas is rolling hills and farm fields. Describe what the Kansas ecosystem (environment + organisms) was like when the sediment in this rock sample (Photograph A) was deposited there about 290 million years ago.

ACTIVITY 9 "Reading" Earth History from a Sequence of Strata

Name: _____   Course/Section: _____

A. Permian strata (about 270 million years old) exposed along Interstate Route 70 in northeastern Kansas. Describe the paleoenvironment (pink column), then apply it to infer the record of change (purple column).

OUTCROP	HAND SAMPLE Bedding plane surface	DESCRIPTION OF ROCK UNIT	DESCRIPTION OF PALEOENVIRONMENT REPRESENTED BY THE ROCK UNIT	RECORD OF CHANGE				
				ocean (marine)	muddy bay/estuary	evaporating bay	peat bog or swamp	land
		Tan skeletal limestone with shells of many kinds of marine organisms, bimodal cross-bedding, oscillation ripple marks, animal burrows, flutes, flute casts, and chert.						
		Gray silty mudstone (shale) with animal burrows, fossil clams, fossil plant fragments, and current ripple marks.						
		Red and gray silty mudstone with raindrop impressions, fossil roots, and mudcracks.						
		Gray silty mudstone with abundant gypsum layers and crystals.						
		Tan skeletal limestone with bimodal cross-bedding.						
		Coal.	peat bog or swamp					
	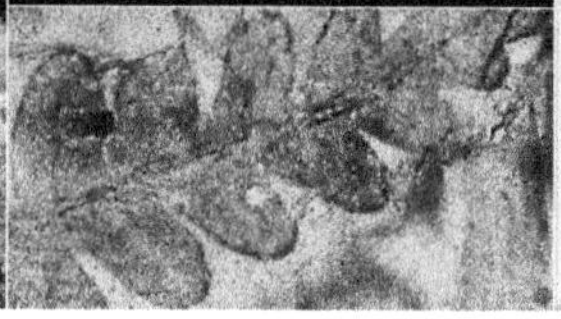	Gray silty mudstone with mudcracks and fossil ferns.	Probably moist muddy land where ferns grew; mudcracks formed in dry periods.					

1 METER

© Richard M. Busch

Metamorphic Rocks, Processes, and Resources

CONTRIBUTING AUTHORS
Harold E. Andrews • *Wellesley College*
James R. Besancon • *Wellesley College*
Margaret D. Thompson • *Wellesley College*

OBJECTIVES AND ACTIVITIES

A. Be able to describe and interpret textural and compositional features of metamorphic rocks.
ACTIVITY 1: Metamorphic Rock Analysis and Interpretation
B. Be able to determine the names, parent rocks (protoliths), and uses of common metamorphic rocks, based on their textures and mineralogical compositions.
ACTIVITY 2: Hand Sample Analysis (Metamorphic Rocks Worksheet)
C. Infer regional geologic history and the relationship of metamorphic facies to plate tectonics using index minerals, pressure-temperature diagrams, and geologic maps.
ACTIVITY 3: Metamorphic Grades and Facies

STUDENT MATERIALS

Pencil, eraser, laboratory notebook, hand magnifying lens (optional), metric ruler, mineral identification materials of your choice, and samples of metamorphic rocks (obtain as directed by your instructor).

INTRODUCTION

The word *metamorphic* is derived from Greek and means "of changed form." **Metamorphic rocks** are rocks changed from one form to another (metamorphosed)

by intense heat, intense pressure, or the action of watery hot fluids (Figures 1, 2, 3). Think of metamorphism as it occurs in your home. *Heat* can be used to metamorphose bread into toast, *pressure* can be used to compact an aluminum can into a flatter and more compact form, and the chemical action of *watery hot fluids* (boiling water, steam) can be used to change raw vegetables into cooked forms. Inside Earth, all of these metamorphic processes are more intense and capable of changing a rock from one form (size, shape, texture, color, and/or mineralogy) to another. Therefore, every metamorphic rock has a **parent rock** (or *protolith*), the rock type that was metamorphosed. Parent rocks can be any of the three main rock types: igneous rock, sedimentary rock, or even metamorphic rock (i.e., metamorphic rock can be metamorphosed again).

Figure 1 illustrates how a regional intrusion of magma (that cooled to form granite) has metamorphosed parent rocks to new metamorphic forms of rock. Mafic and ultramafic igneous rocks were metamorphosed to serpentinite. Sedimentary conglomerate, sandstone, and limestone parent rocks were metamorphosed to *metaconglomerate*, *quartzite*, and *marble*. Shale was metamorphosed to *slate, phyllite, schist,* and *gneiss,* depending on the grade (intensity) of metamorphism from low-grade (slate) to medium-grade (phyllite, schist), to high-grade (gneiss). *Hornfels* formed only in a narrow zone of contact metamorphism next to the intrusion of magma.

Different grades of metamorphism produce characteristic changes in the texture and mineralogy of the

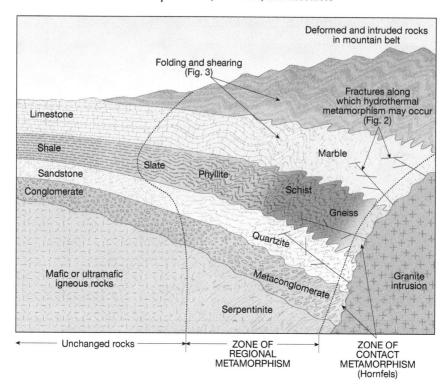

FIGURE 1 Metamorphism of a region by the heat, pressure, and chemical action of watery hot (hydrothermal) fluids associated with a large magma intrusion that cooled to form granite (granite intrusion). Some of the preexisting *parent rocks* are far removed from the intrusion and remain unchanged. Closer to the intrusion, the parent rocks were changed in form within a zone of regional metamorphism. Mafic igneous rocks were metamorphosed to serpentinite. Sedimentary conglomerate, sandstone, and limestone parent rocks were metamorphosed to *metaconglomerate*, *quartzite*, and *marble*. Shale was metamorphosed to *slate*, *phyllite*, *schist*, and *gneiss* depending on the grade (intensity) of metamorphism from low-grade (slate) to medium-grade (phyllite, schist), to high-grade (gneiss).

Notice two scales of metamorphism in the figure. **Contact metamorphism** occurred in narrow zones next to the contact between parent rock and intrusive magma and along fractures in the parent rock that were intruded by hydrothermal fluids. The zone of contact metamorphism next to the intrusive magma was changed to *hornfels* by intense heat and chemical reaction with the magma. Zones of contact metamorphism have widths on the order of millimeters to tens-of-meters. **Regional metamorphism** occurred over a larger region, throughout the mountain belt, and was accompanied by folding and shearing of rock layers.

rock, which you will study below. Some common metamorphic rock-forming minerals include quartz, feldspars, muscovite, biotite, chlorite, garnet, tourmaline, calcite, dolomite, serpentine, talc, kyanite, sillimanite, and amphibole (hornblende). You should familiarize yourself with all of these minerals by reviewing their distinctive properties in the Mineral Database.

PART A: METAMORPHIC PROCESSES AND ROCKS

There are two main scales at which metamorphic processes occur: contact and regional (see Figure 1). **Contact metamorphism** occurs locally, adjacent to igneous intrusions and along fractures that are in contact with watery hot (hydrothermal) fluids. The latter process is called *hydrothermal metamorphism*, and it involves condensation of gases to form liquids, which may precipitate mineral crystals along the fractures such as in Figure 2. Contact metamorphism is caused by conditions of low to moderate pressure, intense heating, and reaction with the metamorphosing magma or hydrothermal fluids over days to thousands of years. The intensity of contact metamorphism is greatest at the contact between parent rock and intrusive magma or hydrothermal fluids. The intensity then decreases rapidly over a short distance from the magma or hydrothermal fluids. Thus, zones of contact metamorphism are narrow, on the order of millimeters to tens-of-meters thick.

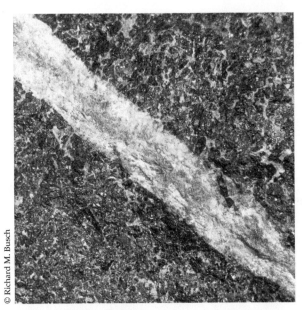

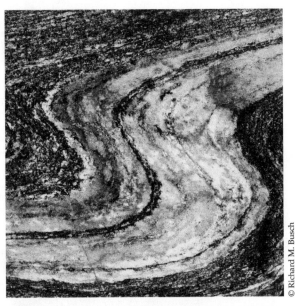

FIGURE 2 Hydrothermal mineral deposits. The dark part of this rock is chromite (chromium ore) that was precipitated from *hydrothermal fluids* (watery hot fluids). The light-colored minerals form a *vein of* zeolites (a group of light-colored hydrous aluminum silicates formed by low-grade metamorphism). The vein formed when directed pressure fractured the chromite deposit, hydrothermal fluids intruded the fracture, and the zeolites precipitated from the hydrothermal fluids as they cooled (making a *healed* fracture and a *vein* of zeolites).

FIGURE 3 Folded and foliated (layered) gneiss. The dark minerals are muscovite, and the white minerals are quartz. Some of the quartz has been stained brown by iron. Regional metamorphism caused this normally rigid and brittle rock to be bent into *folds* without breaking. The flat mica mineral grains have been sheared (smeared) into layers called *foliations*. Metamorphic rocks with a layered appearance or texture are *foliated* metamorphic rocks. Figure 2 is a *nonfoliated* metamorphic rock because it lacks layering.

Regional metamorphism occurs over very large areas (regions), such as deep within the cores of rising mountain ranges (see Figure 1), and generally is accompanied by folding of rock layers (see Figure 3). Regional metamorphism is caused by large igneous intrusions that form and cool over long periods (thousands to tens-of-millions of years), the moderate to extreme pressure and heat associated with deep burial or tectonic movements of rock, and/or the very widespread migration of hot fluids from one region to another along rock fractures and pore spaces.

The distinction between contact and regional metamorphism often is blurred. Contact metamorphism may be caused by small igneous intrusions, or by the local effects of hydrothermal fluids from some distance away that are traveling along fractures or other voids. Regional metamorphism may be caused by large intrusions, tectonism, and/or the action of abundant and widespread hydrothermal fluids associated with large intrusions. One kind of metamorphism replaces another, so that rocks undergo both regional and contact metamorphism. Most major intrusions are preceded by contact metamorphism and followed by regional metamorphism.

The **mineralogical composition** of a metamorphic rock is a description of the kinds and *relative* abundances of mineral crystals that make up the rock. Information about the relative abundances of the minerals is important for constructing a complete name for the rock and understanding metamorphic changes that formed the mineralogy of the rock. Mineralogical composition of a parent rock may change during metamorphism as a result of changing pressure, changing temperature, and/or the chemical action of hydrothermal fluids. Mineralogical composition may also stay the same, whereas the texture of the rock changes. **Recrystallization** is a process whereby small crystals of one mineral will slowly convert to fewer, larger crystals of the same mineral, without melting of the rock. For example, microscopic calcite crystals in seashells that make up biochemical limestone can recrystallize to form a mass of visible calcite crystals in metamorphic marble.

Neomorphism is one way that mineralogical composition actually changes during metamorphism. In this process, minerals not only recrystallize but also form different minerals from the same chemical elements. For example, shales consisting mainly of clay minerals, quartz grains, and feldspar grains may change to a metamorphic rock consisting mainly of muscovite and garnet.

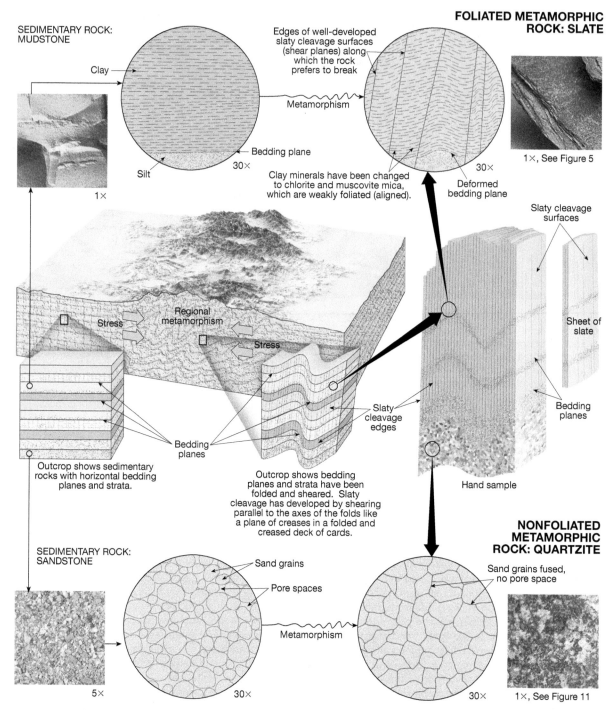

FOLIATED METAMORPHIC ROCK: SLATE

SEDIMENTARY ROCK: MUDSTONE

Clay

Edges of well-developed slaty cleavage surfaces (shear planes) along which the rock prefers to break

Metamorphism

Bedding plane

30×

Silt

1×

1×, See Figure 5

Clay minerals have been changed to chlorite and muscovite mica, which are weakly foliated (aligned).

Deformed bedding plane

Slaty cleavage surfaces

Sheet of slate

Regional metamorphism

Stress

Stress

Bedding planes

Slaty cleavage edges

Bedding planes

Outcrop shows sedimentary rocks with horizontal bedding planes and strata.

Outcrop shows bedding planes and strata have been folded and sheared. Slaty cleavage has developed by shearing parallel to the axes of the folds like a plane of creases in a folded and creased deck of cards.

Hand sample

SEDIMENTARY ROCK: SANDSTONE

Sand grains

Pore spaces

Metamorphism

5×

30×

NONFOLIATED METAMORPHIC ROCK: QUARTZITE

Sand grains fused, no pore space

30×

1×, See Figure 11

FIGURE 4 Foliated and nonfoliated metamorphic rock formed by regional metamorphism. The mudstone and sandstone (sedimentary rocks) occur in layers separated by relatively flat, horizontal, bedding planes. Regional metamorphism compresses the sedimentary rock layers and bedding planes until they are folded (bent) and sheared across the layering into flat, parallel sheets of slate that slide past one another. The flat parallel surfaces between the layers of slate are called *slaty cleavage* surfaces (because they resemble cleavage in minerals).

Photomicrograph illustrations (in circles) show microscopic effects of the metamorphism. The layers of mudstone are metamorphosed to *slate* (Figure 5), in which the chlorite and muscovite mineral crystals are also *foliated* (aligned and layered subparallel to the shear planes). The sandstone (comprised of quartz sand grains and pore spaces) is metamorphosed to the harder, more dense, nonfoliated metamorphic rock *quartzite*, which consists of fused quartz sand grains. Notice that the shear planes are not obvious in the quartzite, because the sand grains roll and move about easily as the rock deforms.

The most significant mineralogical changes occur during **metasomatism.** In this process, chemicals are added or lost. For example, anthracite coal is a relatively pure aggregate of carbon that forms when the volatile chemicals like nitrogen, oxygen, and methane are driven off from peat or bituminous coal by pressure and heating. Hornfels sometimes has a spotted appearance caused by the partial decomposition of just some of its minerals. In still other cases, one mineral may decompose (leaving only cavities or molds where its crystals formerly existed) and be simultaneously replaced by a new mineral of slightly or wholly different composition.

Textures of Metamorphic Rocks

Texture of a metamorphic rock is a description of its constituent parts and their sizes, shapes, and arrangements. Two main groups of metamorphic rocks are distinguished on the basis of their characteristic textures, *foliated* and *nonfoliated.*

Foliated metamorphic rocks (foliated textures) exhibit **foliations**—*layering* and parallel alignment of platy (flat) mineral crystals, such as micas. All metamorphic rocks with a layered appearance are foliated. This usually forms as a result of pressure (shearing and smearing of crystals) and recrystallization. Crystals of minerals such as tourmaline, hornblende, and kyanite can also be foliated because their crystalline growth occurred during metamorphism and had a preferred orientation in relation to the directed

pressure. Specific kinds of foliated textures are described below:

- **Slaty rock cleavage**—*a very flat foliation* (resembling mineral cleavage) developed along flat, parallel, closely spaced shear planes (microscopic faults) in tightly folded clay- or mica-rich rocks (Figure 4). Rocks with excellent slaty cleavage are called *slate* (Figure 5), which is used to make roofing shingles and classroom blackboards. The flat surface of a blackboard or sheet of roofing slate is a slaty cleavage surface.

- **Phyllite texture**—*a wavy and/or wrinkled foliation* of fine-grained *platy minerals* (mainly muscovite or chlorite crystals) that gives the rock a satiny or metallic luster. Rocks with phyllite texture are called *phyllite* (Figure 6). The phyllite texture is normally developed oblique or perpendicular to a weak slaty cleavage, and it is a product of intermediate-grade metamorphism.

- **Schistosity**—*a scaly glittery layering* of visible (medium- to coarse-grained) *platy minerals* (mainly micas and chlorite) *and/or linear alignment of long prismatic crystals* (tourmaline, hornblende, kyanite). Rocks with schistosity break along scaly, glittery foliations and are called *schist* (Figure 7). Schists are a product of intermediate-to-high grades of metamorphism.

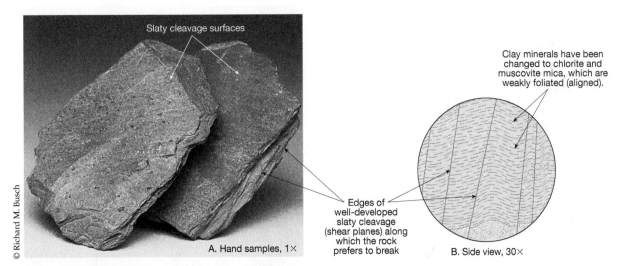

FIGURE 5 Slate—a foliated metamorphic rock with dull luster, excellent slaty cleavage, and no visible grains. Slate forms from low-grade metamorphism of mudstone (shale, claystone). Clay minerals of the mudstone parent rock change to foliated chlorite and muscovite mineral crystals. Slate splits into hard, flat sheets (usually less than 1 cm thick) along its well-developed *slaty cleavage* (Figure 4). It is used to make roofing shingles and classroom blackboards.

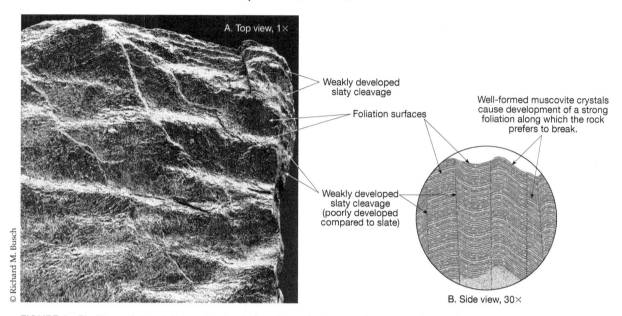

FIGURE 6 Phyllite—a foliated, fine-grained metamorphic rock, with a satiny, green, silver, or brassy metallic luster and a wavy foliation with a wrinkled appearance (*phyllite texture*). Phyllite forms from low-grade metamorphism of mudstone (shale, claystone), slate, or other rocks rich in clay, chlorite, or mica. When the very fine-grained mineral crystals of clay, chlorite, or muscovite in dull mudstone or slate are metamorphosed to form the phyllite, they become recrystallized to larger sizes and are aligned into a wavy and/or wrinkled foliation (*phyllite texture*) that is satiny or metallic. This is the wavy foliation along which phyllite breaks. Slaty cleavage may be poorly developed. It is not as obvious as the wavy and/or wrinkled foliation surfaces. The phyllite grade of metamorphism is between the low grade that produces slate (Figure 5) and the intermediate grade that produces schist (Figure 7).

FIGURE 7 Schist—a medium- to coarse-grained, scaly (like fish scales), foliated metamorphic rock formed by intermediate-grade metamorphism of mudstone, shale, slate, phyllite, or other rocks rich in clay, chlorite, or mica. Schist forms when clay, chlorite, and mica mineral crystals are foliated as they recrystallize to larger, more visible crystals of chlorite, muscovite, or biotite. This gives schist its scaly foliated appearance called *schistosity*. Slaty cleavage or *crenulations* (sets of tiny folds) may be present, but schist breaks along its scaly, glittery schistosity. It often contains porphyroblasts of garnet, kyanite, sillimanite, or tourmaline mineral crystals. The schist grade of metamorphism is intermediate between the lower grade that produces phyllite (Figure 6) and the higher grade that produces gneiss (Figures 3, 8). Also see chlorite schist in Figure 14.

Top view of foliation surfaces, 1×

- **Gneissic banding**—*alternating layers or lenses of light and dark medium- to coarse-grained minerals.* Rock with gneissic banding is called *gneiss* (Figures 3 and 8). Ferromagnesian minerals usually form the dark bands. Quartz or feldspars usually form the light bands. Most gneisses form by high-grade metamorphism (including recrystallization) of clay- or mica-rich rocks such as shale (see Figure 1), but they can also form by metamorphism of igneous rocks such as granite and diorite.

Nonfoliated metamorphic rocks have no obvious layering (i.e., no foliations), although they may exhibit stretched fossils or long, prismatic crystals (tourmaline, amphibole) that have grown parallel to the pressure field. Nonfoliated metamorphic rocks are mainly characterized by the following textures:

- **Crystalline texture (nonfoliated)**—a medium- to coarse-grained aggregate of intergrown, usually equal-sized (equigranular), visible crystals. *Marble* is a nonfoliated metamorphic rock that typically exhibits an equigranular crystalline texture (Figure 9).

- **Microcrystalline texture**—a fine-grained aggregate of intergrown microscopic crystals (as in a sugar

FIGURE 8 Gneiss—a medium- to coarse-grained metamorphic rock with *gneissic banding* (alternating layers or lenses of light and dark minerals). Generally, light-colored layers are rich in quartz or feldspars and alternate with dark layers rich in biotite mica, hornblende, or tourmaline. Most gneisses form by high-grade metamorphism (including recrystallization) of clay or mica-rich rocks such as shale (Figure 1), mudstone, slate, phyllite, or schist. However, they can also form by metamorphism of igneous rocks such as granite and diorite. The compositional name of the rock in this picture is biotite quartz gneiss.

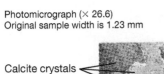

Photomicrograph (× 26.6)
Original sample width is 1.23 mm

Calcite crystals

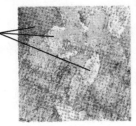

Enlarged 5×

FIGURE 9 Marble—a fine- to coarse-grained, nonfoliated metamorphic rock with a crystalline texture formed by tightly interlocking grains of calcite or dolomite. Marble forms by intermediate- to high-grade metamorphism of limestone or dolostone. Marble is a dense aggregate of nearly equal-sized crystals (see photograph), in contrast to the porous texture and/or odd-sized grains of its parent rock.

cube). *Hornfels* (Figure 10) is a nonfoliated metamorphic rock that has a microcrystalline texture.

- **Sandy texture**—a medium- to coarse-grained aggregate of fused, sand-sized grains that resembles sandstone. *Quartzite* is a nonfoliated metamorphic rock with a sandy texture (Figure 11) remaining from its sandstone parent rock, but the sand grains cannot be rubbed free of the rock because they are fused together.

- **Glassy texture**—a homogeneous texture with no visible grains or other structures and breaks along glossy surfaces; said of materials that resemble glass, such as *anthracite coal* (Figure 12).

Besides the main features that distinguish foliated and nonfoliated metamorphic rocks, there are some features that can occur in any metamorphic rock. They include:

- **Stretched or sheared grains**—deformed pebbles, fossils, or mineral crystals that have been stretched out (Figure 13), shortened, or sheared.

- **Porphyroblastic texture**—an arrangement of large crystals, called *porphyroblasts*, set in a finer-grained

FIGURE 10 Hornfels—a fine-grained, nonfoliated metamorphic rock having a dull luster and a microcrystalline texture (that may appear smooth or sugary). It is usually very hard and dark in color, but it sometimes has a spotted appearance caused by patchy chemical reactions with the metamorphosing magma or hydrothermal fluid. Hornfels forms by contact metamorphism of any rock type.

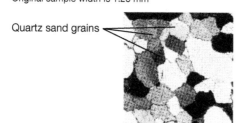

Photomicrograph (× 26.6)
Original sample width is 1.23 mm

Quartz sand grains

FIGURE 11 Quartzite—a medium- to coarse-grained, nonfoliated metamorphic rock consisting chiefly of fused quartz grains that give the rock its *sandy texture*. Compare the fused quartz grains of this quartzite sample (see photomicrograph) with the porous sedimentary fabric of quartz sandstones. Sand grains can often be rubbed from the edges of a sandstone sample, but never from quartzite (because the grains are fused together).

×1

© Richard M. Busch

FIGURE 12 Anthracite coal—a fine-grained, nonfoliated metamorphic rock, also known as *hard coal* (because it cannot easily be broken apart like its parent rock, bituminous or soft coal). Anthracite has a smooth, homogeneous, glassy texture and breaks along glossy, curved (conchoidal) fractures. It is formed by low- to intermediate-grade metamorphism of bituminous coal, lignite, or peat.

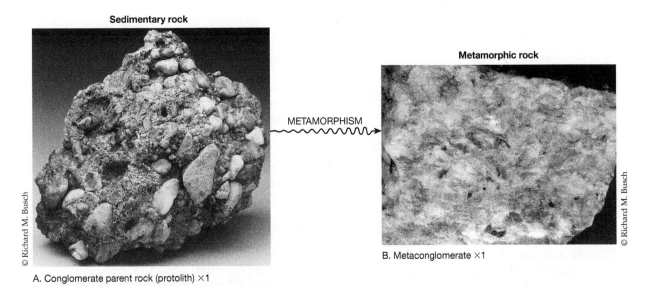

Sedimentary rock

Metamorphic rock

METAMORPHISM

© Richard M. Busch

B. Metaconglomerate ×1

© Richard M. Busch

A. Conglomerate parent rock (protolith) ×1

FIGURE 13 Metaconglomerate—metamorphosed conglomerate. **A.** Conglomerate is a detrital (clastic) sedimentary rock consisting chiefly (>50%) of rounded, odd-sized grains of gravel (grains larger than 2 mm, coarser than sand). Conglomerate breaks around the grains (pebbles, granules, sand grains) that stand out in this image. **B.** Metaconglomerate forms when conglomerate is heated (and softened) under directed pressure or tension. The stout, rounded grains of conglomerate are compressed and fused together to form a denser mass of metaconglomerate. Metaconglomerate breaks through the fused grains rather than around them.

Chlorite

Pyrite
porphyroblast
(brassy cube)

×1

© Richard M. Busch

FIGURE 14 Porphyroblastic texture—large, visible crystals of one mineral occur in a fine-grained groundmass of one or more other minerals. This medium-grained chlorite schist contains porphyroblasts of pyrite (brassy metallic cubes) in a groundmass of chlorite. The rock can be called porphyroblastic chlorite schist or pyrite chlorite schist.

groundmass (Figure 14). It is analogous to porphyritic texture in igneous rocks.

- **Hydrothermal veins**—fractures "healed" (filled) by minerals that precipitated from hydrothermal fluids (see Figure 2).

- **Folds**—bends in rock layers that were initially flat, like a folded stack of paper (see Figure 3).

- **Lineations**—lines on rocks at the edges of foliations, shear planes, slaty cleavage, folds, or aligned crystals.

Classification of Metamorphic Rocks

Metamorphic rocks are mainly classified according to their texture and mineralogical composition. This information is valuable for naming the rock and

determining how it formed from a parent rock (protolith). It is also useful for inferring how the metamorphic rock could be used as a commodity for domestic or industrial purposes. You can analyze and classify metamorphic rocks with the aid of Figure 15, which also provides information about parent rocks and how the metamorphic rocks are commonly used.

ACTIVITY 1

Metamorphic Rock Analysis and Interpretation

Conduct this introductory activity on the analysis and interpretation of metamorphic rocks before proceeding on to hand sample analysis.

METAMORPHIC ROCK ANALYSIS AND CLASSIFICATION

STEP 1: What are the rock's textural features?			STEP 2: What are the rock's mineralogical composition and/or other distinctive features?	STEP 3: Metamorphic rock name	STEP 4: What was the parent rock?	STEP 5: What is the rock used for?
FOLIATED	Fine-grained or no visible grains	Flat slaty cleavage is well developed	Dull luster; breaks into hard flat sheets along the slaty cleavage	SLATE[1]	Mudstone or shale	Roofing slate, table tops, floor tile, and blackboards
		Phyllite texture well developed more than slaty cleavage	Breaks along wrinkled or wavy foliation surfaces with shiny metallic luster	PHYLLITE[1]	Mudstone, shale, or slate	Construction stone, decorative stone, sources of gemstones
	Medium- to coarse-grained	Schistosity: foliation formed by alignment of visible crystals; rock breaks along scaly foliation surfaces; crystalline texture	Mostly blue or violet needle-like crystals (blue amphibole)	Blueschist	Mudstone, shale, slate, or phyllite	
			Mostly visible sparkling crystals of chlorite +/– actinolite (green amphibole)	Greenschist		
			Mostly visible sparkling crystals of muscovite	Muscovite schist		
			Mostly visible sparkling crystals of biotite	Biotite schist		
		Gneissic banding: minerals segregated into alternating layers gives the rock a banded texture in side view; crystalline texture	Visible crystals of two or more minerals in alternating light and dark foliated layers	GNEISS[1]	Mudstone, shale, slate, phyllite, schist, granite, or diorite	Construction stone, decorative stone, sources of gemstones
FOLIATED OR NONFOLIATED		Medium- to coarse-grained crystalline texture	Mostly visible glossy black amphibole (hornblende) in blade-like crystals	AMPHIBOLITE	Basalt, gabbro, or ultramafic igneous rocks	Construction stone
		Crystalline texture	Green pyroxene + red garnet	ECLOGITE	Basalt, gabbro	Titanium ore
NONFOLIATED	Fine-grained or no visible grains	Glassy texture; slaty cleavage may barely be visible	Black glossy rock that breaks along uneven or conchoidal fractures (Figure 7.12)	ANTHRACITE COAL	Peat, lignite, bituminous coal	Highest grade coal for clean burning fossil fuel
		Microcrystalline texture	Usually a dull dark color; very hard	HORNFELS	Any rock type	
		Microcrystalline texture or no visible grains. May have fibrous asbestos form	Serpentine; dull or glossy; color usually shades of green	SERPENTINITE	Basalt, gabbro, or ultramafic igneous rocks	Decorative stone
		Microcrystalline or no visible grains	Talc; can be scratched with your fingernail; shades of green, gray, brown, white	SOAPSTONE	Basalt, gabbro, or ultramafic igneous rocks	Art carvings, electrical insulators, talcum powder
	Fine- to coarse-grained	Sandy texture	Quartz sand grains fused together; grains will not rub off like sandstone; usually light colored	QUARTZITE[1]	Sandstone	Construction stone, decorative stone
		Microcrystalline (resembling a sugar cube) or medium to coarse crystalline texture	Calcite (or dolomite) crystals of nearly equal size and tightly fused together; calcite effervesces in dilute HCl; dolomite effervesces only if powdered	MARBLE[1]	Limestone	Art carvings, construction stone, decorative stone, source of lime for agriculture
		Conglomeratic texture, but breaks across grains	Pebbles may be stretched or cut by rock cleavage	META-CONGLOMERATE	Conglomerate	Construction stone, decorative stone

SCHIST[1] — INCREASING METAMORPHIC GRADE

[1]Modify rock name by adding names of minerals in order of increasing abundance. For example, garnet muscovite schist is a muscovite schist with a small amount of garnet.

FIGURE 15 Five-step chart for metamorphic rock analysis and classification. See text for description of steps (next page).

PART B: DESCRIPTION AND INTERPRETATION OF METAMORPHIC ROCK SAMPLES

The complete classification of a metamorphic rock requires knowledge of its composition, texture(s), and other distinctive properties that you learned in Part A.

ACTIVITY 2

Hand Sample Analysis (Metamorphic Rocks Worksheet)

Obtain a set of metamorphic rocks (as directed by your instructor) and analyze the rocks one at a time. For each sample, complete a row on the Metamorphic Rocks Worksheet using the steps below.

Follow these steps to analyze and classify a metamorphic rock:

Step 1: *Determine and record the rock's textural features.* Determine and record if the rock is foliated or nonfoliated (see Figure 4), and what other specific kinds of textural features are present. Use this information to work from left to right across the three columns of Step 1 in Figure 15, and match the rock texture to one of the specific categories there.

Step 2: *Determine and record the rock's mineralogical composition and/or other distinctive features.* List the minerals in order of increasing abundance, and distinguish between porphyroblasts and mineralogy of the groundmass making up most of the rock. Use this information and any other distinctive features to match the rock to one of the categories in Step 2 of Figure 15.

Step 3: Recall how you categorized the rock in Steps 1 and 2. Use this information to work from left to right across Figure 15 and determine the name of the rock. You can also modify the rock name by adding the names of minerals present in the rock in order of their increasing abundance. If the rock is porphyroblastic, then you can add this to the name as well (e.g., Figure 14).

Step 4: After you have determined the metamorphic rock name in Step 3, look to the right along the same row of Figure 15 and find the name of a parent rock (protolith) for that kind of metamorphic rock.

Step 5: After you have determined the parent rock in Step 4, look to the right along the same row of Figure 15 and find out what the rock is commonly used for.

Example:

Study the metamorphic rock in Figure 16. Step 1— The rock has no obvious layering, so it is nonfoliated. It also has a microcrystalline form with some asbestos. Step 2—The rock is made of the mineral serpentine and is many shades of green color. Step 3—By moving from left to right across the chart in Figure 15, notice that the rock name is serpentinite. Step 4—The parent rock for serpentinite was basalt, gabbro, or an ultramafic igneous rock. Step 5—Serpentinite is commonly used as a green decorative stone.

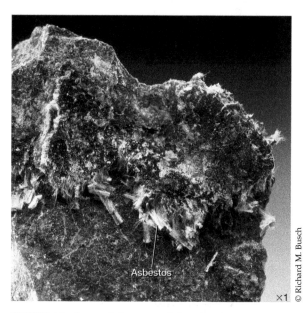

FIGURE 16 Serpentinite—a nonfoliated metamorphic rock made mostly of serpentine, which gives the rock its green color. Serpentinite forms by the low- to intermediate-grade metamorphism of mafic or ultramafic igneous rocks (basalt, gabbro, peridotite). Serpentinite often contains minor amounts of talc, magnetite, and chlorite. This sample contains some fibrous serpentine called *asbestos*.

PART C: USING INDEX MINERALS TO INTERPRET METAMORPHIC GRADES AND FACIES

The changes in metamorphic grade that are indicated by textural changes, like schist to gneiss, are also accompanied by mineralogical changes. Minerals that indicate specific grades of metamorphism are called index minerals. Assemblages of index minerals make up metamorphic facies, which can be interpreted using pressure temperature diagrams.

ACTIVITY 3

Metamorphic Grades and Facies

Conduct this activity to infer regional geologic history and the relationship of metamorphic facies to plate tectonics using index minerals, pressure-temperature diagrams, and geologic maps.

ACTIVITY 1 Metamorphic Rock Analysis and Interpretation

Name: _____   Course/Section: _____

A. Analyze these samples of sedimentary limestone and metamorphic marble.

Limestone ×1

Marble ×1

© Richard M. Busch

1. These rocks are both composed of the same mineral. What is it? _____
What test could you perform on the rocks to be sure?

2. How is the texture of these two rocks different?

B. The sequence of increasing grades of metamorphism of a mudstone (shale, claystone, or siltstone) parent rock (protolith) is: slate (lowest grade), phyllite, schist, gneiss (highest grade).

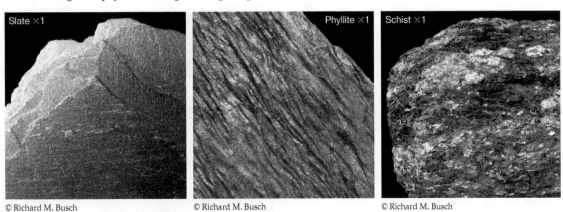

Slate ×1

Phyllite ×1

Schist ×1

© Richard M. Busch   © Richard M. Busch   © Richard M. Busch

1. Describe the change in grain size from slate to schist.

2. How does the texture of phyllite differ from that of schist?

3. Why do you think that the micas (flat minerals) in these rocks are all parallel or subparallel to one another?

C. Analyze the rock sample in Figure 3. The parent rock for this metamorphic rock had flat layers that were folded during metamorphism. Describe a process that could account for how this rigid gneiss was folded without breaking during regional metamorphism. (*Hint*: How could you bend a brittle candlestick without breaking it?)

D. Analyze this metamorphic rock sample using the classification chart in Figure 15.

    1. Is this rock foliated or nonfoliated?

    2. Notice that the rock consists mostly of muscovite but also contains scattered garnet crystals. What is this name for this kind of texture?

    3. What is the name of this metamorphic rock?

    4. What was the likely parent rock (protolith)?

E. Analyze this metamorphic rock sample using the classification chart in Figure 15.

    1. Is this rock foliated or nonfoliated?

    2. What is the name of this metamorphic rock?

    3. What was the likely parent rock (protolith)?

Name: _____   Course/Section: _____

ACTIVITY 2 Hand Sample Analysis (Metamorphic Rocks Worksheet)

METAMORPHIC ROCKS WORKSHEET

Sample Letter or Number	Texture(s) (Figures 4, 15—Step 1)	Mineral Composition and Other Distinctive Properties (Figure 15, Step 2)	Rock Name (Figure 15, Step 3)	Parent Rock (Figure 15, Step 4)	Uses (Figure 15, Step 5)
	☐ foliated ☐ nonfoliated				
	☐ foliated ☐ nonfoliated				
	☐ foliated ☐ nonfoliated				
	☐ foliated ☐ nonfoliated				
	☐ foliated ☐ nonfoliated				

Name: _____   Course/Section: _____

	Texture(s) (Figures 4, 15—Step 1)	Mineral Composition and Other Distinctive Properties (Figure 15, Step 2)	Rock Name (Figure 15, Step 3)	Parent Rock (Figure 15, Step 4)	Uses (Figure 15, Step 5)
	☐ foliated ☐ nonfoliated				
	☐ foliated ☐ nonfoliated				
	☐ foliated ☐ nonfoliated				
	☐ foliated ☐ nonfoliated				
	☐ foliated ☐ nonfoliated				

METAMORPHIC ROCKS WORKSHEET

Sample Letter or Number

Metamorphic Rocks, Processes, and Resources

Name: _____   Course/Section: _____

ACTIVITY 2 Hand Sample Analysis (Metamorphic Rocks Worksheet) (continued)

METAMORPHIC ROCKS WORKSHEET

Sample Letter or Number	Texture(s) (Figures 4, 15—Step 1)	Mineral Composition and Other Distinctive Properties (Figure 15, Step 2)	Rock Name (Figure 15, Step 3)	Parent Rock (Figure 15, Step 4)	Uses (Figure 15, Step 5)
	☐ foliated ☐ nonfoliated				
	☐ foliated ☐ nonfoliated				
	☐ foliated ☐ nonfoliated				
	☐ foliated ☐ nonfoliated				
	☐ foliated ☐ nonfoliated				

Name: _____   Course/Section: _____

METAMORPHIC ROCKS WORKSHEET

Sample Letter or Number	Texture(s) (Figures 4, 15—Step 1)	Mineral Composition and Other Distinctive Properties (Figure 15, Step 2)	Rock Name (Figure 15, Step 3)	Parent Rock (Figure 15, Step 4)	Uses (Figure 15, Step 5)
	☐ foliated ☐ nonfoliated				
	☐ foliated ☐ nonfoliated				
	☐ foliated ☐ nonfoliated				
	☐ foliated ☐ nonfoliated				
	☐ foliated ☐ nonfoliated				

ACTIVITY 3 Metamorphic Grades and Facies

Name: _____   Course/Section: _____

A. How much a parent rock (protolith) is metamorphosed is called its metamorphic **grade** and varies from low grade (low temperature and pressure) to high grade (high temperature and pressure). British geologist George Barrow, mapped rocks in the Scottish Highlands that were metamorphosed by granitic igneous intrusions. He discovered that as he walked away from the granitic intrusive igneous rock, there was a sequence of mineral zones from the high grade to the low grade of metamorphism. He defined the following sequence of **index minerals**, which represent degrees of metamorphism along a gradient from low grade to high grade:

Chlorite (lowest grade), biotite, garnet, staurolite, kyanite, sillimanite (highest grade)

1. Boundaries between the index mineral zones of metamorphism are called isograds and represent lines/surfaces of equal metamorphic grade. In the geologic map below, color in the zone of maximum metamorphic grade.

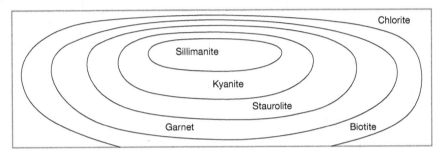

B. Most metamorphism is caused by increases of both temperature and pressure. Geologists represent these relationships on pressure-temperature (P-T) diagrams showing the stability of different index minerals. On this diagram andalusite, kyanite, and sillimanite are *polymorphs*, minerals that have the same chemical composition but different crystalline structure and physical properties that can be used to distinguish them. Note that any two of these minerals can occur together only along lines, and that the three minerals can only occur together at one specific point in temperature and pressure, 500°C and 4 kilobars, which normally occurs about 15 km below Earth's surface.

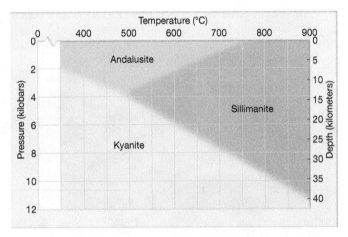

1. Study the mineral zones and isograds on the two maps below. Which region was metamorphosed at higher pressure, and how can you tell?

2. What was the minimum temperature at which the rocks in Map B were metamorphosed? _____

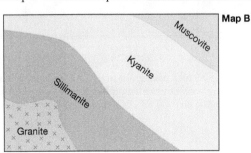

C. Finnish geologist, Pentti Eskola, first recognized in 1921 that basalt volcanic rock could be metamorphosed to distinctly different **metamorphic facies** (unique assemblages of several minerals) under changing conditions of temperature and pressure (depth).

- Amphibolite facies (low pressure, high temperature): black hornblende amphibole, sillimanite
- Greenschist facies (low pressure, low temperature): green actinolite amphibole and chlorite
- Eclogite facies (high pressure, high temperature): red garnet, green pyroxene
- Blueschist facies (high pressure, low temperature): blue amphibole (glaucophane, riebeckite)

1. Write the names of these metamorphic facies where they would occur in this pressure-temperature diagram.

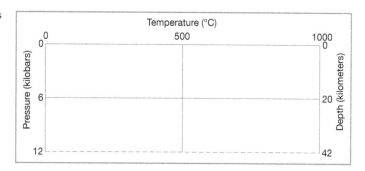

2. At the time that Pentti Eskola discovered these metamorphic facies, the Plate Tectonics Theory had not yet been developed. Geologists now realize that volcanic arcs develop at convergent plate boundaries where the oceanic edge of one plate subducts beneath the continental edge of another plate. Notice (below) how the geothermal gradient (rate of change in temperature with depth) varies relative to the subduction zone and the volcanic arc. Place letters in the white spaces on this illustration to show where Eskola's facies should occur: A = Amphibolite, G = Greenschist, E = Eclogite, B = Blueschist.

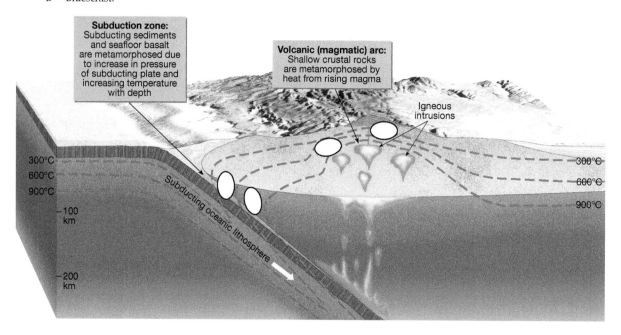

3. Reexamine the map of isograds in Part A1, and notice that the pattern of isograds is not symmetrical. Circle the region on that map where the metamorphic gradient was the steepest (increased the most over the shortest distance). Based on the illustration above (Part 2B), explain one reason that could account for this.

160

Dating of Rocks, Fossils, and Geologic Events

CONTRIBUTING AUTHORS

Jonathan Bushee • *Northern Kentucky University*

John K. Osmond • *Florida State University*

Raman J. Singh • *Northern Kentucky University*

OBJECTIVES AND ACTIVITIES

A. Apply principles of relative age dating to analyze and interpret sequences of events in geologic cross sections

ACTIVITY 1: Sequence of Events in Geologic Cross Sections

B. Use index fossils to determine the relative ages (eras, periods) of rock bodies and infer some of Earth's history.

ACTIVITY 2: Use Index Fossils to Date Rocks and Events

C. Learn and be able to apply techniques for absolute age dating of Earth materials and events.

ACTIVITY 3: Absolute Dating of Rocks and Fossils

D. Be able to apply relative and absolute dating techniques to analyze outcrops and infer their geologic history.

ACTIVITY 4: Infer Geologic History from a New Mexico Outcrop

ACTIVITY 5: Infer Geologic History from a Pennsylvania Outcrop

ACTIVITY 6: CSI (Canyon Scene Investigation) Arizona

E. Be able to construct and interpret a geologic cross section using well data.

ACTIVITY 7: Subsurface Geology Inferred from Well Data

STUDENT MATERIALS

Pencil, eraser, laboratory notebook, calculator, colored pencils, plus a ruler and protractor.

INTRODUCTION

If you could dig a hole deep into Earth's crust, you would encounter the **geologic record,** layers of rock stacked one atop the other like pages in a book. As each new layer of sediment or rock forms today, it covers the older layers of the geologic record beneath it and becomes the youngest layer of the geologic record. Thus, rock layers form a *sequence* from oldest at the bottom to youngest at the top. They also have different colors, textures, chemical compositions, and **fossils** (any evidence of ancient life) depending on the environmental conditions under which they were formed. Geologists have studied sequences of rock layers wherever they are exposed in mines, quarries, river beds, road cuts, wells, and mountain sides throughout the world. They have also *correlated* the layers (traced them from one place to another) across regions and continents. Thus, the geologic record of rock layers is essentially a stack of stone pages in a gi-ant natural book of Earth history. And like the pages in any old book, the rock layers have been folded, fractured (cracked), torn (faulted), and even removed by geologic events.

Geologists tell time based on relative and absolute dating techniques. **Relative age dating** is the process

From Laboratory 8 of *Laboratory Manual in Physical Geology*, Ninth Edition, American Geological Institute, National Association of Geoscience Teachers, Richard M. Busch, Dennis Tasa. Copyright © 2011 by Pearson Education, Inc. Published by Pearson Prentice Hall. All rights reserved.

of determining when something formed or happened in relation to other events. For example, if you have a younger brother and an older sister, then you could describe your relative age by saying that you are younger than your sister and older than your brother. **Absolute age dating** is the process of determining when something formed or happened in exact units of time such as days, months, or years. Using the example above, you could describe your absolute age just by saying how old you are in years.

Geologists "read" and infer Earth history from rocky outcrops and geologic cross sections by observing rock layers, recognizing geologic structures, and evaluating age relationships among the layers and structures. The so-called *geologic time scale* is a chart of named intervals of the geologic record and their ages in both relative and absolute time. It has taken thousands of geoscientists, from all parts of the world, more than a century to construct the present form of the geologic time scale.

Just as authors organize books according to sections, chapters, and pages, geologists have subdivided the rock layers of the geologic record into named eonothems (the largest units), erathems, systems, series, stages, and zones of rock on the basis of fossils, minerals, and other historical features they contained. These physical divisions of rock also represent specific intervals of geologic time. An *eonothem* of rock represents an eon of time, an *erathem* of rock represents an era of time, a *system* of rock represents a period of time, and so on in the table below.

ROCK UNITS (Division of the Geologic Record)	CORRESPONDING GEOLOGIC TIME UNITS
Eonothem (largest)	Eon of time (longest unit)
Erathem	Era of time
System	Period of time
Series	Epoch of time
Stage	Age of time
Zone	Chron of time

PART A: DETERMINING RELATIVE AGES OF ROCKS BASED ON THEIR PHYSICAL RELATIONSHIPS

A geologist's initial challenge in the field is to subdivide the local sequence of sediments and bodies of rock into mappable units that can be correlated from one site to the next. Subdivision is based on color, texture, rock type, or other physical features of the rocks, and the mappable units are called **formations.** Formations can be subdivided into

members, or even individual strata. Surfaces between any of these kinds of units are **contacts.**

Geologists use six basic laws for determining relative age relationships among bodies of rock based on their physical relationships. They are:

- **Law of Original Horizontality**—*Sedimentary layers* (**strata**) *and lava flows were originally deposited as relatively horizontal sheets, like a layer cake. If they are no longer horizontal or flat, it is because they have been displaced by subsequent movements of* Earth's crust.

- **Law of Lateral Continuity**—*Lava flows and strata extend laterally in all directions until they thin to nothing (pinch out) or reach the edge of their basin of deposition.*

- **Law of Superposition**—*In an undisturbed sequence of strata or lava flows, the oldest layer is at the bottom of the sequence and the youngest is at the top.*

- **Law of Inclusions**—*Any piece of rock (clast) that has become included in another rock or body of sediment must be older than the rock or sediment into which it has been incorporated.* Such a clast (usually a rock fragment, crystal, or fossil) is called an **inclusion.** The surrounding body of rock is called the **matrix** (or groundmass). Thus, an inclusion is older than its surrounding matrix.

- **Law of Cross Cutting**—*Any feature that cuts across a rock or body of sediment must be younger than the rock or sediment that it cuts across.* Such cross cutting features include fractures (cracks in rock), faults (fractures along which movement has occurred), or masses of magma (*igneous intrusions*) that cut across preexisting rocks before they cooled. When a body of magma intrudes preexisting rocks, a narrow *zone of contact metamorphism* usually forms in the preexisting rocks adjacent to the intrusion.

- **Law of Unconformities**—*Surfaces called unconformities represent gaps in the geologic record that formed wherever layers were not deposited for a time or else layers were removed by erosion.* Most contacts between adjacent strata or formations are conformities, meaning that rocks on both sides of them formed at about the same time. An unconformity is a rock surface that represents a gap in the geologic record. It is like the place where pages are missing from a book. An unconformity can be a buried surface where there was a pause in sedimentation, a time between two lava flows, or a surface that was eroded before more sediment was deposited on top of it.

There are three kinds of unconformities (Figure 1). A **disconformity** is an unconformity between *parallel* strata or lava flows. Most disconformities are very irregular surfaces, and pieces of the underlying rock

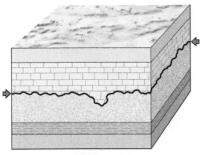

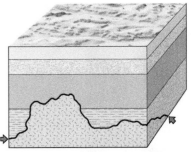

Disconformity

In a succession of rock layers (sedimentary strata or lava flows) parallel to one another, the disconformity surface is a gap in the layering. The gap may be a non-depositional surface where some layers never formed for a while, or the gap may be an erosional surface where some layers were removed before younger layers covered up the surface.

Angular unconformity

An angular unconformity is an erosional surface between two bodies of layered sedimentary strata or lava flows that are not parallel. The gap is because the older body of layered rock was tilted and partly eroded (rock was removed) before a younger body of horizontal rock layers covered the eroded surface.

Nonconformity

A nonconformity is an erosional surface between older igneous and/or metamorphic rocks and younger rock layers (sedimentary strata or lava flows). The gap is because some of the older igneous and/or metamorphic rocks were partly eroded (rock was removed) before the younger rock layers covered the eroded surface.

FIGURE 1 Three kinds of unconformities—surfaces that represent gaps (missing layers) in the geologic record; analogous to a gap (place where pages are missing) in a book. Red arrows point to the unconformity surface (bold black line) in each block diagram.

are often included in the strata above them. An **angular unconformity** is an unconformity between two sets of strata that are not parallel to one another. It forms when new horizontal layers cover up older layers folded by mountain-building processes and eroded down to a nearly level surface. A **nonconformity** is an unconformity between younger sedimentary rocks and subjacent metamorphic or igneous rocks. It forms when stratified sedimentary rocks or lava flows are deposited on eroded igneous or metamorphic rocks.

Analyze and evaluate Figures 2–8 to learn how the above laws of relative age dating are applied in

cross sections of Earth's crust. These are the kinds of two-dimensional cross sections of Earth's crust that are exposed in road cuts, quarry walls, and mountain sides. *Ignore the symbols for fossils until Part 8B (Activity 2). Be sure that you consider all of these examples before proceeding.*

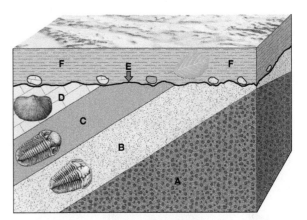

FIGURE 3 This is another sequence of strata, some of which do not have their original horizontality. Formation **A** is the oldest, because it is at the bottom of the sedimentary sequence. Formation **F** is youngest, because it forms the top of the sequence. Tilting and erosion of the sequence occurred after **D** but before deposition of Formation **F**. **E** is an angular unconformity.

The sequence of events began with deposition of **A, B, C,** and **D** in that order and stacked one atop the other. The sequence of **A–D** was then tilted, and its top was eroded **(E)**. Siltstone **F** was deposited horizontally on top of the erosional surface **(E)**, which is now an angular unconformity.

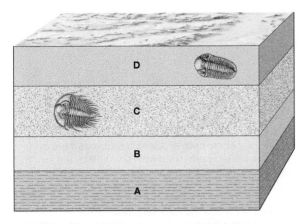

FIGURE 2 This is a sequence of strata that has maintained its original horizontality and does not seem to be disturbed. Therefore, Formation **A** is the oldest, because it is on the bottom of a sedimentary sequence of rocks. **D** is the youngest, because it is at the top of the sedimentary sequence. The sequence of events was deposition of **A, B, C,** and **D,** in that order and stacked one atop the other.

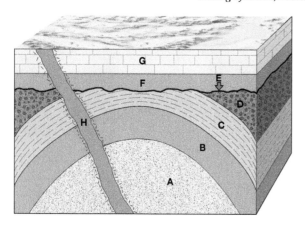

FIGURE 4   The body of igneous rock **H** is the youngest rock unit, because it cuts across all of the others. (When a narrow body of igneous rock cuts across strata in this way, it is called a **dike**.) **A** is the oldest formation, because it is at the bottom of the sedimentary rock sequence that is cut by **H**. Folding and erosion occurred after **D** was deposited, but before **F** was deposited. **E** is an angular unconformity.

The sequence of events began with deposition of formations **A** through **D** in alphabetical order and one atop the other. That sequence was folded, and the top of the fold was eroded. Formation **F** was deposited horizontally atop the folded sequence and the erosional surface, which became angular unconformity **E**. **G** was deposited atop **F**. Lastly, a magma intruded across all of the strata and cooled to form basalt dike **H**.

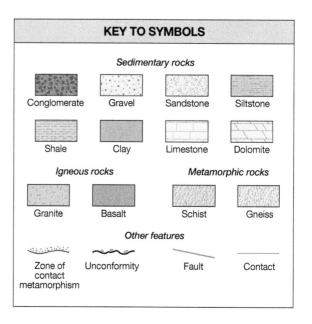

KEY TO SYMBOLS

Sedimentary rocks

Conglomerate   Gravel   Sandstone   Siltstone

Shale   Clay   Limestone   Dolomite

Igneous rocks   *Metamorphic rocks*

Granite   Basalt   Schist   Gneiss

Other features

Zone of contact metamorphism   Unconformity   Fault   Contact

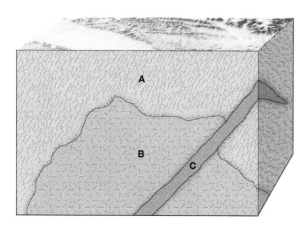

FIGURE 5   The body of granite **B** must have formed from the cooling of a body of magma that intruded the preexisting rock **A**, called **country rock.** The country rock is schist **A** containing a zone of contact metamorphism adjacent to the granite. Therefore, the sequence of events began with a body of country rock **A**. The country rock was intruded by a body of magma, which caused development of a zone of contact metamorphism and cooled to form granite **B**. Lastly, another body of magma intruded across both **A** and **B**. It caused development of a second zone of contact metamorphism and cooled to form basalt dike **C**.

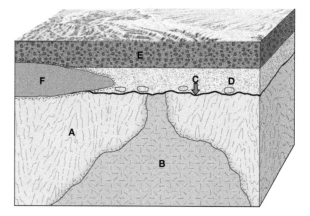

FIGURE 6   At the base of this rock sequence there is gneiss **A**, which is separated from granite **B** by a zone of contact metamorphism. This suggests that a body of magma intruded **A**, then cooled to form the contact zone and granite **B**. There must have been erosion of both **A** and **B** *after* this intrusion (to form surface **C**), because there is no contact metamorphism between **B** and **D**. Formation **D** was deposited horizontally atop the eroded igneous and metamorphic rocks, forming nonconformity **C**. After **E** was deposited, a second body of magma **F** intruded across **A**, **C**, **D**, and **E**. Such an intrusive igneous body that is intruded along (parallel to) the strata is called a **sill** (**F**).

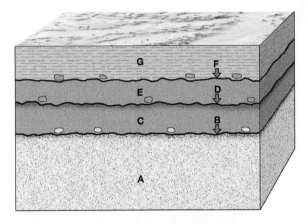

FIGURE 7 Notice that this is a sequence of strata and basalt lava flows (that have cooled to form the basalt). There are zones of contact metamorphism beneath both of the basalt lava flows (**C, E**). The sequence of events must have begun with deposition of sandstone **A**, because it is on the bottom. A lava flow was deposited atop **A** and cooled to form basalt **C**. This first lava flow caused development of the zone of contact metamorphism in **A** and the development of disconformity **B**. A second lava flow was deposited atop **C** and cooled to form basalt **E**. This lava flow caused the development of a zone of contact metamorphism and a disconformity **D**. An erosional surface developed atop **E**, and the surface became a disconformity **F** when shale **G** was deposited on top of it.

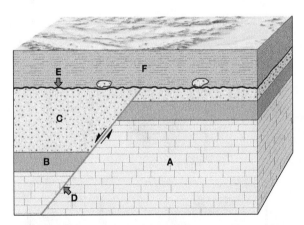

FIGURE 8 This is a sequence of relatively horizontal strata: **A, B, C,** and **F. A** must be the oldest of these formations, because it is on the bottom. **F** is the youngest of these formations, because it is on top. Formations **A, B,** and **C** are cut by a fault, which does not cut **F**. This means that the fault **D** must be younger than **C** and older than **F. E** is a disconformity. The sequence of events began with deposition of formations **A, B,** and **C,** in that order and one atop the other. This sequence was then cut by fault **D**. After faulting, the land surface was eroded. When siltstone **F** was deposited on the erosional surface, it became disconformity **E**.

ACTIVITY 1

Sequence of Events in Geologic Cross Sections

Apply the laws of relative age dating to analyze and interpret the sequence of geologic units and events in four geologic cross sections.

PART B: USING FOSSILS TO DETERMINE AGE RELATIONSHIPS

The sequence of strata that makes up the geologic record is a graveyard filled with the fossils of millions of kinds of organisms that are now extinct. Geologists know that they existed only because of their fossilized remains or the traces of their activities (like tracks and trails). Geologists have also determined that fossil organisms originate, co-exist, or disappear from the geologic record in a definite sequential order recognized throughout the world, so *any rock layer containing a group of fossils can be identified and dated in relation to other layers based on its fossils.* This is known as the **Principle of Fossil Succession.**

The sequence of strata in which fossils of a particular organism are found is called a **range zone,** which represents a chron of time. Organisms whose range zones have been used to represent named divisions of the geologic time scale are called **index fossils.**

The range zones of some well-known Phanerozoic index fossils are presented on the right side of Figure 9. Relative ages of the rocks containing these fossils are presented as *periods* and *eras* on the left side of Figure 9. By noting the range zone of a fossil (vertical black line), you can determine the corresponding era(s) or period(s) of time in which it lived. For example, all of the different species of dinosaurs lived and died during the Mesozoic Era of time, from the middle of the Triassic Period to the end of the Cretaceous Period. Mammals have existed since late in the Triassic Period. If you found a rock layer with bones and tracks of both dinosaurs and mammals, then the age of the rock layer would be represented by the overlap of the dinosaur and mammal range zones (i.e., Middle Triassic to Late Cretaceous). Notice that Figure 9 also includes the following groups:

- **Brachiopods** (pink on chart): marine invertebrate animals with two symmetrical seashells of unequal size. They range throughout the Paleozoic, Mesozoic, and Cenozoic Eras, but they were

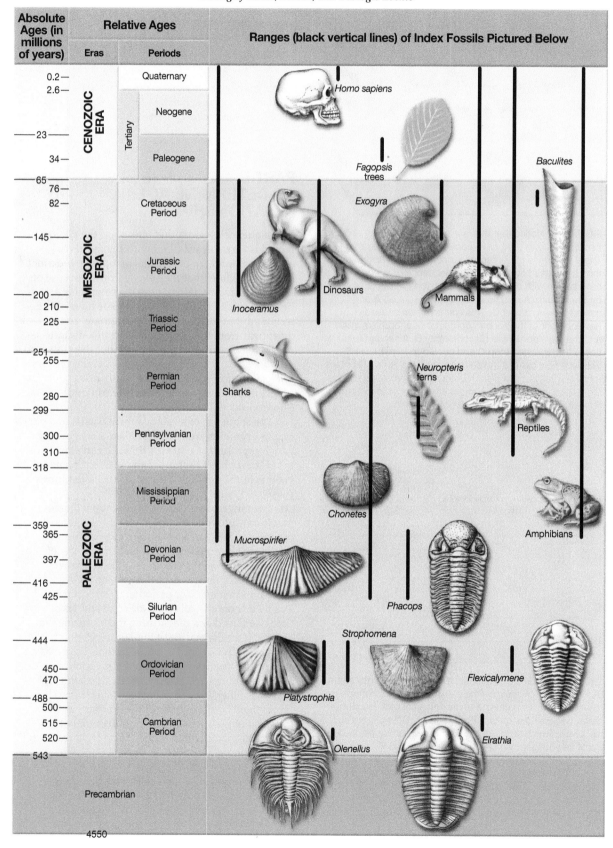

FIGURE 9 Range zones (vertical, bold black lines) of some well-known index fossils relative to the geologic time scale.

most abundant in the Paleozoic Era. Only a few species exist today, so they are nearly extinct.

- **Trilobites** (orange on chart): an extinct group of marine invertebrate animals related to lobsters. They are only found in Paleozoic rocks, so they are a good index fossil for the Paleozoic Era and its named subdivisions.

- **Mollusks** (pink on chart): phylum of snails, cephalopods (squid, octopuses), and bivalves (oysters, clams; two asymmetrical shells of unequal size).

- **Plants** (dark green on chart).

- **Reptiles** (pale green on chart): the group of vertebrate animals that includes lizards, snakes, turtles, and dinosaurs. **Dinosaurs** are only found in Mesozoic rocks, so they are an index fossil for the Mesozoic and its subdivisions.

- **Mammals** (gray on chart): the group of vertebrate animals (including humans) that are warm blooded, nurse their young, and have hair.

- **Amphibians** (brown on chart): the group of vertebrate animals that includes frogs and salamanders.

- **Sharks** (blue on chart).

Notice that absolute ages in millions of years are also presented on Figure 9. Determining absolute ages will be addressed in Part C, but you will need to use the absolute ages in Activity 2.

ACTIVITY 2

Use Index Fossils to Date Rocks and Events

Use fossils to determine the relative ages of rocks and geologic events. Then find the absolute ages on the geologic time scale in Figure 9.

PART C: DETERMINING ABSOLUTE AGES BY RADIOMETRIC DATING

You measure the passage of time based on the rates and rhythms at which regular changes occur around you. For example, you are aware of the rate at which hands move on a clock, the rhythm of day and night, and the regular sequence of the four seasons. These regular changes allow you to measure the passage of minutes, hours, days, and years.

Another way to measure the passage of time is by the regular rate of decay of radioactive isotopes. This technique is called **radiometric dating** and is one way

that geologists determine absolute ages of some geologic materials.

You may recall that **isotopes** of an element are atoms that have the same number of protons and electrons but different numbers of neutrons. This means that the different isotopes of an element vary in atomic weight (mass number) but not in atomic number (number of protons).

About 350 different isotopes occur naturally. Some of these are *stable isotopes*, meaning that they are not radioactive and do not decay through time. The others are *radioactive isotopes* that decay spontaneously, at regular rates through time. When a mass of atoms of a radioactive isotope is incorporated into the structure of a newly formed crystal or seashell, it is referred to as a **parent isotope**. When atoms of the parent isotope decay to a stable form, they have become a **daughter isotope**. A parent isotope and its corresponding daughter are called a **decay pair.**

Atoms of a parent isotope always decay to atoms of their stable daughter isotope at an exponential rate that does not change. The rate of decay can be expressed in terms of **half-life**—the time it takes for half of the parent atoms in a sample to decay to stable daughter atoms.

Radiometric Dating of Geologic Materials

The decay parameters for all radioactive isotopes can be represented graphically as in Figure 10. Notice that the decay rate is exponential (not linear)—during the second half-life interval, only half of the remaining half of parent atoms will decay. All radioactive isotopes decay in this way, but each decay pair has its own value for half-life.

Half-lives for some isotopes used for radiometric dating have been experimentally determined by physicists and chemists, as noted in the top chart of Figure 10. For example, uranium-238 is a radioactive isotope (parent) found in crystals of the mineral zircon. It decays to lead-206 (daughter) and has a half-life of about 4500 million years (4.5 billion years).

To determine the age of an object, it must contain atoms of a radioactive decay pair that originated when the object formed. You must then measure the percent of those atoms that is parent atoms (**P**) and the percent that is daughter atoms (**D**). This is generally done in a chemistry laboratory with an instrument called a *mass spectrometer*. Based on **P** and **D** and the chart at the bottom of Figure 10, find the number of half-lives that have elapsed and the object's corresponding age in number of half-lives. Finally, multiply that number of half-lives by the known half-life for that decay pair (noted in the top chart of Figure 10).

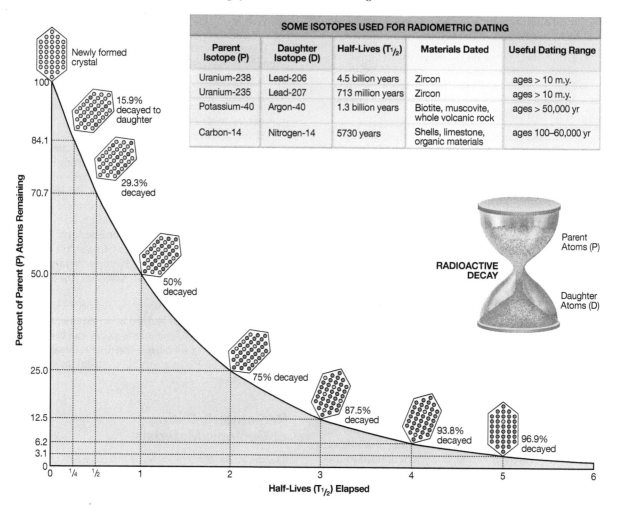

SOME ISOTOPES USED FOR RADIOMETRIC DATING				
Parent Isotope (P)	**Daughter Isotope (D)**	**Half-Lives (T₁/₂)**	**Materials Dated**	**Useful Dating Range**
Uranium-238	Lead-206	4.5 billion years	Zircon	ages > 10 m.y.
Uranium-235	Lead-207	713 million years	Zircon	ages > 10 m.y.
Potassium-40	Argon-40	1.3 billion years	Biotite, muscovite, whole volcanic rock	ages > 50,000 yr
Carbon-14	Nitrogen-14	5730 years	Shells, limestone, organic materials	ages 100–60,000 yr

DECAY PARAMETERS FOR ALL RADIOACTIVE DECAY PAIRS			
Percent of Parent Atoms (P)	**Percent of Daughter Atoms (D)**	**Half-Lives Elapsed**	**Age**
100.0	0.0	0	0.000 x T₁/₂
98.9	1.1	1/64	0.015 x T₁/₂
97.9	2.1	1/32	0.031 x T₁/₂
95.8	4.2	1/16	0.062 x T₁/₂
91.7	8.3	1/8	0.125 x T₁/₂
84.1	15.9	1/4	0.250 x T₁/₂
70.7	29.3	1/2	0.500 x T₁/₂
50.0	50.0	1	1.000 x T₁/₂
35.4	64.6	1½	1.500 x T₁/₂
25.0	75.0	2	2.000 x T₁/₂
12.5	87.5	3	3.000 x T₁/₂
6.2	93.8	4	4.000 x T₁/₂
3.1	96.9	5	5.000 x T₁/₂

FIGURE 10 Some isotopes useful for radiometric dating, their decay parameters, and their useful ranges for dating. The half-life of each decay pair is different (top chart), but the graph and decay parameters (bottom charts) are the same for all decay pairs.

For example, a sample of Precambrian granite contains biotite mineral crystals, so it can be dated using the potassium-40 to argon-40 decay pair. If there are three argon-40 atoms in the sample for every one potassium-40 atom, then the sample is 25.0% potassium-40 parent atoms (**P**) and 75.0% argon-40 daughter atoms (**D**). This means that two half-lives have elapsed, so the age of the biotite (and the granite) is 2.0 times 1.3 billion years, which equals 2.6

billion years. The useful dating ranges are also noted on Figure 10.

ACTIVITY 3

Absolute Dating of Rocks and Fossils

Apply absolute dating techniques to determine the absolute ages of rocks and geologic events.

FIGURE 11 Surface mine (strip mine) in northern New Mexico, from which bituminous coal is being extracted. Note the sill, sedimentary rocks, fossils, isotope data for zircon crystals in the sill, and fault.

WEST

EAST

Piles of mined coal

Coal

Fossiliferous sandstone

Fossiliferous sandstone

Fossil plants

© Richard M. Busch

© Richard M. Busch

© Richard M. Busch

Plant fossil (×1). See if you can find its name and age on Figure 8.9.

FIGURE 12 Surface mine (strip mine) in northeastern Pennsylvania, from which anthracite coal was extracted. Close-ups show plant fossils that were found at the site.

PART D: INFER THE GEOLOGIC HISTORY OF FIELD SITES

Now that you have developed knowledge and skills of relative and absolute dating, use them to analyze and interpret outcrops of rock at three field sites.

ACTIVITY 4

Infer Geologic History from a New Mexico Outcrop

Take a field trip to a surface mine (strip mine) in northern New Mexico, and use field evidence to infer the geologic history of the site.

ACTIVITY 5

Infer Geologic History from a Pennsylvania Outcrop

Take a field trip to a surface mine (strip mine) in northeast Pennsylvania, and use field evidence to infer all that happened to fossil plants that lived there long ago.

ACTIVITY 6

CSI (Canyon Scene Investigation) Arizona

Look into the Grand Canyon and analyze the scene using your geologic knowledge and skills.

PART E: CONSTRUCT AND INTERPRET A SUBSURFACE GEOLOGIC CROSS SECTION

Often geologists must infer geologic relationships that exist underground. One of the main tools available for this comes from wells. Some wells are drilled simply for exploratory purposes, to gather evidence of the subsurface geology. The evidence may be a core of rock or chips of rock from the well. When data from two or more wells are combined, then geologists use them to construct and interpret geologic cross sections.

ACTIVITY 7

Subsurface Geology Inferred from Well Data

Tear out the Activity 7 activity sheet. Part A is a cross section of five wells drilled along a west–east line. At the bottom of Part A are well logs for these wells. These logs are a record of the faults and rock units (layers) intersected by each well. The dip (inclination) of faults or any rock units that are no longer horizontal is also noted. You also need to know these lithologic descriptions of the rock units:

Unit 1: Cross-bedded eolian (wind-blown) sandstone

Unit 2: Brown-to-gray siltstone with shale zones and some coal seams

Unit 3: Parallel-bedded, poorly sorted sandstone

Unit 4: Conglomerate

Unit 5: Poorly sorted sandstone with some clay, silt, pebbles

Unit 6: Black, clayey shale

Unit 7: Parallel-bedded, well-sorted, coarse-grained sandstone

Unit 8: Black shale

Unit 9: Gray limestone

Complete the cross section in Part A like this. On each well (vertical lines), mark with ticks the elevations of the contacts between units (lightly in pencil). For example, in well A, Unit 1 extends from the surface (2400 feet) to 2100 feet, so make tick marks at these points; Unit 2 extends from 2100 to 2050 feet, so make ticks at these points; and so on. Label each unit number lightly beside each column, between the ticks.

Pay careful attention to the *dip* (inclination) *angles* indicated for faults and some rock units that are not horizontal. When you make tick marks, it is very helpful to angle them approximately to indicate dip (use a protractor). This is especially true if you encounter any *faults* in the cross section.

When you have all units plotted in the five wells, connect corresponding points between wells. (You are *correlating* well logs when you do this. You are also preparing a subsurface cross section of the type actually constructed by petroleum-exploration geologists.)

From the lithologic descriptions given, you can fill in some of the rock units with patterns—for example, sandstone (dots), conglomerate (tiny circles), and coal (solid black). Use the symbols given in Figure 4. Then complete the questions in Part B of the activity.

ACTIVITY 1 Sequence of Events in Geologic Cross Sections

Name: _____   Course/Section: _____

Materials: Pencil.

A. Review the legend of symbols at the bottom of this page. On the lines provided for each cross section, write letters to indicate the sequence of events from oldest (first in the sequence of events) to youngest (last in the sequence of events). Refer to Figures 1–8 and the laws of relative age dating, as needed.

Youngest _____
_____
_____
_____
_____
_____
_____
_____
_____
_____
_____
_____
_____
_____
Oldest _____

Geologic Cross Section 1

Youngest _____
_____
_____
_____
_____
_____
_____
_____
_____
_____
_____
_____
_____
Oldest _____

Geologic Cross Section 2

KEY TO SYMBOLS

Sedimentary rocks

Conglomerate   Gravel   Sandstone   Siltstone

Igneous rocks

Granite   Basalt

Metamorphic rocks

Schist   Gneiss

Shale   Clay   Limestone   Dolomite

Zone of contact metamorphism

Other features

Unconformity   Fault   Contact

CONTINUED

173

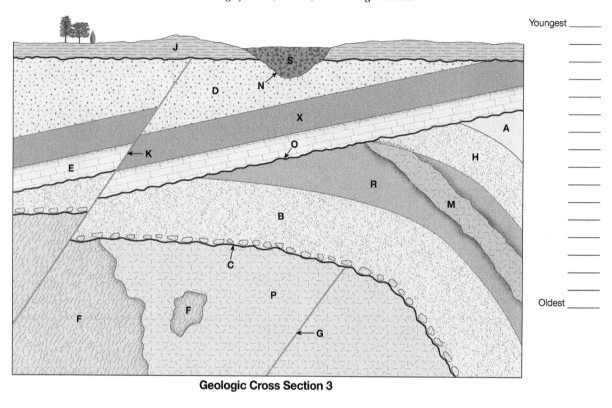

Youngest _____

Oldest _____

Geologic Cross Section 3

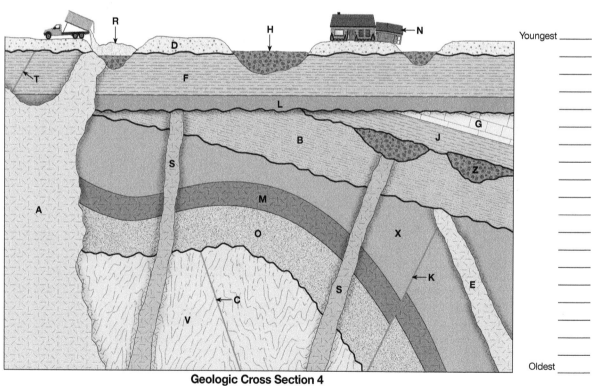

Youngest _____

Oldest _____

Geologic Cross Section 4

ACTIVITY 2 Use Index Fossils to Date Rocks and Events

Name: _____   Course/Section: _____

Materials: Pencil, calculator.

A. Analyze this fossiliferous rock from New York.

  1. What index fossils from Figure 9 are present?

  2. Based on the overlap of range zones for these index fossils what is the relative age of the rock (expressed as the early, middle, or late part of one or more periods of time)?

  3. Using Figure 9, what is the absolute age of the rock in Ma (millions of years old/ago), as a range from oldest to youngest?

B. Analyze this fossiliferous rock from Ohio.

  1. What index fossils from Figure 9 are present?

  2. Based on the overlap of range zones for these index fossils, what is the relative age of the rock (expressed as the early, middle, or late part of one or more periods of time)?

  3. Using Figure 9, what is the absolute age of the rock in Ma (millions of years old/ago), as a range from oldest to youngest?

C. Analyze this fossiliferous sand from Delaware.

  1. What index fossils from Figure 9 are present?

  2. Based on the overlap of range zones for these index fossils what is the relative age of the rock (expressed as the early, middle, or late part of one or more periods of time)?

  3. Using Figure 9, what is the absolute age of the rock in Ma (millions of years old/ago), as a range from oldest to youngest?

D. Using Figure 9, re-evaluate the geologic cross section in Figure 2 based on its fossils.

  1. Which one of the contacts (surfaces) between lettered layers is a disconformity? _____

  2. A system is the rock/sediment deposited during a period of time. What system of rock is completely missing at the disconformity?

  3. What amount of absolute time in m.y. (millions of years) is missing at the disconformity? _____ m.y.

E. What geologic event occurred during the Mesozoic Era in the region where Figure 3 is located? Explain.

ACTIVITY 3 Absolute Dating of Rocks and Fossils

Name: _____   Course/Section: _____

Materials: Pencil, calculator.

A. A solidified lava flow containing zircon mineral crystals is present in a sequence of rock layers that are exposed in a hillside. A mass spectrometer analysis was used to count the atoms of uranium-235 and lead-207 isotopes in zircon samples from the lava flow. The analysis revealed that 71% of the atoms were uranium-235, and 29% of the atoms were lead-207. Refer to Figure 10 to help you answer the following questions.

  1. About how many half-lives of the uranium-235 to lead-207 decay pair have elapsed in the zircon crystals? _____

  2. What is the absolute age of the lava flow based on its zircon crystals? Show your calculations.

  3. What is the age of the rock layers beneath the lava flow? _____

  4. What is the age of the rock layers above the lava flow? _____

B. Astronomers think that Earth probably formed at the same time as all of the other rocky materials in our solar system, including the oldest meteorites. The oldest meteorites ever found on Earth contain nearly equal amounts of both uranium-238 and lead-206. Based on Figure 10, what is Earth's age? Explain your reasoning.

C. If you assume that the global amount of radiocarbon (formed by cosmic-ray bombardment of atoms in the upper atmosphere and then dissolved in rain and seawater) is constant, then decaying carbon-14 is continuously replaced in organisms while they are alive. However, when an organism dies, the amount of its carbon-14 decreases as it decays to nitrogen-14.

  1. The carbon in a buried peat bed has about 6% of the carbon-14 of modern shells. What is the age of the peat bed? Explain.

  2. In sampling the peat bed, you must be careful to avoid any young plant roots or old limestone. Why?

D. Zircon ($ZrSiO_4$) forms in magma and lava as it cools into igneous rock. It is also useful for absolute age dating (Figure 10).

  1. If you walk on a modern New Jersey beach, then you will walk on some zircon sand grains. Yet if you determine the absolute age of the zircons, it does not indicate a modern age (zero years) for the beach. Why?

  2. Suggest a rule that geologists should follow when they date rocks according to radiometric ages of crystals inside the rocks.

E. An "authentic dinosaur bone" is being offered for sale on the Internet. The seller claims that he had it analyzed by scientists who confirmed that it is a dinosaur bone and used carbon dating to determine that it is 400 million years old. Give two reasons why you should be suspicious of this bone's authenticity. (See Figures 9, 10).

  1.   **2.**

ACTIVITY 4   Infer Geologic History from a New Mexico Outcrop

Name: _____   Course/Section: _____

Materials: Ruler, pencil.

A. Refer to Figure 11, an outcrop in a surface mine (strip mine) in northern New Mexico.

   1. What is the relative age of the sedimentary rocks in this rock exposure? Explain.

   2. What is the absolute age of the sill? Show how you calculated the answer.

   3. Locate the fault. How much displacement has occurred along this fault? _____ meters

   4. Make a numbered list of the geologic events of this region, starting with deposition of the sandstone (oldest event: a) and ending with the time this picture was taken. Use names of relative ages of geologic time and absolute ages in your writing. *Your reasoning and number of events may differ from other students.*

      a.

      b.

      c.

      d.

      e.

      f.

      g.

ACTIVITY 5   Infer Geologic History from a Pennsylvania Outcrop

Name: _____   Course/Section: _____

Materials: Pencil.

A. Carefully examine Figure 12, a surface mine (strip mine) in northeastern Pennsylvania's anthracite coal mining district. Make a list of all of the events that have happened to the fossil plants from the time when they were alive to the time when they were fossils exposed by bulldozers. *Your reasoning and number of events may differ from that of other students, because more than one inference is possible about the geologic history of the site. Be prepared to discuss your reasoning with other members of your class.*

   1.

   2.

   3.

   4.

   5.

   6.

   7.

   8.

ACTIVITY 6 CSI (Canyon Scene Investigation) Arizona

Name: _____   Course/Section: _____

Materials: Ruler, pencil.

This is a photograph of the bottom of the Grand Canyon, which runs east to west across northern Arizona. You are standing on the south rim of the canyon and looking at the bottom of the north side of the canyon.

Carefully analyze the photograph for rock layering. The very bottom rock layers in the foreground are folded Precambrian metamorphic rock called the "Vishnu Schist," which contains narrow bodies of granite (colored white). The Vishnu Schist is overlain here by relatively horizontal layers of sedimentary rock.

A. Using a pen, draw a line exactly along the contact (boundary) between the Vishnu Schist and the relatively horizontal sedimentary rocks above it.

B. Based on Figure 1, what specific kind of unconformity did you trace above?

C. The Vishnu Schist has an absolute age of about 1700 million years. The Lower Cambrian Tapeats Sandstone sits on top of the unconformity that you drew in Part A. If you assume that the Tapeats Sandstone includes strata (sedimentary layers) that were deposited at the very start of the Cambrian Period, then how much of a gap in time exists at the unconformity (where you traced it with a pen)?

ACTIVITY 7 Subsurface Geology Inferred from Well Data

Name: _____   Course/Section: _____

Materials: Ruler, protractor, pencil, one colored pencil.

A. Use the well data provided here, and instructions in the text (Part E), to construct a geologic cross section.

West
Well A   Well B   Well C   Well D   East
                                                                         Well E

Elevation (feet)

2400
2200
2000
1800
1600
1400
1200
1000
800
600
400
200
Sea level

Well A

2400–2100	Unit 1, horizontal
2100–2050	Unit 2, horizontal
2050–1700	Unit 3, dips westward 15°
1700–1150	Unit 4, dips westward 15°
1150–800	Unit 5, dips westward 15°
800–550	Unit 6, dips westward 15°
550–200	Unit 7, dips westward 15°
Bottom of well	

1150–800	Unit 5, dips westward 15°
800–550	Unit 6, dips westward 15°
550–200	Unit 7, dips westward 15°
200	Fault; dips eastward 60°
200–100	Unit 9, dips westward 15°
Bottom of well	

Well B

2300–2100	Unit 1, horizontal
2100–1980	Unit 2, horizontal
1980–1650	Unit 3, dips westward 15°
1650	Fault; dips eastward 60°
1650–1350	Unit 4, dips westward 15°
1350–1000	Unit 5, dips westward 15°
1000–750	Unit 6, dips westward 15°
750–200	Unit 7, dips westward 15°
200–sea level	Unit 8, dips westward 15°
Bottom of well	

Well C

2350–2100	Unit 1, horizontal
2100–1900	Unit 2, horizontal; coal seam at 1950
1900–1700	Unit 3, dips westward 15°
1700–1150	Unit 4, dips westward 15°

Well D

2300–2100	Unit 1, horizontal
2100–1800	Unit 2, horizontal; coal seam at 1950
1800–1350	Unit 4, horizontal
1350–1000	Unit 5, horizontal
1000–750	Unit 6, horizontal
750–200	Unit 7, horizontal
200–100	Unit 8, horizontal
Bottom of well	

Well E

2400–2100	Unit 1, horizontal
2100–1650	Unit 2, horizontal; coal seams at 1950 and 1850
1650–1450	Unit 3, dips eastward 21°
1450–900	Unit 4, dips eastward 21°
900–550	Unit 5, dips eastward 21°
550–300	Unit 6, dips eastward 21°
300–200	Unit 7, dips eastward 21°
Bottom of well	

CONTINUED

B. Refer to the geologic cross section that you completed in Part A.

1. What is the nature and geologic origin of the bottom contact of Unit 2?

2. Why is coal not found in wells A and B, whereas two coal seams are found in well E?

3. Wells A and E are **dry holes,** so-called because they produced no petroleum. But the others produce petroleum. An oil pool is penetrated in well B from 750 feet to 650 feet, in well C from 550 down to 500 feet, and in well D from 750 down to 500 feet. Color and label the oil pools on the cross section and explain why the oil was trapped there.

4. Why is there no oil in either well A or well E?

5. Using the laws of original horizontality, superposition, and cross cutting (page 176) describe the sequence of events that developed this geologic cross section.

Topographic Maps, Aerial Photographs, and Orthoimages

CONTRIBUTING AUTHORS

Charles G. Higgins • *University of California*

Evelyn M. Vandendolder • *Arizona Geological Survey*

John R. Wagner • *Clemson University*

James R. Wilson • *Weber State University*

OBJECTIVES AND ACTIVITIES

A. Be able to locate and characterize features on topographic maps using printed information, compass bearings, scales, symbols, contour lines, and three geographic survey/grid systems: latitude and longitude, the U.S. Public Land Survey System (PLSS), and the Universal Transverse Mercator System (UTM).

   ACTIVITY 1: Introduction to Topographic Maps

B. Be able to construct a topographic profile and calculate its vertical exaggeration.

   ACTIVITY 2: Topographic Profile Construction

C. Become familiar with the U.S. Geological Survey's newest generation of free digital topographic maps and orthoimages and be able to use them to do geologic mapping.

   ACTIVITY 3: Map CA Geology with a Topo Map and Orthoimage

   ACTIVITY 4: Map AZ Geology with a Topo Map and Orthoimage

   ACTIVITY 5: Obtain and Analyze a Topo Map or Orthoimage

D. Understand how stereo pairs (stereograms) of aerial photographs are obtained and used in geological studies.

   ACTIVITY 6: Aerial Photographs

STUDENT MATERIALS

Pencil, pen (black or blue), eraser, laboratory notebook, topographic quadrangle map (obtained by you or provided by your instructor), calculator, colored pencils, and pocket stereoscope (optional); millimeter ruler, protractor, and UTM templates from GeoTools Sheets 2–4.

INTRODUCTION

In 1937, American aviator Amelia Earhart and her navigator Fred Noonan attempted to make the first round-the-world flight. But two-thirds of the way around the globe, they disappeared in the South Pacific Ocean. Earhart and Noonan were trying to reach tiny Howland Island, a mere speck of land just north of the Equator, when they vanished. It appears that their flight plan gave the wrong coordinates for the island.

Earhart's flight plan listed the island's coordinates as 0°49′ north latitude, 176°43′ west longitude. But the actual coordinates are 0°48′ north latitude, 176°38′ west longitude (Barker, V., *New Haven Register*, Dec. 21, 1986:A48). In the open ocean, with nothing else to guide them and limited fuel, such a miss was fatal. Investigators who researched their disappearance thought that Earhart and Noonan were on course and would certainly have reached Howland Island—had they been given the correct coordinates. Thus, their demise probably was due to a mapmaker's mistake or to the flight planner's inability to correctly read a map.

Earhart's story illustrates that map errors, or errors in reading a map, can have drastic effects. Your ability to read topographic maps is essential for geologic studies, but it is also useful for safely planning a hike or wisely using/developing land. Therefore, topographic maps are often integrated with stereo pairs of aerial photographs (taken from an airplane at two different angles) and **orthoimages** (images of the landscape that have the same uniform scale as the map but also show buildings, trees, and other visual attributes of the landscape).

PART A: INTRODUCTION TO TOPOGRAPHIC MAPS

A **topographic map** is a two-dimensional (flat) representation (model) of a three-dimensional land surface (landscape). It shows landforms (hills, valleys, slopes, coastlines, gullies) and their **relief** (difference in elevation) by using **contour lines** to represent elevations of hills and valleys. The contour lines are the distinguishing features of a topographic map. They are what make a topographic map different from the more familiar *planimetric* map, such as a highway map, which has no contour lines and does not show relief of the land. Yet topographic maps still have many of the features of the planimetric maps (roads, buildings, streams, etc.).

Topographic Quadrangles, Symbols, and Revisions

Most United States topographic maps are published by the U.S. Geological Survey (USGS) and available at their US Topo website **(http://store.usgs.gov)**. Canadian topographic maps are produced by the Centre for Topographic Information of Natural Resources Canada (NRCAN: **http://maps.nrcan.gc.ca**). State and provincial geological surveys, and the national geological surveys of other countries, also produce and/or distribute topographic maps of their political jurisdictions.

Some topographic maps cover areas defined by political boundaries (such as a state, county, or city) but most depict rectangular sections of Earth's surface, called quadrangles. A **quadrangle** is a section of Earth's surface that is bounded by lines of *latitude* at the top (north) and bottom (south) and by lines of *longitude* on the left (west) and right (east)—see Figure 1.

Latitude and longitude are both measured in *degrees* (°). Latitude is measured from 0° at the Equator to 90°N (at the North Pole) or 90°S (at the South Pole). Longitude is measured in degrees east or west of the *prime meridian*, a line that runs from the North Pole to the South Pole through Greenwich, England. Locations in Earth's Eastern Hemisphere are east of the prime meridian, and locations in the Western

Hemisphere are west of the prime meridian. For finer measurements each degree can be subdivided into 60 equal subdivisions called *minutes* ('), and the minutes can be divided into 60 equal subdivisions called *seconds* (").

Quadrangle maps are published in many different sizes but two USGS sizes are most common: 15-minute quadrangle maps and $7\frac{1}{2}$-minute quadrangle maps (Figure 1). The numbers refer to the amount of area that the maps depict, in degrees of latitude and longitude. A *15-minute topographic map* represents an area that measures 15 minutes of latitude by 15 minutes of longitude. A $7\frac{1}{2}$-minute topographic map represents an area that measures $7\frac{1}{2}$ minutes of latitude by $7\frac{1}{2}$-minutes of longitude. Each 15-minute map can be divided into four $7\frac{1}{2}$ maps (Figure 1).

A reduced copy of a $7\frac{1}{2}$-minute USGS topographic map is provided in Figure 2. Notice that it is identified by name (Ritter Ridge, CA) and size (7.5 Minute Series, SW/4 of the Lancaster 15' Quadrangle) in the upper right and lower right corners of the map, respectively. Also notice that the map has colors, patterns, and symbols (Figure 3) that are used to depict water bodies, vegetation, roads, buildings, political boundaries, place names, and other natural and cultural features of the landscape. The lower right corner of the map indicates that the map was originally published in 1958, but it was photorevised in 1974. *Photorevised* means that aerial photographs (from airplanes) were used to discover changes on the landscape, and the changes are overprinted on the maps in a standout color like purple, red, or gray. The main new features shown on this 1974 photorevised map are the California Aqueduct (that carries water south, from the Sierra Nevada Mountains to the southern California desert) and several major highways.

Declination and Compass Bearings

Notice the trident-shaped symbol in the lower left corner of the Ritter Ridge Quadrangle (UTM Grid and 1974 Magnetic North Declination at Center of Sheet). Because longitude lines form the left and right boundaries of a topographic map, north is always at the top of the quadrangle. This is called grid north (GN) and is usually the same direction as *true north* on the actual Earth. Unfortunately, magnetic compasses are not attracted to true north (the geographic North Pole). Instead, they are attracted to the *magnetic north pole* (MN), currently located northwest of Hudson Bay in Northern Canada, about 700 km (450 mi) from the true North Pole. The trident-shaped symbol on the bottom margin of topographic maps shows the **declination** (difference in degrees) between compass north (MN) and true north (usually a *star* symbol). Also shown is the declination between compass north (*star* symbol) and grid north (GN). The magnetic pole migrates very slowly, so the declination is exact only for the year listed on the map. You can obtain the most

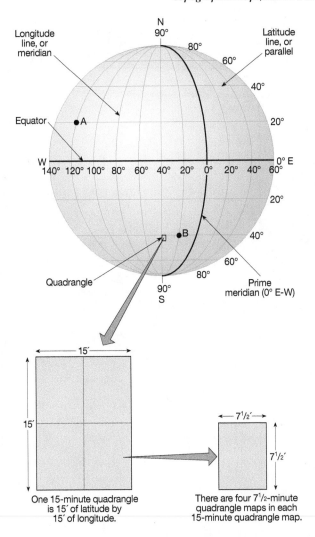

FIGURE 1 Latitude and longitude geographic grid and co-ordinate system. Earth's spherical surface is divided into lines of latitude (*parallels*) that go around the world parallel to the Equator, and lines of longitude (*meridians*) that go around the world from pole to pole. There are 360 degrees (360°) around the entire Earth, so the distance from the Equator to a pole (one-fourth of the way around Earth) is 90° of latitude. The Equator is assigned a value of zero degrees (0°) latitude, the North Pole is 90 degrees north latitude (90°N), and the South Pole is 90 degrees south latitude (90°S). The *prime meridian* is zero degrees of longitude and runs from pole to pole through Greenwich, England. Locations in Earth's Eastern Hemisphere are located in degrees east of the prime meridian, and points in the Western Hemisphere are in located in degrees west of the prime meridian. Therefore, any point on Earth (or a map) can be located by its latitude-longitude coordinates. The latitude coordinate of the point is its position in degrees north or south of the Equator. The longitude coordinate of the point is its position in degrees east or west of the prime meridian. For example, point **A** is located at coordinates of: 20° north latitude, 120° west longitude.

For greater detail, each degree of latitude and longitude can also be subdivided into 60 minutes (60′), and each minute can be divided into 60 seconds (60″). Note that a 15-minute (15′) quadrangle map represents an area of Earth's surface that is 15 minutes of longitude wide (E–W) and 15 minutes of latitude long (N–S). A 7.5-minute quad-rangle map (Figure 2) is one-fourth of a 15-minute quadrangle map.

One 15-minute quadrangle is 15′ of latitude by 15′ of longitude.

There are four 7¹/₂-minute quadrangle maps in each 15-minute quadrangle map.

recent magnetic data from the NOAA National Geophysical Data Center **(http://www.ngdc.noaa.gov/geomagmodels/Declination.jsp).**

A **bearing** is the *compass direction* along a line from one point to another. If expressed in degrees east or west of true north or south, it is called a *quadrant bearing*. Or it may be expressed in degrees between 0 and 360, called an *azimuth bearing*, where north is 0° (or 360°), east is 90°, south is 180°, and west is 270°. Linear geologic features (faults, fractures, dikes), lines of sight and travel, and linear property boundaries are all defined on the basis of their bearings. But because a compass points to Earth's *magnetic north* (MN) pole rather than the true North Pole or *grid north* (GN), one must correct for this difference. If the MN arrow is to the (east) right of true north (star symbol), then subtract the degrees of declination from your compass reading. If the MN arrow is to the west (left) of true north, then add the degrees of declination to your compass readings. These adjustments will mean that your compass readings are synchronized with the

map (so long as you used the latest declination values obtained from NOAA, as noted above).

Some compasses allow you to rotate their basal ring graduated in degrees to permanently correct for the magnetic declination. If the MN arrow is 5° east (right) of true north, then you would rotate the graduated ring 5° east (clockwise, to permanently subtract 5° from the reading). If the MN arrow is 5° west (left) of true north, then you would rotate the graduated ring 5° west (counter-clockwise, to permanently add 5° to the reading).

To determine a compass bearing on a map, draw a straight line from the starting point to the destination point and also through any one of the map's borders. Align a protractor (left drawing, Figure 4) or the N–S or E–W directional axis of a compass (right drawing, Figure 4) with the map's border, and read the bearing in degrees toward the direction of the destination. Imagine that you are buying a property for your dream home. The boundary of the property is marked by four metal rods driven into the ground, one at each

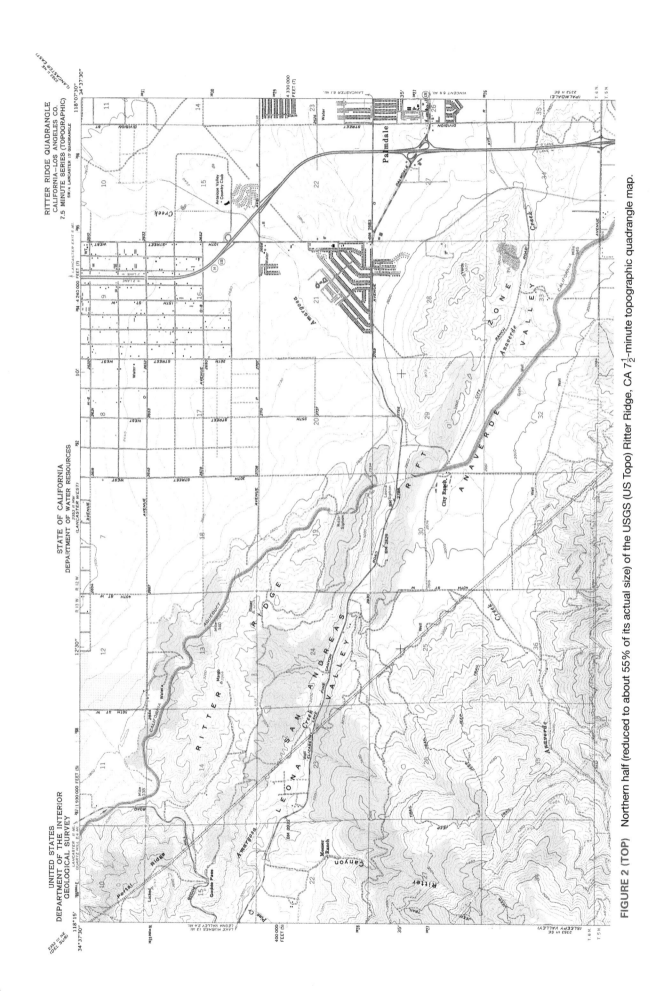

FIGURE 2 (TOP) Northern half (reduced to about 55% of its actual size) of the USGS (US Topo) Ritter Ridge, CA $7\frac{1}{2}$-minute topographic quadrangle map.

184

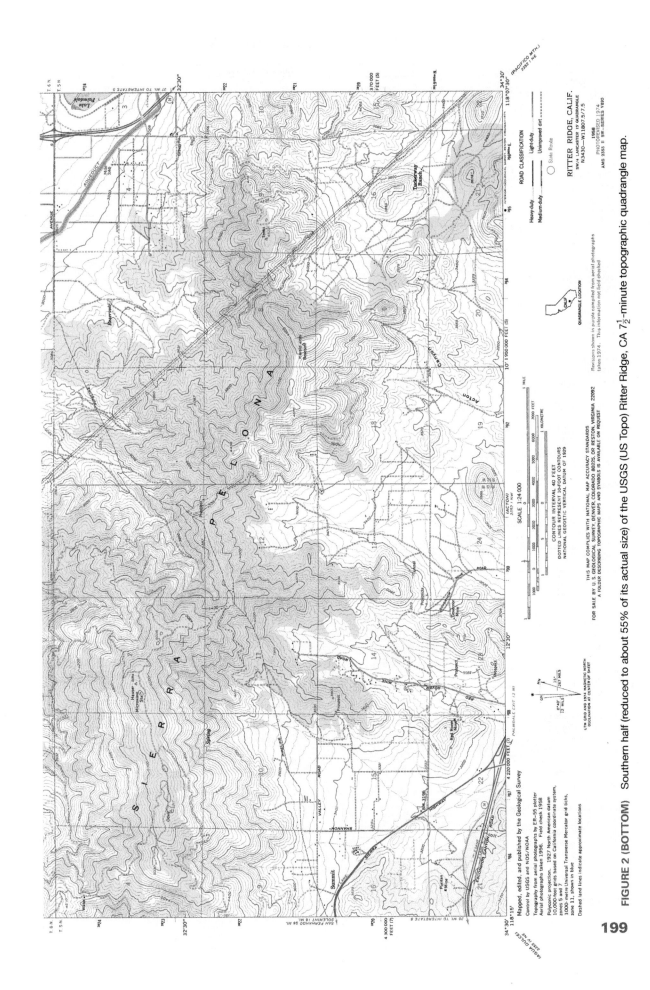

FIGURE 2 (BOTTOM)   Southern half (reduced to about 55% of its actual size) of the USGS (US Topo) Ritter Ridge, CA 7½-minute topographic quadrangle map.

185

Control data and monuments

Vertical control

Third order or better, with tablet	BM×16.3
Third order or better, recoverable mark	×120.0
Bench mark at found section corner	BM 18.6
Spot elevation	×5.3

Contours

Topographic

Intermediate	
Index	
Supplementary	
Depression	
Cut; fill	

Bathymetric

Intermediate	
Index	
Primary	
Index primary	
Supplementary	

Boundaries

National	
State or territorial	
County or equivalent	
Civil township or equivalent	
Incorporated city or equivalent	
Park, reservation, or monument	

Surface features

Levee	Levee
Sand or mud area, dunes, or shifting sand	Sand
Intricate surface area	Strip mine
Gravel beach or glacial moraine	Gravel
Tailings pond	Tailings pond

Mines and caves

Quarry or open pit mine	
Gravel, sand, clay, or borrow pit	
Mine tunnel or cave entrance	
Mine shaft	
Prospect	X
Mine dump	Mine dump
Tailings	Tailings

Vegetation

Woods	
Scrub	
Orchard	
Vineyard	
Mangrove	Mangrove

Glaciers and permanent snowfields

Contours and limits	
Form lines	

Marine shoreline

Topographic maps

Approximate mean high water	
Indefinite or unsurveyed	

Topographic-bathymetric maps

Mean high water	
Apparent (edge of vegetation)	

Submerged areas and bogs

Marsh or swamp	
Submerged marsh or swamp	
Wooded marsh or swamp	
Submerged wooded marsh or swamp	
Rice field	Rice
Land subject to inundation	Max pool 431

Coastal features

Foreshore flat	Mud
Rock or coral reef	
Rock bare or awash	*
Group of rocks bare or awash	
Exposed wreck	
Depth curve; sounding	
Breakwater, pier, jetty, or wharf	
Seawall	

Rivers, lakes, and canals

Intermittent stream	
Intermittent river	
Disappearing stream	
Perennial stream	
Perennial river	
Small falls; small rapids	
Large falls; large rapids	
Masonry dam	
Dam with lock	
Dam carrying road	
Perennial lake; Intermittent lake or pond	
Dry lake	Dry lake
Narrow wash	
Wide wash	Wide wash
Canal, flume, or aquaduct with lock	
Well or spring; spring or seep	

Buildings and related features

Building	
School; church	
Built-up area	
Racetrack	
Airport	
Landing strip	
Well (other than water); windmill	
Tanks	
Covered reservoir	
Gaging station	
Landmark object (feature as labeled)	
Campground; picnic area	
Cemetery: small; large	Cem

Roads and related features

Roads on Provisional edition maps are not classified as primary, secondary, or light duty. They are all symbolized as light duty roads.

Primary highway	
Secondary highway	
Light duty road	
Unimproved road	
Trail	
Dual highway	
Dual highway with median strip	

Railroads and related features

Standard gauge single track; station	
Standard gauge multiple track	
Abandoned	

Transmission lines and pipelines

Power transmission line; pole; tower	
Telephone line	Telephone
Aboveground oil or gas pipeline	
Underground oil or gas pipeline	Pipeline

FIGURE 3 Symbols used on topographic quadrangle maps produced by the U.S. Geological Survey.

READING BEARINGS WITH A PROTRACTOR

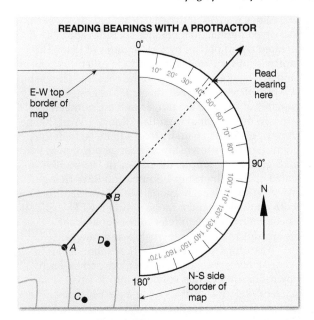

READING BEARINGS WITH A COMPASS

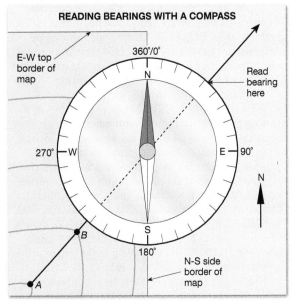

FIGURE 4 Examples of how to read the *bearing* (compass direction) from one point to another using a map and protractor (left) or compass (right). To determine a compass bearing on a map, draw a straight line from the starting point to the destination point and also through any one of the map's borders. For example, to find the bearing from *A* to *B*, a line was drawn through both points and the east edge of the map. Align a protractor (left drawing) or the N-S or E-W directional axis of a compass (right drawing) with the map's border and read the bearing in degrees toward the direction of the destination. In this example, notice that the *quadrant bearing* from point *A* to *B* is North 43° East (left map, using protractor) or an *azimuth bearing* of 43°. If you walked in the exact opposite direction, from *B* to *A*, then you would walk along a quadrant bearing of South 43° West or an azimuth bearing of 223° (i.e., 43° + 180° = 223°). Remember that a compass points to Earth's *magnetic north* pole (MN) rather than true north (GN, grid north). When comparing the bearing read directly from the map to a bearing read from a compass, you must adjust your compass reading to match grid north (GN) of the map, as described in the text.

corner of the property. The location of these rods is shown on the map in Figure 4 (left side) as points *A, B, C,* and *D.* The property deed notes the distances between the points *and* bearings between the points. This defines the shape of the property. Notice that the northwest edge of your property lies between two metal rods located at points *A* and *B.* You can measure the distance between the points using a tape measure. How can you measure the bearing?

First, draw a line (very lightly in pencil so that it can be erased) through the two points, *A* and *B.* Make sure the line also intersects an edge of the map. In both parts of Figure 4, a line was drawn through points *A* and *B* so that it also intersects the east edge of the map. Next, orient a protractor so that its 0° and 180° marks are on the edge of the map, with the 0° end toward geographic north. Place the origin of the protractor at the point where your line *A–B* intersects the edge of the map. You can now read a bearing of 43° east of north. We express this as a quadrant bearing of "North 43° East" (written N43°E) or as an azimuth bearing of 43°. If you were to determine the opposite bearing, from *B* to *A*, then the bearing would be pointing southwest and would be read as "South 43° West," or as an azimuth of 223°. Remember that a compass points to Earth's *magnetic north* pole (MN)

rather than true north or grid north (GN). When comparing the bearing read directly from the map to a bearing read from a compass, you must adjust your compass reading to match true north or grid north (GN) of the map, as described above.

You also can use a compass to read bearings, as shown in Figure 4 (right). Ignore the compass needle and use the compass as if it were a circular protractor. Some compasses are graduated in degrees, from 0–360, in which case you read an azimuth bearing from 0–360°. Square azimuth protractors for this purpose are provided in GeoTools Sheets 3 and 4.

Scales of Maps and Models

Maps are scale models, like toy cars or boats. To make a model of anything, you must first establish a model scale. This is the proportion by which you will reduce the real object to the model size. For example, if you make a $\frac{1}{4}$-scale model of a 16-ft car, your model would be 4 ft long. The ratio scale of model-to-object is 4:16, which reduces to 1:4. A house floorplan, which really is a map of a house, commonly is drawn so that one foot on the plan equals 30 or 40 ft of real house, or a **ratio scale** of 1:30 or 1:40.

Topographic maps often model large portions of Earth's surface, so the ratio scale must be much greater—like 1:24,000. This ratio scale can also be expressed as a **fractional scale** (1/24,000), indicating that the portion of Earth represented has been reduced to the fraction of 1/24,000th of its actual size.

Therefore, a *ratio scale* of 1:24,000 equals a *fractional scale* of 1/24,000. They both are ways of indicating that any unit (inch, centimeter, foot, etc.) on the map represents 24,000 of the same units (inches, centimeters, feet) on Earth's actual surface. For example, 1 cm on the map represents 24,000 cm on the ground, or your thumb width on the map represents 24,000 thumb widths on the ground. Other common map scales are 1:25,000, 1:50,000, 1:62,500, 1:63,360, 1:100,000, 1:125,000, and 1:250,000. Everything looks small and not very detailed on a small-scale map (1:100,000). Everything looks larger and more detailed on a larger-scale map (1:24,000).

Drawing a map at 1:24,000 scale provides a very useful amount of detail. But knowing that 1 inch on the map = 24,000 inches on the ground is not very convenient, because no one measures big distances in inches! However, if you divide the 24,000 inches by 12 to get 2000 ft, the scale suddenly becomes useful: "1 in. on the map = 2000 ft on the ground." An American football field is 100 yards (300 ft) long, so: "1 in. on the map = $6\frac{2}{3}$ football fields." Such scales expressed with words are called **verbal scales.**

On a map with a scale of 1:63,360, 1 in. = 63,360 in. again not meaningful in daily use. But there are 63,360 in. in a mile. So, the verbal scale, "1 in. = 1 mi" is very meaningful. A standard 1:62,500 map (15-minute quadrangle map commonly used in parts of Alaska) is very close to this scale, so it is common practice to say that "one inch equals approximately one mile" on such a map. Note that verbal scales are often approximate because their sole purpose is to increase the convenience of using a map.

Finally, all topographic maps have one or more **graphic bar scales** printed in their lower margin. They are essentially rulers for measuring distances on the map. U.S. Geological Survey topographic maps generally have four different bar scales: miles, feet, kilometers, and meters.

PLSS—Public Land Survey System

The **U.S. Public Land Survey System (PLSS)** was initiated in the late 1700s. All but the original thirteen states, and a few states derived from them, are covered by this system. Other exceptions occur in the southwestern United States, where land surveys may be based upon Spanish land grants, and in areas of rugged terrain that were never surveyed.

The PLSS scheme was established in each state by surveying **principal meridians,** which are north–south lines, and **base lines,** which are east–west lines (Figure 5A). Once the initial principal meridian and

base lines were established, additional lines were surveyed parallel to them and six miles apart. This created a grid of 6 mi by 6 mi squares of land. The north–south squares of the grid are called **townships** and are numbered relative to the base line (Township 1 North, Township 2 North, etc.). The east–west squares of the grid are **ranges** and are numbered relative to the principal meridian (Range 1 West, Range 2 West, etc.). Each 6 mi by 6 mi square is, therefore, identified by its township and range position in the PLS grid. For example, the square in Figure 5B is located at T1S (Township 1 South) and R2W (Range 2 West). Although each square like this is identified as both a township and a range within the PLSS grid, it is common practice to refer to the squares as townships rather than township-and-ranges.

Townships are used as political subdivisions in some states and are often given place names. Each township square is also divided into 36 small squares, each having an area of 1 square mile (640 acres). These squares are called **sections.**

Sections are numbered from 1 to 36, beginning in the upper right corner (Figure 5B). Sometimes these are shown on topographic quadrangle maps (Figure 2, red-brown grid). Any point can be located precisely within a section by dividing the section into quarters (labeled NW, NE, SW, SE). Each of these quarters can itself be subdivided into quarters and labeled (Figure 5C).

GPS—Global Positioning System

The **Global Positioning System (GPS)** is a constellation of 28 navigational communication satellites in 12-hour orbits approximately 12,000 miles above Earth (about 24 of these are operational at any given time). The GPS constellation is maintained by the United States (NOAA and NASA) for operations of the U.S. Department of Defense, but it is free for anyone to use. Because GPS receivers can be purchased for as little as $100 and come with most cell phones, they are widely used by airplane navigators, automated vehicle navigation systems, ship captains, hikers, and scientists to map locations on Earth. More expensive and accurate receivers with millimeter accuracy are used for space-based geodesy measurements that reveal plate motions over time.

Each GPS satellite communicates simultaneously with fixed ground-based Earth stations and other GPS satellites, so it knows exactly where it is located relative to the center of Earth and Universal Time Coordinated (UTC, also called Greenwich Mean Time). Each GPS satellite also transmits its own radio signal on a different channel, which can be detected by a fixed or handheld GPS receiver. If you turn on a handheld GPS receiver in an unobstructed outdoor location, then the receiver immediately *acquires* (picks up) the radio channel of the strongest signal it can detect from a GPS satellite. It downloads the navigational

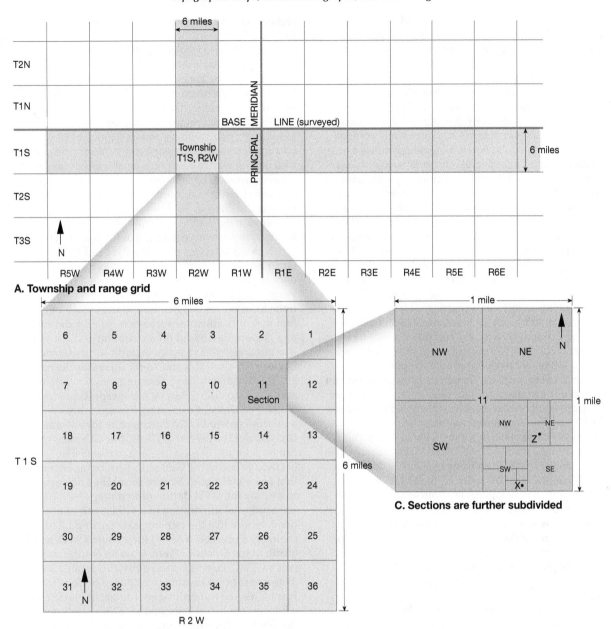

A. Township and range grid

B. A township contains 36 sections

C. Sections are further subdivided

FIGURE 5 U.S. Public Land Survey System (PLS) is based on a grid of townships and ranges unique to specific states or regions. **A.** Townships and ranges are located relative to a state's *principal meridian* (N-S line) of longitude and its *base line* (E-W line, surveyed perpendicular to the principal meridian). *Township* strips (columns) of land are 6 miles long and parallel to the base line. North of the base line, townships are numbered T1N, T2N, and so on. South of the base line, townships are numbered T1S, T2S, and so on. *Range* strips (rows) of land are 6 miles wide and parallel to the principal meridian. East of the principal meridian, ranges are numbered R1E, R2E, and so on. West of the principal meridian, ranges are numbered R1W, R2W, and so on. Each intersection of a township strip of land with a range strip of land forms a square, called a *township*. Note the location of Township T1S, R2W. **B.** Each township is 6 miles wide and 6 miles long, so it contains 36 square miles. Each square mile (640 acres) is called a *section,* and each section is numbered exactly as shown above. **C.** Sections are subdivided according to a hierarchy of square *quarters* listed in order of increasing size and direction. For example, point **x** is located in the southeast quarter, of the southeast quarter, of the southwest quarter, of the southeast quarter, of section 11. This is written: $SE\frac{1}{4}$, $SE\frac{1}{4}$, $SW\frac{1}{4}$, $SE\frac{1}{4}$, sec. 11, T1S, R2W.

information from that satellite channel, followed by a second, third, and so on. A receiver must acquire and process radio transmissions from at least four GPS satellites to triangulate a determination of its exact position and elevation—this is known as a *fix*.

Many GPS receivers are *12-channel parallel receivers*, which means that they can receive and process radio signals from as many as twelve satellites at the same time (the maximum possible number for any point on Earth). Older models cycle through the channels one at a time, or have fewer parallel channels, so they take longer to process data and usually give less accurate results. Newer models may have 20 or more channels that process simultaneously. They can receive faint signals from satellites that are moving out of range at the same time that other channels are picking up satellites well within range and still more channels are available to independently start to pick up new satellites that are moving within range. An unobstructed view is also best (GPS receivers cannot operate indoors). If the path from satellite to receiver is obstructed by trees, canyon walls, or buildings, then the receiver has difficulty acquiring that radio signal. It is also possible that more or fewer satellites will be nearly overhead at one time than another, because they are in constant motion within the constellation. Therefore, if you cannot obtain a fix at one time (because four satellite channels cannot be acquired), you may be able to obtain a fix in another half hour or so. Acquiring more than four satellite channels will provide more navigational data and more accurate results. Most handheld, 12-channel parallel receivers have an accuracy of about 10–15 meters.

When using a GPS receiver for the first time in a new region, it generally takes about one to three minutes for it to triangulate a fix. This information is stored in the receiver, so readings taken over the next few hours at nearby locations normally take only seconds. Consult the operational manual for your receiver so you know the time it normally takes for a *cold* fix (first time) or *warm* fix (within a few hours of the last fix).

GPS navigation does not rely on the latitude-longitude or the public land survey system. It relies on an Earth-centered geographic grid and coordinate system called the *World Geodetic System 1984 or WGS 84*. WGS 84 is a **datum** (survey or navigational framework) based on the Universal Transverse Mercator (UTM) grid described below.

UTM—Universal Transverse Mercator System

The U.S. National Imagery and Mapping Agency (NIMA) developed a global military navigation grid and coordinate system in 1947 called the **Universal Transverse Mercator System (UTM).** Unlike the latitude-longitude grid that is spherical and measured in degrees, minutes, seconds, and nautical miles (1 nautical mile = 1 minute of latitude), the UTM grid is rectangular and measured in decimal-based metric units (meters).

The UTM grid (top of Figure 6) is based on sixty north–south **zones,** which are strips of longitude having a width of 6°. The zones are consecutively numbered from Zone 01 (between 180° and 174° west longitude) at the left margin of the grid, to Zone 60 (between 174° and 180° east longitude) at the east margin of the grid. The location of a point within a zone is defined by its **easting** coordinate—its distance within the zone measured in meters from west to east, and a **northing** coordinate—its distance from the Equator measured in meters. In the Northern Hemisphere, northings are given in meters north of the Equator. To avoid negative numbers for northings in the Southern Hemisphere, NIMA assigned the Equator a reference northing of 10,000,000 meters.

Because satellites did not exist until 1957, and GPS navigational satellites did not exist until decades later, the UTM grid was applied for many years using regional ground-based surveys to determine locations of the grid boundaries. Each of these regional or continental surveys is called a **datum** and is identified based on its location and the year it was surveyed. Examples include *North American Datum 1927 (NAD27)* and *North American Datum 1983 (NAD83)*, which appear on many Canadian and U.S. Geological Survey topographic quadrangle maps. The Global Positioning System relies on an Earth-centered UTM datum called the *World Geodetic System 1984* or *WGS 84*, but GPS receivers can be set up to display regional datums like *NAD27*. When using GPS with a topographic map that has a UTM grid, be sure to set the GPS receiver to display the UTM datum of that map.

Study the illustration of a GPS receiver in Figure 6. Notice that the receiver is displaying UTM coordinates (based on *NAD27*) for a point **X** in Zone 18 (north of the Equator). Point **X** has an easting coordinate of E384333, which means that it is located 384333 meters east of the starting (west) edge of Zone 18. Point **X** also has a northing coordinate of N4455250, which means that it is located 4455250 meters north of the Equator. Therefore, point **X** is located in southeast Pennsylvania. To plot point **X** on a 1:24,000 scale, $7\frac{1}{2}$ minute topographic quadrangle map, see Figure 7.

Point **X** is located within the Lititz, PA $7\frac{1}{2}$ minute (USGS, 1:24,000 scale) topographic quadrangle map (Figure 7). Information printed on the map margin indicates that the map has blue ticks spaced 1000 m apart along its edges that conform to *NAD27*, Zone 18. Notice how the ticks for northings (blue) and eastings (green) are represented on the northwest corner of the Lititz map—Figure 7B. One northing label is written out in full ($^{44}56^{000m}$ N) and one easting label is written out in full ($^{3}84^{000m}$ E), but the other values are given in UTM shorthand for thousands of meters (i.e., do not end in ^{000m}). Because point **X** has an easting of E384333 within Zone 18, it must be located 333 m east of the tick mark labeled $^{3}84^{000m}$ E along the

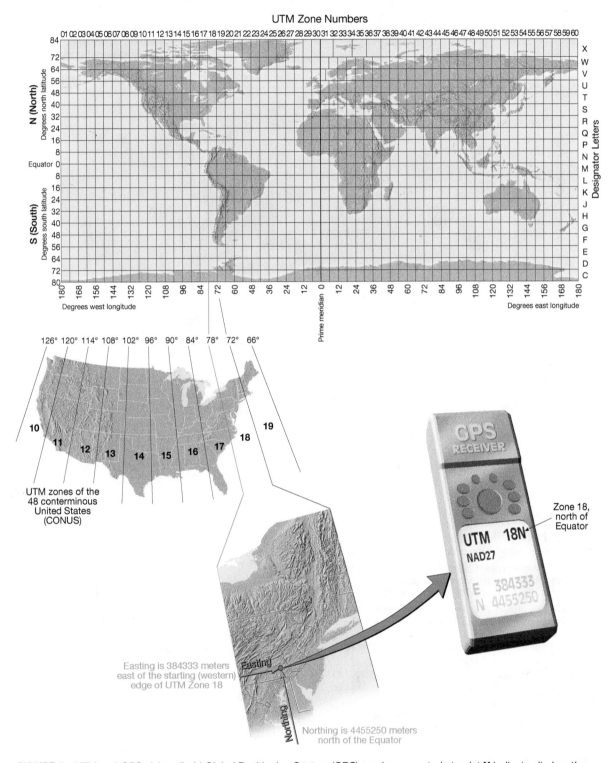

FIGURE 6 UTM and GPS. A handheld Global Positioning System (GPS) receiver operated at point **X** indicates its location according to the Universal Transverse Mercator (UTM) grid and coordinate system, *North American Datum 1927 (NAD27)*. Refer to text for explanation.

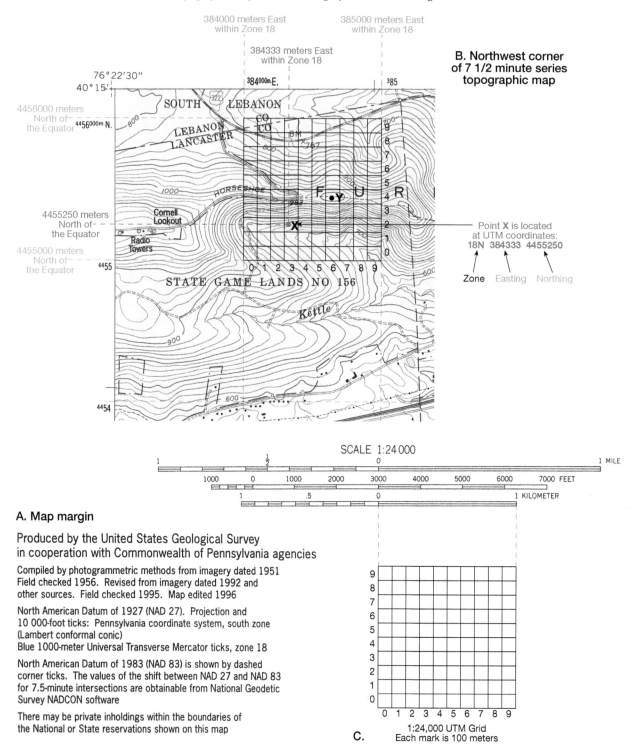

FIGURE 7 UTM and topographic maps—refer to text for discussion. Point **X** (from Figure 6) is located within the Lititz, PA $7\frac{1}{2}$-minute (USGS, 1:24,000 scale) topographic quadrangle map. **A.** Map margin indicates that the map includes UTM grid data based on *North American Datum 1927* (NAD27, Zone 18) and represented by blue ticks spaced 1000 meters (1 km) apart along the map edges. **B.** Connect the blue 1000-m ticks to form a grid square, each representing 1 square kilometer. Northings (blue) are read along the N-S map edge, and eastings (green) are located along the E-W map edge. **C.** You can construct a 1-km grid (1:24,000 scale) from the map's bar scale, then make a transparency of it to form a grid overlay (see GeoTools Sheets 2 and 4). Place the grid overlay atop the 1-kilometer square on the map that includes point **X**, and determine the *NAD27* coordinates of **X** as shown (red).

top margin of the map. Because Point **X** has a northing of N4455250, it must be located 250 m north of the tick mark labeled as ⁴⁴55 in UTM shorthand. Distances east and north can be measured using a ruler and the map's graphic bar scale as a reference (333 m = 0.333 km, 250 m = 0.250 km). However, you can also use the graphic bar scale to construct a UTM grid like the one in Figure 7C. If you construct such a grid and print it onto a transparency, then you can use it as a UTM *grid overlay*. To plot a point or determine its coordinates, place the grid overlay on top of the square kilometer in which the point is located. Then use the grid as a two-dimensional ruler for the northing and easting. Grid overlays for many different scales of UTM grids are provided in GeoTools Sheets 2–4 for you to cut out and use.

The UTM system described above is known as the *civilian UTM grid and coordinate system*, and it is the system that has been used on most published

topographic maps to date. However, newer USGS topographic maps use the U.S. Department of Defense, Military Grid Reference System (MGRS) that divides the zones into horizontal sections identified by *designator letters* (Figure 6). These sections are 8° wide and lettered consecutively from **C** (between 80° and 72° south latitude) through **X** (between 72° and 84° north latitude). Letters I and O are not used.

Contour Lines

Examine the image of one of the Galapagos Islands in Figure 8, a perspective view of the landscape that has been false colored to show relief. It was made by transmitting imaging radar from an airplane (flying at a constant altitude). Timed pulses of the radar measured the distance between the airplane (flying at a constant elevation) and the ground. Overlapping pulses of the radar produced the three-dimensional perspective similar to the way that overlapping lines

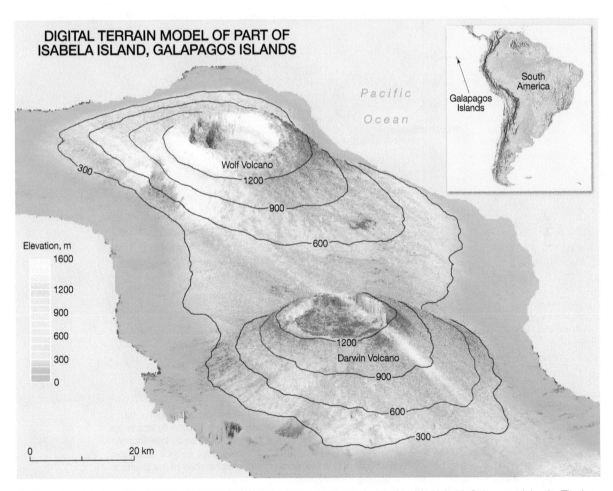

FIGURE 8 Digital model (AIRSAR/TOPSAR 3-dimensional perspective) of part of Isabela Island, Galapagos Islands. The image has been false colored to show relief. It was made with imaging radar transmitted from an airplane (flying at a constant altitude of 33,000 ft). Timed pulses of the radar measured the distance between the airplane (flying at a constant elevation) and the ground. Overlapping pulses of the radar produced the three-dimensional perspective. (Image courtesy of NASA/JPL–Caltech)

of sight from your eyes enable you to see in stereo. Notice that the island has a distinct coastline, which has the same elevation all of the way around the island (zero feet above sea level). Similarly, all points at the very top of the green (including yellow-green) regions form a line at about 300 ft above sea level. These lines of equal elevation (e.g., the coastline and 300-ft line) are called **contour lines.** Unfortunately, the 1200-ft contour line (located at the boundary between yellow and pink) is not visible behind Darwin and Wolf Volcanoes in this perspective view. The only way that you could see all of the 0-ft, 300-ft, 600-ft, 900-ft, and 1200-ft contour lines at the same time would be if you viewed the island from directly above. This is how topographic maps are constructed (Figure 9).

Topographic maps are made from overlapping pairs of photographs, called *stereo pairs.* Each stereo pair is taken from an airplane making two closely spaced passes over a region at the same elevation. The passes are flown far enough apart to provide the stereo effect, yet close enough to be almost directly above the land that is to be mapped. After the stereo

pairs are used to define contour lines and construct a first draft of the topographic map, angular distortion is removed and the exact elevations of the contour lines on the map are "ground truthed" (checked on the ground) using very precise altimeters and GPS.

Therefore, topographic maps are miniature models of Earth's three-dimensional surface, printed on two-dimensional pieces of paper. Two of the dimensions are the lengths and widths of objects and landscape features. But the third dimension, elevation (height), is shown using contour lines. Each **contour line** connects all points on the map that have the same elevation above sea level (Figure 10, rule 1). Look at the topographic map in Figure 2 and notice the light brown and heavy brown contour lines. The heavy brown contour lines are called **index contours,** because they have elevations printed on them (whereas the lighter contour lines do not; Figure 10, rule 6). Index contours are your starting point when reading elevations on a topographic map. For example, notice that every fifth contour line on Figure 2 is an index contour. Also notice that the index contours are labeled with el-

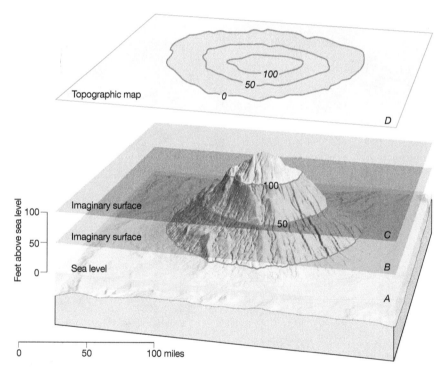

FIGURE 9 Topographic map construction. A *contour line* is drawn where a horizontal plane (such as **A, B,** or **C**) intersects the land surface. Where sea level (plane **A**) intersects the land, it forms the 0-ft contour line. Plane **B** is 50 ft above sea level, so its intersection with the land is the 50-ft contour line. Plane **C** is 100 ft above sea level, so its intersection with the land is the 100-ft contour line. **D** is the resulting topographic map of the island. It was constructed by looking down onto the island from above and tracing the 0, 50, and 100-ft contour lines. The elevation change between any two contour lines is 50 ft, so the map is said to have a 50-ft *contour interval.* The topographic datum (reference level) is sea level, so all contour lines on this map represent elevations in feet above sea level and are *topographic contour lines.* (Contours below sea level are called *bathymetric contour lines* and are generally shown in blue.)

RULES FOR CONTOUR LINES

1. Every point on a contour line is of the exact same elevation; that is, contour lines connect points of equal elevation. The contour lines are constructed by surveying the elevation of points, then connecting points of equal elevation.

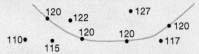

2. Interpolation is used to estimate the elevation of a point B located in line between points A and C of known elevation. To estimate the elevation of point B:

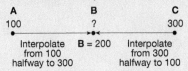

3. Extrapolation is used to estimate the elevations of a point C located in line beyond points A and B of known elevation. To estimate the elevation of point C, use the distance between A and B as a ruler or graphic bar scale to estimate in line to elevation C.

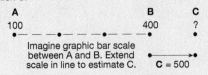

4. Contour lines always separate points of higher elevation (uphill) from points of lower elevation (downhill). You must determine which direction on the map is higher and which is lower, relative to the contour line in question, by checking adjacent elevations.

5. Contour lines always close to form an irregular circle. But sometimes part of a contour line extends beyond the mapped area so that you cannot see the entire circle formed.

6. The elevation between any two adjacent contour lines of different elevation on a topographic map is the *contour interval*. Often every fifth contour line is heavier so that you can count by five times the contour interval. These heavier contour lines are known as *index contours*, because they generally have elevations printed on them.

7. Contour lines never cross each other except for one rare case: where an overhanging cliff is present. In such a case, the hidden contours are dashed.

8. Contour lines can merge to form a single contour line only where there is a vertical cliff or wall.

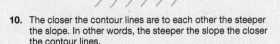

9. Evenly spaced contour lines of different elevation represent a uniform slope.

10. The closer the contour lines are to each other the steeper the slope. In other words, the steeper the slope the closer the contour lines.

11. A concentric series of closed contours represents a hill:

12. *Depression contours* have hachure marks on the downhill side and represent a closed depression:

See Figure 9.12

13. Contour lines form a V pattern when crossing streams. The apex of the V always points upstream (uphill):

14. Contour lines that occur on opposite sides of a valley or ridge always occur in pairs. See Figure 9.13.

FIGURE 10 Rules for constructing and interpreting contour lines on topographic maps.

evations in increments of 200 ft. This means that the map has five contours for every 200 ft of elevation, or a **contour interval** of 40 ft. This contour interval is specified at the center of the bottom margin of the map (Figure 2). All contour lines are multiples of the contour interval above a specific surface (almost always sea level). For example, if a map uses a 10-ft contour interval, then the contour lines represent elevations of 0 ft (sea level), 10 ft, 20 ft, 30 ft, 40 ft, and so on. Most maps use the smallest contour interval that will allow easy readability and provide as much detail as possible.

Additional rules for contour lines are also provided in Figure 10. For example, contour lines never cross, except in the rare case where an overhanging cliff is present. If contour lines merge into one line, then that line indicates a cliff. The spacing of contour lines can be used to interpret the steepness of a slope and whether it is uniform or variable in steepness. The apex (tip) of a V-shaped notch in a contour line always points up hill.

Be sure to review all of the rules for contour lines in Figure 10 and the common kinds of landforms represented by contour lines on topographic maps (Figure 11). Your ability to use a topographic map is based on your ability to interpret what the contour lines mean (imagine the topography).

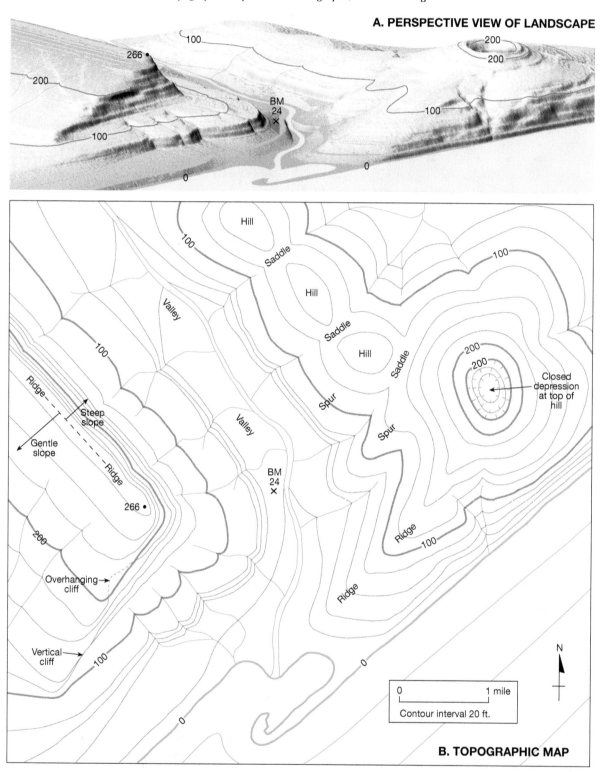

FIGURE 11 Names of landscape features observed in perspective view **(A)** and on topographic maps **(B)**: **valley** (low-lying land bordered by higher ground), **hill** (rounded elevation of land; mound), **ridge** (linear or elongate elevation or crest of land), **spur** (short ridge or branch of a main ridge), **saddle** (low point in a ridge or line of hills; it resembles a horse saddle), **closed depression** (low point/area in a landscape from which surface water cannot drain; contour lines with hachure marks), **steep slope** (closely spaced contour lines), **gentle slope** (widely spaced contour lines), **vertical cliff** (merged contour lines), **overhanging cliff** (dashed contour line that crosses a solid one; the dashed line indicates what is under the overhanging cliff).

Reading Elevations

If a point lies on an index contour, you simply read its elevation from that line. If the point lies on an unnumbered contour line, then its elevation can be determined by counting up or down from the nearest index contour. For example, if the nearest index contour is 300 ft, and your point of interest is on the fourth contour line *above* it, and the contour interval is 20 ft, then you simply count up by 20s from the index contour: 320, 340, 360, 380. The point is 380 ft above sea level. (Or, if the point is three contour lines *below* the index contour, you count down: 280, 260, 240; the point is 240 ft above sea level.)

If a point lies between two contour lines, then you must estimate its elevation by interpolation (Figure 6, rule 2). For example, on a map with a 20-ft contour interval, a point might lie between the 340 and 360-ft contours, so you know it is between 340 and 360 ft

above sea level. If a point lies between a contour line and the margin of the map, then you must estimate its elevation by extrapolation (Figure 6, rule 3).

Figure 12 shows how to read topographic contour lines in and adjacent to a depression. *Hachure marks* (short line segments pointing downhill) on some of the contour lines in these maps indicate the presence of a closed depression (a depression from which water cannot drain) (Figure 10, rule 12). At the top of a hill, contour lines repeat on opposite sides of the rim of the depression. On the side of a hill, the contour lines repeat only on the downhill side of the depression.

Figure 13 shows how topographic contour lines represent linear ridge crests and valley bottoms. Ridges and valleys are roughly symmetrical, so individual contour lines repeat on each side (Figure 10, rule 14). To visualize this, picture yourself walking along an imaginary trail across the ridge or valley (dashed lines in Figure 13).

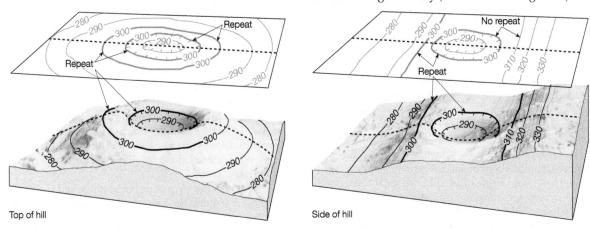

FIGURE 12 Contour lines repeat on opposite sides of a depression (left illustration), except when the depression occurs on a slope (right illustration).

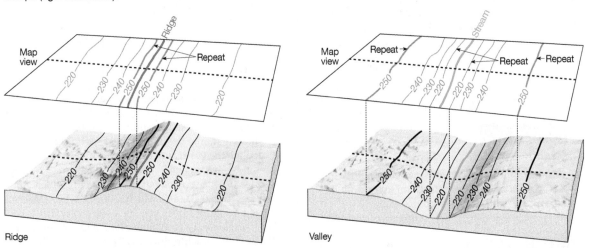

FIGURE 13 Contour lines repeat (occur in pairs) on opposite sides of linear ridges and valleys. For example, in the left illustration, if you walked the dashed line from left to right, you would cross the 220, 230, 240, and 250-ft contour lines, go over the crest of the ridge, and cross the 250, 240, 230, and 220-ft contour lines again as you walk down the other side. Note that the 250-ft contour lines on these maps are heavier than the other lines because they are *index contours*. On most maps, every fifth contour line above sea level is an index contour, so you can count by five times the contour interval. The *contour interval* (elevation between any two contour lines) of these maps is 10 ft, so the index contours are every 50 feet of elevation.

Every time you walk up the side of a hill or valley, you cross contour lines. Then, when you walk down the other side of the hill or valley, you recross contour lines of the same elevations as those crossed walking uphill.

Elevations of specific points on topographic maps (tops of peaks, bridges, survey points, etc.) sometimes are indicated directly on the maps beside the symbols indicated for that purpose. The notation "BM" denotes a **benchmark**, a permanent marker (usually a metal plate) placed by the U.S. Geological Survey or Bureau of Land Management at the point indicated on the map (Figure 7). Elevations usually are given. The elevations of prominent hilltops, peaks, or other features are sometimes identified specifically, even if there is no benchmark on the ground. For example, the highest point on the ridge in the west central part of Figure 11B has an elevation of 266 ft above sea level.

Relief and Gradient

Recall that **relief** is the difference in elevation between landforms, specific points, or other features on a landscape or map. *Regional relief* (total relief) is the difference in elevation between the highest and lowest points on a topographic map. The highest point is the top of the highest hill or mountain; the lowest point is generally where the major stream of the area leaves the map, or a coastline. **Gradient** is a measure of the steepness of a slope. One way to determine and express the gradient of a slope is by measuring its steepness as an angle of ascent or descent (expressed in degrees). On a topographic map, gradient is usually determined by dividing the relief (rise or fall) between two points on the map by the distance (run) between them (expressed as a fraction in feet per mile or meters per kilometer). For example, if points **A** and **B** on a map have elevations of 200 ft and 300 ft, and the points are located two miles apart, then:

$$\text{gradient} = \frac{\text{relief (amount of rise or fall between } \mathbf{A} \text{ and } \mathbf{B})}{\text{distance between } \mathbf{A} \text{ and } \mathbf{B}}$$

$$= \frac{100 \text{ ft}}{2 \text{ mi}} = 50 \text{ ft/mi}$$

ACTIVITY 1

Introduction to Topographic Maps
Complete this activity to enhance your ability to locate and characterize features on topographic maps and construct topographic maps.

PART B: TOPOGRAPHIC PROFILES AND VERTICAL EXAGGERATION

A topographic map provides an overhead (aerial) view of an area, depicting features and relief by means of its symbols and contour lines. Occasionally a cross section of the topography is useful. A **topographic profile** is a cross section that shows the elevations and slopes along a given line (Figure 14).

Follow these steps and Figure 14 to construct a topographic profile:

Step 1: On the map, draw a **line of section** along which the profile is to be constructed. Label the section line **A–A'**. Be sure that the line intersects all of the features (ridges, valleys, streams, etc.) that you wish the profile to show.

Step 2: On a strip of paper placed along section line **A–A'**, make tick marks at each place where a contour line intersects the section line and note the elevation at the tick marks. Also note the location and elevation of points **A**, **A'**, and any streams crossed.

Step 3: Draw the profile. On a separate sheet of paper, draw a series of equally spaced parallel lines that are the same length as the line of section (graph paper can be used). Each horizontal line on this sheet represents a *constant elevation* and therefore corresponds to a contour line. The total number of horizontal lines that you need, and their elevations, depends on the total relief along the line of section and on whether you make the space between the lines equal to the contour interval, or to multiples of it (vertical exaggeration, which will be discussed shortly). Label your lines so that the highest and lowest elevations along the line of section will be within the grid.

Then, take the strip of paper you marked in Step 2 and place it along the base of your profile. Mark a dot on the grid above it for each elevation. Smoothly connect these dots to complete the topographic profile. (This line should not make angular bends. Make it a smoothly curving line that reflects the relief of the land surface along the line of section.)

Step 4: The vertical scale of your profile will vary greatly depending on how you draw the grid. It almost certainly will be larger than the horizontal scale of the map. This difference causes an exaggeration in the vertical dimension. Such exaggeration almost always is necessary to construct a readable profile, for without vertical exaggeration, the profile might be so shallow that only the highest peaks would be visible. Calculate the **vertical exaggeration** by one of two methods. *You can divide the horizontal ratio scale (1:24,000) by the vertical ratio scale (1:1440)*, which reduces to 24,000/1440, which reduces to 16.7 (Method 1, Step 4, Figure 14). Or *you can divide the vertical fractional scale (1/1440) by the horizontal fractional scale (1/24,000)*, which reduces to 24,000/1440, which reduces to 16.7 (Method 2, Step 4, Figure 14). The number 16.7 (usually written 16.7 ×) indicates that the relief shown on the profile is 16.7 times greater than the true relief. This makes the slopes on the profile 16.7 times steeper than the corresponding real slopes on the ground.

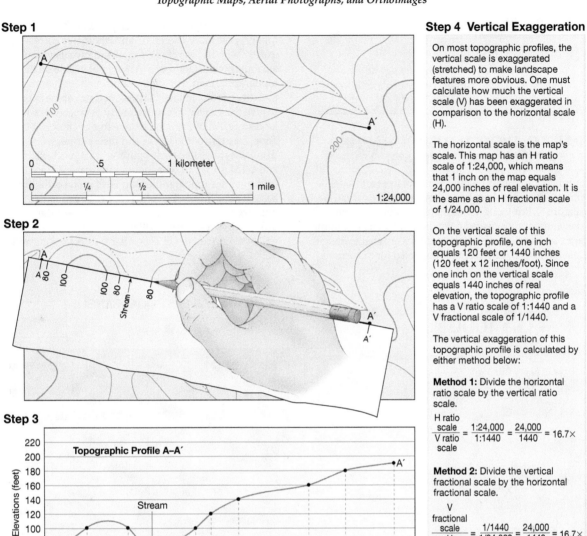

Step 1

Step 2

Step 3

Topographic Profile A–A′

Paper strip with elevations noted beside tick marks.

Step 4 Vertical Exaggeration

On most topographic profiles, the vertical scale is exaggerated (stretched) to make landscape features more obvious. One must calculate how much the vertical scale (V) has been exaggerated in comparison to the horizontal scale (H).

The horizontal scale is the map's scale. This map has an H ratio scale of 1:24,000, which means that 1 inch on the map equals 24,000 inches of real elevation. It is the same as an H fractional scale of 1/24,000.

On the vertical scale of this topographic profile, one inch equals 120 feet or 1440 inches (120 feet x 12 inches/foot). Since one inch on the vertical scale equals 1440 inches of real elevation, the topographic profile has a V ratio scale of 1:1440 and a V fractional scale of 1/1440.

The vertical exaggeration of this topographic profile is calculated by either method below:

Method 1: Divide the horizontal ratio scale by the vertical ratio scale.

$$\frac{\text{H ratio scale}}{\text{V ratio scale}} = \frac{1{:}24{,}000}{1{:}1440} = \frac{24{,}000}{1440} = 16.7\times$$

Method 2: Divide the vertical fractional scale by the horizontal fractional scale.

$$\frac{\text{V fractional scale}}{\text{H fractional scale}} = \frac{1/1440}{1/24{,}000} = \frac{24{,}000}{1440} = 16.7\times$$

FIGURE 14 Topographic profile construction and vertical exaggeration. Shown are a topographic map (Step 1), topographic profile constructed along line **A–A'** (Steps 2 and 3), and calculation of vertical exaggeration (Step 4).
Step 1—Select two points (**A, A'**), and the line between them (line **A–A'**), along which you want to construct a topographic profile. **Step 2**—To construct the profile, the edge of a strip of paper was placed along line **A–A'** on the topographic map. A tick mark was then placed on the edge of the paper at each point where a contour line and stream intersected the edge of the paper. The elevation represented by each contour line was noted on its corresponding tick mark. **Step 3**—The edge of the strip of paper (with tick marks and elevations) was placed along the bottom line of a piece of lined paper, and the lined paper was graduated for elevations (along its right margin). A black dot was placed on the profile above each tick mark at the elevation noted on the tick mark. The black dots were then connected with a smooth line to complete the topographic profile.
Step 4—*Vertical exaggeration* of the profile was calculated using either of two methods. Thus, the vertical dimension of this profile is exaggerated (stretched) to 16.7 times greater than it actually appears in nature compared to the horizontal/map dimension.

ACTIVITY 2

Topographic Profile Construction

Construct a topographic profile using the graph paper provided beneath it, then calculate its vertical exaggeration.

PART C: DIGITAL TOPOGRAPHIC MAPS AND ORTHOIMAGES

Aerial photographs (taken from airplanes) and satellite images are taken at angles oblique to the landscape (Figure 8), but topographic maps are representations of the landscape as viewed from directly above. **Orthoimages** are digitized aerial photographs or satellite images that have been orthorectified, corrected for distortions until they have the same geometry and uniform scale as a topographic map. Therefore, an orthoimage correlates exactly with its topographic map and reveals visual attributes of the landscape that are not visible on the topographic map. The topographic map, orthoimage, and other orthorectified "layers" of data can be overlain to give the viewer an extraordinary perspective of the landscape. All of this can be done free of charge at US Topo, courtesy of the USGS and their partners. One can display features like hydrography (water bodies), roads, and UTM grid lines on a topographic base (Figure 15A), or display the topographic map layer on an orthoimage base (Figure 15B). All layers can be enlarged with outstanding resolution (Figure 15C). Some of the orthoimages are currently "Digital Maps— Beta," which will be upgraded to US Topo after the beta testing and periodically thereafter.

The National Map
US Topo

COFFEYVILLE EAST QUADRANGLE
KANSAS
7.5-MINUTE SERIES

KANSAS

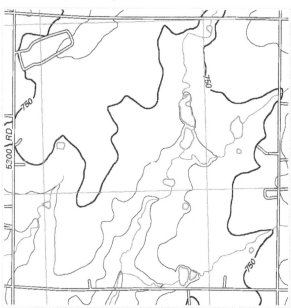

A. Topographic map base (contour lines), UTM grid lines (WGS84, Zone 15S), hydrography, and transportation features.

B. Orthoimage base with all other data layers: contour lines, UTM grid lines (WGS84, Zone 15S), geographic names and boundaries, hydrography, and transportation features.

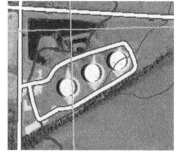

C. Enlarged portion of B.

FIGURE 15 US Topo—Free USGS digital topographic maps, orthoimages of quadrangles, and other data layers. Choose layers displayed on a topographic map base **(A),** or else combine the topographic base as one layer of data on an orthoimage base **(B)** that can be enlarged with high resolution **(C).** Use Adobe Reader® (or Adobe Acrobat®) to print products in GeoPDF® format. Using Adobe Acrobat®, you can save products as JPEG images for enhancement with any photo processing software.

ACTIVITY 3

Map CA Geology with a Topo Map and Orthoimage

Analyze a US Topo topographic map and orthoimage of part of the Ritter Ridge, CA $7\frac{1}{2}$-minute Quadrangle, and use them to practice mapping geologic features.

ACTIVITY 4

Map AZ Geology with a Topo Map and Orthoimage

Analyze a US Topo topographic map and orthoimage of part of the Grand Canyon (Havasu Falls, AZ $7\frac{1}{2}$-minute Quadrangle) and use them to practice mapping geologic features.

ACTIVITY 5

Obtain and Analyze a Topo Map or Orthoimage

Use US Topo to obtain and analyze (for free) a topographic map or orthoimage of a 7.5-minute quadrangle of your choice (or as noted by your instructor). You will need to follow the instructions below to obtain your map or orthoimage.

Follow these steps to view and download or print free maps and orthoimages from US Topo:

Step 1: Go to the USGS Store (http://store.usgs. gov). If your computer does not have Adobe Reader® (or Adobe Acrobat®), then download and install it from that site or Adobe (http://get .adobe.com/reader/). All of the US Topo maps and images are displayed in GeoPDF® format and can only be viewed with Adobe Reader® or Adobe Acrobat®.

Step 2: Go to *US Topo*. At the USGS Store, select US Topo. This will take you to the US Topo map locator. An orange bar (Show US Topo and "Digital Maps—Beta") beneath the map locator allows you to view the parts of the United States where final versions of US Topo are complete (yellow on the locator map) and where Digital Maps—Beta orthoimages are available (red on the locator map). Parts of the locator map that are not yellow or red have no orthoimages available on this site at this time. You can obtain topographic maps for those areas, but you cannot add or subtract layers from them. Check often for updates.

Step 3: Search for a place/quadrangle on US Topo. Follow "Step 1" at the right-hand side of the US Topo map locator. You can search for an address or place name, or use the pull-down menu to search for a specific quadrangle by name. The place will appear on the map locator as a red balloon marker. Alternatively, you can use the map locator to zoom in and view a region in map, satellite, or hybrid image mode until you find the place you are looking for. Click on that place to set a balloon marker.

Step 4: Obtain digital products for that location. Left click on the black dot in the center of the red balloon marker to obtain a list of products available for the Step-3 location. If an orthoimage is available, then it will appear as "US Topo" or "Digital Map— Beta." Other maps are also listed. Left click on "download" to display your selection. The US Topo and Digital Map—Beta files are large (10–20 MB) and may take some time to open or download. The beta orthoimage products do not include the topographic map layer at this time (2010). That layer will be available in the final US Topo version after the beta phase, so check for updates. To obtain the topographic map, go back to the list of downloadable files (that appeared when you clicked on the red balloon marker) and choose the topographic map.

If you obtain and open a US Topo or Digital Maps—Beta orthoimage or layered $7\frac{1}{2}$-minute quadrangle, then you can add or subtract layers from them by using the menu along the left-hand side of the image. You will also be given the option of downloading a free TerraGo Toolbar (Windows OS only) that allows you to measure distances, add comments, and merge products with Google Maps™ or your GPS.

Step 5: Printing and Downloading Tips. You can print all or parts of the maps and orthoimages that you display in US Topo. The GeoPDF® files are very large (10–20 MB), so be patient and allow time for them to load, display, and print. If you are using Adobe Acrobat®, then you can use the "save as" function to easily convert and save the GeoPDF® file as a high resolution JPEG file, which can be enhanced with any photo processing software. If you have a snipping tool on your computer (Windows 7), then you can also snip the images as low-resolution JPEG files.

PART D: AERIAL PHOTOGRAPHS

Aerial photographs are pictures of Earth taken from airplanes, with large cameras that generally make 9-by-9-inch negatives. Most of these photographs are black and white, but color pictures sometimes are available. The photographs may be large scale or small scale, depending on the elevation at which they were taken, on the focal length of the camera lens, and on whether the pictures have been enlarged or reduced from the negatives.

Aerial photographs can be taken nearly straight down from the plane, termed *vertical*, or they may be taken at a large angle to the vertical, termed *oblique*. Oblique views help reveal geological features and landforms; however, vertical aerial photographs are even more useful in geological studies. The photographs used in this exercise are verticals.

Vertical aerial photos are taken in a series during a flight so that the images form a continuous view of the area below. They are taken so that approximately 60% image overlap occurs between any two adjacent photos. The view is straight down at the very center of each picture (called the *center point* or *principal point*), but all other portions of the landscape are viewed at an angle that becomes increasingly oblique away from the center of the picture.

The scale of any photographic image cannot be uniform, because it differs with the distance of the camera lens from the ground. Thus, in photos of flat terrain, the scale is largest at the center of the photo, where the ground is closest to the camera lens, and decreases away from the center. Also, hilltops and other high points that are closer to the camera lens are shown at larger scales than are valley bottoms and other low places.

Aerial photos commonly are overlapped to form a **stereogram,** or **stereo pair,** to be viewed with a *stereoscope* (Figures 16, 17). When the photos

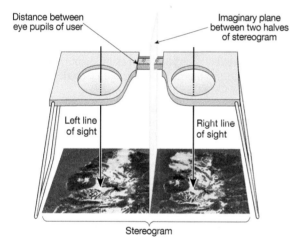

FIGURE 16 How to use a pocket stereoscope. First, have a partner measure the distance between the pupils of your eyes, in millimeters. Set the distance on the stereoscope. Then, position the stereoscope so that your lines of sight are aimed at a common point on each half of the stereogram (stereopair). As you look through the stereoscope, move it around slightly until the image "pops" into three dimensions. Be patient during this first attempt so that your eyes can focus correctly.

Most people do not need a stereoscope to see the stereograms in stereo (three-dimensions). Try holding the stereogram at a comfortable distance (one foot or so) from your eyes. Cross your eyes until you see four photographs (two stereograms), then relax your eyes to let the two center photographs merge into one stereo image.

are viewed through the stereoscope, the image appears three-dimensional (stereo). This view is startling, dramatic, and reveals surprises about the terrain, as you shall see shortly. Stereoscopes can be of many types, but the most commonly used variety is a *pocket stereoscope* such as the one shown in Figure 16.

Figure 17 shows parts of three overlapping vertical aerial photos. They have been cropped (trimmed) and mounted in sequence. The view is of Garibaldi Provincial Park in British Columbia, Canada. All three pictures show a dark volcanic cinder cone bulging out into Garibaldi Lake from the edge of Mount Price. Each photo shows it from a different overhead viewpoint. These landscape features are depicted by contours on the topographic map in Figure 18.

The center point of each photo is marked with a circled **X.** In the right-hand photo (BC 866:50), the center point is in the lake. In the middle photo (BC 866:49), it is near the cinder cone. In the left-hand photo (BC 866:48), it is near the margin of the page. By locating these center points on the map and connecting them with straight lines, you can see the **flight line,** or route flown by the photographing aircraft.

Locating the centers of these photos on the topographic map (Figure 18) is not easy, because the map and the photos show different types of features. However, you can plot the centers fairly accurately by referring to recognizable topographic features such as stream valleys and angles in the lakeshore.

ACTIVITY 6

Aerial Photographs

Complete this activity to learn more about stereograms (stereo pairs) of aerial photographs and how they can be used to reveal geologic features.

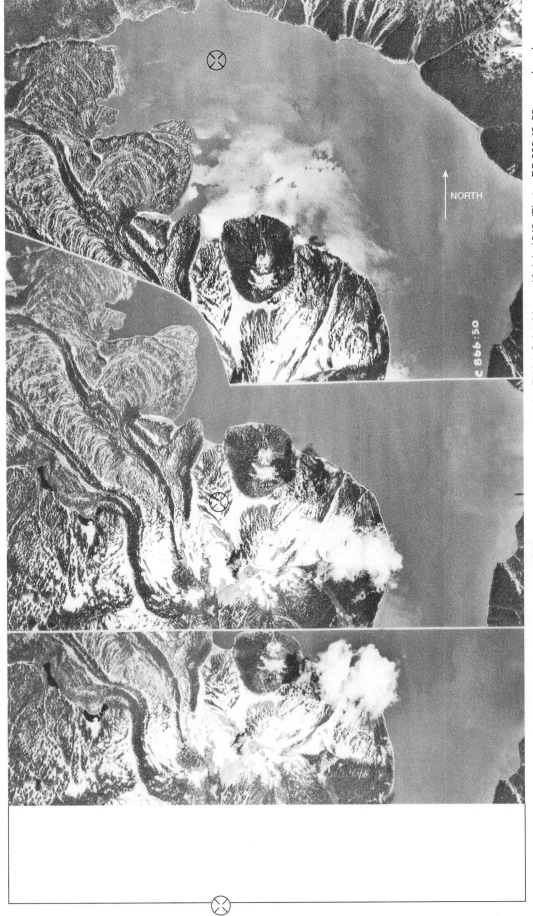

FIGURE 17 Stereogram comprised of three aerial photographs taken at Garibaldi Lake and vicinity, British Columbia, on 13 July 1949. (Photos BC 866:48–50, reproduced courtesy of Surveys & Resource Mapping Branch, Ministry of Environment, Government of British Columbia, Canada.)

203

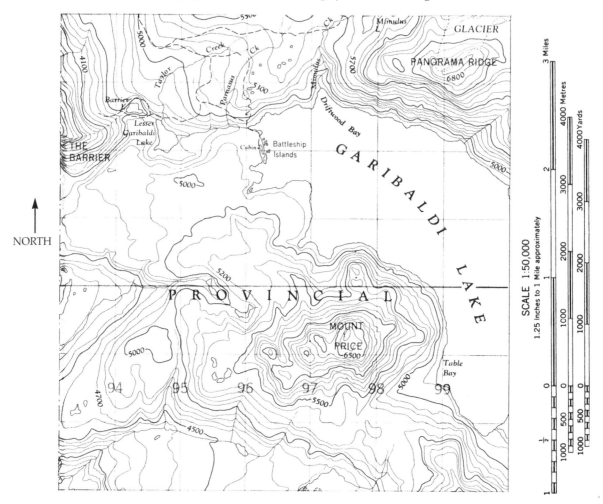

FIGURE 18 Portion of the Cheakamus River, East, topographic quadrangle map, British Columbia, on 13 July 1949; the same time at which the stereogram Figure 17 was made. (Reproduced courtesy of Surveys & Resource Mapping Branch, Ministry of Environment, Government of British Columbia, Canada.)

ACTIVITY 1 Introduction to Topographic Maps

Name: _____   Course/Section: _____

Materials: Pencil, calculator.

A. What are the latitude-longitude coordinates   Latitude: _____ Longitude: _____
of point **B** in Figure 1?

B. Refer to Figure 4.

    1. What is the bearing   **2.** What is the bearing
       from point C to point D? _____   from point D to point C? _____

C. Refer to Figure 5 (PLSS).

    1. Review how the location of point **x** in Figure 5C was determined using PLSS shorthand (see the caption for Figure 5).
       What is the location of point **z** in Figure 5C in PLSS shorthand?

    2. How many acres are present in the township in Figure 5B? (*Hint:* There are 640 acres in 1 mi^2.) Show your work.

    3. Imagine that you wanted to purchase the NE 1/4 of the SE 1/4 of section 11 in Figure 5C. If the property costs $500
       per acre, then how much must you pay for the entire property? Explain.

D. Examine Figure 2.

    1. In what UTM zone is this map located? _____

    2. What are the exact UTM (NAD 27) coordinates of Puritan Mine near the southwest corner of this map?

    3. Notice that the southwest corner of this map bears evidence of significant mining activity. Gold, copper, and titanium
       were mined here until the early 1900s, and it is still possible to find gold nuggets. There are several different symbols
       used on this map to indicate different kinds of mining activity. Draw the different symbols below and label them with
       what they mean (see Figure 3 for help).

    4. What linear geologic feature cuts across this map from sec.15 T6N, R13W to sec. 34 T6N, R12W?

    5. What is the total relief of this map area, and how did you determine it?

E. USGS 30 × 60 minute maps have a scale of 1:100,000.

    1. One inch on such maps equals about how many miles?
       Show your work.

    2. One cm on such maps equals about how many meters?
       Show your work.

F. Most handheld 12-channel parallel GPS receivers have an error of about 5 m when they fix on their position, and most
geologists plot their data on $7\frac{1}{2}$-minute topographic quadrangle maps that have a ratio scale of 1:24,000. If an object is
5 meters long in real life, then exactly how long (in millimeters) would it be on the 1:24,000 scale map?

CONTINUED

G. Use interpolation and extrapolation to estimate and label elevations of all points below that are not labeled (see Figure 10 for help). Then add contour lines using a contour interval of 100 feet. Notice how the 0-foot and 100-foot contour lines have already been drawn.

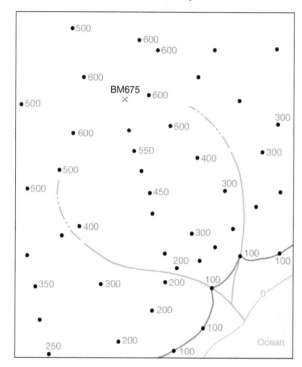

H. Contour the elevations on the map below using a contour interval of 10 feet. Refer to Figure 10 as needed.

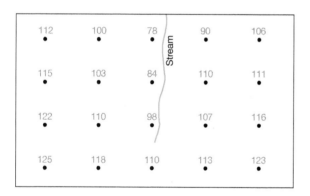

I. Using a contour interval of 10 feet, label the elevation of every contour line on the map below. (*Hint:* Start at sea level and refer to Figures 12 and 13.)

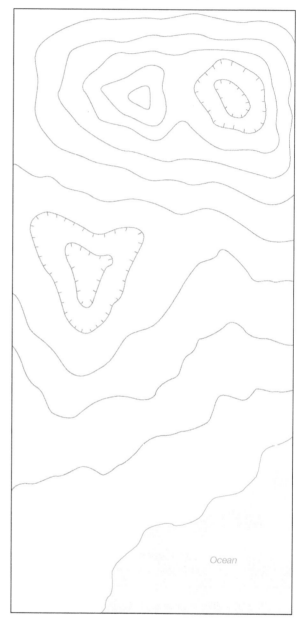

J. Analyze the topographic map below.

1. The contour lines on this map are labeled in meters.
   What is the contour interval of this map in meters? _____

2. What is the regional (total) relief of the land represented in this map in meters? _____

3. What is the gradient from **Y** to **X**? Show your work.

4. How could you find the areas of this map that have a gradient of 20 meters per kilometer or greater? (*Hint:* Think of the contour interval and how many contour lines of map elevation must occur along one kilometer of map distance.)

5. Imagine that you need to drive a truck from point **A** to point **B** in this mapped area and that your truck cannot travel up any slopes having a gradient over 20 m/km. Trace a route that you could drive to get from point **A** to point **B**. (More than one solution is possible.)

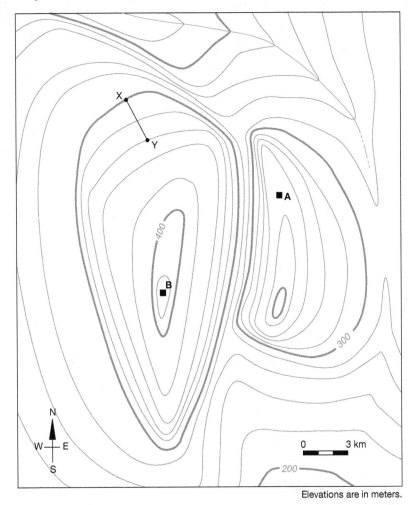

Elevations are in meters.

ACTIVITY 2 Topographic Profile Construction

Name: _____   **Course/Section:** _____

Materials: Pencil, calculator, ruler.

A. Construct a topographic profile for **A–A′** on the graph paper provided.

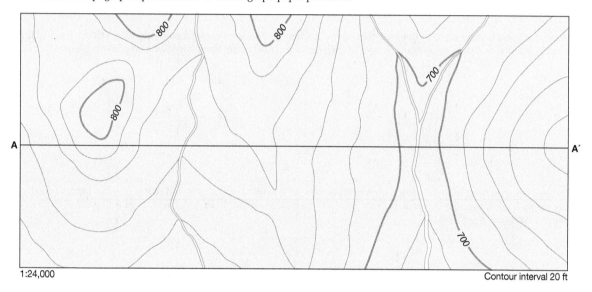

1:24,000   Contour interval 20 ft

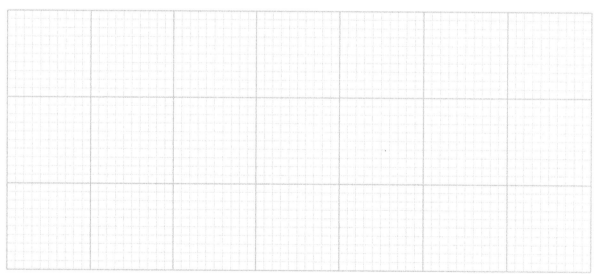

B. What is the vertical exaggeration of the topographic profile that you constructed above? Show your work.

ACTIVITY 3 Map CA Geology with a Topo Map and Orthoimage

Name: _____   **Course/Section:** _____

Materials: Pencil, colored pencils, pen (black or blue).

Analyze part of the Ritter Ridge, CA topographic map (part of Figure 2) and orthoimage below, to see if you can locate the exact line of the San Andreas Fault. The Pelona Schist is located all along the north side of the fault here and in the hills like Ritter Ridge. North and east of Ritter Ridge, the lowlands are Quaternary gravel.

A. On the orthoimage, draw a pen line along the exact trace of the San Andreas Fault. Be as exact as you can.

B. On the topographic map:

  1. Plot the same fault line (with pen) that you drew on the orthoimage.

  2. Based on the change in topography, draw a second pen line that is the contact (boundary) between the Pelona Schist and Quaternary gravel.

  3. Use colored pencils to color the Quaternary gravel yellow and the Pelona Schist another contrasting color of your choice.

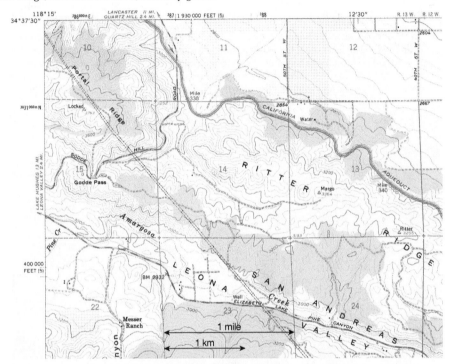

ACTIVITY 4 Map AZ Geology with a Topo Map and Orthoimage

Name: _____ **Course/Section:** _____

Materials: Pencil, red and blue colored pencils, pen (black or blue).

Analyze part of the Havasu Falls, AZ topographic map and orthoimage below (courtesy of U.S. Geological Survey, US Topo). A 1-km NAD27 UTM grid is visible on the map.

A. Find the Sinyala Fault zone in the orthoimage (cuts across the eastern half of the image). Map the fault by tracing the exact line(s) of its path with a black or blue pen on the orthoimage (first) and the topographic map.

B. The Cambrian Mauv Limestone Formation forms the floor of the canyon and has been labeled "**M**" at several places on the orthoimage. The location of the Pennsylvanian Watahomigi Formation has also been labeled "**W**." Notice that you can locate the two formations based on their topographic expression on the orthoimage and map. Map both formations onto the topographic map by coloring (as neatly and exact as you can) the Mauv red and the Watahomigi blue everywhere that they appear on the topographic map. Are these formations horizontal or dipping (tilted)?

ACTIVITY 5 Obtain and Analyze a Topo Map or Orthoimage

Name: _____   Course/Section: _____

Materials: Ruler, pencil.

A. Refer to Part C of your manual for instructions on how to obtain USGS topographic maps and orthoimages from US Topo. Follow the steps in Part C and on the US Topo web site to display and print a copy of a topographic map or orthoimage of your choice. Write your name on the print and staple a copy of it to this activity sheet to hand in.

B. Analyze the map/image that you printed. Be prepared to share your work with other members of the class/lab.

1. What quadrangle did you choose? Why?

2. In what year was the quadrangle published (or most recently photorevised)? _____

3. **Recall that** the trident-shaped symbol on the bottom margin of the quadrangle (topographic map or orthoimage) shows the **declination** (difference in degrees) between compass north (MN) and true north (usually a *star* symbol). Also shown is the declination between compass north (*star* symbol) and grid north (GN). The magnetic pole migrates very slowly, so the declination is exact only for the year listed on the map. What was the magnetic declination between MN and true north when the quadrangle was published?

4. Obtain the most recent magnetic data from the Geomagnetic Data page of the NOAA National Geophysical Data Center (http://www.ngdc.noaa.gov/geomagmodels/Declination.jsp). Enter a zip code, or latitude and longitude coordinates, to find the current declination for the quadrangle. What is the declination now?

5. Find one geological feature in the quadrangle. Describe the feature and its location.

ACTIVITY 6 Aerial Photographs

Name: _____   Course/Section: _____

Materials: Pencil, pocket stereoscope (provided in the laboratory), calculator.

Figure 17 shows parts of three overlapping vertical air photos. They have been cropped (trimmed) and mounted in sequence. The view is of Garibaldi Provincial Park in British Columbia, Canada. All three pictures show a dark volcanic cinder cone bulging out into Garibaldi Lake from the edge of Mount Price. Each photo shows it from a different overhead viewpoint. These landscape features are depicted by contours on the topographic map in Figure 18. The center point of each photo is marked with a circled **X.** In the right-hand photo (BC 866:50), the center point is in the lake. In the middle photo (BC 866:49), it is near the cinder cone. In the left-hand photo (BC 866:48), it is near the margin of the page. By locating these center points on the map and connecting them with straight lines, you can see the **flight line,** or route flown by the photographing aircraft. Locating the centers of these photos on the topographic map (Figure 18) is not easy, because the map and the photos show different types of features. However, you can plot the centers fairly accurately by referring to recognizable topographic features such as stream valleys and angles in the lakeshore.

A. Notice how the image of the cinder cone in Figure 17 is distorted when you compare the three successive pictures. Not only is the base of the cone different in each picture, but the round patch of snow in the central crater appears to shift position relative to the base. In which photograph (left, middle, or right) does the image of the cone appear to be least distorted? Why?

The same varying-perspective view that distorts features in air photos also makes it possible to view them **stereoscopically.** Thus, when any two overlapping photos in a sequence are placed side-by-side and viewed with the stereoscope, you see the overlap area as a vertically exaggerated three-dimensional image of the landscape. (With practice, you can train your eyes to do this without a stereoscope.)

B. Features of the Garibaldi Lake region appear larger in the photos than they do on the topographic map (Figure 18). The topographic map has a scale of 1:50,000 (1/50,000, features are 0.00002 times their actual size). The scale of the photos is larger (more magnified). Calculate their scale by measuring corresponding distances on the photos and on the topographic map, setting these distances as a ratio, and then multiplying the map scale by this ratio. What is the nominal scale thus derived? (You must write "nominal scale" because the actual scale differs with elevation and distance from the camera lens, as mentioned above.)

C. Photograph BC 866:48 shows two broad pathways that sweep down the slopes of Mount Price from a point near the summit. One trends down to the south and southeast and the other to the northwest. Both are bordered by narrow ridges. What are these features, and of what rock type are they probably made?

D. On the map and stereogram, examine both sides of the outlet channel where Garibaldi Lake overflows into Lesser Garibaldi Lake, near the northwest corner of BC 866:50.

  1. Is the rock that forms the slopes on the north side of the outlet channel the same or different from that on the south side?

  2. Name two features in the photos that lead you to this interpretation.

E. Lakes, and the basins they occupy, can be formed in many ways. Based on these photos, how do you think Garibaldi Lake formed?

Geologic Structures, Maps, and Block Diagrams

CONTRIBUTING AUTHORS

Michael J. Hozik • *Stockton State College*
William R. Parrott, Jr. • *Stockton State College*
Raymond W. Talkington • *Stockton State College*

OBJECTIVES AND ACTIVITIES

A. Understand how to determine and record the attitude of structural elements on orthoimages and maps, apply the data to construct geologic maps and geologic cross sections, and identify geologic structures.

ACTIVITY 1: Introduction to Structural Geology

ACTIVITY 2: Geologic Mapping in Wyoming (Orthoimage Base)

ACTIVITY 3: Geologic Mapping in Colorado (Topo Map Base)

B. Know symbols used to describe the attitude of structural elements and use them to interpret and label geologic structures on block diagrams and three dimensional cardboard models.

ACTIVITY 4: Cardboard Model Analysis and Interpretation

ACTIVITY 5: Block Diagram Analysis and Interpretation

C. Be able to analyze and interpret geologic structures from geologic maps and construct detailed geologic cross sections.

ACTIVITY 6: Appalachian Mountains Geologic Map

ACTIVITY 7: Geologic Map of Colorado National Monument

STUDENT MATERIALS

Pencil, pen, eraser, laboratory notebook, ruler, set of colored pencils, scissors, Models 1–6 (located at the end of this chapter) and protractor.

INTRODUCTION

Sediment and lava are deposited in relatively flat horizontal layers called *beds* or *strata* (plural of stratum) like a layer cake. This is known as the geologic Law of Original Horizontality. So wherever strata are folded (no longer relatively flat) or tilted (no longer horizontal), they have been deformed. Many bodies of igneous and metamorphic rock that were originally massive (lacking internal structures; not layered) also show evidence of deformation, both internally (faulting, folding) and in general shape. **Structural geology** is the study of how bodies of rock are deformed and the study of structures like faults and folds that formed during deformation.

When a body of rock or sediment is subjected to severe *stress* (directed pressure), then it may eventually *strain* (undergo deformation: change in position or shape by tilting, faulting, folding, or shearing). Much of the study of structural geology involves deciphering stress and strain relationships recorded in geologic structures, which are used to infer regional geologic history. Structural geologists also decipher the shapes

From Laboratory 10 of *Laboratory Manual in Physical Geology*, Ninth Edition, American Geological Institute, National Association of Geoscience Teachers, Richard M. Busch, Dennis Tasa. Copyright © 2011 by Pearson Education, Inc. Published by Pearson Prentice Hall. All rights reserved.

and internal characteristics of geologic structures to help locate Earth resources (like petroleum and coal) that may be hidden within them.

PART A: INTRODUCTION TO STRUCTURAL GEOLOGY

Generally, geologists can see how bodies of rock or sediment are positioned three dimentionally where they *crop out* (stick out of the ground as an outcrop) at Earth's surface. They record this outcrop data on flat (two-dimensional) **geologic maps** using different colors and symbols to represent the locations of different layers or formations of rock and their directions and angles of tilting or other deformation. This map data are used to infer the geometry of geologic structures.

Formations and Contacts

Formations are mappable rock units (Figure 1). This means that they can be distinguished from one another "in the field" and are large enough to appear on a geologic map (which usually covers a $7\frac{1}{2}$-minute quadrangle). The surfaces between formations are called **contacts** and appear as lines on geologic maps and cross sections. Formations may be subdivided into mappable **members** composed of **beds** (individual strata, layers of rock or sediment). Individual beds/strata are rarely mapped because they are not wide enough to show up on a typical $7\frac{1}{2}$-minute quadrangle map (where a pencil line equals about 6 meters, 20 ft). An exception is a "marker bed," like a volcanic ash layer, which is so distinctive and easy to recognize that it can serve as a datum or time marker that can be traced over long distances or through complex geologic structures. Geologists assign each formation a formal name, which is capitalized (e.g., Yellow Formation or Yellow Fm in Figure 1) and published with a description of its distinguishing features and a "type locality" upon which the name and distinguishing features are based. The formal name can include the word "formation" or the name of the rock type that makes up the formation. For example, the Dakota Formation is also formally called the Dakota Sandstone. You can search for U.S. geologic maps and formation descriptions with the National Geologic Map Database and Geologic Names Lexicon **(http://ngmdb.usgs .gov).** This site also has links to state geologic maps.

Formations are three-dimensional bodies of rock that are represented on two-dimensional (planar) geologic maps by distinctive colors, patterns, and symbols. The widths of formations vary in outcrops and on maps because of variations in formation thickness, angle of tilting, and the angle of the landscape in which they crop out. The geologic map in Figure 1 shows the part of the map where each formation occurs but it does not yet include any information about the orientation of each unit relative to its original horizontality.

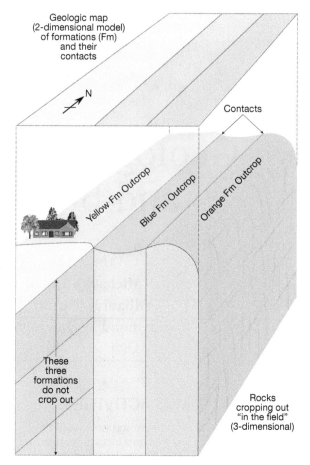

FIGURE 1 Geologic map of sedimentary rock formations (made of beds/strata) and contacts. Formations are mappable rock units, meaning that they can be distinguished from one another "in the field" and are large enough to appear on a geologic map (which usually covers a $7\frac{1}{2}$-minute quadrangle). Each formation has a capitalized formal name (e.g., Yellow Formation or Yellow Fm). Notice that all of the formations in this figure have the same thickness underground, but their outcrop and map widths are not the same. This is caused by steepness of the landscape and the angle of formation tilting (dip). All of the formations are deformed (no longer horizontal). The Blue and Orange Formations are vertical and the other formations are tilted (dip) about 40° toward the west.

A geologist must obtain such information in the field and add it to the map.

Strike and Dip

Attitude is the orientation of a rock unit, surface (contact), or line relative to horizontal and/or a compass direction. Geologists have devised a system of strike-and-dip for measuring and describing the attitude of tilted rock layers or surfaces, so they can visualize how they have been deformed from their original horizontality (Figures 2). Strike and dip are usually

STRIKE AND DIP

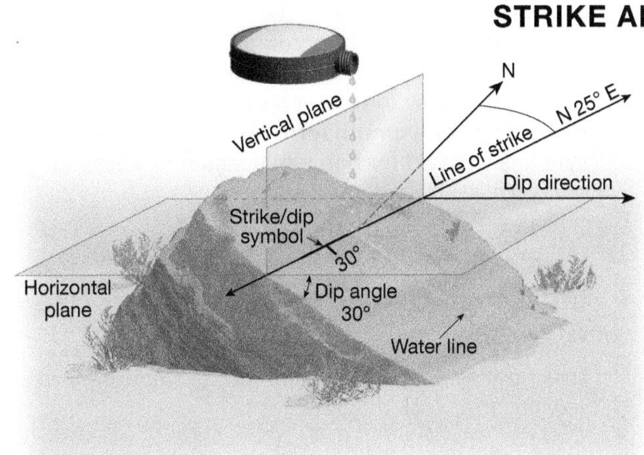

STRIKE–is the direction (bearing) of a line formed by the intersection of the surface (dip slope) of an inclined rock layer and a horizontal plane. (In this case: quadrant N25°E or azimuth 025°)

DIP–is the maximum angle of inclination of the rock layer, always measured perpendicular to strike. Water poured on a dip slope always runs along the dip and in the direction of dip (in this case 30°SE or azimuth 30° @ compass 115°).

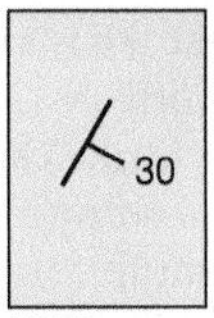

MAP SYMBOL FOR THIS STRIKE AND DIP–The long top line of the "T" represents the line of strike and the short line represents the dip direction. Degrees of dip are indicated beside the symbol. If the rock layer is horizontal, then a plus sign inside of a circle is used (or just a plus sign).

OUTCROP OF ROCK

MAP

DETERMINING STRIKE AND DIP FROM ORTHOIMAGES, AERIAL PHOTOGRAPHS, AND SATELLITE IMAGES

Flatiron–a triangular ridge of steeply dipping resistant rock between two V-shaped notches (cut by streams) and resembling the flat pointed end of a clothing iron. A jagged ridge of flatirons is parallel to strike, and the flatiron surfaces are dip slopes.

Hogback–a sharp-crested ridge of resistant rock that slopes equally on both sides, so it resembles the back of a razorback hog. The ridge crest is parallel to strike and dip is > 30°.

Cuesta–a ridge or hill of resistant rock with a short steep slope on one side (scarp) and a long gentle dip slope on the other side. The ridge is parallel to strike and the long gentle slope is a dip slope. Dip is < 30°.

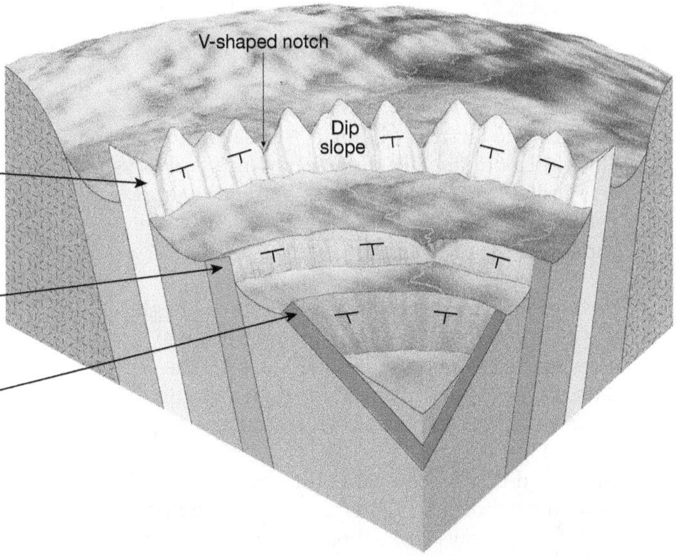

RULE OF Vs FOR FINDING DIP DIRECTION

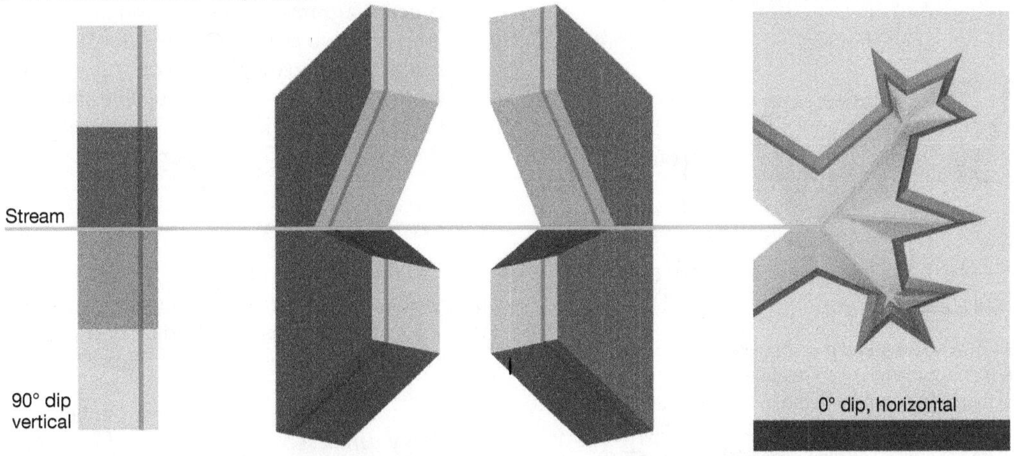

Vertical strata: No V-shapes in the rock layers or contacts can be seen on orthoimages and maps.

Tilted strata: Streams cut V-shapes into the rock layers and contacts that point in the direction of dip (except in rare cases when the slope of the stream bed is greater than the dip of the strata).

Horizontal strata: Streams cut V-shapes into the rock layers and contacts that point upstream and form a characteristic dendritic drainage (streams branching like a plant).

FIGURE 2 Strike and dip of a rock layers.

measured directly from an outcrop using a compass and clinometer (device for measuring the angle of inclined surfaces). However, they can be measured or estimated by the shapes of landforms observed from a distance or on aerial photographs, orthoimages, and satellite images (Figure 2):

- **Strike**—the *compass bearing* (line of direction or trend) of a line formed by the intersection of a horizontal plane (such as the surface of a lake) and an inclined surface (contact) or rock layer (bed, stratum, formation) (Figure 2, 3). When the strike is expressed in degrees east or west of true north or true south, it is called a *quadrant bearing*. Strike can also be expressed as a three-digit *azimuth bearing* in degrees between 000 and 360. In azimuth form, north is 000° (or 360°), east is 090°, south is 180°, and west is 270°.

- **Dip**—the *angle* between a horizontal plane and the inclined (tilted) stratum, fault, or fracture. As you can see in Figure 2, a thin stream of water poured onto an inclined surface always runs downhill along the **dip direction**, which is always perpendicular to the line (bearing, trend) of strike. The inclination of the water line, down from the horizontal plane, is the **dip angle.**

Dip is always expressed in terms of its dip angle and dip direction (bearing). The dip angle is always expressed in two digits (e.g., 30° in Figure 2). The dip direction can be expressed as a three-digit azimuth direction or as a quadrant direction like southeast or northwest (Figures 2, 3).

Strike-and-dip is shown on maps by use of a "T"-shaped symbol (see Figures 2–3). The long line (top of the "T") shows strike (line of direction), and the short line (upright of the "T") shows dip

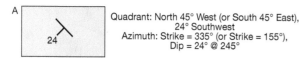

A Quadrant: North 45° West (or South 45° East),
24° Southwest
Azimuth: Strike = 335° (or Strike = 155°),
Dip = 24° @ 245°

B Quadrant: North 90° East (or South 90° West),
43° North
Azimuth: Strike = 090° (or Strike = 270°),
Dip = 43° @ 000°

FIGURE 3 The strike and dip symbol is used on maps to indicate the attitude (position relative to horizontal) of rock layers. The long line segment in the symbol indicates strike (a compass direction), and the short line segment points in the compass direction of dip (always perpendicular to strike). A number beside the symbol (if given) indicates the angle of dip (tilting). Compass directions can be expressed as bearings in quadrant or azimuth form. Azimuth bearings should be expressed as three digits in order to distinguish them from two-digit dip angles. Strike can be expressed as a bearing in either direction. See related symbols on Figure 4.

direction (bearing). Note that the dip direction is always perpendicular to strike. The short line of the "T" points *downdip*. The accompanying numerals indicate the dip angle in degrees. Refer to Figure 3 for examples of how to read and express strike and dip in quadrant or azimuth form. Also note that special symbols are used for horizontal strata (rock layers) and vertical strata (Figure 4).

Geologic Maps, Cross Sections, and Block Diagrams

Three representations of Earth are commonly used by structural geologists. These are the geologic map, cross section, and block diagram:

- **Geologic map**—a two-dimensional representation of the locations and attitudes of formations and contacts at Earth's surface, viewed from directly above. Most geologic maps also show the topography of the land surface with contour lines, so they are both a geologic *and* topographic map. This is useful, because some formations weather as topographic "highs" (hills, ridges) and others as topographic "lows" (depressions, valleys).

- **Geologic cross section**—a drawing of a vertical slice through Earth, with the material in front of it removed: a two-dimensional cutaway view. It shows the arrangement of formations and their contacts. A good cross section also shows the topography of the land surface, like a topographic profile. Vertical exposures of rocks in road cuts, cliffs, and canyon walls are natural geologic cross sections. Geologists often sketch them in their notebooks, then combine them with geologic maps to get a three-dimensional sense of subsurface geology.

- **Block diagram**—a combination of the geologic map and two cross sections. It looks like a solid block, with a geologic map on top and a geologic cross section on each of its visible sides (e.g., Figure 5). Each block diagram is a small three-dimensional model of a portion of Earth's crust.

Unconformities

Structural geologists must locate, observe, and interpret many different structures. Fundamentally, these include unconformities, faults, and folds. There are three common types of *unconformities* (see Figure 5):

- **Disconformity**—an unconformity between relatively *parallel* strata.

- **Angular unconformity**—an unconformity between *nonparallel* strata.

- **Nonconformity**—an unconformity between sedimentary rock/sediment and subjacent *nonsedimentary* (igneous or metamorphic) rock.

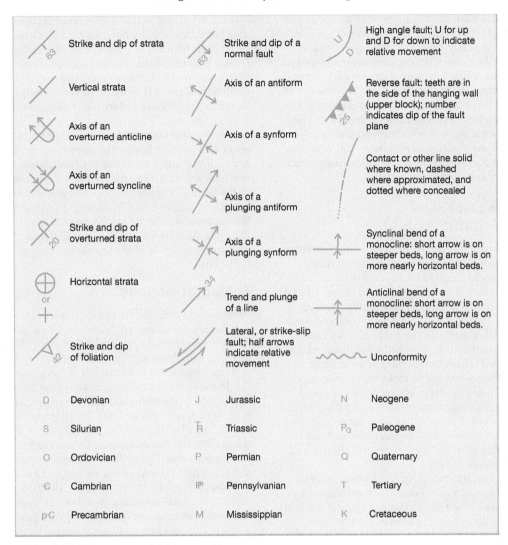

	Strike and dip of strata		Strike and dip of a normal fault		High angle fault; U for up and D for down to indicate relative movement
	Vertical strata		Axis of an antiform		Reverse fault: teeth are in the side of the hanging wall (upper block); number indicates dip of the fault plane
	Axis of an overturned anticline		Axis of a synform		Contact or other line solid where known, dashed where approximated, and dotted where concealed
	Axis of an overturned syncline		Axis of a plunging antiform		Synclinal bend of a monocline: short arrow is on steeper beds, long arrow is on more nearly horizontal beds.
	Strike and dip of overturned strata		Axis of a plunging synform		Anticlinal bend of a monocline: short arrow is on steeper beds, long arrow is on more nearly horizontal beds.
	Horizontal strata		Trend and plunge of a line		Unconformity
	Strike and dip of foliation		Lateral, or strike-slip fault; half arrows indicate relative movement		

D	Devonian	J	Jurassic	N	Neogene
S	Silurian	Ʀ	Triassic	Pɢ	Paleogene
O	Ordovician	P	Permian	Q	Quaternary
Ꞓ	Cambrian	ℙ	Pennsylvanian	T	Tertiary
pꞒ	Precambrian	M	Mississippian	K	Cretaceous

FIGURE 4 Structural geology symbols and abbreviations used on geologic maps.

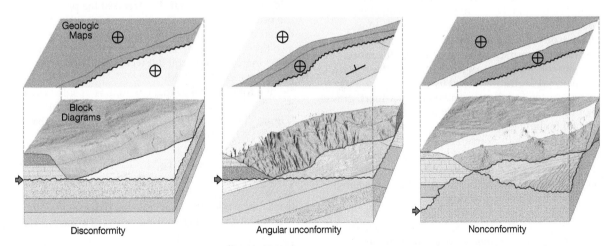

FIGURE 5 Unconformities. Arrows point to the unconformity surface (black line). A *disconformity* is an unconformity between relatively *parallel* strata. An *angular unconformity* is an unconformity between *nonparallel* strata. A *nonconformity* is an unconformity between sedimentary rock/sediment and either igneous or metamorphic rock.

Unconformities are usually uneven or irregular surfaces, because they usually are surfaces of erosion that were eventually buried by younger strata. For example, bedrock surfaces exposed on the slopes of hills and mountains in your region are part of a regional surface of erosion that could become an unconformity. If sea level were to rise and cover your region with a fresh layer of mud or sand, then the uneven regional surface of erosion would become a regional unconformity. Usually, the younger superjacent strata contain pieces of the older eroded rock within them, called *inclusions*.

Fractures and Faults (Brittle Deformation)

Brittle deformation is said to occur when rocks **fracture** (crack) or **fault** (slide in opposite directions along a crack in the rock). Fault surfaces usually have *slickensides*, linear grooves and ridges (mm to cm wide) that indicate the direction of movement along the fault. If you gently rub the palm of your hand back and forth along the slickensides, then one direction will seem smoother than the other. That is the relative direction of the side of the fault represented by your hand.

Faults form when brittle rocks experience one of these three kinds of severe stress: *tension* (pulling apart or lengthening), *compression* (pushing together, compacting, and shortening), or *shear* (smearing or tearing). The three kinds of stress produce three different kinds of faults: normal, reverse/thrust, and strike-slip (Figure 6).

Normal and reverse/thrust faults both involve vertical motions of rocks. These faults are named by noting the *sense of motion* of the top surface of the fault (top block) relative to the bottom surface (bottom block), regardless of which one actually has moved. The top surface of the fault is called the **hanging wall** and is the base of the **hanging wall** (top) **block** of rock. The bottom surface of the fault is called the **footwall** and forms the top of the **footwall block.** Whenever you see a fault in a vertical cross section, just imagine yourself walking on the fault surface. The surface that your feet would touch is the footwall.

Normal faults are caused by tension (rock lengthening). As tensional stress pulls the rocks apart, gravity pulls down the hanging wall block. Therefore, normal faulting gets its name because it is a normal response to gravity. You can recognize normal faults by recognizing the motion of the hanging wall block relative to the footwall block. First, imagine that the footwall block is stable (has not moved). If the hanging wall block has moved downward in relation to the footwall block, then the fault is a normal fault.

Reverse faults are caused by compression (rock shortening). As compressional stress pushes the rocks together, one block of rock gets pushed atop another. You can recognize reverse faults by recognizing the motion of the hanging wall block relative to the footwall

block. First, imagine that the footwall block is stable (has not moved). If the hanging wall block has moved upward in relation to the footwall block, then the fault is a reverse fault. **Thrust faults** are reverse faults that develop at a very low angle and may be very difficult to recognize (Figure 6). Reverse faults and thrust faults generally place older strata on top of younger strata.

Strike-slip faults (lateral faults) are caused by shear and involve horizontal motions of rocks (Figure 6). If you stand on one side of a strike-slip fault and look across it, then the rocks on the opposite side of the fault will appear to have slipped to the right or left. Along a *right-lateral (strike-slip) fault*, the rocks on the opposite side of the fault appear to have moved to the right. Along a *left-lateral (strike-slip) fault*, the rocks on the opposite side of the fault appear to have moved to the left.

Folded Structures

Folds are upward, downward, or sideways bends of rock layers. **Synclines** are "downfolds" or "concave folds," with the *youngest* rocks in the middle (Figure 7A). **Anticlines** are "upfolds" or "convex folds" with the *oldest* rocks in the middle (Figure 7B).

In a fold, each stratum is bent around an imaginary axis, like the crease in a piece of folded paper. This is the **fold axis** (or **hinge line**). For all strata in a fold, the fold axes lie within the **axial plane** of the fold (Figure 7A–D). The axial plane divides the fold into two **limbs** (sides, Figure 7B). For symmetric anticlines and synclines, the fold axis is vertical, but most anticlines and synclines are asymmetric. The axial plane of asymmetric folds is leaning to one side or the other, so one limb is steeper and shorter than the other.

The fold axis may not be horizontal, but rather it may plunge into the ground. This is called a **plunging fold** (Figure 7C, D). **Plunge** is the angle between the fold axis and horizontal. The **trend** of the plunge is the bearing (compass direction), measured in the direction that the axis is inclined downward. You can also think of the trend of a plunging fold as the direction a marble would roll if it were rolled down the plunging axis of the fold.

If a fold is tilted so that one limb is upside down, then the entire fold is called an **overturned fold** (Figure 7H). **Monoclines** have two axial planes that separate two nearly horizontal limbs from a single, more steeply inclined limb (Figure 7G).

Domes and **basins** (Figure 7E, F) are large, somewhat circular structures formed when strata are warped upward, like an upside-down bowl (dome) or downward, like a bowl (basin). Strata are oldest at the center of a dome, and youngest at the center of a basin.

Homoclines

A **homocline** is a geologic structure in which all of the formations/strata dip in one same direction. This can

FAULTED GEOLOGIC STRUCTURES (Brittle Deformation)

STRESS TYPES
and the strain (deformation)
they cause

FAULT TYPES
developed when brittle rocks
deform so much that they break

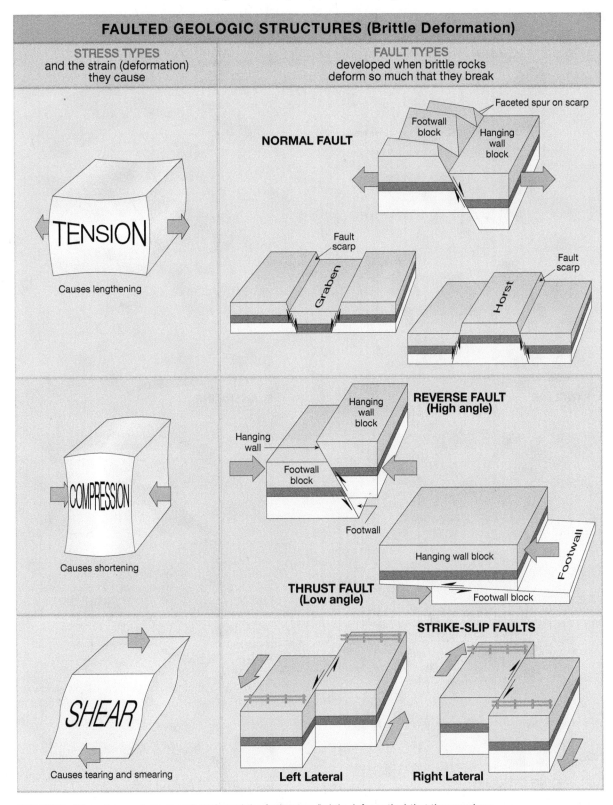

FIGURE 6   Three types of stress and strain and the fault types (brittle deformation) that they produce.

FOLDED GEOLOGIC STRUCTURES (Ductile Deformation)

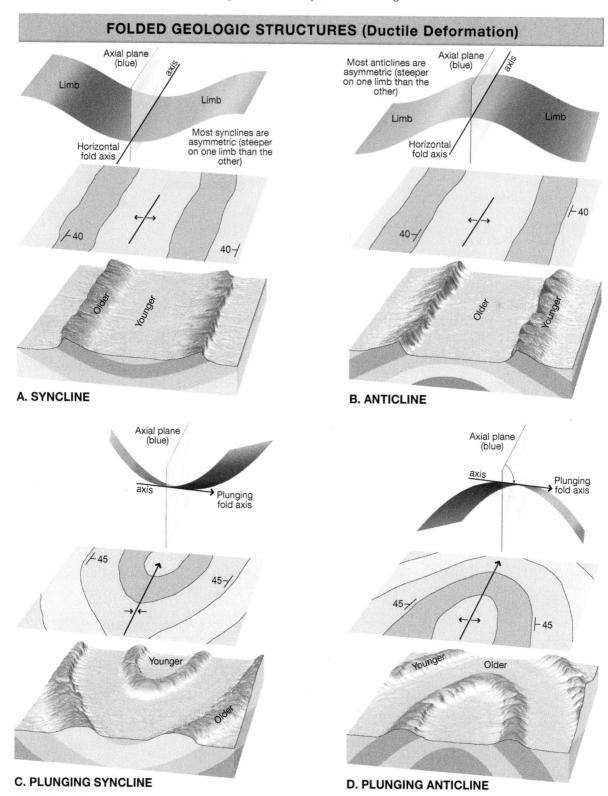

A. SYNCLINE

B. ANTICLINE

C. PLUNGING SYNCLINE

D. PLUNGING ANTICLINE

FIGURE 7 Folds—types of ductile deformation, in block diagrams and geologic maps. Fold axes and limbs are blue and red, respectively. Note how and where symbols from Figure 4 are used on the geologic maps.

FOLDED GEOLOGIC STRUCTURES (Ductile Deformation)

Basins are somewhat circular
or oval, with the youngest
strata in the middle

Domes are somewhat circular
or oval, with the oldest strata
in the middle

Youngest
strata

Oldest
strata

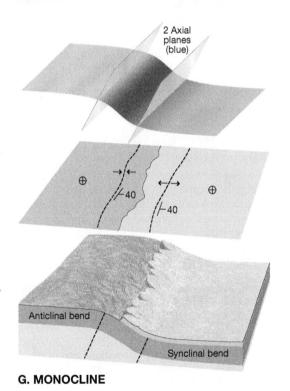

E. BASIN

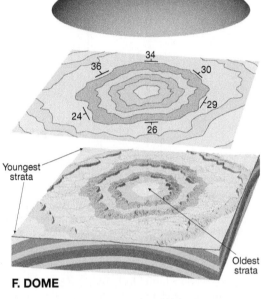

Youngest
strata

Oldest
strata

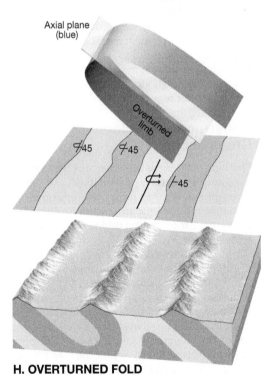

F. DOME

2 Axial
planes
(blue)

Anticlinal bend

Synclinal bend

G. MONOCLINE

Axial plane
(blue)

Overturned
limb

H. OVERTURNED FOLD

FIGURE 7 Folds. (CONTINUED)

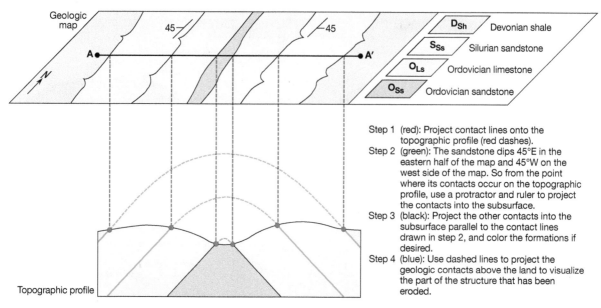

Step 1 (red): Project contact lines onto the topographic profile (red dashes).

Step 2 (green): The sandstone dips 45°E in the eastern half of the map and 45°W on the west side of the map. So from the point where its contacts occur on the topographic profile, use a protractor and ruler to project the contacts into the subsurface.

Step 3 (black): Project the other contacts into the subsurface parallel to the contact lines drawn in step 2, and color the formations if desired.

Step 4 (blue): Use dashed lines to project the geologic contacts above the land to visualize the part of the structure that has been eroded.

FIGURE 8 Geologic cross section construction. After you have selected a map location line for your profile (A–A') and constructed a topographic profile or rectangular box for that line segment, then follow these directions to add the geologic information that completes the cross section.

happen when a fault block (block of bedrock bounded by faults) is tilted, when the limb of a broad gentle "fold" is tilted but remains relatively planar, or when the edge of a continent is uplifted or subsides (and causes once-horizontal coastal plain strata to tilt regionally). It is useful to know the extent of the homocline in order to infer how it may be connected to another geologic structure or uplift/subsidence over a broader region.

Constructing Geologic Cross Sections

Geologic maps contain evidence of the surface locations and orientations of formations and the structures into which they have been deformed. To help visualize the geologic structures, geologists convert this surface information into vertical geologic cross sections.

Geologic cross sections are drawn perpendicular to strike. Most are drawn beneath a topographic profile (Figure 8), so you can see the topographic expression of the formations and geologic structures. However, some geologic cross sections are just rectangular cross sections that do not show the topography. Once you have constructed a topographic profile (or drawn a rectangular space) for the map line segment of the cross section (**A–A'**), then follow the directions in Figure 8 to add the geologic information. You will need to use a pencil (with a good eraser), protractor, ruler, and colored pencils and be very neat and exact in your work.

ACTIVITY 1

Introduction to Structural Geology

The activity is designed for you to practice the skills that you will apply in the remainder of the lab.

ACTIVITY 2

Geologic Mapping in Wyoming (Orthoimage Base)

Geologists often use orthoimages to help them do geologic mapping. In this activity you will determine strike and dip, map formations, sketch a geologic cross section, and identify and map a geologic structure.

ACTIVITY 3

Geologic Mapping in Colorado (Topo Map Base)

Geologists commonly map formations and information about structural elements onto a $7\frac{1}{2}$-minute map like this one. You will see how the topographic map can be used to map geology, conduct a geologic cross section, and determine the dip angle of a formation.

PART B: BLOCK DIAGRAMS, GEOLOGIC CROSS SECTIONS, AND GEOLOGIC MAPS

Block diagrams are either physical models (3-dimensional) of a block of bedrock or else a two-dimensional drawing rendered to appear three-dimensional. Both types look like a solid block, with a geologic map on top and a geologic cross section on each of its visible sides (e.g., Figure 5). You will need to know symbols used to describe the attitude of structural elements (Figure 4) and use them to interpret and label geologic structures on block diagrams and three dimensional cardboard models.

edges, so you can fold them into blocks. To fold them, follow the procedure printed in red on each model. You will also need to understand and apply the symbols for geologic structures (Figure 4) and follow the set of simple rules for interpreting geologic maps on the tops of the block diagrams (Figure 9, below).

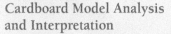

ACTIVITY 4

Cardboard Model Analysis and Interpretation

Six cardboard block diagrams (Models 1–6) are provided at the end of this chapter. Carefully remove them from the book and cut off the torn

ACTIVITY 5

Block Diagram Analysis and Interpretation

Illustrated block diagrams and geologic maps are provided for you to develop your skills of identifying, describing, and interpreting geologic structures. You will need to understand and apply the symbols in Figure 4 and follow the set of simple rules for interpreting geologic maps (Figure 9). Refer back to Figures 4–7 as needed.

RULES FOR INTERPRETING GEOLOGIC MAPS

1. Anticlines have their oldest beds in the center, and their limbs (sides) dip away from the fold axis.

2. Synclines have their youngest beds in the center, and their limbs (sides) dip toward the fold axis.

3. Plunging anticlines plunge toward the nose (closed end) of the V-shaped outcrop belt.

4. Plunging synclines plunge toward the open end of the V-shaped outcrop belt.

5. Streams cut "V" shapes into tilted beds and formation contacts that point in the direction of dip (except in rare cases when the slope of the stream is greater than the dip of the beds and formation contacts).

6. Streams cut "V" shapes into horizontal beds and formation contacts that point upstream. The formation contacts are parallel to topographic contour lines, and the stream drainage system developed on horizontal and/or unstratified formations has a dendritic pattern that resembles the branching of a tree.

7. Vertical beds do not "V" where streams cut across them.

8. The upthrown blocks of faults tend to be eroded more (down to older beds) than downthrown blocks.

9. Contacts migrate downdip upon erosion.

10. True dip angles can only be seen in cross section if the cross section is perpendicular to the fault or to the strike of the beds.

FIGURE 9   Some common rules used by geologists to interpret geologic maps.

PART C: ANALYSIS OF GEOLOGIC MAPS

Review the summary list of rules for interpreting geologic maps (Figure 9) that you learned in Parts A and B. A few useful additional rules have also been added. Then complete the activities below.

Appalachian Mountains Geologic Map

Analyze a geologic map from the Valley and Ridge Physiographic Province of the Appalachians, construct a detailed geologic cross section, and identify and map the geologic structures.

Geologic Map of Colorado National Monument

Analyze a geologic map from Colorado National Monument, construct a detailed geologic cross section, and identify and map the geologic structures.

ACTIVITY 1 Introduction to Structural Geology

Name: _____ Course/Section: _____

Materials: Pencil, pen; protractor and ruler from **GeoTools** sheets at the back of the manual.

A. This is a copy of the geologic map from Figure 1.

1. Add symbols (Figure 4) to show the attitude (strike and dip) of the formations.

2. Notice the abrupt change in dip at the contact between the Blue Fm and Yellow Fm Figure 1. This contact could be at least two different kinds of geologic structures. What are they?

   _____ _____

3. If you could see this contact in the field, and gather more evidence of exactly what kind of structure it is, then what evidence would you look for and how would you use it to decide which of the two structures is actually present at the contact?

B. For each map below, record the strike of the formations and their contacts. Then use the Rule of Vs (Figure 2) to determine the dip direction and sketch formation contacts on the geologic cross section (Figure 8, steps 1 and 2).

Hint: Cut a V-shaped notch into the top edge of a 3 x 5 card. Hold card vertically and look down on edge. See Vs at different dips of the card.

1. Strike: _____

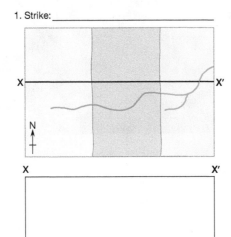

2. Strike: _____

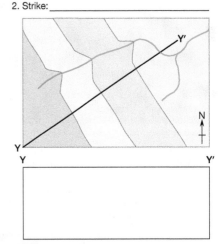

C. This is an aerial photograph taken from directly above the landscape. The view is 1 km wide.

1. Circle a V-shaped notch.

2. Add a strike and dip symbol to one of the flatirons.

3. What is the strike: _____

4. What is the dip direction: _____

CONTINUED

D. This orthoimage was acquired about 7 km east of Las Vegas, Nevada (US Topo: Frenchman Mtn. Quad.). The Nevada Geological Survey has determined that faulting occurred here 11–6 Ma. Use a pen to neatly and precisely trace the fault line that crosses this area and add half-arrow symbols (Figure 4) to show its relative motion. Scale: 1 cm = 0.11 km.

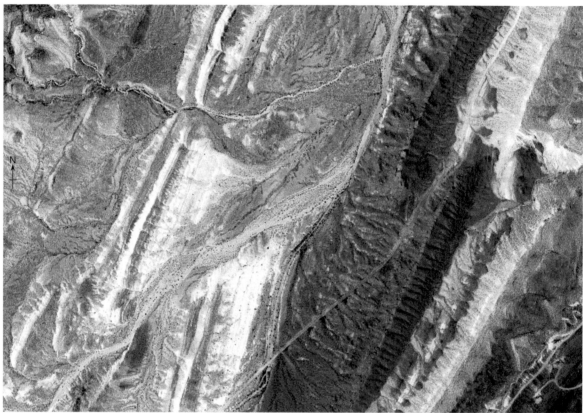

© Richard M. Busch

Exactly what kind of fault have you mapped above? _____

E. Below is a more detailed orthoimage of part of central Wyoming (US Topo). Yellow lines are the UTM square km grid. The striped red-brown and beige rock unit in the southeast corner of the image is interbedded sandstone and shale of the Triassic Dinwoody Fm. The smooth-looking brown rock unit at the top of the image is shale of the Permian Phosphoria Fm.

1. Draw one strike and dip symbol on the Dinwoody Fm and another one on a flatiron of the Phosphoria Fm to show their attitudes.

2. Notice, in the western half of the image, that sediment weathering from the Phosphoria Formation is moving downslope and covering parts of the Dinwoody Formation. This is forming what kind of geologic structure?

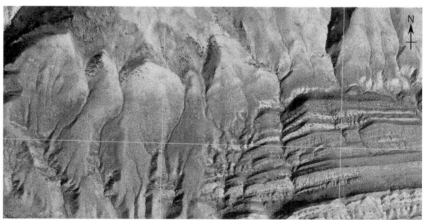

© Richard M. Busch

ACTIVITY 2 Geologic Mapping in Wyoming (Orthoimage Base)

Name: _____   Course/Section: _____

Materials: Pencil, pen; protractor and ruler.

This orthoimage is from central Wyoming's Wind River Basin. Four formations are labeled on the image and can be identified on the basis of how they weather: Lower Cretaceous Cloverly Sandstone (**C**), Lower to Upper Cretaceous Thermopolis and Mowry Shale (**TM**), Upper Cretaceous Frontier Sandstone (**F**), and Quaternary alluvial (stream) sediment (**Qal**).

A. Use a pen to carefully and precisely map the contacts between the formations on the orthoimage.

B. Add six strike and dip symbols to flatirons throughout the Frontier Formation (F) outcrop belt.

C. Sketch a geologic cross section for **X–Y**. In the bottom half, sketch the rocks at and below the ground. In the top half, use dashed lines to show what has eroded away as in Figure 8. Label formations in the sketch.

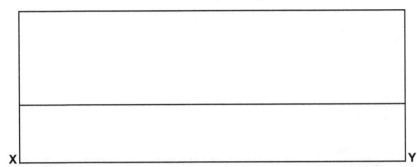

D. Exactly what kind of structure is this?

E. Map the axis of this structure onto the orthoimage with the correct symbol from Figure 4

ACTIVITY 3 Geologic Mapping in Colorado (Topo Map Base)

Name: _____   **Course/Section:** _____

Materials: Pencil, pen; protractor and ruler.

This is a 4-square-mile portion of the Boulder, Colorado $7\frac{1}{2}$-minute quadrangle (US Topo). The map has been selected to show the eastern edge of the Front Range of the Rocky Mountains (western part of the map) and western edge of the Great Plains (eastern margin of map). Notice that five formations crop out here and have been labeled on the image: Precambrian igneous and metamorphic rocks (**PC**), Permian Fountain and Lyons Sandstone (**Pfly**), Triassic and Jurassic Lykins and Morrison Mudstones (**TJ**), Cretaceous Dakota Sandstone (**Kd**), and Cretaceous Benton Shale Group (**Kb**).

A. Notice that the **PC** bedrock has a dendritic drainage, which indicates horizontal strata or homogeneous rock (in this case, homogeneous **PC** igneous and metamorphic rocks). What are the landforms that formed on **Pfly** and **Kd** here, and what do they indicate about the bedrock and its dip direction?

B. Each formation here weathers in a way that gives it a unique topography, which is visible on this map. Some formations are more resistant and form ridges. Less resistant rocks form gentle slopes and valleys. Streams flow along contacts or cut across formations at V-shaped notches. Based on topography, map (with lines) the formation contacts as accurately as possible.

C. Complete a geologic cross section A–A′ using the four steps in Figure 8.

D. The geologic cross section has vertical exaggeration (1.9 ×). To find the dip angle here, use the dip slope located in the SE corner of sect. 26. Plot its elevation change (ft) vs. distance (ft) on the graph below, then draw the slope and measure and record the dip.

E. Add a strike and dip symbol to the map based on D.

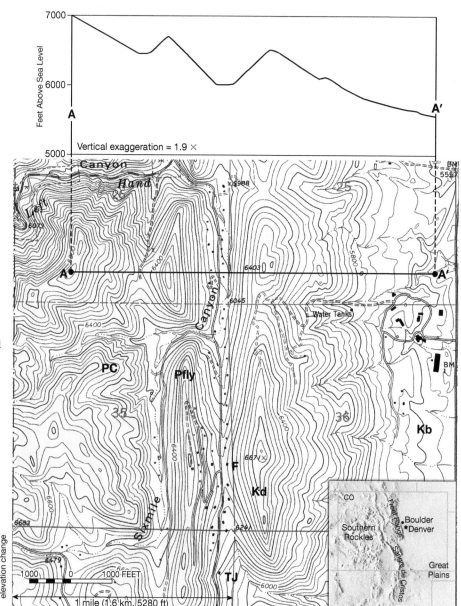

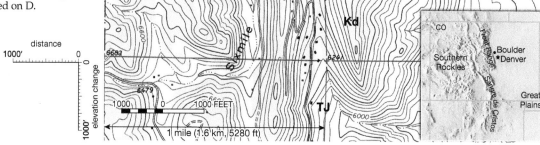

ACTIVITY 4 Model Analysis and Interpretation

Name: _____   Course/Section: _____

Materials: Pencil, scissors; protractor and ruler.

Tear Models 1–6 from the end of the chapter. Cut and fold them as noted in red on each model.

A. Model 1

This model shows Ordovician (green), Silurian (light gray), Devonian (bule-gray), Mississippian (dark gray), Pennsylvanian (yellow), and Permian (salmon) formations striking due north and dipping 24° to the west. Provided are a complete geologic map (the top of the diagram) and three of the four vertical cross sections (south, east, and west sides of the block diagram).

1. Finalize Model 1 as follows. First construct the vertical cross section on the north side of the block so it shows the formations and their attitudes (dips). On the map, draw a strike and dip symbol on the Mississippian sandstone that dips 24° to the west (see Figures 3 and 4 for the strike and dip symbol).

2. Explain the sequence of events that led to the existence of the formations and the relationships that now exist among them in this block diagram.

B. Model 2

This model is slightly more complicated than the previous one. The geologic map is complete, but only two of the cross sections are available. Letters **A–G** are ages from oldest (**A**) to youngest (**G**).

1. Finalize Model 2 as follows. First, complete the north and east sides of the block. Notice that the rock units define a fold. This fold is an anticline, because the strata are convex upward and the oldest formation (**A**) is in the center of the fold. It is symmetric (non-plunging), because its axis is horizontal. (Refer back to Figure 7 for the differences between plunging and non-plunging folds if you are uncertain about this.) On the geologic map, draw strike and dip symbols to indicate the attitudes of formation **E** (gray formation) at points **I, II, III,** and **IV**. Also draw the proper symbol on the map (top of model) along the axis of the fold (refer to Figure 4).

2. How do the strikes at all four locations compare with each other?

3. How does the dip direction at points **I** and **II** compare with the dip direction at points **III** and **IV**? *In your answer, include the dip direction at all four points.*

C. Model 3

This model has a complete geologic map. However, only one side and part of another are complete.

Letters **A–E** are ages from oldest (**A**) to youngest (**E**).

1. Finalize Model 3 as follows. Complete the remaining two-and-a-half sides of this model, using as guides the geologic map on top of the block and the one-and-a-half completed sides. On the map, draw strike and dip symbols showing the orientation of formation **C** at points **I, II, III,** and **IV**. Also draw the proper symbol along the axis of the fold (refer to Figure 4).

2. How do the strikes of all four locations compare with each other?

3. How does the dip direction (of formation **C**) at points **I** and **II** compare with the dip direction at points **III** and **IV**? *Include the dip direction at all four points in your answer.*

4. Is this fold plunging or non-plunging? _____

CONTINUED

5. Is it an anticline or a syncline? _____

6. On the basis of this example, how much variation is there in the strike at all points in a non-plunging fold?

D. Model 4

Letters **A–H** are ages from oldest (**A**) to youngest (**H**). This model shows a plunging anticline and an unconformity. The anticline plunges to the north, following the general rule that *anticlines plunge in the direction in which the fold closes.*

1. Finalize Model 4 as follows. Complete the north and east sides of the block. Draw strike and dip symbols on the map at points **I, II, III, IV,** and **V.** Draw the proper symbol on the map along the axis of the fold, including its direction of plunge. Also draw the proper symbol on the geologic map to indicate the orientation of beds in formation **J.**

2. How do the directions of strike and dip differ from those in Model 3?

3. What type of unconformity is at the base of formation **J**?

E. Model 5

Letters **A–H** are ages from oldest (**A**) to youngest (**H**). This model shows a plunging syncline. Two of the sides are complete and two remain incomplete.

1. Finalize Model 5 as follows. Complete the north and east sides of the diagram. Draw strike and dip symbols on the map at points **I, II, III, IV,** and **V** to show the orientation of layer **G.** *Synclines plunge in the direction in which the fold opens.* Draw the proper symbol along the axis of the fold (on the map) to indicate its location and direction of plunge.

2. In which direction (bearing, trend) does this syncline plunge?

F. Model 6

This model shows a fault that strikes due west and dips 45° to the north. Three sides of the diagram are complete, but the east side is incomplete.

1. Finalize Model 6 as follows. At point **I,** draw a symbol from Figure 4 to show the *orientation of the fault.* On the west edge of the block, draw arrows parallel to the fault, indicating relative motion. Label the hanging wall and the footwall. Complete the east side of the block. Draw half-arrows (Figure 4) parallel to the fault, to indicate its relative motion. Now look at the geologic map and at points **II** and **III.** Write **U** on the side that went up and **D** on the side that went down. At points **IV** and **V,** draw strike and dip symbols for formation **B.**

2. Is the fault in this model a normal fault or a reverse fault? Why?

3. On the geologic map, what happens to the contact between units **A** and **B** where it crosses the fault?

4. There is a general rule that, as erosion of the land proceeds, *contacts migrate downdip.* Is this true in this example? Explain.

5. Could the same offset along this fault have been produced by strike-slip motion?

ACTIVITY 5 Block Diagram Analysis and Interpretation

Name: _____   **Course/Section:** _____

Materials: Pencil.

For each block diagram: **1.** Complete the diagram so that contact lines between rock formations are drawn on all sides. **2.** Add symbols (Figures 4–7) to indicate the attitudes of all structures. **3.** On the line provided, write the exact name of the geologic structure represented in the diagram.

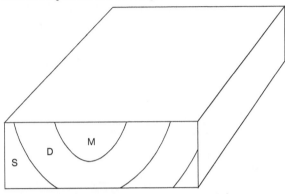

A. Complete top and side. Add appropriate symbols from Figure 4. What geologic structure is present?

_____

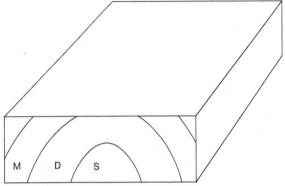

B. Complete top and side. Add appropriate symbols from Figure 4. What geologic structure is present?

_____

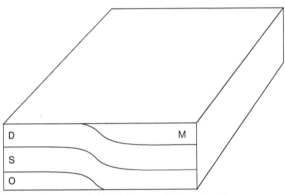

C. Complete top and side. Add appropriate symbols from Figure 4. What geologic structure is present?

_____

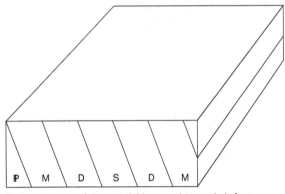

D. Complete top of diagram. Add appropriate symbols from Figure 4. What geologic structure is present?

_____

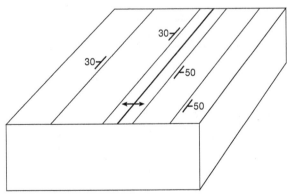

E. Complete the sides of the diagram. What geologic structure is present?

_____

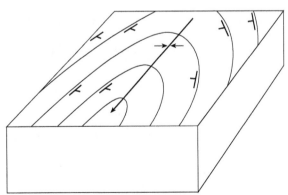

F. Complete the sides of the diagram. What geologic structure is present?

_____

For each block diagram: **1.** Complete the diagram so that contact lines between rock formations are drawn on all sides.
2. Add symbols (Figures 4–7) to indicate the attitudes of all structures. **3.** On the line provided, write the exact name of the geologic structure represented in the diagram.

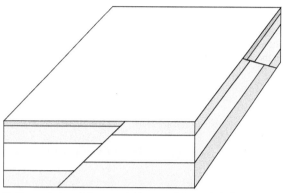

G. Complete top of diagram. Add appropriate symbols from Figure 4. What geologic structure is present?

_____

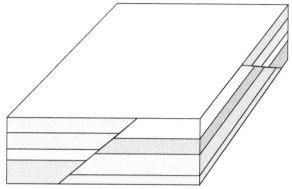

H. Complete top of the diagram. Add appropriate symbols from Figure 4. What geologic structure is present?

_____

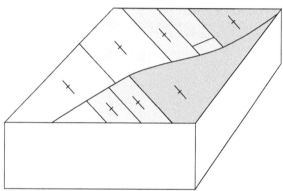

I. Complete the sides of the diagram. Add half-arrows. What geologic structure is present?

_____

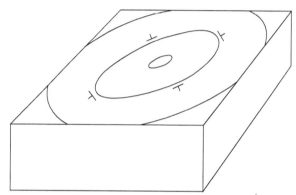

J. Complete the sides of the diagram. What geologic structure is present?

_____

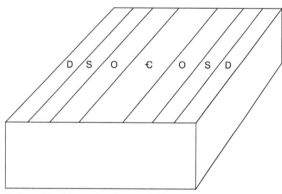

K. Complete sides of the diagram. Add appropriate symbols from Figure 4. What geologic structure is present?

_____

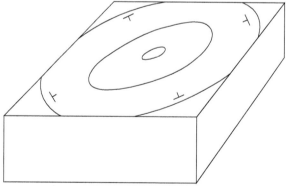

L. Complete the sides of the diagram. What geologic structure is present?

_____

ACTIVITY 6 Appalachian Mountains Geologic Map

Name: _____   Course/Section: _____

Materials: Pencil, scratch paper; protractor and ruler.

Directions: A. Complete the geologic cross section using the steps in Figure 8. **B.** Label the kind(s) of geologic structure(s) revealed by your work. Then add the appropriate symbols from Figure 4 to the geologic map to show the axes of the folds. **C.** Add half-arrows to the fault near the center of the geologic map to show the relative motions of its two sides. Exactly what kind of fault is it (refer to Figure 6)?

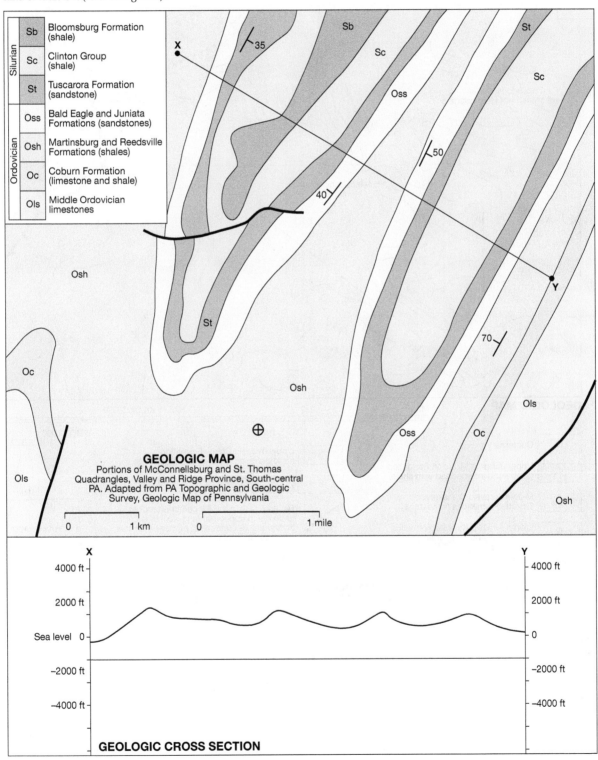

GEOLOGIC MAP
Portions of McConnellsburg and St. Thomas
Quadrangles, Valley and Ridge Province, South-central
PA. Adapted from PA Topographic and Geologic
Survey, Geologic Map of Pennsylvania

GEOLOGIC CROSS SECTION

233

ACTIVITY 7 Geologic Map of Colorado National Monument

Name: _____   Course/Section: _____

Materials: Pencil, scratch paper; protractor and ruler.

Directions: A. Complete the geologic cross section using the steps in Figure 8. **B.** What kind of geologic structure is present, and how do you think it formed? **C.** Modify the geologic map by adding the appropriate symbols from Figure 4 to show the location and orientation of the structure.

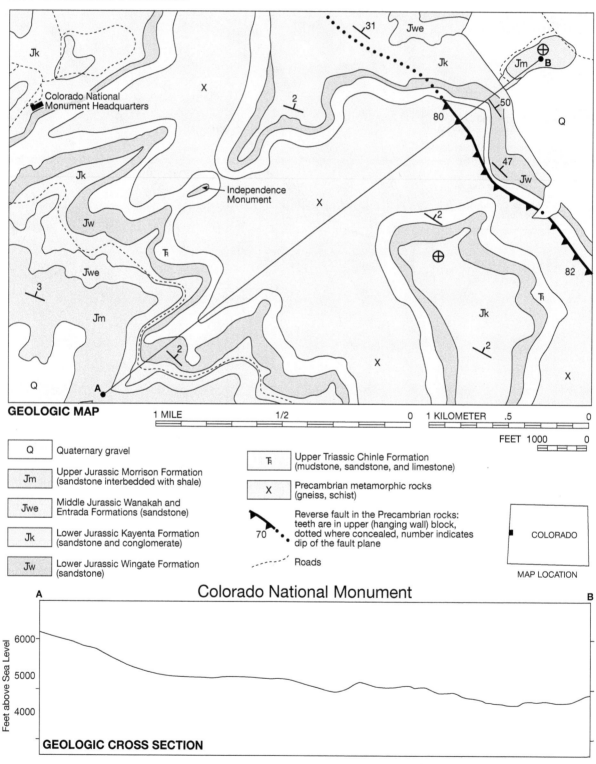

GEOLOGIC MAP

1 MILE   1/2   0   1 KILOMETER   .5   0

FEET 1000   0

Q	Quaternary gravel
Jm	Upper Jurassic Morrison Formation (sandstone interbedded with shale)
Jwe	Middle Jurassic Wanakah and Entrada Formations (sandstone)
Jk	Lower Jurassic Kayenta Formation (sandstone and conglomerate)
Jw	Lower Jurassic Wingate Formation (sandstone)

Ŧ	Upper Triassic Chinle Formation (mudstone, sandstone, and limestone)
X	Precambrian metamorphic rocks (gneiss, schist)
70 ⟋••	Reverse fault in the Precambrian rocks: teeth are in upper (hanging wall) block, dotted where concealed, number indicates dip of the fault plane
------	Roads

COLORADO

MAP LOCATION

Colorado National Monument

A   B

Feet above Sea Level

6000

5000

4000

GEOLOGIC CROSS SECTION

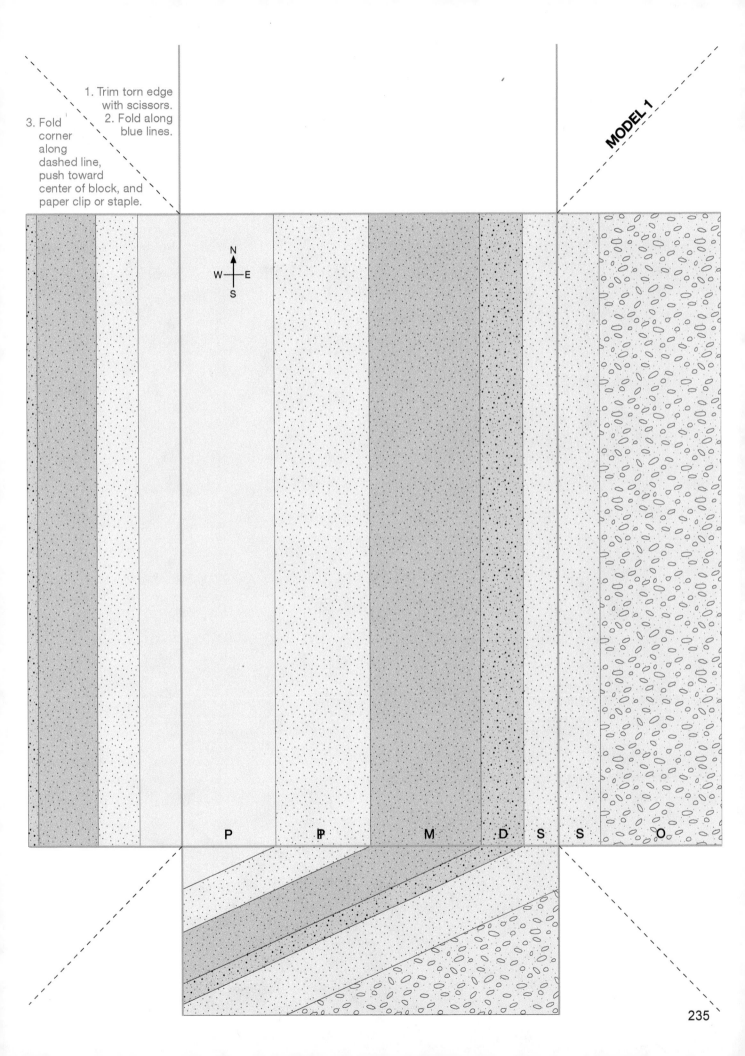

1. Trim torn edge
   with scissors.
2. Fold along
   blue lines.

3. Fold
   corner
   along
   dashed line,
   push toward
   center of block, and
   paper clip or staple.

MODEL 1

N
W—E
S

P   P   M   D S S   O

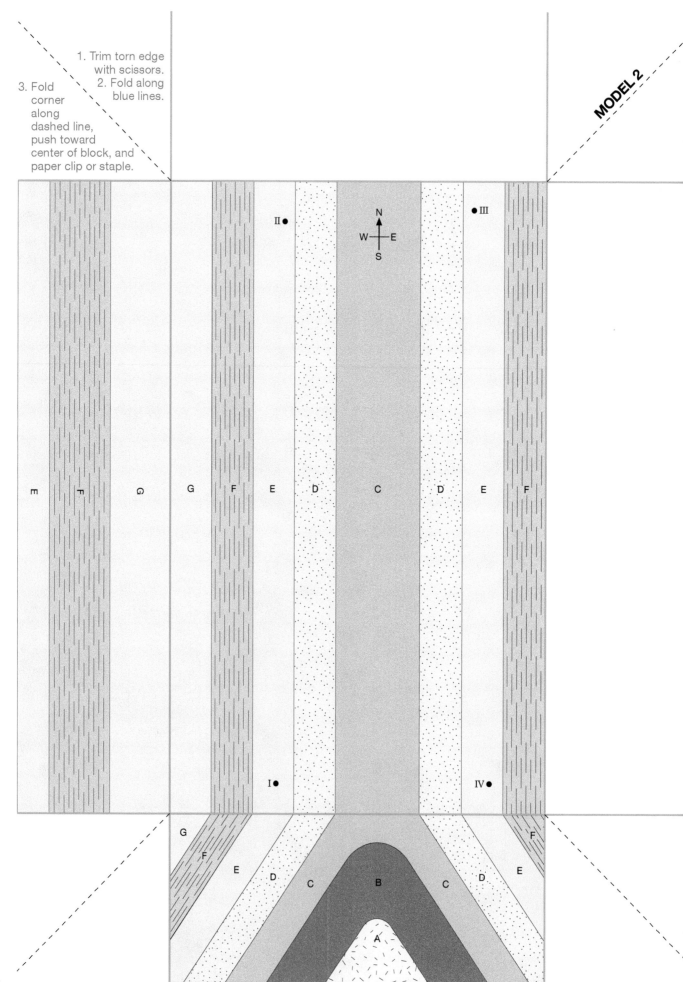

1. Trim torn edge with scissors.
2. Fold along blue lines.
3. Fold corner along dashed line, push toward center of block, and paper clip or staple.

MODEL 2

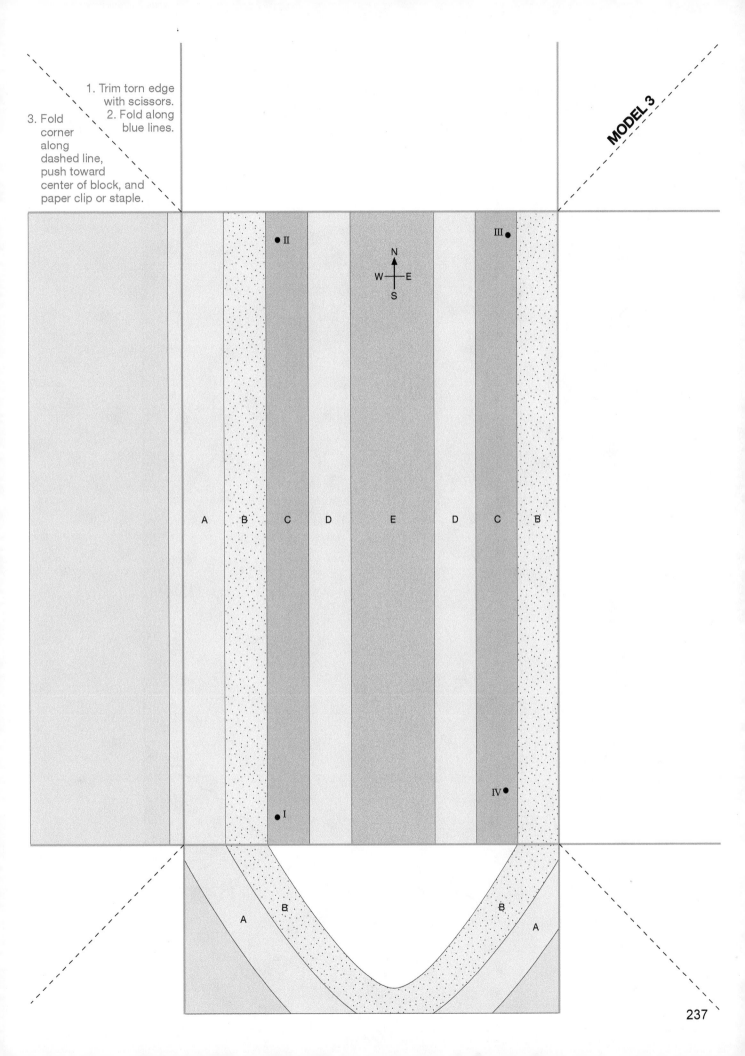

1. Trim torn edge with scissors.
2. Fold along blue lines.
3. Fold corner along dashed line, push toward center of block, and paper clip or staple.

MODEL 3

237

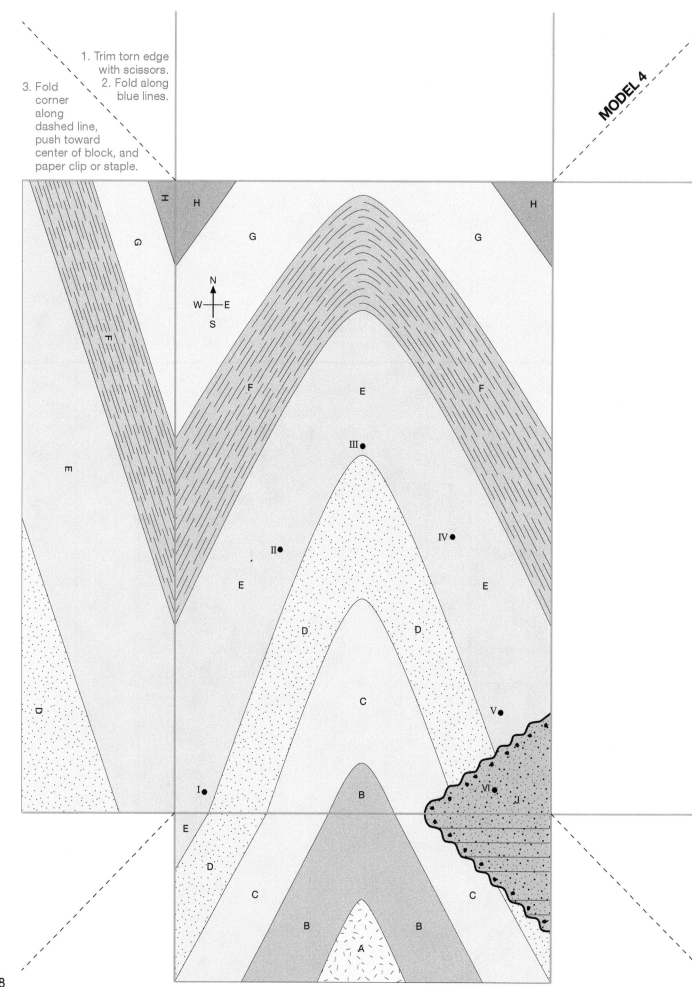

1. Trim torn edge with scissors.
2. Fold along blue lines.

3. Fold corner along dashed line, push toward center of block, and paper clip or staple.

MODEL 4

N
W—E
S

H
H
G
G
H
F
F
E
E
F
III•
II•
IV•
E
E
E
D
D
D
C
V•
D
I•
VI•
J
E
B
D
C
B
B
C
A

238

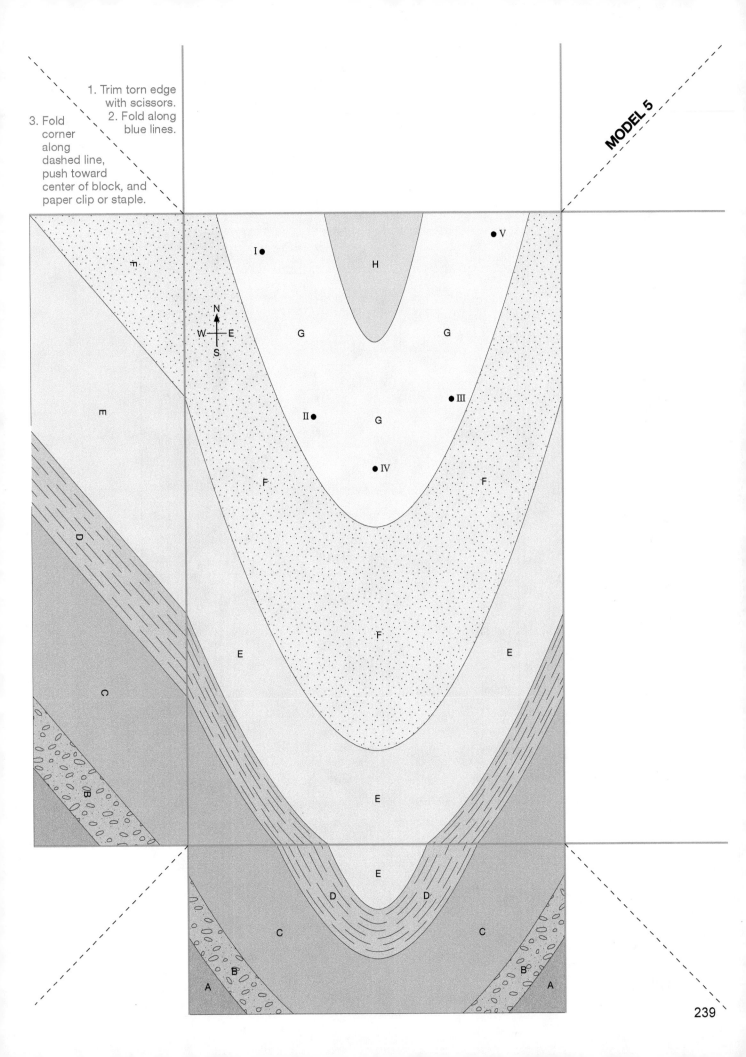

1. Trim torn edge with scissors.
2. Fold along blue lines.
3. Fold corner along dashed line, push toward center of block, and paper clip or staple.

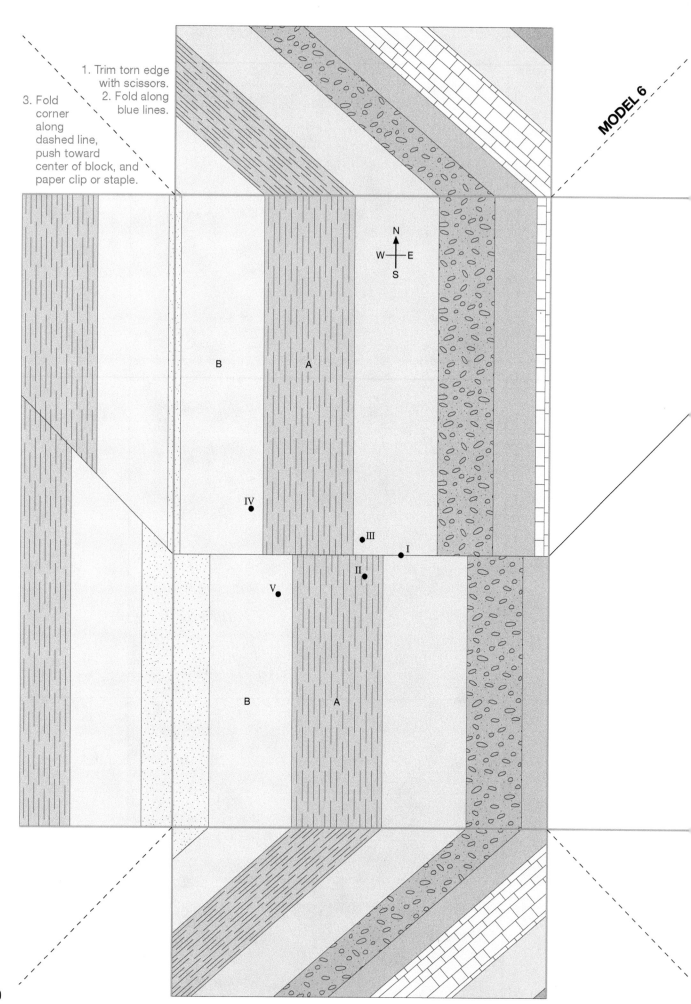

1. Trim torn edge
   with scissors.
2. Fold along
   blue lines.

3. Fold
   corner
   along
   dashed line,
   push toward
   center of block, and
   paper clip or staple.

N
W—E
S

B   A

IV

III
I
II

V

B   A

240

Earthquake Hazards and Human Risks

CONTRIBUTING AUTHORS

Thomas H. Anderson • *University of Pittsburgh*

David N. Lumsden • *University of Memphis*

Pamela J.W. Gore • *Georgia Perimeter College*

OBJECTIVES AND ACTIVITIES

A. Experiment with models to determine how earthquake damage to buildings is related to the Earth materials on which they are constructed. Apply your experimental results to evaluate earthquake hazards and human risks in San Francisco.

ACTIVITY 1: Simulate Earthquake Hazards and Infer Risks

B. Graph seismic data to construct and evaluate travel time curves for P-waves, S-waves, and L-waves, then use seismograms and travel time curves to locate the epicenter of an earthquake.

ACTIVITY 2: How Seismic Waves Travel Through Earth

ACTIVITY 3: Locate the Epicenter of an Earthquake

C. Analyze and evaluate active faults using remote sensing and geologic maps.

ACTIVITY 4: San Andreas Fault Analysis at Wallace Creek

D. Interpret seismograms and first motion studies to infer fault motion in the blind New Madrid Fault within the North American Plate.

ACTIVITY 5: New Madrid Blind Fault Zone

STUDENT MATERIALS

Pencil, eraser, ruler, and calculator. Drafting compass, several coins, a small plastic or paper cup containing dry sediment (fine sand, sugar, or salt), and a wash bottle of water will be provided in the laboratory.

INTRODUCTION

Earthquakes are shaking motions and vibrations of the Earth caused by large releases of energy that accompany volcanic eruptions, explosions, and movements of Earth's bedrock along fault lines. News reports usually describe an earthquake's **epicenter,** which is the point on Earth's surface (location on a map) directly above the **focus** (underground origin of the earthquake, in bedrock). The episodic releases of energy that occur along fault lines strain the bedrock like a person jumping on a diving board. This strain produces elastic waves of vibration and shaking called **seismic waves** (earthquake waves). Seismic waves originate at the earthquake's focus and travel in all directions through the rock body of Earth and along Earth's surface. The surface seismic waves travel in all directions from the epicenter, like the rings of ripples (small waves) that form when a stone is cast into a pond. In fact, people who have experienced strong surface seismic waves report that they saw and felt wave after wave of elastic motion passing by like the above-mentioned ripples on a pond. These waves are strongest near the epicenter and grow weaker with distance from the epicenter. For example, when a strong earthquake struck Mexico City in.1985, it caused massive property damage and 9500 deaths in a circular area radiating about 400 km (250 mi) in every direction from the city. By the time these same surface seismic waves of energy had traveled 3200 km to Pennsylvania, they were so weak that people could not even feel them passing beneath their feet. However, they did cause water levels in wells and swimming pools to fluctuate by as much as 12 cm. They also were recorded by earthquake-detecting instruments called *seismographs*. Therefore, although most damage from an earthquake usually occurs close to its epicenter, seismographs can detect the earthquake's waves of energy even when they travel through Earth's rocky body or along Earth's surface to locations thousands of kilometers away from the epicenter.

Fault motions (movements of Earth's crust along breaks in the rocks) are the most common source of earthquakes felt by people. These motions can occur along faults that do not break the Earth's surface or along faults that break the Earth's surface. Fault motions at Earth's surface can directly cause *hazards* such as the destruction of buildings, breakage of pipes and electric lines, development of open fissures in the soil, change in the course of streams, and generation of tsunamis (destructive ocean waves, generally 1–10 m high, that devastate coastal environments). However, *all* earthquakes cause some degree of vibration and shaking of the Earth, which can also cause most of the above-mentioned hazards.

Therefore, people who live where strong earthquakes occur are at *risk* for experiencing personal injury, property damage, and disruption of their livelihoods and daily routines. Geologists study seismic waves, map active faults, determine the nature of earthquake-induced hazards, assess human risk where such hazards occur, and assist in the development of government policies related to public safety in earthquake-prone regions.

PART A: EARTHQUAKE HAZARDS AND RISKS

Earthquakes can have very different effects on buildings in different parts of the same city. To understand why, geologists compare earthquake damage to maps of bedrock. They also simulate earthquakes in the laboratory to observe their effects on models of construction sites, buildings, bridges, and so on. All of this information is used to construct earthquake hazard maps and revise building codes for earthquake prone regions.

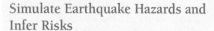

ACTIVITY 1

Simulate Earthquake Hazards and Infer Risks

In this activity, you will construct simple models of buildings constructed on different sedimentary substrates (e.g., Figure 1), simulate earthquakes to determine what substrates are most and least hazardous, and apply what you learned to explain the effects that one earthquake had on different parts of San Francisco (Figures 2, 3).

FIGURE 1 Photograph of Model 1 being subjected to a simulated earthquake.

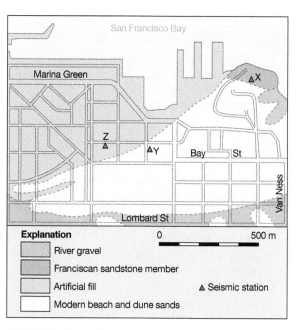

FIGURE 2 Map of the nature and distribution of Earth materials on which buildings and roads have been constructed for a portion of San Francisco, California. (Courtesy of U.S. Geological Survey)

PART B: GRAPHING SEISMIC DATA AND LOCATING THE EPICENTER OF AN EARTHQUAKE

An earthquake produces three main types of seismic waves that radiate from its focus/epicenter at different

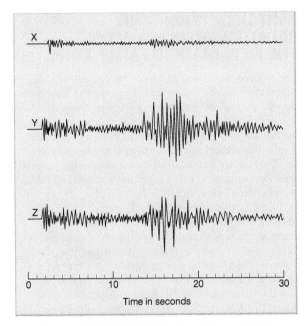

FIGURE 3 Seismograms recorded at Stations **X, Y,** and **Z,** for a strong (Richter Magnitude 4.6) aftershock of the Loma Prieta, California, earthquake. During the earthquake, little damage occurred at **X,** but significant damage to houses occurred at **Y** and **Z**. (Courtesy of U.S. Geological Survey)

these body waves are used to locate earthquake epicenters:

- **P-waves:** *P* for primary, because they travel fastest and arrive at seismographs first. (They are compressional, or "push–pull" waves.)

- **S-waves:** *S* for secondary, because they travel more slowly and arrive at seismographs after the P-waves. (They are perpendicular, shear, or "side-to-side" waves.)

Seismographs also detect the surface seismic waves, called **L-waves** or *Love waves* (named for A. E. H. Love, who discovered them). L-waves travel along Earth's surface (a longer route than the body waves) and thus are recorded after the S-waves and P-waves arrive at the seismograph.

Figure 4 is a seismogram recorded at a station located in Australia. Seismic waves arrived there from an earthquake epicenter located 1800 kilometers (1125 miles) away in New Guinea. Notice that the seismic waves were recorded as deviations (vertical zigzags) from the nearly horizontal line of normal background vibrations. Thus, the first pulse of seismic waves was P-waves, which had an **arrival time** of 7:14.2 (i.e., 14.2 minutes after 7:00). The second pulse of seismic waves was the slower S-waves, which had an arrival time of 7:17.4. The final pulse of seismic waves was the L-waves that traveled along Earth's surface, so they did not begin to arrive until 7:18.3. The earthquake actually occurred at the New Guinea epicenter at 7:10:23 (or 10.4 minutes after 7:00, written 7:10.4). Therefore the **travel time of the main seismic waves** (to go 1800 km) was 3.8 minutes for P-waves (7:14.2 minus 7:10.4), 7.0 minutes for S-waves (7:17.4 minus 7:10.4), and 7.9 minutes for L-waves (7:18.3 minus 7:10.4).

rates. Seismographs are instruments used to detect these seismic waves and produce a **seismogram**—a record of seismic wave motions obtained at a specific recording station (Figure 4).

Seismograms can detect and record several types of *body waves*, which are seismic waves that travel through Earth's interior (rather than along its surface) and radiate in all directions from the focus. Two of

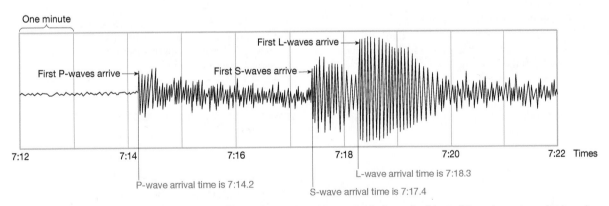

FIGURE 4 Seismogram of a New Guinea earthquake recorded at a location in Australia. Most of the seismogram shows only minor background deviations (short zigzags) from a horizontal line, such as the interval recorded between 7:12 and 7:14. Large vertical deviations indicate motions caused by the arrival of P-waves, S-waves, and L-waves of the earthquake (note arrows with labels). By making detailed measurements with a ruler, you can determine that the arrival time of the P-waves was 7:14.2 (14.2 minutes past 7:00), the arrival time of the S-waves was 7:17.4, and the arrival time of the L-waves was 7:18.3.

ACTIVITY 2

How Seismic Waves Travel Through Earth

Conduct this activity using Figure 5 to see how seismic P-waves, S-waves, and L-waves travel through Earth at the same rates as those from other earthquakes. Apply this knowledge to understand how graphs of seismic wave travel time and distance can be used to determine the distance between a seismograph station and an earthquake epicenter.

ACTIVITY 3

Locate the Epicenter of an Earthquake

See if you can use the travel time curves and seismograms recorded in Alaska, North Carolina, and Hawaii to locate the epicenter (point on a map) of the earthquake that produced the seismograms.

PART C: ANALYSIS OF ACTIVE FAULTS USING AERIAL PHOTOGRAPHS

There are many faults that can be imaged, photographed, mapped, and studied where they break Earth's surface. Some of these faults are **active faults,** meaning that they can move and generate earthquakes at the present time.

ACTIVITY 4

San Andreas Fault Analysis at Wallace Creek

In this activity, you will examine an aerial photograph of a portion of southern California for evidence of the San Andreas Fault and its motions and effects on the landscape.

PART D: DETERMINING RELATIVE MOTIONS ALONG THE NEW MADRID FAULT ZONE

The relative motions of blocks of rock on either side of a fault zone can be determined by mapping the way the pen on a seismograph moved (up or down on the seismogram) when P-waves first arrived at various seismic stations adjacent to the fault. This pen motion is called **first motion** and represents the reaction of the P-wave to dilation (pulling rocks apart) or compression (squeezing rocks together) as observed on seismograms (see Figure 6, left).

If the first movement of the P-wave was up on a seismogram, then that recording station (where the seismogram was obtained) experienced compression during the earthquake. If the first movement of the P-wave was down on a seismogram, then that recording station was dilational during the earthquake. What was the first motion at all of the seismic stations in Figure 3? (Answer: The first movement of the pen was up for each P-wave, so the first motion at all three sites was compressional.)

By plotting the first motions observed at recording stations on both sides of a fault that has experienced an earthquake, a picture of the relative motions of the fault emerges. For example, notice that the first motions observed at seismic stations on either side of a hypothetical fault are plotted in relation to the fault in Figure 6 (right side). The half-arrows indicate how motion proceeded away from seismic stations where dilation was recorded and toward seismic stations where compression was recorded (for each side of the fault). So the picture of relative motion along this fault is that Block **X** is moving southeast and Block **Y** is moving northwest.

ACTIVITY 5

New Madrid Blind Fault Zone

Use the seismograms in Figure 7 to determine fault motions within the New Madrid Fault Zone of the Mississippi Embayment in Arkansas, Tennessee, Missouri, and Kentucky.

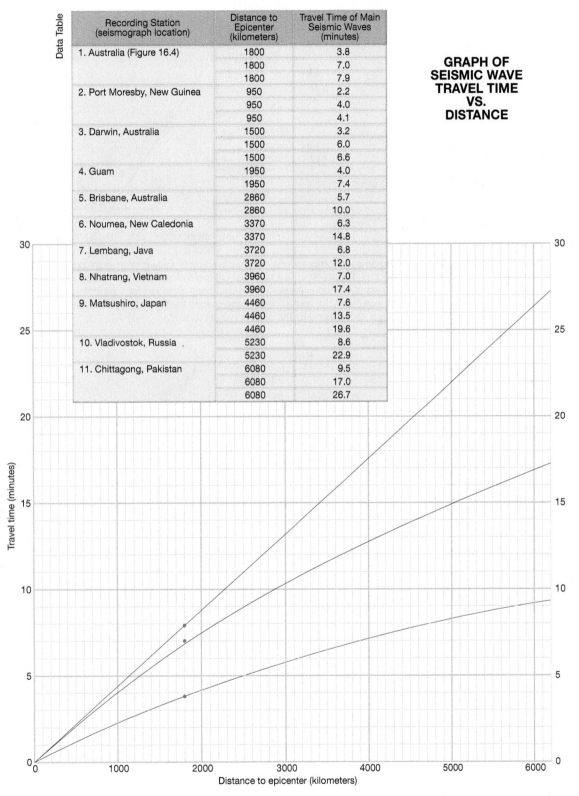

Data Table	Recording Station (seismograph location)	Distance to Epicenter (kilometers)	Travel Time of Main Seismic Waves (minutes)
	1. Australia (Figure 16.4)	1800	3.8
		1800	7.0
		1800	7.9
	2. Port Moresby, New Guinea	950	2.2
		950	4.0
		950	4.1
	3. Darwin, Australia	1500	3.2
		1500	6.0
		1500	6.6
	4. Guam	1950	4.0
		1950	7.4
	5. Brisbane, Australia	2860	5.7
		2860	10.0
	6. Noumea, New Caledonia	3370	6.3
		3370	14.8
	7. Lembang, Java	3720	6.8
		3720	12.0
	8. Nhatrang, Vietnam	3960	7.0
		3960	17.4
	9. Matsushiro, Japan	4460	7.6
		4460	13.5
		4460	19.6
	10. Vladivostok, Russia .	5230	8.6
		5230	22.9
	11. Chittagong, Pakistan	6080	9.5
		6080	17.0
		6080	26.7

GRAPH OF SEISMIC WAVE TRAVEL TIME VS. DISTANCE

FIGURE 5 Seismic wave data for an earthquake that occurred in New Guinea (at 3° North latitude and 140° East longitude) at Greenwich Mean Time of 10.4 minutes past 7:00 (7:10.4). The travel time of a main seismic wave is the time interval between when the earthquake occurred in New Guinea and when that wave first arrived at a recording location. The surface distance is the distance between the recording location and the earthquake epicenter. Graph is for plotting points that represent the travel time of each main seismic wave at each location versus the surface distance that it traveled.

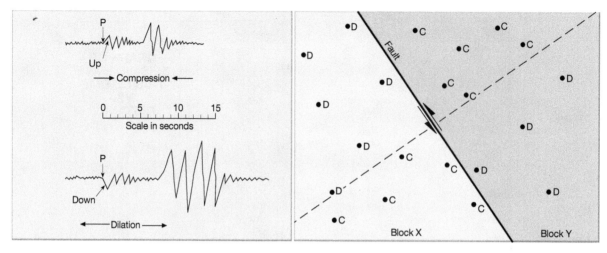

FIGURE 6 **Left**—Sketch of typical seismograms for compressional first motion (first P-wave motion is up) compared with dilational first motion (first P-wave motion is down). **Right**—Map of a hypothetical region showing a fault along which an earthquake has occurred, and the P-wave first motions (C = compressional, D = dilational) observed for the earthquake at seismic stations adjacent to the fault. Stress moves away from the field of dilation and toward the field of compression on each side of the fault, so the relative motion of the fault is as indicated by the smaller half-arrows.

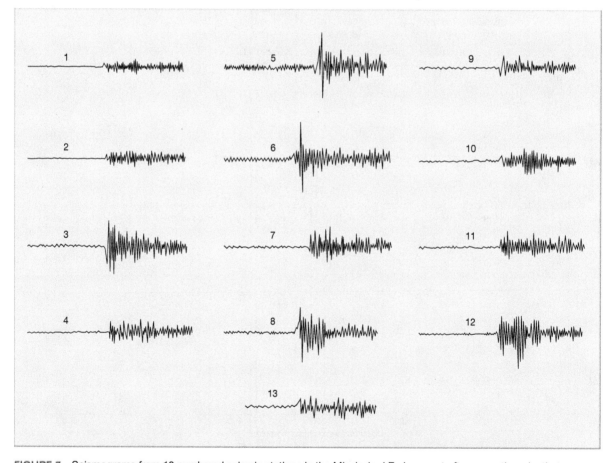

FIGURE 7 Seismograms from 13 numbered seismic stations in the Mississippi Embayment after an earthquake that occurred in the New Madrid Fault System. Numbers in this figure correspond to the numbered sites on the map in Activity 5.

ACTIVITY 1 Simulate Earthquake Hazards and Infer Risks

Name: _____   Course/Section: _____

Materials: Pencil. Cups, sand, coins, and water provided in the laboratory.

A. Obtain a small plastic or paper cup. Fill it three-quarters full with a dry sand. Place several coins in the sediment so they resemble vertical walls of buildings constructed on a substrate of uncompacted sediment (as in Figure 1). This is Model 1. Observe what happens to Model 1 when you *simulate an earthquake* by tapping the cup on a table top while you also rotate it counterclockwise.

    1. What happened to the vertically positioned coins in the uncompacted sediment of Model 1 when you simulated an earthquake?

    2. Now make Model 2. Remove the coins from Model 1, and add a small bit of water to the sediment in the cup so that it is moist (but not soupy). Press down on the sediment in the cup so that it is well compacted, and then place the coins into this compacted sediment just as you placed them in Model 1 earlier. *Simulate an earthquake* as you did for Model 1. What happened to the vertically positioned coins in the compacted sediment of Model 2 when you simulated an earthquake?

    3. Based on your experimental Models 1 and 2 above, which kind of Earth material is more hazardous to build on in earthquake-prone regions: compacted sediment or uncompacted sediment? (Justify your answer by citing evidence from your experimental models.)

    4. Consider the moist, compacted sediment in Model 2. Do you think this material would become *more* hazardous to build on, or *less* hazardous to build on, if it became totally saturated with water during a rainy season? To find out, design and conduct another experimental model of your own. Call it Model 3, describe what you did, and tell what you learned.

    5. Write a statement that summarizes how water in a sandy substrate beneath a home can be beneficial or hazardous. Justify your reasoning with reference to your experimental models.

CONTINUED

B. San Francisco, California is located in a tectonically active region, so it occasionally experiences strong earthquakes. Figure 2 is a map showing the kinds of Earth materials upon which buildings have been constructed in a portion of San Francisco. These materials include hard compact Franciscan Sandstone, uncompacted beach and dune sands, river gravel, and artificial fill. The artificial fill is mostly debris from buildings destroyed in the great 1906 earthquake that reduced large portions of the city to blocks of rubble. Also note that three locations have been labeled **X, Y,** and **Z** on Figure 2. Imagine that you have been hired by an insurance company to assess what risk there may be in buying newly constructed apartment buildings located at **X, Y,** and **Z** on Figure 2. Your job is to infer whether the risk of property damage during strong earthquakes is **low** (little or no damage expected) or **high** (damage can be expected). All that you have as a basis for reasoning is Figure 2 and knowledge of your experiments with models in Part A of this activity.

1. Is the risk at location **X** low or high? Why?

2. Is the risk at location **Y** low or high? Why?

3. Is the risk at location **Z** low or high? Why?

C. On October 17, 1989, just as Game 3 of the World Series was about to start in San Francisco, a strong earthquake occurred at Loma Prieta, California, and shook the entire San Francisco Bay area. Seismographs at locations **X, Y,** and **Z** (see Figure 2) recorded the shaking, and the resulting seismograms are shown in Figure 3. Earthquakes are recorded on the seismograms as deviations (vertical zigzags) from a flat, horizontal line. Thus, notice that much more shaking occurred at locations **Y** and **Z** than at location **X.**

1. The Loma Prieta earthquake caused no significant damage at location **X,** but there was moderate damage to buildings at location **Y** and severe damage at location **Z.** Explain how this damage report compares to your above predictions of risk (Part B).

2. The Loma Prieta earthquake shook all of the San Francisco Bay region. Yet Figure 3 is evidence that   the earthquake had very different effects on properties located only 600 m apart. Explain how the kind of substrate (uncompacted vs. firm and compacted) on which buildings are constructed influences how much the buildings are shaken and damaged in an earthquake.

D. Imagine that you are a member of the San Francisco City Council. Name two actions that you could propose to **mitigate** (decrease the probability of) future earthquake hazards such as the damage that occurred at locations **Y** and **Z** in the Loma Prieta earthquake.

ACTIVITY 2 How Seismic Waves Travel Through Earth

Name: _____   **Course/Section:** _____

Materials: Pencil, calculator, ruler.

Notice the seismic data provided with the graph in Figure 5. There are data for 11 recording stations where seismograms were recorded after the same New Guinea earthquake (at 3° North latitude and 140° East longitude). The **distance from epicenter** (surface distance between the recording station and the epicenter) and travel time of main seismic waves are provided for each recording station. Notice that the data from most of the recording stations include travel times for all three main kinds of seismic waves (P-waves, S-waves, and L-waves). However, instruments at some locations recorded only one or two kinds of waves. Location 1 is the Australian recording station where the seismogram in Figure 4 was obtained.

A. On the graph in Figure 5, plot points from the data table in pencil to show the travel time of each main seismic wave in relation to its distance from the epicenter (when recorded on the seismogram at the recording station). For example, the data for location 1 have already been plotted as red points on the graph. Recording station 1 was located 1800 km from the earthquake epicenter and the main waves had travel times of 3.8 minutes, 7.0 minutes, and 7.9 minutes. Plot points in pencil for data from all of the remaining recording stations in the data table, and then examine the graph.

Notice that your points do not produce a *random pattern*. They fall in *discrete paths* close to the three narrow black lines (or curves) already drawn on the graph. These black lines (or curves) were formed by plotting many thousands of points from hundreds of earthquakes, exactly as you just plotted your points. Explain why you think that your points, and all of the points from other earthquakes, occur along three discrete lines (or curves).

B. Study the three discrete, narrow black lines (or curves) of points in Figure 5. Label the line (curve) of points that represents travel times of the P-waves. Label the line or curve that connects the points representing travel times of the S-waves. Label the line or curve that connects the points representing travel times of the L-waves. Why is the S-wave curve steeper than the P-wave curve?

C. Why do the L-wave data points that you plotted on Figure 5 form a straight line whereas data points for P-waves and S-waves form curves? (*Hint:* The curved lines are evidence of how the physical environments and rocks deep inside Earth are different from the physical environments and rocks just beneath Earth's surface.)

D. Notice that the origin on your graph (travel time of zero and distance of zero) represents the location of the earthquake epicenter and the start of the seismic waves. The time interval between first arrival of P-waves and first arrival of S-waves at the same recording station is called the **S-minus-P time interval.** How does the S-minus-P time interval change with distance from the epicenter?

CONTINUED

E. Imagine that an earthquake occurred this morning. The first P-waves of the earthquake were recorded at a recording station in Houston at 6:12.6 a.m. and the first S-waves arrived at the same Houston station at 6:17.1 a.m. Use the travel time graph (Figure 5) to determine an answer for each question below.

1. What is the S-minus-P time interval of the earthquake?

2. How far from the earthquake's epicenter is the Houston recording station located?

3. You have determined the distance (radius of a circle on a map) between Houston and the earthquake epicenter. What additional data would you require to determine the location of the earthquake's epicenter (point on a map), and how would you use the data to locate the epicenter?

ACTIVITY 3 Locate the Epicenter of an Earthquake

Name: _____   Course/Section: _____

Materials: Pencil, ruler. Drafting compass will be provided in the laboratory.

A single earthquake produced the seismograms below at three different locations (Alaska, North Carolina, and Hawaii). Times have been standardized to Charlotte, North Carolina to simplify comparison. See if you can use these seismograms and a seismic-wave travel time curve to locate the epicenter of the earthquake that produced the seismograms.

A. Estimate, to the nearest tenth of a minute, the times that P-waves and S-waves first arrived at each recording station (seismograph location) in Figure 6. Then, subtract P from S to get the S-minus-P time interval:

	First P arrival	First S arrival	S-minus-P
Sitka, AK	_____	_____	_____
Charlotte, NC	_____	_____	_____
Honolulu, HI	_____	_____	_____

B. Using the S-minus-P time intervals and the travel time curves in Figure 5, determine the distance from the epicenter (in kilometers) for each recording station.

Sitka, AK: _____ km   Charlotte, NC _____ km   Honolulu, HI _____ km

CONTINUED

C. Next, find the earthquake's epicenter on the map below using the distances just obtained.

1. First use the geographic coordinates below to locate and mark the three recording stations on the world map below. Plot these points as exactly as you can.

Sitka, AK: 57°N latitude, 135°W longitude
Charlotte, NC: 35°N latitude, 81°W longitude
Honolulu, HI: 21°N latitude, 158°W longitude

2. Use a drafting compass to draw a circle around each recording station. Make the radius of each circle equal to the *distance from epicenter* determined for the station in Part B. (Use the scale on the map to set this radius on your drafting compass.) The circles you draw should intersect approximately at one point on the map. This point is the epicenter. (If the three circles do not quite intersect at a single point, then find a point that is equidistant from the three edges of the circles, and use this as the epicenter.) Record the location of the earthquake epicenter:

N Latitude _____ W Longitude _____

D. What is the name of a major fault that occurs near this epicenter?

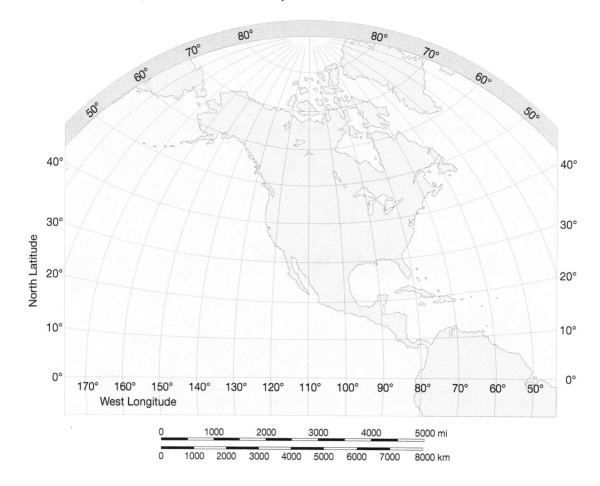

ACTIVITY 4 San Andreas Fault Analysis at Wallace Creek

Name: _____   Course/Section: _____

Materials: Pencil, ruler.

Below is an aerial photograph of the San Andreas Fault (a tectonic plate boundary) at Wallace Creek, Carrizo Plain, southern California. (Photo courtesy of Randall Marrett, University of Texas, Austin). Notice the fence line, small streams, and fine features of the landscape. Also notice that the figure shows a portion of the strike-slip San Andreas Fault, which is a transform plate boundary separating the Pacific Plate from the North American Plate.

A. Geologists have inferred that the San Andreas Fault is an active fault separating the North American and Pacific tectonic plates.

   1. Draw a line along the exact line of the fault as exactly as you can.

   2. Based on evidence visible in this photograph, add half-arrows on both sides of the fault to show the direction that each side is moving relative to the other.

   3. How much has the San Andreas Fault offset the present-day channel of Wallace Creek?

   4. Is the San Andreas Fault a left-lateral fault or a right-lateral fault?

B. How wide is the San Andreas Fault (tectonic plate boundary) here?

C. Notice the small dry valley in the lower-left part of the photograph. Infer how this valley may have formed.

ACTIVITY 5 New Madrid Blind Fault Zone

Name: _____   **Course/Section:** _____

Materials: Pencil, ruler.

The New Madrid Fault System is located within the *Mississippi Embayment*, a basin filled with Mesozoic and Cenozoic rocks that rest unconformably on (and are surrounded by) Paleozoic and Precambrian rocks (see map below). Faults of the New Madrid System are not visible on satellite images and photographs, because they are **blind faults** (faults that do not break Earth's surface). These blind faults occur in the Paleozoic and Precambrian rocks that are buried beneath approximately a kilometer of Mesozoic and Cenozoic rocks.

The main fault of the New Madrid System is plotted in red on the map below. It is well known, because a series of strong earthquakes occurred along it in 1811 and 1812. One of these earthquakes was the strongest earthquake ever recorded in North America, and the potential for more strong earthquakes here is a lingering hazard. The locations of 13 seismic stations are also plotted on the map below. Seismograms obtained at these stations (after an earthquake along the New Madrid Fault System) are plotted on the map.

A. Analyze the seismograms in Figure 7 to determine if their P-wave first motions indicate compression or dilation (refer to Figure 6 as needed). Plot this information on the map below by writing a *C* beside the stations where compression occurred and a *D* beside the stations where dilation occurred.

B. When you have finished plotting the letters above, draw half-arrows on the map to indicate the relative motions of the blocks of rock on either side of the main fault. Does the main fault have a right-lateral motion or a left-lateral motion? Explain your answer.

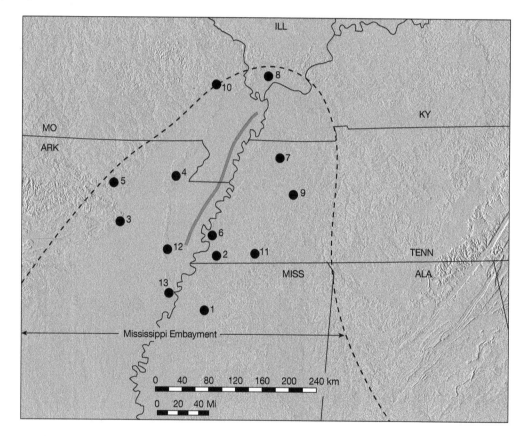

Index

Page references followed by "f" indicate illustrated figures or photographs; followed by "t" indicates a table.

A

Absolute time, 162
Amphibole, 41, 66, 91-94, 142
Amphiboles, 67
Andesite, 92
Angular unconformity, 163-164, 217
Anthracite, 145, 170
Apatite, 64
Aphanitic texture, 90
Aragonite, 58, 117
Archaeopteryx, 4
Arkose, 117
Atomic number, 167
Augite, 66-67, 91-92
Axial plane, 220-221

B

Base line, 189
Bauxite, 72-73
Biotite, 58, 91, 142, 168-169
Bituminous coal, 117, 145, 169
Blueschist facies, 160
Body waves, 243
Boundaries
    divergent, 32-33, 95
    geometric, 58
Bowen's reaction series, 89

C

Calcareous ooze, 116
Calcite, 58, 117-121, 142-143
Carbon-14, 168
Cephalopods, 167
Chalk, 116-118
Chemical sedimentary rocks
    chert, 77, 116-118
    dolostone, 116-117, 147
    evaporites, 116
    identification of, 70
Chert, 71-72, 116-118
Chromium, 74, 143
Clasts, 114
Cleavage, 57, 91, 144-146
Cocos plate, 36
Confining pressure, 40
Conglomerate, 116-117, 151, 164, 234
Continental margins
    continental slope, 116
Continental slope, 116
Convection
    plate tectonics and, 31-36
Coquina, 116-117
Cross-bedding, 122
Cross-stratification, 122
Crystal form, 58
Crystalline rocks, 61
Crystals
    shapes of, 89

D

Decompression melting, 40
Dendritic pattern, 223
Detrital sedimentary rocks
    breccia, 91-93, 116-117
    conglomerate, 116-117, 151, 164, 234
Detrital sediments, 118
Dinosaurs, 113, 165-167
Diorite, 91-92, 127, 147
Dip, 171, 214-218
Disconformities, 162
Disconformity, 162-163, 217

Divergent boundary, 33
Divergent plate boundaries, 40
Divergent plate boundary, 46, 95
Dolostone, 116-117, 147
Ductile deformation, 220-221

E

Earth
    radius of, 7
Earth, evolution through geologic time
    Mesozoic era, 165-166
    Paleozoic era, 166-167
Earthquakes
    catastrophic, 31
    convergent boundaries, 32
    interplate, 35
    intraplate, 35
    safety, 242
Electrolysis, 8-9
Electron, 81
Eons, 3

F

Facies, 141
Felsic rocks, 93
Ferromagnesian, 67, 93, 147
Ferromagnesian minerals, 93, 147
Foliated metamorphic rock, 145-146
Fossils
    index, 3, 161
    Precambrian, 4, 166
Fractures
    conchoidal, 65-66, 151

G

Galena, 59-61
Garnet, 41, 67-68, 142-143
Geologic time
    radiometric dating, 167-168
Geothermal gradient, 40, 160
Glassy texture, 90-91, 149
Global change, climate
    sea level rise, 18
Graded beds, 122
Granules, 114, 149
Graphite, 70
Graywacke, 117
Groundwater movement
    scales of, 7
Gulf Stream
    turbidity, 116

H

Habit, 57
Half-life, 167-168
Halite, 66, 114
Hanging wall block, 34, 218-219
Hawaiian Islands
    age of, 4, 53
Hess, Harry, 34
Himalaya Mountains, 29
Hinge line, 218
Holmes, Arthur, 34
Hornblende, 66-67, 92, 142
Hornfels, 141-142
Hydrothermal metamorphism, 142

I

Igneous rocks
    classifying, 93-94, 121
    compositions, 123, 141, 161
    felsic, 91-97
Igneous rocks, naming
    intermediate (andesitic), 111
    mafic (basaltic), 111
International Union of Geological Sciences, 4

Intraplate earthquakes, 35
Isostatic adjustment
    of Earth's crust, 18
Isotopes
    radioactive, 167-168

J

Jasper, 72, 117

K

Kilauea, 38
Kilauea Volcano, 38

L

Land use
    sequential, 165
Lava
    tubes, 100
Limestones, 233
Lithosphere
    subduction of, 35
Lithospheric mantle, 32-33
Lobsters, 167
Lodestone, 69
Lombard, 242
Luster, 57, 115, 145-146

M

Mafic rocks, 95
Magma
    crystallization of, 95
Magnetite, 69-70, 99, 152
Mantle plumes
    hot spots and, 95
Marine environment
    divisions of, 165
Metallic minerals, 61
Metamorphic environments
    burial, 143
    interpreting, 94, 113
Metamorphic facies, 141
Metamorphic rocks
    foliated, 145-146
Metamorphic textures
    foliation, 146-147, 217
Metamorphism
    contact, 141-143, 164-165
Metasomatism, 145
Mica, 71-73, 91, 144-147
Micas, 66-67, 145
Mid-ocean ridges
    fracture zones, 35
Mohs scale, 63-64
Monocline, 217
Monoclines, 218
Mountain belts, 31
Mudstone, 116-118, 144-147, 234
Muscovite, 65-67, 91-95, 142-146, 168

N

Neutrons, 167
Nonconformity, 163-164, 217
Nonmetallic minerals, 61

O

Ocean
    layering, 122
Oolitic limestone, 116-117

P

Peru-Chile Trench, 36
Phaneritic texture, 90
Phenocrysts, 90
Phyllite, 141-142
Physical geology, 1, 31, 57, 89, 113, 141, 161, 181,